Unified Modeling Language: Systems Analysis, Design and Development Issues

Table of Contents

Preface

This book provides a set of readings on the Unified Modeling Language (UML), currently the most popular language for modeling object-oriented software. To set the scene for these readings, this preface provides a brief historical and structural overview of UML, and then identifies the specific focus of each of the contributing chapters.

Initially based on a combination of the Booch, OMT (Object Modeling Technique) and OOSE (Object-Oriented Software Engineering) methods, UML was refined and extended by a consortium of several companies, and is subject to ongoing revisions by the Object Management Group (OMG). UML was first adopted in November 1997 by the OMG as a language for object-oriented analysis and design (UML version 1.1). Within the OMG, the UML specification is the responsibility of the Analysis and Design Task Force (ADTF). Minor changes to the UML specification that led to point releases (e.g., 1.2, 1.3, 1.4) are managed by a subgroup of the ADTF known as a UML Revision Task Force (RTF).

In late 1999, UML version 1.3 was approved and work began on version 1.4, which was expected to be ratified around the end of 2000. Following UML's adoption by the OMG, the language has gained wide acceptance in industry for object-oriented modeling. Some preliminary work has begun on a major revision (2.0), for release some years later (possibly 2002). Though not yet an official standard, UML has been proposed for standardization by the International Standards Organization (ISO), and approval is anticipated sometime in 2001. The UML specification itself, as well as details about current work on its revisions, can be accessed online at www.omg.org/technology/uml/.

From a semiotic viewpoint, UML can be examined in relation to its syntax (notation), semantics (meaning) and pragmatics (use). The UML notation includes hundreds of symbols, from which various diagrams may be constructed to model different perspectives of an application. Different kinds of diagrams provide different views of the overall model. The UML specification includes the following canonical diagram types:

- Use case diagram
- Class diagram
- Behavior diagrams
    o Statechart diagram
    o Activity diagram
    o Interaction diagrams
        § Sequence diagram
        § Collaboration diagram
- Implementation diagrams
    o Component diagram
    o Deployment diagram

Use case diagrams are used primarily for requirements analysis to provide a high level view of how actors interact with the system. Class diagrams are used to capture the static aspects (or data model). Behavior diagrams are used to model the dynamic aspects of the system, while implementation diagrams indicate how components are packaged and deployed. Although the syntax and semantics of these diagrams are described in the UML specification, very little is said about pragmatics, or how a modeler may use these notations to construct models. The only advice given as to the modeling process is that it should be "use-case driven, architecture centric and iterative." Various companies have made their own proposals for a detailed modeling process, and the OMG itself has begun preliminary work on a "Unified Process" to provide advice on the use of UML in developing software.

In spite of its good points, UML is a large and complex language, with many features in need of refinement or clarification, and there are different views about how to use UML to develop software systems. This book sheds light on such issues, by illustrating how UML can be used successfully in practice as well as identifying some problematic aspects of UML and suggesting possible solutions. As an edited collection of insightful contributions from both industry and academia, the book should be of interest to researchers, practitioners and instructors of UML.

The book is divided into the following four sections: Applying UML, Evaluating UML, Extending UML and Formalizing UML. Although each individual chapter appears in the section most closely related to its primary focus, a chapter may include some material relevant to another section. For example, most chapters include a brief critical evaluation of some aspects of UML.

Applying UML

In "Systematic Design of Web Applications with UML," Rolf Hennicker and Nora Koch propose a systematic design method for Web applications that addresses both navigation and presentation aspects, based on a UML profile for the Web domain. In "A Systematic Approach to Transform UML Static Models to Object-Oriented Code," Lilian Favre and Silvia Clérici discuss a reuse-based method for mapping UML static models to object-oriented code, using Eiffel as the sample target language. In "Data Modeling and UML," Devang Shah and Sandra Slaughter discuss how to map a data model expressed as a UML class diagram to a relational database schema, illustrating their technique with a drug dispensing application.

Evaluating UML

In "RUP, A Process Model for Working with UML," Wolfgang Hesse provides a critical evaluation of a popular modeling process proposed for use with UML, and offers an alternative component-based, multi-variant approach. In "UML Modeling Support for Early Reuse Decisions in Component-Based Development," Jim Sykes and Pramila Gupta evaluate UML's support for reuse in terms of the need for composable, business-oriented abstractions and a functional mental model. In "Using a Semiotic Framework to Evaluate UML for the Development of Models of High Quality," John Krogstie provides a critique of UML as supported in a popular UML modeling tool, drawing upon a general framework for evaluating the quality of conceptual models as well as practical experience. In "Rational Unified Process and Unified Modeling Language, A GOMS Analysis," Keng Siau introduces GOMS (Goals, Operators, Methods and Selection rules) and discusses the use of GOMS for evaluating the Rational Unified Process and UML.

Extending UML

In "Extension of the Unified Modeling Language for Mobile Agents," Cornel Klein, Andreas Rausch, Marc Sihling and Zhaojun Wen present extensions to UML for modeling mobile agents, and demonstrate their approach using a prototype of an advanced telecommunication system. In "Rendering Distributed Systems in UML," Patricia Lago identifies problems with using UML for design distributed systems and proposes extensions to address these problems. In "Temporal OCL: Meeting Specification Demands for Business Components," Stefan Conrad and Klaus Turowski discuss difficulties with specifying software contracts for business components, and suggest temporal extensions to UML's Object Constraint language to provide a possible solution. In "Supplementing UML with Concepts from ORM," Terry Halpin identifies deficiencies in UML's class diagram notation for data modeling, and shows how to compensate for these defects by augmenting UML with concepts and techniques from the Object Role Modeling approach. In "The Whole-Part Relationship in the Unified Modeling Language: A New Approach," Franck Barbier, Brian Henderson-Sellers, Andreas Opdahl and Martin Gogolla provide a thorough analysis of the whole-part relationship, and suggest various extensions that go beyond UML's basic aggregation and composition approach.

Formalizing UML

In "Linking UML with Integrated Formal Techniques," Jing Liu, Jin Song Dong and Brendan Mahony investigate the links between static and dynamic aspects of UML and the Timed Communicating Object Z formalism, illustrating the connections with an example light control application. In "Seamless Formalizing the UML Semantics Through Metamodels," José Luis Fernández Alemán and Ambrosio Toval Álvarez use the algebraic specification language, Maude, to provide a framework for formalizing UML that caters for evolution of the UML metamodel. In "An Interactive Viewpoint on the Role of UML," Dina Goldin, David Keil and Peter Wegner provide a theoretical framework for modeling interactive computing, and discuss its use for strengthening the formal foundations of UML.

The editors:

> Keng Siau (University of Nebraska, USA)
> Terry Halpin (Microsoft Corporation, USA)

August 2000

Chapter I

Systematic Design of Web Applications with UML

Rolf Hennicker
Ludwig-Maximilians-University Munich, Germany

Nora Koch
Ludwig-Maximilians-University Munich, Germany
F.A.S.T. Applied Software Technology GmbH

We propose a systematic design method for Web applications which takes into account the navigation space and the presentational aspects of the application. The method is based on a UML profile for the Web domain. Starting with a use case analysis and a conceptual model of the application, we first provide guidelines for modeling the navigation space. From the navigation space model we can derive, in a subsequent step, a navigational structure model which shows how to navigate through the navigation space using access elements like indexes, guided tours, queries and menus. Finally, a static and dynamic presentation model is constructed. The different models of the design process are represented by using a Web extension of UML.

The strength of the presented methodology is that most steps can be performed in a semiautomatic way, thus providing the basis for a systematic mechanism for Web design.

INTRODUCTION

Web engineering is a new and still evolving discipline. The process of learning how to develop large Web applications has just begun. Web applications are mostly the result of an ad hoc implementation, growing usually from small to large applications that very quickly become difficult to maintain. Some guidelines and tools are beginning to appear that assist developers of Web applications, but these current practices often fail due to inappropriate techniques, processes and methodologies. The objective is to develop a suitable method that allows high-quality Web applications to be produced through the systematic construction of high-quality models.

People with different skills are involved in the process of Web systems development, such as authors, layout designers, programmers, multimedia experts and marketing specialists. The role of the user is augmented and makes it more difficult to capture the requirements of the application. The non-linearity of the hyperdocuments as well as the possibility to connect easily to other Web applications increases the complexity and risk of lost in the hyperspace." Web engineering has also to take into account aesthetic and cognitive aspects that general software engineering environments do not support (Lowe & Hall, 1999). Moreover, the development process tends to be more fine grained, more incremental and iterative. Maintenance is an even more significant part of the lifecycle of Web applications than in traditional systems since Web technologies and user require-ments change continuously. In addition, nonfunctional requirements such as security have to be addressed by a Web development process.

If we restrict ourselves to the design steps, the main differences we can observe between design of Web solutions and other software applications are the heterogeneity of the designer group, the hypertext structure of nodes and links, the need for navigational assistance, the inclusion of searching and indexing mechanisms, and the presentation of the multimedia contents and the contents, e.g., for different browsers. Thus, the design is centered around three main aspects of Web systems: the content, the navigational structure and the presentation. Treating these aspects separately during design will payoff in the maintenance phase.

In this work we concentrate our attention on the analysis and design workflows of an engineering process based on the Unified Process (Jacobson, Booch & Rumbaugh, 1999) adapted for Web applications. The approach we propose consists of a method and a notation. The notation is a UML profile that defines a set of appropriate stereotypes for the Web by using the UML extension mechanism. The stereotypes are used to indicate the descriptive and restrictive properties that the modeling elements have in comparison to standard UML elements.

The method consists of three steps that are performed in an iterative design process. The steps are the conceptual, navigational and presentational design. The artifacts produced as results of the application of the method are models represented by UML diagrams.

They are:
- a conceptual model for the content,
- a navigation space model and a navigational structure model,
- a static and a dynamic presentation model.

The conceptual model is built by taking into account the functional requirements captured with use cases. Traditional object-oriented techniques are used to construct the conceptual model, such as finding classes, defining inheritance structures and specifying constraints. It is represented by a UML class diagram.

Based on this conceptual model, the navigation space model is constructed. It is also represented as a static class diagram showing which objects can be visited through navigation. A set of guidelines is proposed for modeling the navigation space. A detailed specification of (navigation) associations, their multiplicity and role names establish the base for deriving a navigational structure model. In this step, access structures such as indexes, guided tours, queries and menus are incorporated. The navigational structure model defines the structure of nodes and links of the Web application showing how navigation is supported by the access structures.

Navigational design is a critical step in the design of Web applications. Even simple applications with a non-deep hierarchical structure become complex very quickly by the addition of new links. Additional links improve navigability on the one hand but imply on the other hand higher risk for loss of orientation. Building a navigation model is not only helpful for the documentation of the application structure, it also allows for a more structured increase of navigability. Navigational models are also represented as UML class diagrams that are built with particular stereotypes.

In the last step of our method, we construct a presentational model which consists of two parts: a static model of an abstract user interface based on framesets and a model of the dynamic aspects of the presentation. The dynamic presentation model takes into account multi-window techniques. UML class diagrams and interaction diagrams are used for the representation of these models.

The focus of our methodology is on the structure of the navigation rather than on the dynamics and architecture of Web applications which are considered in Conallen (1999). The strength of our method is the fact that a systematic approach for the construction of the models is described, identifying as many steps as possible that can be performed in an automatic way. This consequently provides the basis for a systematic mechanism for Web design.

This chapter is structured as follows: Section 2 provides a brief description of related work. Section 3 describes the starting points for the modeling process: use cases and a conceptual model. Section 4 gives guidelines to build a navigation space model based on the conceptual model. In Section 5 we present a procedure to derive the navigational structure model from the navigation space model. Section 6 shows how a static presentation model is obtained from the navigational structure model and, in Section 7, the dynamic aspects of the presentation are modeled. Finally, Section 8 gives some concluding remarks and an overview of future trends.

BACKGROUND

Over the last few years, many methods for Web design have been proposed; see Lowe and Hall (1999) for an overview. Most of them are not based on the UML, like RMM (Relationship Management Methodology) of Isakowitz, Stohr and Balasubramanian (1995) and OOHDM (Object-Oriented Hypermedia Design Method) of Schwabe and Rossi (1998). They utilize entity-relationship diagrams, OMT or their own notation and techniques.

Recently, some new approaches have proposed UML extensions for the Web domain, such as the development process of Conallen (1999), the extension for multimedia applications in Sauer and Engels (1999) and the UML extension of Baumeister, Koch and Mandel (1999). The first approach is based on the Rational Unified Process, RUP (Kruchten, 1998) and focuses particularly on the architecture of Web applications. The second extends UML sequence diagrams to model multimedia processes and the third one provides modeling elements for the navigational and presentational design that we have used in our method.

The methodology presented in this chapter differs from the other Web design methods in that it provides guidelines about the activities to be performed systematically by the designer for modeling the navigation space, structure and presentation. The advantage of such guidelines is that they provide a basis for developing case tools for the semiautomatic generation of the Web navigational structure and of presentation templates.

For further details on design and development methods for Web systems, see the comparative study of Web development methods in Koch (1999).

FROM REQUIREMENTS TO A CONCEPTUAL MODEL

The design of Web applications builds on the requirements specification, just like the design of software applications in general. Following the Unified Process (Jacobson, Booch & Rumbaugh, 1999), we propose use cases for capturing the requirements. They provide a user-centered technique that forces developers to define who are the users (actors) of the application and offer an intuitive way to represent the functionality that an application has to fulfill for each actor.

The conceptual design of the domain is based on these use cases and includes the objects involved in the typical activities users will perform with the application. The conceptual design aims to build a domain model trying to take into account as little as possible of the navigation paths, presentation and interaction aspects. These aspects are postponed to the navigational and presentational steps of the design.

Modeling Elements

The main modeling elements used in the conceptual model are: *class* and *association*. They are represented graphically by the UML notation (Booch, Rumbaugh & Jacobson, 1999). If the conceptual model consists of many classes, it is recommended to group them using the UML *package* modeling element.

Classes defined in this step are used during navigational design to derive nodes of the Web structure. Associations will be used to derive links.

Example

As a running example to illustrate the design process, through the whole chapter we use the Web site of a service company. This Web site offers information about the company itself, the employees and their relationships to projects, customers and departments. We restrict ourselves in the example to these concepts, although many other aspects should be included in an incremental and iterative process, such as information about products, documents, events, press releases and job offers. Figure 1 shows a use case model for the project administration, which is part of the use case model of the company's Web application. The company's, department's and employee's administration can be modeled in a similar way. The conceptual model for the Web site of the service company is shown in Figure 2.

Figure 1. Use Cases for the Project Administration

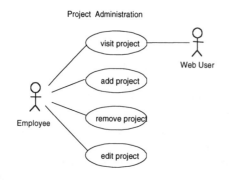

Method

For each use case identified during the requirement analysis a detailed description is provided in terms of (primary and secondary) scenarios, for instance, following the guidelines of Schneider and Winters (1998). Thus, for Web applications particular emphasis is placed on the information exchanged between the user and the

Figure 2. Conceptual Model

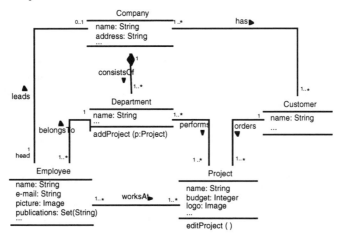

system. The use case descriptions serve as an input for modeling the content of the application.

Well-known object-oriented modeling activities are performed to obtain a conceptual model, such as:

1. finding classes,
2. specifying the most relevant attributes and operations,
3. determining associations between classes,
4. defining inheritance hierarchies,
5. finding dependencies, and
6. defining constraints.

The result of these activities is a UML class model of the problem domain.

FROM A CONCEPTUAL MODEL
TO A NAVIGATION SPACE MODEL

In this section we present guidelines to construct a navigation space model from a conceptual model. The navigation space model specifies *which* objects can be visited by navigation through the Web application. *How* these objects are reached is defined by the navigational structure model that is constructed in the next section. In the process of building the navigation space model, the developer takes crucial design decisions, such as which view of the conceptual model is needed for the application and what navigation paths are required to ensure the application's functionality. The decisions of the designer are based on the conceptual model, use case model and the navigation requirements that the application must satisfy.

Modeling Elements

For the construction of the navigation space model, two modeling elements are used: navigational classes and navigation associations which express direct navigability.

- *Navigational Class*
  A navigational class models a class whose instances are visited by the user during

navigation. Navigational classes will be given the same name as conceptual classes. For their representation we use the UML stereotype «navigational class» which is shown in Figure 3.

- *Direct Navigability*
  Associations in the navigation space model are interpreted as representing direct navigability from the source navigation class to the target navigation class. Hence their semantics are different from the associations used in the conceptual model. To determine the directions of the navigation, the associations of this model are directed (possibly bi-directed). This is shown by an arrow that is attached to one or both ends of the association. Moreover, each directed end of an association is named with a role name and is equipped with an explicit multiplicity. If no explicit role name is given, the following convention is used: if the multiplicity is less than or equal to one, the target class name is used as the role name; if the multiplicity is greater than one, the plural form of the target class name is used. In the following diagrams all associations with the exception of composition are implicitly assumed to be stereotyped by «direct navigability».

Example

The navigation space model built with the navigational classes and navigability associations is graphically represented by a UML class diagram. Figure 3 shows the navigation space model for the Web Site of our service company.

The Method

Although there is obviously no way to automate the construction of the navigation space model, there are several guidelines that can be followed by the developer:

1. Classes of the conceptual model that are relevant for the navigation are included as navigational classes in the navigation space model (i.e., navigational classes can be mapped to conceptual classes). If a conceptual class is not a visiting target in the use case model, it is irrelevant in the navigational process and therefore is omitted in the

Figure 3. Navigation Space Model

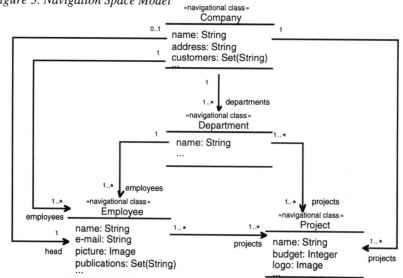

navigation space model (like the class Customer in our example).

2. Required information on the omitted classes can still be kept as attributes of other classes in the navigation space model (e.g., the newly introduced attribute customers of the navigational class Company). All other attributes of navigational classes map directly to attributes of the corresponding conceptual class. Conversely, attributes of the conceptual classes that are considered to be irrelevant for the presentation are excluded in the navigation space model.

3. Associations of the conceptual model are directed in the navigational model. Often additional associations are added for direct navigation to avoid navigation paths of length greater than one. Examples are the newly introduced navigation associations between Company and Employee and between Company and Project. Scenarios described by the use case model give the input for the choice of direct navigations.

FROM A NAVIGATION SPACE MODEL TO A NAVIGATIONAL STRUCTURE MODEL

The navigation space model tells us which objects can be visited by direct navigation from other objects. In this section we proceed by describing how the navigation can be performed using access elements like indexes, guided tours, queries and menus. Technically, the navigation paths together with the access elements are presented by a navigational structure model which can be systematically constructed from the navigation space model in two steps: First, we enhance the navigation space model by indexes, guided tours and queries. Then we can directly derive menus which represent possible choices for navigation.

Defining Indexes, Guided Tours and Queries

Indexes, guided tours and queries, so called access primitives, are additional navigational nodes required to access instances of navigational classes. Another access primitive is menu which is treated separately in the next subsection.

Modeling Elements

For describing indexes, guided tours and queries, we use the following modeling elements. Their stereotypes and associated icons originate from Baumeister et al. (1999).

- *Index*
  An index is modeled by a composite object which contains an arbitrary number of index items. Each index item is in turn an object which has a name and owns a link to an instance of a navigational class. Any index is a member of some index class which is stereotyped by «index» with a corresponding icon. An index class must be built to conform to the composition structure of classes shown in Figure 4. Hence the stereotype «index» is a restrictive stereotype in the sense of Berner, Glinz and Joos (1999). In practice, we will always use the shorthand notation shown in Figure 5. Note that in the short form the association between MyIndex and MyNavigationalClass is derived from the index composition and the association between MyIndexItem and MyNavigationalClass.

- *Guided Tour*
  A guided tour is modeled by an object which provides sequential access to the

instances of a navigational class.
For classes which contain guided
tour objects, we use the stereotype
«guidedTour» and its corresponding icon depicted in Figure 6. As
shown in Figure 6, any guided tour
class must be connected to a navigational class by a directed association which has the property {or-
dered}.

Figure 4. Index Class

Figure 5. Shorthand Notation for Index Class

- *Query*
  A query is modeled by an object
  which has a query string as an
  attribute. (This string may be given,
  for instance, by an OCL select operation.) For query classes we use
  the stereotype «query» and the icon
  depicted in Figure 7. As shown in
  Figure 7, any query class is the
  source of two directed associations

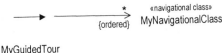

Figure 6. Guided Tour Class

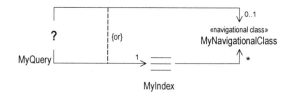

related by the constraint {or}. In this way we can model the fact that a query with
several result objects must first lead to an index supporting the selection of a
particular instance of a navigational class.

Example

Fig. 8 shows how the navigation space model for the Web site of our service company
can be enhanced by indexes,
guided tours and queries. Note
that we have included two possible ways to access the employees of a department, by an index
and by a query.

Figure 7. Query Class

The Method

The enhancement of a navigation space model by access elements of type index, guided tour
and query follows certain rules which can be summarized as follows:

1. Consider only those associations of the navigation space model which have multiplicity greater than one at the directed association end.
2. For each association of this kind, choose one or more access elements to realize the
   navigation.
3. Enhance the navigation space model correspondingly. It is therefore important that
   the role names of the navigation in the navigation space model are now moved to the
   access elements (compare Figure 3 and Figure 8).

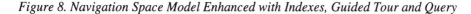

Figure 8. Navigation Space Model Enhanced with Indexes, Guided Tour and Query

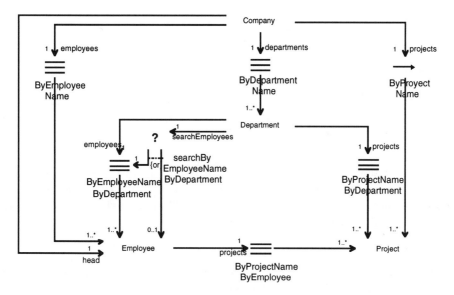

In step 2 it is the task of the designer to choose appropriate access elements. However, it is important to note that it is also possible to fully automate this step by making as a default design decision the choice of an index according to a selected key attribute of the target navigational class.

Defining Menus

In this step, access primitives of type menu are added to the navigational structure model.

Modeling Elements

The modeling element menu is a stereotyped class that is defined as follows:

- *Menu*

A menu is modeled by a composite object which contains a fixed number of menu items. Each menu item has a constant name and owns a link either to an instance of a navigational class or to an access element. Any menu is an instance of some menu class which is stereotyped by «menu» with a corresponding icon. A menu class must be built to conform to the composition structure of classes shown in Figure 9. Hence the stereotype «menu» is again a restrictive stereotype according to the classification of stereotypes given in Berner et al. (1999).

Since menu items are assumed to have fixed names, the property {frozen} is attached to each name attribute in a menu item class. Nevertheless, the same menu item class may have different instances since there may be menu items with the same name but linked to different objects. To provide a convenient notation for menu classes in navigational structure models, we will use in the following the shorthand notation shown in Figure 10.

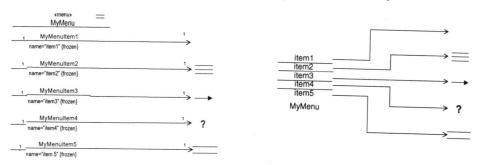

Figure 9. Menu Class

Figure 10. Shorthand for Menu Class

Figure 11 shows how the navigational structure model of the previous section is enriched by menus where each menu class is associated by a composition association to a navigational class. Note that the role names occurring in the previous model are now names of corresponding menu items.

The Method

The enhancement of a navigation space model by access elements of type menu follows certain rules which can be summarized as follows:

1. Consider those associations which have as their source a navigational class.
2. Associate to each navigational class which has (in the previous model) at least one outgoing association a corresponding menu class. The association between a

Figure 11. Navigational Structure Model

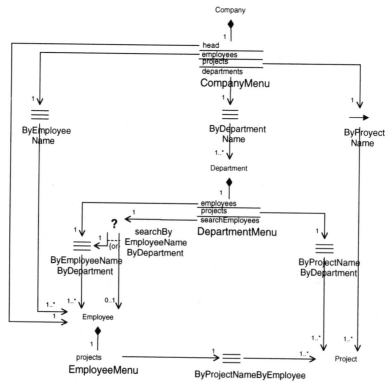

navigational class and its corresponding menu class is a composition.

3. Introduce for each role which occurs in the previous model at the end of a directed association a corresponding menu item. By default, the role name is used as the constant name of the menu item.

4. Any association of the previous model which has as its source a navigational class becomes now an association of the corresponding menu item introduced in step 3.

Navigational Structure Pattern

As a result of our method, we obtain a comprehensive navigational structure model of a Web application. It is guaranteed by our method that this model is built to conform to the pattern shown in Figure 12.

FROM A NAVIGATIONAL STRUCTURE MODEL TO A STATIC PRESENTATION MODEL

The navigational structure model shows how to navigate through the navigation space by using the access elements defined in the previous section. In the next step of our methodology, we describe how the information within the navigation space and the access structures are presented to the user. This is done by constructing a presentation model which shows an abstract interface design in a similar way to a user interface sketch. The presentation model focuses on the structural organization of the presentation and not on the physical appearance in terms of special formats, colors, etc. Such decisions are left to the implementation phase which is beyond the scope of this paper. However, the layout of modeling elements in the presentation model may provide hints, for example, about the position and the size of these elements relative to each other.

The following subsections show how a presentation model is derived from the navigational structure model. There are various different types of presentations that can be constructed. Two common alternatives are presented here: a menu-based presentation and a map-based presentation. The last one is also known as tree-structured technique and supports the visualization of the (total or partial) navigation space. It reduces the problem of the "lost in the hyperspace" syndrome. Sometimes both presentation types are combined in one application.

Modeling Elements

For constructing a presentation model, one has to decide which presentation elements will be used for the presentation of the instances of navigational classes and which for the presentation of the access elements. For this purpose we use several presentation modeling elements (with corresponding stereotypes):

- *Frameset*
  A frameset is a container of

Figure 12. Navigational Structure Pattern

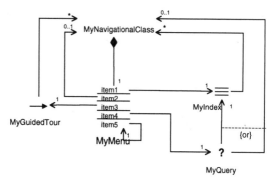

presentational objects or other framesets. It is an instance of a frameset class stereotyped by «frameset» with a corresponding icon. (The same stereotype and a similar icon is also used in Conallen (1999). A frameset must be built to conform to the composition structure shown in Figure 13.

- *Presentational class*
  A presentational class models the presentation of a navigational class or an access primitive, such as an index, a guided tour, query or menu. Instances of a presentational class are containers which comprise modeling elements like texts, images, video sequences, audio sequences, anchors, collections (i.e., lists of texts, images, etc.), anchored collections (i.e., lists of anchors), etc. It is stereotyped by «presentational class» with a corresponding icon and follows the composite rules depicted in Figure 14.

Figure 13. Frameset

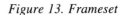
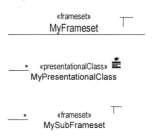

- *Text*
  A text is a sequence of characters.
- *Anchor*
  An anchor is a clickable piece of text which is the starting point of a navigation establishing the relationship to other nodes.
- *Button*
  A button is a clickable area which has an associated action. Examples of actions are playVideo, displayImage, stopAudio and runApplet. Note that buttons can also be triggers of navigation.
- *Image, audio* and *video*
  Image, audio and video are multimedia objects. An image can be displayed; audio and video can be started, stopped, rewinded and forwarded.
- *Form*
  A form is used to request information from the user who supplies information in one or more input fields or selects options from a browser or checkbox.
- *Collection and anchored collection*
  Collection and anchored collection are model elements, such as lists of text elements and lists of anchors introduced to pro-vide a convenient representation of composites. It is not specified whether the collection will be laid out horizon-tally or vertically.

The stereotypes for text, form, button, image, audio, video, anchor, collection and anchored collection are depicted in Figure 14. Figure 15 shows how these modeling elements can be used to construct a template for the presentation of employees.

Figure 14. Presentational Class

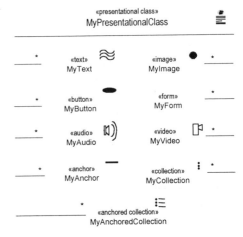

Example for a Menu-Based Presentation

Figures 16 to 19 show part of a presentation model for our sample application. In this example we use framesets to partition the presentation into frames, where the left frame always shows the main menu and the right frame shows the actual content. How this presentation model can be systematically derived from the navigational structure model is explained in the following section. For the moment, it is sufficient to point out that Figure 16 shows the presentation of the company, Figure 17 shows the presentation of the head of the company (after having selected Head), Figure 18 shows the presentation of the department index by means of a list of anchors (after having selected Departments) and Figure 19 shows how a selected department is presented. Thus we have not detailed the presentational class for department which can be done in a similar way to employee (in Figure 15).

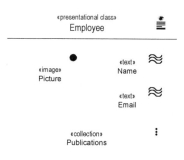

Figure 15. Presentational Class for Employee

The Method for a Menu-Based Presentation

The presentation model consists of a set of presentational classes (Web pages). The following rules can be used as a guide:

1. Construct a presentation for each navigational class occurring in the navigational structure model. It has to provide a template for presenting the instances of the class, taking into account the given attributes. Stereotyped classes, such as «text», «image», «audio», «video», are used for attributes of primitive types and «collections» are used for lists, etc. For instance, Figure 15 shows the presentation constructed for the navigational class Employee.

2. Choose one navigational class as a root for navigation and construct a presentational class for the menu of this navigational class (called main menu). In our example we select the class Company with the main menu CompanyMenu shown in Figure 16. We add an anchor Home, such that it is always possible to go back to the root.

3. Construct a presentational class for each index and menu occurring in the navigational structure model. For the presentation of an index or a menu class, we use modeling elements with stereotypes «anchored collection» or «anchor». Examples for menus and indexes are the EmployeeMenu, the DepartmentIndex and the DepartmentMenu included in Figures 17, 18 and 19, respectively.

4. Construct a presentational class for each query and each guided tour. Use forms for representing queries, and for guided tours introduce additional menu items ("next," "prev") which allow navigation to the next and previous object within the guided tour.

5. Combine each presentational class (constructed in 1) with the presentational class of its menu (constructed in 3) in a frameset. Eventually, add the main menu to the frameset. Such combinations can be seen in Figure 17 and Figure 19.

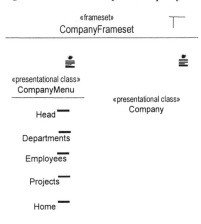

Figure 16. Frameset for Company

Example for a Map-Based Presentation

Figures 20 to 23 show a map-based presentation model for our sample application which is an alternative to the following section. In this case the left frame shows the actual navigation tree and the right frame shows the corresponding content. How this presentation model can be systematically derived from the navigational structure model is explained in Section 5.5.

Figure 20 shows the presentation of the company, Figure 21 shows the presentation of the head of the company (after having selected Head), Figure 22 shows the presentation of the department index by a list of anchors (after having selected Departments) and Figure 23 shows how a selected department (for instance the i-th department Dep_i) is presented.

Figures 17. Frameset for Head

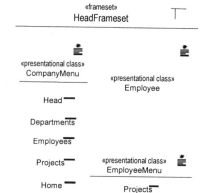

The Method for a Map-Based Presentation

The map-based presentation method is again based on the use of framesets which allow us to visualize the navigation structure. The idea is therefore to always divide a presentation into two basic parts: one part provides a presentation of the navigation tree (showing the user's actual navigation path and hence the context of navigation) and the other part shows the corresponding content.

On this basis we define the following procedure for deriving a presentation model from a navigational structure model in an entirely systematic way.

1. Construct a presentation for each navigational class, and model each index class occurring in the navigational structure in a similar way as above.
2. Choose one navigational class as a root for navigation. In our example we select the class Company.
3. For each navigational class and for each index class, consider all possible paths (in the navigational structure model) from the root class to the actual class. For each path

Figure 18. Frameset for Department Index

Figure 19. Frameset for Department

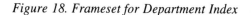

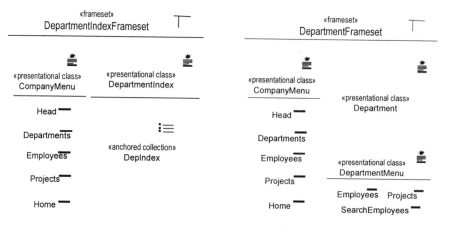

construct a presentation of the corresponding navigation tree.

Let us explain this step in more detail by considering our example. We start with the class Company. The corresponding navigation tree is represented by the presentational class NavigationalTreeCompany in the left frame of Figure 20. Since Company is the root of the navigation the corresponding tree is trivial and shows only the menu associated with Company.

The presentational class NavigationalTreeHead in Figure 21 shows the navigation tree if one moves to the head of the company. Note that the root of this tree is represented by the anchor Home for going back to the company. The anchor Projects is inserted at depth 2 of the tree to present the menu associated to employees (remember that the head is indeed an employee).

The presentational class NavigationalTreeDepartmentIndex in Figure 22 shows the navigation tree if one moves from the company to the department index, and the presentational class NavigationalTree-Department_i in Figure 23 shows the navigation tree if one navigates further to a particular department (for instance, the i-th department Dep_i). Note that in this case the anchors Employees, Projects and Search Employees are inserted at depth 3 of the tree for presenting the menu associated with a department.

4. Combine the results of step 1 and step 3 to framesets. Any frameset has two parts where the right frame contains the presentation of the navigational class or index class (constructed in step 1) and the left frame represents the navigation tree (constructed in step 3) corresponding to one possible navigation to this class.

Figure 20. Frameset for Company

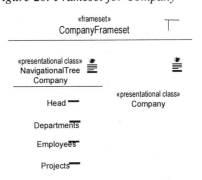

Figure 21. Frameset for Head

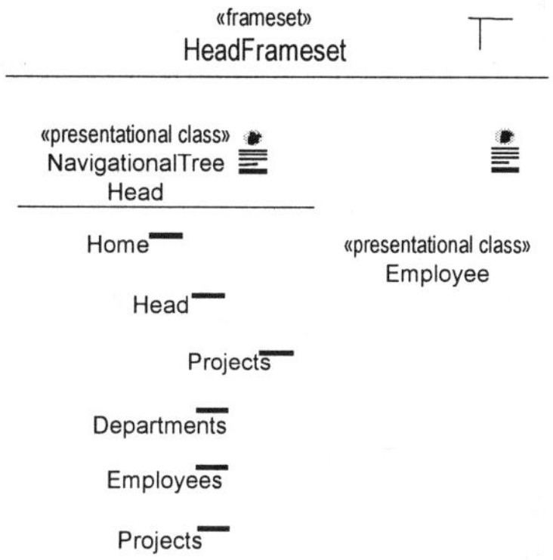

Figure 22. Frameset for Department Index

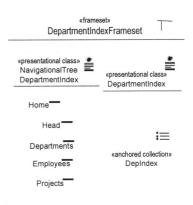

In our example, this leads to the framesets shown in Figures 20 to 23 which of course have to be completed by taking into account all other possible navigations shown in the navigational structure model in Figure 11. In particular, Figure 11 also contains guided tours and queries whose presentation is not detailed here. The idea is to present a guided tour simply by two additional anchors Next and Prev (with an obvious meaning) which extend the menu of the corresponding navigational class. As a straightforward presentation of queries, one will usually choose forms.

In step 3 we must ensure that there is only a finite set of navigation paths from the root class to each navigational or index class. For this purpose we assume that the given navigational structure model has no cycles, i.e., forms a directed acyclic graph. This is not a proper restriction since in any case we provide a presentation of the navigation tree that allows us to move backwards. Concerning the presentation of a navigation tree, it is obvious that in practice the depth of the tree must be limited. For a convenient representation of such trees, one may also use several frames, for instance a top frame and a left frame. In this case the left frame in Figure 23 would be split into a top frame which contains the main menu and into a left frame presenting the subtree with the anchor Dep_i as a root.

Let us note that there is also a variant of the above procedure which treats the presentation of indexes differently. With this variant the department index would be included in the navigation tree on the left-hand side while the right frame could include, for instance, some additional general information on all departments. This variant is shown in Figure 24.

DYNAMIC PRESENTATION MODEL

In addition to the static presentation model, we model the dynamic aspects of the presentation by a window flow model that describes the behavior of the presentational objects, i.e., the changes on the user interface when the user interacts with the system. The construction of a window flow model is mainly recommended when a multiple-window technique is chosen. It specifies when windows are open, closed and when they coexist.

Control flow between windows can be represented by interaction models showing which windows are open and which frameset is displayed in each window at a certain moment. For this purpose we use UML sequence diagrams.

Figure 23. Frameset for Department   *Figure 24. Department Index Frameset (Variant)*

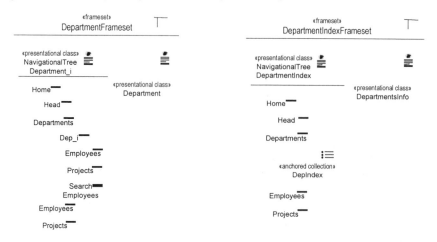

Modeling Elements

The following modeling element *window* is used for describing user interactions with the user interface of the Web application:

* *Window*
  A window is the area of the user interface where framesets or presentational objects are displayed. A window can be moved, resized and reduced to an icon. It includes at least two buttons, one to transform the window into an icon and one to close the window. Figure 25 depicts a stereotyped class for windows.

Figure 25: Window

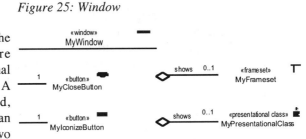

Example

Figure 26 shows part of a window flow model for the sample application corresponding to the search of employees by department. The window flow model describes the dynamics of the map-based presentation of the last section. It shows an abstract representation since the eventual implementation will include more objects, in particular control objects that collaborate in this interactive process (Conallen, 1999).

The Method

The steps to build a window flow model cannot be automated as the developer has to decide how many windows are used, when and which additional windows are opened and

Fig. 26: Window Flow Model

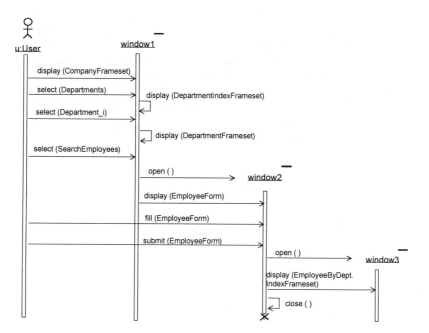

closed. The following is a set of guidelines to assist the developer in the modeling of the window flow model based on the navigational structure model and the static presentation model:

1. Set the context for the interaction model, i.e., define which navigation path of the navigational structure diagram will be modeled . A navigation path is always related to a use case. In Figure 26 it is the use case search employee by department that is part of the employee's administration.
2. Decide how many windows are needed in this context. Three windows are used in our example. Represent the user and these window objects in the horizontal dimension.
3. Specify a display message for each presentational object and frameset that should be presented to the user (in a window). The parameter of the display message is the corresponding frameset.
4. Include a select message for each user action that selects an anchor or a button. The anchor or button names are the parameters of the message.
5. Specify a fill and a submit message for each user action that consist of supplying data in a query form. This form is the parameter of the message.
6. Include a message for each open and each close of a window.
7. Use "balking" to specify the period of time that a window is visible.

UML sequence diagrams are used to represent the window control flow. Note that the representation does not include additional classes needed in the implementation to facilitate the communication between windows.

FUTURE TRENDS

Let us return to the first sentence of this chapter, Web engineering is a new and still evolving discipline. The methodology presented in this chapter is part of this Web engineering discipline and is not expected to be an exception.

There are many open issues to be addressed and integrated, such as database and distributed systems aspects, changing technologies in the Web field or new versions of the UML. Another aspect that will play an important role in the future development of hypermedia systems is the personalization of applications, i.e., adaptation of the presentation or navigation according to the user interests, knowledge or preferences. Adaptation can be based on the information provided by agents that observe the users' behavior. A future methodology for Web design also has to cope with the design of multi-modal interfaces including speech for example. Synchronization problems also have to be solved in these kinds of flexible Web applications.

Tools for UML are developing fast, but there is an enormous scope for improvement; indeed there is widespread dissatisfaction with the state of the art. There are good drawing tools, but these need to increase their capabilities to provide automatic verification of models, to support the use of patterns and to allow for constraint specification with OCL.

There is still much work needed to improve the Web engineering discipline. This will be done mostly in little steps through the continuous adjustment of methodologies, techniques, notations and tools.

CONCLUSIONS

In this chapter we have presented a methodology for the design of Web applications that uses a UML profile for the Web domain. The methodology consists of a notation and a method that extends previous approaches of Baumeister et al. (1999) and Hennicker & Koch (2000). The deliverables of our method are models represented by UML diagrams. Some of the modeling elements occurring in such diagrams are defined by stereotypes using the UML extension mechanism. The definition of many new stereotypes causes extra effort to read the diagrams, but once one gets used to them, the diagrams are more meaningful in terms of Web design. The advantages of the methodology are the use of the UML, the consideration of specific Web aspects in design of Web applications through the definition of specialized modeling elements and the creation of the tailored models to express navigation and presentation.

The methodology describes how to build:
- the navigation space model based on the conceptual model,
- the navigational structure model from the navigation space model, and
- the static and dynamic presentation model from the navigational structure model.

The strength of this approach is that for each model a detailed list of construction steps is provided. We have therefore tried to identify as many steps as possible that can be performed automatically, for instance, when constructing the navigational structure model from the navigation space model. In addition, the method describes how templates for the Web application can be systematically generated from the navigational structure model. However, there are still several steps where decisions of the designers are essential. This concerns, in particular, the construction of the navigation space model based on the conceptual model.

The design steps presented here are part of a development process (Koch, 2000) based on the Unified Process (Jacobson et al., 1999) that covers the whole lifecycle of Web applications. The methodology still requires validation and testing for a wide spectrum of Web applications. Moreover it has to be extended to model the dynamic and database aspects related to Web applications, in particular for e-commerce applications. A further next step will be the construction of a case tool that supports our methodology.

ACKNOWLEDGMENT

We would like to thank Luis Mandel and Hubert Baumeister for common work related to the UML extension. We wish to thank Martin Wirsing for the various discussions, reviews and comments. We thank also Andy Schürr and other participants of the GROOM 2000 Workshop for helpful suggestions.

REFERENCES

Baumeister, H., Koch, N., & Mandel, L. (1999). Towards a UML extension for hypermedia design. In Proceedings «UML»'99, France, R., Rumpe, B. (Eds), LNCS, Vol. 1723. Springer-Verlag, 614-629.

Berner, S., Glinz, M., & Joos, S. (1999). A classification of stereotypes for object-oriented modeling languages. In Proceedings «UML»'99, France, R., Rumpe, B. (Eds), LNCS, Vol. 1723. Springer-Verlag, 249-264.

Booch, G., Rumbaugh, J., & Jacobson, I. (1999). The Unified Modeling Language: A User Guide. Addison-Wesley.

Conallen, J. (1999). *Building Web Applications with UML*. Addison-Wesley.

Hennicker R., & Koch N.(2000). A UML-based methodology for hypermedia design. *In*

Proceedings UML (2000), LNCS, Springer-Verlag.

Isakowitz, T., Stohr, E., & Balasubramanian, P. (1995). *A methodology for the design of structured hypermedia applications*. Communications of the ACM, 8(38), 34-44.

Jacobson, I., Booch, G., & Rumbaugh, J. (1999). *The Unified Software Development Process*. Addison-Wesley.

Koch, N. (1999). A comparative study of methods for hypermedia development. Technical Report 9901, Ludwig-Maximilians-University Munich.

Koch, N. (2000). Hypermedia systems development based on the Unified Process. Technical Report 0003, Ludwig-Maximilians-University Munich.

Kruchten, P. (1998). *The Rational Unified Process: An Introduction*. Addison-Wesley.

Lowe D., & Hall W.(1999). *Hypermedia & the Web: An Engineering Approach*. John Wiley & Sons.

Nanard, J., & Nanard, M. (1995). Hypertext design environments and the hypertext design process. *Communication of the ACM*, Vol. 38(8), 49-56.

Sauer, S., & Engels, G. (1999). *Extending UML for modeling of multimedia applications. In Proceedings of the IEEE Symposium on Visual Languages – VL99*, IEEE Computer Society, 80-87.

Schneider, G., & Winters, J. (1998). *Applying Use Cases: A Practical Guide*. Addison-Wesley Object Technology Series.

Schwabe, D., & Rossi, G. (1998). *Developing hypermedia applications using OOHDM*. In *Proceedings of Workshop on Hypermedia Development Process, Methods and Models, Hypertext98*.

Chapter II

A Systematic Approach to Transform UML Static Models to Object-Oriented Code

Liliana Favre
Universidad Nacional del Centro de la Pcia. de Buenos Aires, Argentina

Silvia Clérici
Universidad Politécnica de Cataluña
España

Formal and semi-formal techniques can play complementary roles in object-oriented software development. The purpose of this chapter is to present a reuse-based rigorous method to forward engineering UML static models. This approach is based on the integration of semi-formal notations in UML with the algebraic style. The main contributions of this chapter are the definition of the GSBL[oo] algebraic language to cope with concepts of the UML models, the definition of the SpReIm model for the description of the structure of reusable components and the definition of a rigorous process with reuse that assists in the transformation of UML class diagrams to object-oriented code. Eiffel was the language of choice in which to demonstrate the feasibility of our approach.

INTRODUCTION

The Unified Modeling Language, UML, is rapidly becoming a de-facto standard for modeling software systems (OMG, 1999). It is a set of graphical and textual notations for specifying, visualizing and documenting object-oriented systems. An important feature of UML is that it is a modeling language, not a method, and therefore it does not prescribe any particular development process. UML is not a visual programming language, but its models can be directly connected to a variety of object-oriented programming languages through forward engineering processes. These processes transform UML models into code through a mapping to an implementation language (Booch, Rumbaugh & Jacobson, 1999).

UML is too imprecise and ambiguous when it comes to simulation, verification, validation and forecasting of system properties and even when it comes to generating implementations from specifications. Another problem is that models written in UML are semantically richer than any other current object programming language. For example, an object-oriented language does not possess an explicit syntax to express UML associations. These can be simulated by pointers and references, but then the structure of the system is not apparent. This often leads to problems during forward/reverse engineering between the specification and code. A variety of advantages have been attributed to the use of formal software specification to solve these problems. It is commonly accepted that a formal specification can reveal gaps, ambiguities and inconsistencies. Furthermore, a precise semantics provides the basis for automated forward engineering and reverse engineering (the process of transforming code into a model through a mapping from a specific implementation language).

However, semi-formal approaches still dominate even in areas where formal approaches should provide a competitive advantage. The success of graphical modeling techniques is due to several reasons. On the one hand, they provide a set of graphical and textual descriptions that are easily understandable for both system developers and expert users. In general, there are also good tools to support them. On the other hand, formal methods provide minimal guidelines for eliciting and structuring requirements, and the notation of formal specification languages requires familiarity with symbolic logic that most designers and implementers do not currently have. Besides, the learning curve for the application of these new techniques requires considerable time.

Formal and informal techniques can play complementary roles in software development. The integration should be based on the following considerations:

- Formal models must preserve the interpretation of object-oriented models, constructions and underlying concepts reinforcing the informal interpretations.
- Specification and reasoning must be integrated with code.
- It is necessary to define mappings between formal models and object-oriented model constructs and concepts that provide the basis for assisted generation of formal specifications from informal specifications without forcing the user to change specification style.
- Only those parts that can benefit from more rigorous specification and analysis must be formalized.

In this chapter we present a rigorous process with reuse to forward engineer UML static models. This approach is based on the integration of semi-formal notations in UML with algebraic specifications. The primary objective of this integration is to make easier the analysis, reuse, evolution and maintenance of the software. Rather than requiring that developers manipulate formal specifications, we want to provide formal semantics for graphical modeling notations and develop rigorous tools that permit developers to directly manipulate models they have created.

The bases of our approach are:

- The definition of the GSBL$^{\infty}$ algebraic language.
- The definition of the *SpReIm* model for the description of the structure of a reusable component.
- The definition of a method with reuse that assists in the transformation of UML class diagrams to object-oriented code.

The GSBL$^{\infty}$ language enriches GSBL (Clérici & Orejas,1988) with constructs that allow us to express different kinds of UML relations: generalization/specialization, dependency, associations and realizations. The *SpReIm* model allows us to describe object-oriented hierarchies at different levels of abstraction that integrate algebraic specifications and classes in an object-oriented language. The method is based on the transformation of a library of reusable components. The manipulation of *SpReIm* components by means of building operators (*Rename, Hide, Combine, Extend*) is the basis for the reusability. Eiffel (Meyer, 1997) was chosen as the language in which to demonstrate the feasibility of our approach.

The chapter has the following structure. We first take a look at related work. Then we describe the GSBL$^{\infty}$ object-oriented algebraic language, the *SpReIm model* and a rigorous process for forward engineering. Next we outline experimental results and advantages of our approach. This is followed by conclusions.

RELATED WORK

At the end of the '80s, new specification languages or extensions of formal languages to support object-oriented concepts began to develop. Among them the different extensions of the Z language (Spivey, 1992), for example Z++ (Lano, 1990), OBJECT-Z (Carrington et al., 1989) or OOZE (Alencar & Goguen, 1989) can be mentioned. Another language with object-oriented characteristics and based on OBJ3 (Goguen & Malcolm, 1989) is FOOPS (Rappanotti & Socorro, 1992). Among the most recent ones, the OBLOG language is being developed as the basis for a commercial product (Junclauss, Saake & Sernadas, 1991). Within the academic world there exists other developments associated with the OBLOG family: TROLL (Junclauss, Saake, Hartmann & Sernadas, 1996), GNOME (Sernadas & Ramos, 1994), LCM (Feenstra & Wieringa, 1993) and ALBERT (Wieringa & Dubois, 1998) whose common semantic basis is the temporal logic. CASL (COFI, 1999) is a language used to specify requirements and designs. It was designed to combine the most successful characteristics of the existing languages and to give a unified basis for the algebraic specification languages. CASL wants to be the central member of a language family that includes simple languages obtained by restriction and more advanced ones obtained by extension (for example to specify reactive systems). Reflexive languages based upon the rewriting logic such as MAUDE (Clavel et al., 1999) and CafeOBJ (Diaconescu & Futatsugi, 1998) are being already designed and implemented.

Among the classical references associated to the generation of object-oriented code from formal specifications, we can mention FRESCO and the LARCH specification language family. FRESCO is a programming environment to develop object-oriented software from VDM specifications (Wills, 1992). Larch/Smalltalk was the first language with subtype and inheritance specification (Cheon & Leavens, 1994). LARCH/C++ is another language with similar characteristics.

Further works analyzed the integration of semi-formal techniques and object-oriented design with formal techniques. For example, France, Bruel and Larrondo-Petri,1997 describe the formalization of FUSION models in Z. Bordeau and Cheng, 1995 introduce a method to derive LARCH algebraic specifications from class diagrams.

The UML formalization is an open problem yet, and many research groups have already achieved the formalization of parts of the language. It is difficult to compare the existing results and to see how to integrate them in order to define standard semantics since they specify a different UML subset and they are based on different formalisms. Bruel and France (1998) describe how to formalize UML models using Z, Lano (1995) using Z++;

Breu et al.(1997) do a similar job using stream-oriented algebraic specifications, Gogolla and Ritchers (1997) do this by transforming UML to TROLL, Overgaard (1998) achieves it by using operational semantics and Kim and Carrington do it through using OBJECT-Z. Firesmith and Henderson-Sellers (1998) describe advanced metamodeling and notation techniques that allow the enhancement of UML. The Precise UML Group, pUML, is created in 1997 with the goal of giving precision to UML (Evans, France, Lano & Rumpe, 1998).

OCL (OMG, 1999) is a formal language developed as a business-modeling language within the IBM Insurance Division and it has its roots in the Syntropy method. UML users can make use of OCL to specify constraints and other expressions associated to their models. It can also be applied to specify invariants on classes, to describe preconditions and postconditions on operations and methods, to specify constraints on operations and as a navigation language. Currently there are few development methods that include OCL. The most important is Catalysis (D'Souza & Wills, 1999). Bidoit, Hennicker, Tort and Wirsing (1999) present an approach for specifying UML interface constraints and proving the correctness of implementation relations between interfaces and classes. Their approach includes a proposal for an interface constraint language OCL-like. Mandel and Cengarle (1999) have examined the expressive power of OCL in terms of navigability and computability. They have shown that OCL is less expressive than the relational calculus, and they also hinted it is not equivalent to a Turing machine. Vaziri and Jackson (1999) argue that OCL is too implementation-oriented and therefore not well-suited for conceptual modeling.

What the latter formalizations have in common is the fact that they give semantics to UML and certainly this is also another goal in our work. However, it is not an end in itself; we want to give semantics to UML static models in order to transform design artifacts into code by means of a rigorous process that facilitates software and design reuse.

As examples of commercial CASE tools that support UML, we can mention Rational Rose, Together, GDPro, Stp/UML, Argo/UML, MagicDraw UML, etc. On the one hand the existing tools are hardly flexible since the programmer has little participation in design decisions associated to the standard translations from the model into code; on the other hand, they free the programmer to such an extent that he can introduce code modification wherever adequate. It is the programmer's responsibility to preserve integrity between code and model. In addition these tools do not support transformation of all the information captured in the UML models (e.g., associations, their cardinality, associated constraints and OCL specifications). The aim of this chapter is to contribute to the solution of these issues.

Algebraic specifications allow association of UML models to a base of reusable components that can be formally manipulated to obtain not only probably correct code but also a "design history" that can support forward and reverse engineering. Our approach emphasizes reusability by manipulating components through reuse operators.

THE GSBL^{OO} LANGUAGE

The GSBL^{oo} language has been designed as an extension of the algebraic specification language GSBL (Clérici & Orejas, 1988) to cope with concepts of the UML models.

The main idea of the algebraic approach is to describe data structures by just giving the names of the different sets of data (sorts), the names of the basic functions (operations) and their properties, which are described by means of a logic (like the equational logic).

GSBL (Generic Specification Base Language) is a kernel language for the incremental construction and organization of specifications. In GSBL genericity goes together with incompleteness and there is not explicit parameterization. Every incomplete specification (i.e., one where there are not enough equations to specify an operation or there are not enough operations to "generate" all values of a given sort) is, implicitly, generic. The only kind of unit specification is the class that can describe incomplete (deferred) and/or complete (effective) parts. In GSBL specifications are considered structured objects. This structure is based on relations associated to two specification-building mechanisms for combining classes. The first one is by extension of a given specification, in this case a new class is built over previously existing ones (its components). The second way is by an inheritance mechanism (which can be considered a generalized parameter-passing). Subclasses are defined by specializing consistently some incompletely defined part of a given specification (its superclass). Both mechanisms correspond respectively to client and inheritance relations that are central notions of object-oriented structuring. On the other hand GSBL provides powerful binding mechanisms to define new specifications in a very concise way.

GSBL$^{\infty}$ adds primitives to directly express constructs and concepts of UML class diagrams. In particular, it provides an explicit syntax for UML relations.

Booch et al. (1999) distinguish four kinds of UML relations: dependency, generalization, association and realization. A detailed description of them may be found in OMG (1999).

- A dependency is "a relationship between two modeling elements, in which a change to one modeling element (the independent element) will affect the other modeling element (the dependent element)" (OMG, 1999, B-6).
- An association is a structural relation that specifies that objects of one class be connected to objects of another. An association that connects two classes is called a binary association. A plain association between classes means that both classes are conceptually at the same level, neither of them is more important than the other. An aggregation is "a special form of association that specifies a whole-part relation between the aggregate (whole) and a component part" (OMG, 1999, B-2). A composition is "a form of aggregation association with strong ownership and coincident lifetime as part of the whole. Parts with non-fixed multiplicity may be created after the composite itself, but once created they live and die with it (i.e., they share lifetimes). Such parts can also be explicitly removed before the death of the composite" (OMG, 1999, B-5). A composite implies propagation semantics. A "shared" aggregation denotes weak ownership (i.e, the part may be included in several aggregates), its owner may also change over time and deletion of the whole does not imply deletion of the parts.
- A generalization is "a taxonomic relation between a more general element and a more specific element. The more specific is fully consistent with the more general element and contains additional information. An instance of a more specific element may be used where the more general element is allowed" (OMG, 1999, B-9).
- A realization is a semantic relation between classifiers (classes, interfaces, components, etc.), in which one classifier specifies a contract that another classifier guarantees to carry out (Booch et al., 1999, p. 149). For example, we can use realizations to specify the relation between an interface and the class or component that provides an operation or service for it. The relation between interface and class is not necessarily one-to-one.

There is no single accepted definition of the difference between aggregation and association. In UML, the shared aggregate is loosely defined. In Henderson-Sellers (1998) and Henderson-Sellers and Barbier (1999), whole-part relations that could allow enhancing UML are defined more precisely.

The treatment of associations and aggregations in object-oriented languages as little more than pointer-value attributes has confined them to a second-class status. But associations are semantic constructions of equal weight to the classes and generalizations in the UML models. In fact, the associations allow abstracting the interaction between classes in the design of large systems and they affect the partition of the systems into modules.

GSBL^{oo} includes a library of generic relations that captures the semantics of associations. New relations can be defined just like an existing one, but with its own special properties. This approach allows us to shape and grow the GSBL^{oo} to our needs and to define associations as an independent unit, thus relieving the designer writing the specification from the burden of replicating that generic semantics for each concrete application. Following, we describe in more detail the GSBL^{oo} syntax.

Representing Object Classes

In Figure 1 we show the syntax of an GSBL^{oo} object class specification. In GSBL^{oo} strictly generic components can be distinguished by means of explicit parameterization. The elements of <parameterlist> are pairs C1:C2, where C1 is the formal generic parameter constrained by an existing class C2 (only subclasses of C2 will be a valid actual parameter).

GSBL^{oo} provides mechanisms for expressing inheritance and dependency relations. The USES clause expresses dependency relations. The specification of the new class is based on the imported specifications declared, and their visible constituents may be used in the new specification. In GSBL^{OO} it is possible to specify any of the three levels of visibility: public, protected and private. They are expressed by prefixing the symbols: +(public), #(protected) and -(private). If we don't decorate an operation with a symbol of visibility, it can be assumed that it is public.

The power of the inheritance comes from the fusion of a type mechanism (the definition of a new type as a special case of existing types) with module mechanisms (the definition of a module as an extension of existing modules). Since it has been recognized that the two views of inheritance have different methodological and semantic background, GSBL^{OO} distinguishes two different mechanisms: REFINES and RESTRICTS. The first one relies on the module viewpoint of classes while the second one relies on the type viewpoint.

In the REFINES clause the specification of the class is built from the union of the specifications of the classes appearing in the <refineslist>. The components of each one of them becomes com-

Figure 1. GSBL^{oo} Class Syntax

```
OBJECT CLASS class-name[<parameterlist>]
USES <useslist>
REFINES <refinestlist>
RESTRICTS < restrictslist>
BASIC CONSTRUCTORS <constructorlist>
DEFERRED
SORTS <sortlist>
OPS <opslist>
EQS <varlist> <equationlist>
EFFECTIVE
SORTS <sortlist>
OPS <opslist>
EQS <varlist> <equationlist>
END-CLASS
```

ponents of the new class, and its own sorts and operations become sorts and operations of the new class. On the other hand, the RESTRICTS clause builds the specification of the new class by adding a value-constraint in the specification of the old one. Note that both REFINES and RESTRICTS are based on subset relations, but at different conceptual levels. While the REFINES relation describes a subset relation at the level of models, the RESTRICTS relation describes a subset relation at the level of carrier set containing objects.

GSBL^{oo}, as GSBL, distinguishes incomplete and complete parts. The DEFERRED clause declares new sorts, operations or equations that are incompletely defined. The EFFECTIVE clause either declares new sorts, operations or equations that are completely defined, or completes the definition of some inherited sort or operation. The syntax of a complete class can include the BASIC CONSTRUCTORS clause that refers to generator operations. A class may introduce any number of sorts; if one of them has the same name as the class, this sort is considered the *sort of interest* of the class.

GSBL^{oo} preserves the GSBL binding mechanisms. In particular, local instances of a class may also be defined in the USES and REFINES clauses by the following syntax:

Class-name [*<binding-list>*]

where the elements of <binding-list> can be pairs of class names C1:C2, C2 being a component of *Class-name;* pairs of sorts *s1:s2,* and/or pairs of operations *o1: o2* with *o2* and *s2* belonging to the own part of *Class-name*. There are different kinds of bindings:

- A[C:B] where C is a class already existing in the environment and B is a component of A and C is a subclass of B. The effect in this case is the creation of an instance of A in which the component B is substituted by C.
- A[C:B] where C is not the name of a previously existing class in the environment and B is a component of A. The effect of this declaration is, simply, the creation of an instance of A in which the name of component B is renamed by C.
- A [s1:s1] or A[o1:o1'] in which a sort or operation of A is renamed.

The sort of interest of a class (if any) is also implicitly renamed each time the class is substituted or renamed. Instances of parameterized classes can be defined with the usual syntax *Class-name*[*<actual-parameter-list>*] when no additional renaming or substitution are needed.

In Figure 2 we give a GSBL^{oo} specification of the OCL Collection Type (see Warner and Kleppe, 1999, pp. 94-95). For example, the *select$_i$* operation specifies a selection from a collection. The predicate p_i specifies which elements we want to select from a collection ANY is a predefined class that only has a deferred sort ANY.

Defining Associations

Associations are defined as standard elements in GSBL^{oo}. ASSOCIATION is a taxonomy of constructor types that classifies associations according to:

- Its kind (aggregation, composition, association, etc). An association can be a simple association, an aggregation, a qualified association or a class association. An aggregation can be "shared " or "non-shared" (composition).
- Its degree (unary, binary, ternary and in general as n-ary).
- Its navigability, for example a binary association can be unidirectional or bi-directional.
- Its connectivity (one-to-one, one-to-many, many-to-many, etc.).

Figure 3 shows hierarchy of associations. Figure 4 partially depicts the GSBL^{oo} specifications of some of them (Binary Association, Aggregation and "shared" aggregation

Figure 2. GSBL^{oo} Specifications

OBJECT CLASS Operation [X:ANY]
USES Boolean, $Z_1,...Z_m$
DEFERRED
OPS
$p_i : X \rightarrow$ Boolean | $1 \leq i \leq n$
$base_j : \rightarrow Z_j$ | $1 \leq j \leq n$
$g_j : Z_j \times X \rightarrow Z_j$ | $1 \leq j \leq n$
.....
END-CLASS
OBJECT CLASS Collection[Elem:ANY]
USES Boolean, Nat, OP: Operation[Elem]
BASIC CONSTRUCTORS create, add
DEFERRED
SORT Collection
OPS
create: $\rightarrow$ Collection
add: Collection x Elem $\rightarrow$ Collection
size: Collection $\rightarrow$ Nat
count: Collection x Elem $\rightarrow$ Nat.
.....
EFFECTIVE
OPS
is-empty: Collection $\rightarrow$ Boolean
includes: Collection x Elem $\rightarrow$ Boolean
includes-all: Collection x Collection $\rightarrow$ Boolean
$select_i$: Collection$\rightarrow$ Collection | $1 \leq i \leq n$

$reject_i$: Collection$\rightarrow$ Collection | $1 \leq i \leq n$
$for-all_i$: Collection$\rightarrow$ Boolean |$1 \leq i \leq n$
$exists_i$: Collection$\rightarrow$ Boolean | $1 \leq i \leq n$
$iterate_j$: Collection$\rightarrow Z_j$ | $1 \leq j \leq n$
....
EQS { c,c1:Collection; e:Elem}
is-empty(create) = true
is-empty(add(c,e))= false
includes(create,e)=false
includes(add(c,e),e1)=
if e=e1 then true else includes(c,e1)
includes-all(c, create)= true
includes-all(c,add (c1,e)) =
includes(c,e) and includes-all(c,c1)
$select_i$ (create)= create
$select_i$ (add(c,e))=
if p_i(e) then add($select_i$(c),e) else $select_i$ (c)
$reject_i$ (create)= create
$reject_i$ (add(c,e))= if not p_i(e)
then add($reject_i$(c),e) else $reject_i$ (c)
$for-all_i$ (create)= true
$for-all_i$(add(c,e))= p_i(e) and $for-all_i$(c)
$exists_i$ (create)= false
$exists_i$ (add(c,e))= p_i(e) or $exists_i$(c)
$iterate_j$(create) = $base_j$
$iterate_j$(add(c,e))= g_j(e, $iterate_j$(c))...
.....
END-CLASS

Figure 3. Association Component

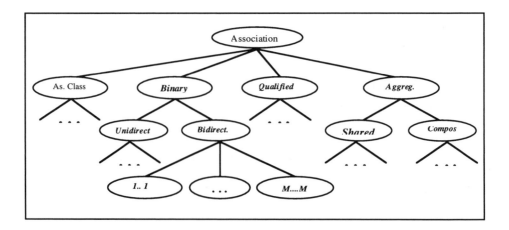

Figure 4. Relation Classes

```
RELATION CLASS                          is-related: Aggregation x Part x Whole→ Boolean
Binary[Class1:ANY; Class2:ANY]          EFFECTIVE
USES String, Multiplicity,              OPS
Pair:CartesProd_2 [Class1,Class2]       get_Part: Aggregation → Part
REFINES Set[Pair]                       get_Whole: Aggregation → Whole ...
DEFERRED                                EQS {p:Part; w:Whole; a:Aggregation;
SORTS Binary                            get_Part(inic (p,w))= p
OPS                                     get_Whole(inic(p,w))=w
role1: Binary → String                  ...
role2: Binary → String                  END- CLASS
mult1: Binary → Multiplicity
mult2:Binary → Multiplicity             RELATION CLASS Aggreg_1to* [P:ANY;W:ANY] ,
......                                   USES P_1to*: Collection[P]
END-RELATION                            REFINES Aggregation[P_1to*; W]...
                                        EFFECTIVE
RELATION CLASS                          OPS
Aggregation[Part:ANY;Whole:ANY]         remove_Part: Aggreg_1to* (c)x P_1to* (p) x W (w) → Aggreg_1to*
USES Boolean, Multiplicity,             pre: is-related(c,p,w) and not frozen(c ) and not add-only(c)
DEFERRED                                add_Part: Aggreg_1to*(c) x P_1to* (p) x W (w) → Aggreg_1to*
SORTS Aggregation                       pre: is-related(c,p,w) and not  frozen(c)
OPS                                     is-related: Aggreg_1to* x P_1to* x W  → Boolean
mult1: Aggregation → Multiplicity       modify: Aggreg_1to* x P_1to*  x P_1to*→ Aggreg_1to*
mult2: Aggregation → Multiplicity       ....
inic:Part x Whole → Aggregation         EQS{ a:Aggreg_1to*;...
frozen: Aggregation → Boolean           not frozen(a)
changeable: Aggregation → Boolean       not add-only(a)
add-only:Aggregation → Boolean          END-CLASS
```

with connectivity one-to many).

Generic relations can be used in the definition of concrete relations by the mechanism of instantiation. It is indicated by the keyword IS, defined by textual substitution (similar to "macro expansion") of the body and coupled with the possibility to specify static constraints in first-order logic that may be applied to the association. New associations and whole-part relations (aggregation and composition) can be defined by means of the following syntax:

```
ASSOCIATION <relation name>
IS <component-relation name> [ Class1:...;Class2:....role1:...;role2:....;
mult1:...;mult2:...;visibility1:...;visibility2:...]
CONSTRAINED BY <constraint-list>
```

```
WHOLE-PART <relation name> IS
<component-relation name> [ Whole:...; Part:....; mult1:...; mult2:...]
CONSTRAINED BY <constrained-list>
```

The IS clause expresses the instantiation of <component-relation name> with roles, visibility, multiplicity, etc. The CONSTRAINED-BY clause allows one to specify static constraints in first order logic.

New relations are specified in an Object Class by placing the relation name, enclosed in quotation marks, above the keywords ASSOCIATES or HAS-A. These keywords identify ordinary association or aggregation respectively. The keywords SHARED and NON-SHARED refer to simple aggregation and composition respectively.

OBJECT CLASS C...
"<relation name>"**ASSOCIATES** <class name>
"<relation name>" **HAS-A SHARED** <class-name>
　　　　　　"<relation name>" **HAS-A NON-SHARED** <class-name>
......
END-CLASS

An association may be refined to have its own set of operations and properties, i.e., operations that do not belong to any of the associated classes, but rather to the association itself. Such an association is called an Association Class. The semantics of such an association are a combination of the semantics of an ordinary association and an object class. Here is the syntax of an ASSOCIATION CLASS (the IS clause includes the specification of an ordinary association and <body> respects the syntax of an object class body):

ASSOCIATION CLASS <class name>
IS <component-relation name> [Class1:...;Class2:....role1:...;role2:...;
mult1:...;mult2:...;visibility1:...;visibility2:...]
<body>
END-CLASS

Packages

The mechanism provided by GSBL^{OO} for grouping classes and relations is the package. Packages have the following general form:

　　PACKAGE package-name
　　IMPORTING <importing-list>
　　INHERITS <inherit-list>
　　<elements>
　　END-PACKAGE

Here *package-name* names a package; *importing-lists* lists the imported packages; *inherit-list* lists the inherited packages and <elements> are the classes, associations and packages. Every element is uniquely owned by exactly one package. Prefixing the element's name with an appropriate visibility symbol specifies the visibility of an element owned by a package. An element can be designated as public, protected or private. "Importing" grants a one-way permission for the elements in one package to access the elements in another package. If X's package imports Y's package, X can now see Y, although Y cannot see X.

It is possible to specify families of packages by generalization. Packages involved in generalization relations follow the same principle of substitutability as classes do. A specialized package can be used anywhere a more general package can be used. Elements made available to another package by generalization have the same visibility in the heir as they have in the owning package.

In the next sections we give several examples that illustrate GSBL$^{\infty}$ specifications. In particular, a package specifying a class diagram for a School System (where the different kinds of associations appear) is shown in Figure 8.

The *SpReIm* Model

It is impossible to manage a library with a large number of components without a systematic classification scheme, which splits object domains into identifiable-subdomains. It is also convenient to reflect this division in the components. Software reusability takes many different requirements into account, some of which are abstract and conceptual, while others are concrete and bound to implementation properties. All must be specified in an appropriate way. Considering the issues described above, we introduce the *SpReIm* model for the definition of the structure of a reusable component (Favre, 1998).

The SpReIm model takes advantage of the power given by algebraic formalism to describe behavior in an abstract way while respecting the domain classification principles adopted for the design of the class libraries in object-oriented languages. It allows us to describe object hierarchies at three different abstraction levels: specialization, realization and implementation.

The specialization level describes a hierarchy of incomplete algebraic specifications as an acyclic graph $G=(V,E)$, where V is a non-empty set of incomplete algebraic specifications and $E \subseteq V \times V$ defines a specialization relation between specifications. In this context, it must be verified that if P(x) is a provable property of objects x of type T, then P(y) must be verified for every object y of type S, where S is a specialization of T.

In order to integrate the *SpReIm* model with UML diagrams, the specialization level has two views. One of them is based on GSBL$^{\infty}$ specifications and the other on OCL. We propose an integration of OCL and GSBL$^{\infty}$ algebraic specifications. OCL helps the user in the component identification process without forcing him to change the specification formalism. The algebraic view will allow early validations and automation of the components' transformation.

Every leaf in the specialization level is associated with a sub-component at the realization level. A realization sub-component is a tree of algebraic specifications:
- The root is the most abstract definition.
- The internal nodes correspond to different realizations of the root.
- Leaves correspond to sub-components at the implementation level.

If E and E1 are specifications, then E can be realized by E1 if E and E1 have the same signature and every model of E1 is a model of E (Hennicker & Wirsing, 1992). Every specification at the realization level corresponds to a subcomponent at the implementation level, which groups a set of implementation schemes associated with a class in an object-oriented language.

There is a relation between the other two levels and the implementation level. Every incomplete algebraic specification in the specialization level is associated with a deferred class in an object-oriented language that matches the specified incomplete behavior. Internal nodes of the realization level components, including the root, correspond to an abstract class that defers implementation in the object-oriented level,b and leaves in the realization level correspond to concrete classes in an object-oriented language. The implementation level can contain classes that are not related to the specifications in the

Figure 5. ASSOCIATION Component

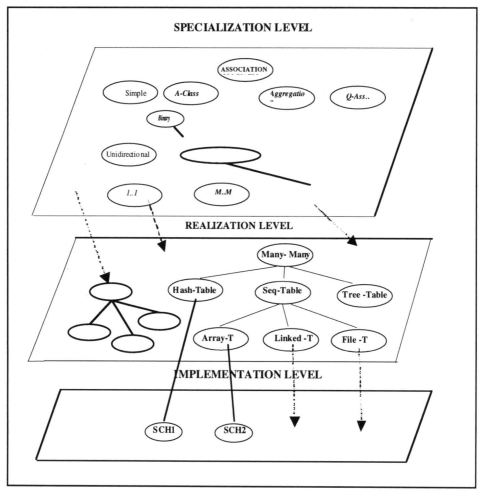

specialization and realization levels. They reflect implementation aspects.

SpReIm components can be manipulated by means of reuse operators:

Rename: changes the name of sorts or operations.

Hide: forgets those parts of a specification that are not necessary for the current application.

Extend: adds sorts, operations or axioms to a specification.

Combine: combines two or more specifications in only one.

These operators were formally defined on the three levels: specialization, realization and implementation. A formal description of the transformation-building operators and examples are included in Favre 1998.

Relations Hierarchy

As we have said, the specifications of different kinds of associations are organized in the component Association whose first level was shown in Figure 3. Figure 5 depicts all the three levels.

The specialization level describes the different relations through incomplete specifications classified according to its kind, its degree and its connectivity.

The realization level describes a hierarchy of specifications associated to different realizations. For example for an association (binary, bi-directional and many-to-many), different realizations through hashing, sequences or trees could be associated. The implementation level associates each leaf of the realization level with different implementations in an object-oriented language.

Implementation sub-components express how to implement associations and aggregations. For example, a bi-directional binary association with multiplicity "one to one" will be implemented as an attribute in each associated class containing a reference to the related object. On the contrary, if the association is "many to many" the best approach is to implement the association as a different class, in which each instance represents one link and its attributes.

A RIGOROUS FORWARD ENGINEERING METHOD

In this section we describe a reuse-based rigorous process to forward engineering UML static models. In the marketplace there exists CASE tools for code generation starting from UML models. Unfortunately, the current techniques available in these tools are not sufficient for the complete automated generation of source code. As an example, we will analyze Rational Rose (Quatrani, 1998). This one allows generating, through standard translations, the definitions of the databases, the class interfaces and the relations in which the class participates. The current modeling languages available in Rational Rose (Booch, OMT, UML) do not have precisely defined semantics. This hinders the code generation processes. Another source of problems in these processes is that, on the one hand, the UML models contain information that cannot be explicited in object-oriented languages and on the other hand, the object-oriented languages express implementation characteristics that have no counterpart in the UML models. For example, languages like C++, Java and Eiffel do not allow us explicit associations, their cardinality and their constraints. It is the responsibility of the designer to make good use of this information, selecting from a limited repertoire of implementations one that would be appropriate or else implementing by himself the association. The forward and reverse processes in Rational Rose are facilitated by means of the insertion of annotations in the generated code (they are treated by compilers as comments). These annotations are the link between the model elements and the language and they should be kept intact and not be moved. It is the responsibility of the programmer to know what he can modify and what he cannot.

The programmer must implement the new operations. In order to solve implementation problems, he can modify the code by adding or removing classes, modifying class attributes or operations, changing operation signatures, modifying class relations and moving functionality to a superclass. These code modifications must be incorporated back into the model. Rational Rose enables the programmer to solve this by means of a concurrent process (each change in the code is expressed in the model) or a deferred process (based upon the reengineering of the modified code). Both processes require the programmer's ability to keep the model and language integration. For example the deferred process requires the programmer to analyze the model obtained by the reverse engineering, mainly associations and cardinalities, checking that attributes do not confuse with associations, etc.

On the other hand, the existing tools do not exploit all the information contained in the UML models, for example, cardinality and constraints of associations, preconditions, postconditions and class invariants in OCL are only translated as annotations. Assertions in OCL could be translated to assertions in an object-oriented language that support them, as it is the case in Eiffel. Furthermore, reuse is based on object-oriented language libraries and not on specifications that describe relations between classes and their operations free from implementation details.

In order to overcome these problems, we define a rigorous process based on the integration of UML static models and algebraic specifications.

From UML Class Diagram to GSBL[00] Specifications

Given a basic UML diagram with OCL annotations, a PACKAGE whose components will be OBJECT CLASS, ASSOCIATION CLASS and relation definitions, is generated semi-automatically. For each class shown in the diagram, an OBJECT CLASS is built and for each association (ordinary, qualified or class-association), a new association is defined. These specifications are obtained by instantiating reusable schemes and classes that already exist in a GSBL[00]'s predefined library. Some of them are shown in Figure 6.

Box specifies the class interface (attributes and methods). It is a refinement of Cartes-

Figure 6. Box and Cartesian-Product

```
OBJECT CLASS Box                          OBJECTCLASS
USES  TP1:ANY, ..,TPm:ANY                 Cartes-Prod[T1:ANY,....,Tn:ANY]
REFINES                                   EFFECTIVE
Cartes-Prod[T-attr1:T1; T- attr2:T2;..;   create: T1 x ... x Tn→ Cartes-Prod
attr1:select-1;  attr2:select-2;........]  modif_i: Cartes-Prod x Ti → Cartes-Prod
DEFERRED                                   ....
OPS                                        select_i: Cartes-Prod  → Ti
meth1:Box x TPi_1 x TPi_2 x .....TPi_n→TPi_j   EQS
....                                       {cp:Cartes-Prod;...;ti, ti´:Ti...tn:Tn}
methr: Box x TPr_1 xTPr_2.....x TPr_p→ TPr_k   select_i (Create(t1,t2,...,tn)) = ti
END-CLASS                                  ...
                                           modif_i (create(t1,t2,....tn),ti´) =
                                           create(t1,t2,..,ti´,..tn)
                                           END-CLASS
```

Prod that allows us to specify cartesian product of different arity.

Each OBJECT CLASS is obtained by instantiating the following scheme:

```
OBJECT CLASS A
REFINES S1, ....Si,...
Box[...:attr1;...:attri;...:meth1;..:methi,..]
"Aggreg_name-i" HAS-A SHARED B
"Compos_name-i" HAS-A NON-SHARED C
"Assoc-name-i" ASSOCIATES D
....
EQS {
<equations>
END-CLASS
```

Generalization/specialization relations are expressed by means of the REFINES clause. Aggreg_name-i, Compos_name-i and Assoc_name-i are new relations defined by instantiating schemes existing in the Association hierarchy.

On the other hand, preconditions, postconditions and invariants in OCL will be translated to preconditions and axioms in GSBL[OO]. This translation required the definition of a number of types in GSBL[∞] for dealing with collections, which conform to the OCL types. Within OCL there are four collection types: Collection, Set, Bag and Sequence. Collection is the abstract supertype of the other ones and it is used to define operations which are common to all collection types (see Figure 2). A detailed description of the translation process may be found in Favre, Martinez and Pereira (2000).

Thus, an incomplete algebraic specification can be built semi-automatically. It contains the highest information that can be extracted from the UML class diagram.

It allows us to carry out a rigorous analysis of the modeled behavior as well as to create more informative and precise UML models.

An Example

We will use a class diagram taken from Booch (1999, p 112) to illustrate the specifications of class diagrams in GSBL[∞]. Figure 7 shows a set of classes modeling an information system for a school, and Figure 8 partially depicts its specification in GSBL[∞]. There's an association between *Student* and *Course,* specifying that students attend courses. The relations between the class *School* and the classes *Student* and *Department*

Figure 7. A Class Diagram

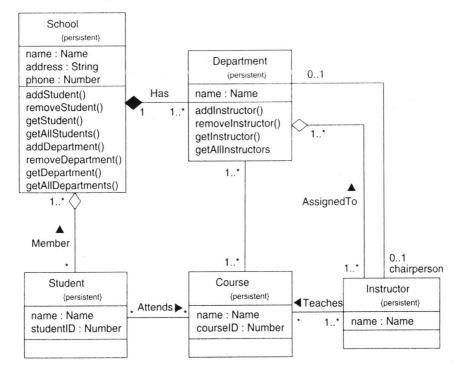

are aggregation relations. On the one hand, a school has zero or more students; each student may be a registered member of one or more schools. The relation between *School* and *Student* is a simple aggregation. On the other hand, a school has one or more departments; each department belongs to exactly one school; once created they live and die with it and they can also be explicitly removed before the death of the composite. Then, the relation between *School* and *Department* is a composition. There is an association between *Department* and *Instructor,* specifying that for every department there is one instructor who is the department chair. Also, there is an aggregation between *Department* and *Instructor.*

Booch et al. (1999, p 73) say "this is modeled as an aggregation because organizationally, departments are at a higher level in the school's structure than are instructors."

Figure 9 shows an instantiation for School class and the resulting class. Some operations come from the BOX instantiation (create, get-phone, get-address, ...) and others come from the "School-Department" and "School-Student" specifications such as get-Student, get-Department and remove-Student (see Figure 8 and Figure 4).

Constructing Realizations

In this phase a more detailed specification is developed. This specification is constructed from the *SpReIm* library to obtain a specification "as complete as possible." The process is based on a number of components that admit a high degree of generality and can be manipulated in order to adapt them to new applications. The library of reusable components should provide such searching mechanisms that users can find appropriate

Figure 8. A Package

```
PACKAGE Information-System-School            OBJECT-CLASS Student
....                                         ........................
OBJECT-CLASS School                          END-CLASS
USES Name, String, Number                    OBJECT CLASS Course
"School-Department" HAS-A SHARED             ........................
Department                                   END-CLASS
"School-Student" HAS-A NON-SHARED            OBJECT CLASS Instructor
Student                                      ......
DEFERRED                                     END-CLASS
SORTS School                                 ASSOCIATION Department-Instructor
OPS                                          IS Bidirectional0..1to0..1[Department:E1;
create-School:                               Instructor:E2 ;"chairperson": role1; 0..1:mult1;
Name x String x Number  → School             0..1:mult2;;....]
add-student: School x Student  → School      CONSTRAINED-BY  frozen
add-department:                              END
 School x Department → School                WHOLE_PART School-Student
get-name: School →Name                       IS Aggregation _1..*to* [Whole:School; Part:
get-phone: School →Number                    Student;mult1:1..*; mult2: *]
.....                                         CONSTRAINED-BY changeable
EQS                                          END
...                                          WHOLE_PART School-Department
END-CLASS.                                   IS Composit_1to1..* [Whole: School;
OBJECT-CLASS Department                       Part:Department, mult1:1;mult2:1..*]
USES Name, Number                            CONSTRAINED-BY frozen, addOnly
"Assigned to" HAS-A SHARED Instructor        ..........
... END-CLASS                                END-PACKAGE
```

components easily. It has to be organized in categories of components that include basic components (constructors types Box, Collection, Association, etc), components of general use, such as Data Structures, Design Patterns and components linked to specific application domains. Next, we describe the steps of this sub-process.

Identification: For every OBJECT CLASS *O* in the PACKAGE obtained in the previous stage will exist, in general, classes of the *SpRelm* library that can be adapted to the wished behavior. As we had said, the designer has an OCL view of the *SpRelm* library, which can be used to identify candidate specifications associated to the diagram's classes while it is being constructed. Let us suppose that an *S* specification has been identified in the component *C*. If *S* is a leaf, it will be associated to the root of a sub-component in the realization level, being *CR* that sub-component. Otherwise, it will be selected a leaf L in the specialization level of *C,* so that there is a path in the graph from *S to L,* as a candidate to be transformed.

Adaptation: The identification of *L* is correct if *Rename*, *Hide*, *Combine* and *Extend* operators can modify it to match *O*. The sorts and operations must be connected with the *O*'s ones by an appropriate renaming. The renamed version must be extended with sorts, operations and axioms. The visible signature must be restricted to the visible signature of *O*. Let *L´* be the specification obtained from transforming *L* by means of the sequence of operators *OP1,OP2,...,OPk*; the next step is to obtain a realization of *L'*. That is, a leaf R has to be selected in the realization level of C, and the sequence of operators used in the previous stage must be applied to it giving *R'*. As the operators preserve realizability, we

Figure 9. Constructing Object Class School

OBJECT CLASS School
REFINES
Box[Name:T-attr$_1$;String:T-attr$_2$; Number:T-attr$_3$; get-name:attr1; get-address:attr2;get-phone: attr3; ...]
"School-Department" **HAS-A NON-SHARED** Department
"School-Student" **HAS-A SHARED** Student

....
END-CLASS

OBJECT CLASS School
USES Name, String, Number
"School-Department" **HAS-A NON-SHARED** Department
"School-Student" **HAS-A SHARED** Student
DEFERRED
SORTS School
OPS create-School: Name x String x Number → School
add-Student: School x Student → School
add-Department: School x Department → School
get-name: School →Name
get-phone: School →Number
get-Student: School →Collection[Student]
get-Department: School →Collection[Department].............
EQS{name n; String s; number x..}
get-name(create(n,s,x))= n
get-phone(create(n,s,x))= x

....
END-CLASS

have that $R'=OP1(.........(OPK(R)....)$ is a realization of $L'=OP1(.........(OPK(L)....)$. The identification and adaptation of association relations is made in the same way. In this case, the specifications reused are in the component Association.

Composition: Compose the specifications of classes and associations in a specification *SC*. This specification allows to carry out behavior simulations, enrich the UML class diagrams and will be the base for the code generation.

Constructing Implementations

For each subspecification R' in *SC*, an implementation scheme I in the implementation sub-component associated to R has to be selected. The implementation associated to R' is $OP1(.........(OPK(I)....)$. If the *Extend* operator was applied in the previous steps, the scheme should probably be extended with new relations and operations. The relations expressed using the USES clause will be translated to a client relation in an object-oriented language. The relations expressed with the REFINES and RESTRICTS clauses will be translated to inheritance relations. For each HAS-A clause an implementation scheme will be selected in the Association component and the "aggregate" and the "part" will be instantiated. For example, if the aggregation is "one-to-many" for an attribute in the "aggregate," a reference to a sequence of pointers to the "part" will be generated.

Analogously, for every ASSOCIATES clause, a scheme in the implementation level of the Association component will be selected and instantiated. In these cases, the implementation level's schemes suggest to include "references" attributes in the classes or to introduce an intermediate class or container. Notice that the transformation of an association does not necessarily imply the existence of an associated class in the code generated, as an efficient implementation can suggest to include "references" attributes in the classes.

Every new operation will be translated into a new method (feature) in Eiffel that could be deferred or effective. Preconditions and axioms are used to construct preconditions and postconditions for features and invariants for Eiffel classes. In Favre (1998) the transformation process from axioms to assertions Eiffel is described. The programmer only completes the implementation of the new methods.

EXPERIMENTAL RESULTS
AND FUTURE TRENDS

Although a tool prototype that assists the proposed method does not exist, key phases of this one have been prototyped. The first results of this research were the reusable component model definition and its adaptation mechanisms. A prototype that assists in the identification, adaptation of reusable components by means of reuse operators and in the generation of the Eiffel code from formal specifications has been proposed. The results were already introduced in Favre (1998). The prototype offers, within its environment, tools for:

Specification editing
Syntatic analysis of specifications written in GSBL
Specification validation: This operation does semantic verifications from a symbolic execution based in the class axioms.
Component reuse: Implementation of reuse operators (Rename, Hide, Combine and Extend) in the three levels of the SpReIm model.

Transformation of GSBL specifications to Eiffel code
Design maintenance: This module stores the decisions and transformations performed during the reuse of components and code generation. It also allows the user to undo some previous steps.

For the construction of this prototype a subset of the libraries provided by the Eiffel language was specified. An essential problem in our approach is how to find appropriate reusable components. We have defined an identification process. It has two steps: *Signature Matching* and *Semantic Matching*. The signature matching enables a syntactic comparison of a query specification with specifications existing in *SpReIm* reusable components. The semantic matching compares the dynamic behavior of specifications. We explore not just the exact matching between components, but many kinds of relaxed matches. The identification process was prototyped (Fariña & Reale, 1999). If the component library is large, many candidate components could be selected as an answer to a query. Hence, it might be useful to consider specification matching as a complementary approach to more traditional information retrieval techniques.

Later works introduced an integration of the proposed method with UML. This originated the formalization of the mapping from semiformal specifications in UML to GSBL$^\infty$ specifications. Nowadays the prototyping of this phase is being considered. An important aspect is the transformation of OCL specifications (preconditions, postconditions and invariants) into GSBL$^\infty$ axioms. A system of transformation rules and strategies to apply them was defined (Favre et al., 2000).

The obtained results prove the feasibility of the proposed framework, however we cannot make an analysis of the pragmatic implications of it.

In the future, we foresee the following evolutions for the proposed framework:
- Compatibility with existing tools for theorem prover such as Isabelle (Paulson, 1994)
- Translation of other UML diagrams
- Definition of a reusable component that captures the semantics of different types of inheritance
- Retrieval of *SpReIm* components
- Integration in the Rational Rose environment.

CONCLUSIONS

In this work we outline a rigorous framework for code generation. The primary purpose of this approach is helping developers to construct more reliable systems. Our contribution is towards an embedding of the code generation within a rigorous process that facilitates reuse, evolution and maintenance of the software.

Our research relates different but interdependent conceptual bases: the algebraic language, the model of a reusable component, the definition and organization of the library of components and the transformational process. These bases are still evolving and it is anticipated that, as new proposals influence future versions of UML, additional issues will have to be tackled. Considering that GSBL$^\infty$ is opened-ended, it will be possible to define new relations in controlled ways.

We believe that our approach provides several advantages:
- It allows deriving knowledge from UML models with annotations in OCL, in order to support assessment of solutions and to verify implementations against specifica-

tions.

- The transitions between the UML diagrams and all intermediate specifications of the program can be done exclusively by applying transformation operators, the correctness of which is proved with respect to the semantics of algebraic specifications . All the transitions preserve the integrity between specifications and code.
- Software developers could perform maintenance and evolution on the system specification, not on implementations. Modifications at specification levels must be applied again to produce a new efficient implementation. Most of the transformations can be undone which provides great flexibility in software development.
- All the information contained in the UML models (associations, their cardinality, OCL constraints, etc) is translated to specifications and will have implementation implications.
- The proposed method forces systematic reuse of behavior from structured algebraic specifications that describe relations between classes and its operations free from implementation details.
- UML models, formal specifications, resulting program and all transitions relating one to the other provides a good basis for reverse engineering
- Code is generated in its purest form, using dynamic binding and polymorphism only where needed and omitting such mechanisms as method redefinition, direct repeated inheritance, etc.

ENDNOTE

This work is partially supported by the Catalan Government (CIRIT-SGR00150/1999) and Comisión de Investigaciones Cientificas de la Pcia.de Buenos Aires.

REFERENCES

Alencar, A. & Goguen, J. (1991). OOZE: An object-oriented Z environment. Proceedings of the European Conference on object-oriented programming, ECOOP 91. *Lecture Notes in Computer Science,* 512. 180-199. Springer-Verlag.

Bidoit, M., Hennicker, R., Tort, F. & Wirsing, M. (1999) Correct Realizations of Interface Constraints with OCL. In The Unified Modeling Language-Beyond the Standard, Proc, 2nd Int. Conference. UML'99. *Lecture Notes in Computer Science 1723.*399-415. Springer Verlag.

Booch, G., Rumbaugh, J. & Jacobson, I. (1999). *The Unified Modeling Language User Guide.* Addison-Wesley.

Bourdeau, R. & Cheng, B. (1995). A formal semantics for object model diagrams. *IEEE Transactions on Software Engineering,* 21(10), 799-821.

Breu, R., Hinkel, U., Hofmann, C., Klein, C., Paech, B., Rumpe & B.,Thurner, V. (1997) *Towards a Formalization of the Unified Modeling Language.* TUM-I9726 Technische Universitat Munchen.

Bruel, J. & France, R. (1998) Transforming UML Models to Formal Specifications. In Proc. of UML'98 Beyond the Notation. *Lecture Notes in Computer Science 1618.* 78-92. Springer-Verlag.

Carrington, D., Duke, R., King, P., Rose, G. & Smith, G. (1989) OBJECT-Z: An Object-oriented extension to Z. In *Proc. Formal Description Techniques FORTE'89.* 281-296. Amsterdam, North-Holland.

Clavel, M., Durán, F., Eker, S., Meseguer, J. & Oliver-Stehr. (1999) MAUDE as a formal meta-tool. In *Proc. of FM'99, The World Congress on Formal Methods in the Development of Computing Systems.* Toulouse, France.

Clérici, S. & Orejas, F. (1988) GSBL: An Algebraic Specification Language Based on Inheritance. In *Proc. of the European Conference on Object-Oriented Programming ECOOP 88.* 78-92.

Cheon, Y. & Leavens, G. (1994) The Larch/Smalltalk Interface Specification Language. *ACM Trans. on Soft. Eng. and Meth.* 3(3) ,221-253.

COFI Task Group on Language Design (1999). *CASL The Common Algebraic Specification Language.* Available: http://www.bricks.dk/Projects/CoFi/Documents/CASL.

Diaconescu, R. & Futatsugi, K. (1998) The CAFEOBJ Report, The Language, Proof Techniques, and Methodologies for Object-oriented Algebraic Specification. *AMAST Series in Computing 6.*

D'Souza, D. & Wills, A. (1999) *Objects, Components, and Frameworks with UML.* Addison-Wesley.

Evans, A., France, R., Lano, K. & Rumpe, B. (1998) The UML as a Formal Modeling Notation. In Proceedings of UML'98-Beyond the Notation, *Lecture Notes in Computer Science 1618.* Springer-Verlag.

Favre, L. (1998) Object-oriented Reuse through Algebraic Specifications. In Proc. Technology of Object-Oriented Languages and Systems. TOOLS 28. *IEEE Computer Society,* 101-112.

Favre, L. & Clérici, S. (1999) Integrating UML and Algebraic Specification Techniques. In Proc. Technology of Object-oriented Languages and Systems. TOOLS 32. *IEEE Computer Society.*

Favre, L., Martínez, L. & Pereira, C. (2000) From OCL to Algebraic Specifications. Technical Report. Departamento de Computación. Universidad Nacional del Centro. Argentina.

Fariña, K. & Reale, M. (1999). *Object-Oriented Reusability Through Formal Specifications.* Undergraduate Thesis. Departamento de Computación. Universidad Nacional del Centro. Argentina.

Feenstra, R. & Wieringa, R. (1993) *LCM 3.0: A Language for Describing Conceptual Models-Syntax Definition.* Rapport IR-344, Vrije Universiteit Amsterdam.

Firesmith, D.G. & Henderson-Sellers, B. (1998) Clarifying specialized forms of association in UML and OML. *JOOP,* 11(2). 47-50.

France, R., Bruel, J. & Larronde-Petri, M. (1997) An Integrated Object-oriented and Formal Modeling Notations. *JOOP,* Nov/Dec. 25-34.

Gogolla, M. & Ritchers, M. (1997) On combining Semi-formal and Formal Object Specification Techniques. In Proc. WADT97, *Lecture Notes in Computer Science 1376,* 238-252. Springer-Verlag.

Goguen, J. & Malcolm, G. (Eds.). (1999). *Software Engineering with OBJ: Algebraic Specification in Action.* Kluwer.

Henderson-Sellers, B. (1998) OPEN Relationships-Associations, Mappings, Dependencies and Uses. *JOOP,* 10(9), 49-57.

Henderson-Sellers, B. & Barbier, F. What Is This Thing Called Aggregation. In Proc. Technology of Object-Oriented Languages and Systems. TOOLS EUROPE 99. 236-250. *IEEE Computer Society Press.*

Hennicker, R. & Wirsing, M. (1992) A Formal Method for the Systematic Reuse of Specifications Components. *Lecture Notes in Computer Science 544.* Springer-Verlag.

Junclauss, R., Saake, G. & Sernadas, C. (1991) Formal Specifications of Object Systems. In Proc.of the International Joint Conference on Theory and Practice of Software Development. TAPSOFT'91. *Lecture Notes in Computer Science 494.* 60-62. Springer-Verlag.

Junclauss, R., Saake, G., Hartmann, T. & Sernadas, C. (1996) TROLL-A Language for Object-oriented Specification of Information Systems. *ACM Transactions on Information Systems,* 14(2), 175-211.

Kim, S. K. & Carrington, D. (1999) Formalizing the UML class diagram using Object-Z. In Proc. UML 99, *Lecture Notes in Computer Science 1723.* 83-98.

Lano, K. (1990) Z++, an Object-Oriented Extension of Z. In *Proc. Z USER Workshop, Oxford, Springer Workshops in Computing.* 151-172.

Lano, K. *Formal Object-Oriented Development.* Springer-Verlag.

Mandel, L. & Cengarle, V. (1999) *On the Expressive Power of the Object Constraint Language OCL.* Available: http://www.fast.de/projeckte/forsoft/ocl .

Meyer, B (1997) *Object-oriented Software Construction.* Prentice Hall.

OMG. (1999). *Unified Modeling Language Specification, v. 1.3. document.* ad/99-06-08, Object Management Group.

Overgaard, G. (1998) A Formal Approach to Relationships in the Unified Modeling Language. In *Proc. of Workshop on Precise Semantic of Modeling Notations, International Conference on Software Engineering, ICSE'98,* Japan.

Paulson, L. (1994) Isabelle: A Generic Theorem Prover. *Lecture Notes in Computer Science 828.* Springer.

Quatrani, T. (1998) *Visual Modeling with Rational Rose and UML.* Addison-Wesley.

Rapanotti, L. & Socorro, A. (1992) *Introducing FOOPS.* Report PRG-TR-28-92, Programming Research Group, Oxford University Computing Laboratory.

Sernadas, A. & Ramos, J. (1994) *The GNOME Language: Syntax, Semantics and Calculus.* Technical Report, Instituto Superior Técnico, Lisboa.

Spivey, J. (1992) *The Z Notation, A Reference Manual.* Prentice Hall

Varizi, M. & Jackson, D. *Some Shortcomings of OCL, The Object Constraint Language of UML.* Available: http://sdg.lcs.mit.edu/~dnj/publications.htm.

Warner, J. & Kleppe, A. (1999) *The Object Constraint Language. Precise Modeling with UML.* Addison-Wesley.

Wieringa, R. & Dubois, E. (1998) Integrating Semi-formal and Formal Software Specification Techniques. *Information System,* 23, 159-178.

Wills, A. (1992). Specification in Fresco. In *Object Orientation in Z. Workshops in Computing.* 127-135. Cambridge: Springer-Verlag.

Chapter III

Data Modeling and UML

Devang Shah and Sandra Slaughter
Carnegie Mellon University, USA

Over the past two decades, the Entity-Relationship (ER) method has become the most popular and widely used method for conceptual database design. On the other hand, the Unified Modeling Language (UML) is widely used in the object-oriented analysis and design world. Despite the dominance of object-oriented techniques during the software development design and development phase, object-oriented databases are still not in widespread use. Software designers and developers often turn to the relational databases to make their application objects persistent. This adds one more task in the 'to-do' list of the designer: to map objects into entities. Considering the fundamental differences between the two methods, this task could be a non-trivial task. The purpose of this chapter is to describe a process that can be used to map a class diagram into an ER diagram, and to discuss the potential of using the UML notation to draw the ER diagrams. An example of an actual systems design is used throughout to illustrate the mapping process, the associated problems encountered and how they could be resolved.

INTRODUCTION

The Entity–Relationship (ER) model is the most widely used data model for the conceptual design of databases. It focuses solely on data, representing a "data network" that exists for a given system. It has emerged as the leading formal structure for conceptual data representation, becoming an industry standard. The ER model is based on only a few modeling concepts and has a very effective graphic representation in which each element of the model is mapped to a distinct graphic symbol (Batini, Ceri & Navathe, 1992).

In the past few years, the Unified Modeling Language (UML) has emerged as a prominent modeling language in the object-oriented analysis and design world (see Booch, Rumbaugh & Jacobson, 1999; Rumbaugh, Jacobson & Booch, 1999). The Class Diagram is an important part of the UML, and it captures the static view of the system. The class diagram models classes in the real world and specifies the relationships between them. The underlying concept of class diagrams may seem to be similar to that of ER diagrams;

however, there are a few fundamental differences between the two modeling languages. Usually, the ER model is used with the method (Structured System Analysis and Design) which is primarily process centric (see Pressman, 1997). On the other hand, object modeling is a part of the method (Object-Oriented Analysis and Design) which is primarily function/ data centric (see Bahrami, 1999; Dewitz, 1995). Having said that, if we ignore the method/ operation property of objects, we can say that object modeling in concept is very similar to data modeling. As Rumbaugh et al. (1991) have observed, the Object Modeling Technique (OMT) is an enhanced form of ER that includes some new concepts (such as qualification). UML is an enhanced form of OMT and thus an enhanced form of the ER model[1] (Ou, 1997).

Although object-oriented methods enjoy some success in the software development field, software engineers often turn to ER diagrams and relational databases to implement the objects, i.e., to make them persistent (Muller, 1999). This raises a number of important issues. If the class diagram is a superset of the ER diagram, then why do we need a separate notation to draw the ER diagrams? Can the UML class diagram notation be used to draw the ER diagrams? What would be the advantage of that? How would the UML class diagram handle different constructs of the ER diagrams such as primary key constraint, referential integrity constraint or unique key constraint? What about normalization?

Translating a class diagram into an ER diagram could be a non-trivial task, as several symbols and notations used in the class diagram (for example: n-ary relationships[2], aggregation) do not have a direct mapping to the ER diagram. A logical and a physical relational database design will require a systematic step-by-step process to translate a class diagram into the ER diagram. This chapter discusses a process that can be used to simplify the database design task of making an object persistent. It demonstrates how the Unified Modeling Language can be used for data modeling. Some have argued that object modeling is the same as relational modeling, and others have confronted this view; however, we do not delve into that issue in this chapter. Our intent is to examine the efficacy of the UML class diagram as a vehicle to draw the ER diagram. We illustrate data modeling in UML using a real example from an extranet-based retail pharmacy drug dispensing system that was designed for a regional health care network of hospitals, pharmacies, pharmacy brokers, patients and drug manufacturers.

The rest of this chapter is organized as follows: we first review related work and provide some background information. We then discuss the notational differences between UML and the ER diagram; the following section describes the mapping steps that can be followed to convert the conceptual view into the logical schema. We then present the result of the work on the complete class diagram, and draw a number of conclusions and implications.

BACKGROUND

The topic of making objects persistent and the relationship between class diagrams and ER diagrams are not novel (e.g., see Bahrami, 1999; Banerjee, 1987; Dewitz, 1995; Muller, 1999). Ever since the emergence of object-oriented technologies, system designers have struggled with how to resolve the mismatch that exists between the two different methodologies while making objects persistent. In a recent article, Ou (1997) defines a mapping from UML to the ER Model. Ou's work addresses many of the UML constructs; however it provides a mapping at the conceptual schema level and not at the logical schema level. Other significant work on this topic has been done by Muller (1999). On the other hand, using the class diagram notation to draw the ER diagrams can be complex. In order to understand the relationship between the two models, one must consider the underlying principles from which both notations have evolved.

As noted by Ling and Teo (1994), even though the object-oriented approach is very popular, it has a number of inadequacies, e.g., lack of a formal foundation, lack of a standard query language, etc. Over the past couple of years, significant research has been done to address the formality issue. As a result, the Object Constraint Language (OCL) has been introduced by IBM to formally represent the constructs in the UML diagrams. Gogolla discusses the notation differences and the work-around solution (Gogolla & Richters, 1998). Today, very few of the existing UML-based CASE tools provides support of forward and reverse engineering between UML/Class diagrams and the relational database schema. Some tools that do provide support for this mapping include the Rose Data Modeler from Rational Corporation, and ObjectF developed by Microtool, Inc. However, the effectiveness of these tools in the CASE tool market is yet to be determined.

As we have mentioned earlier, our purpose in this chapter is two-fold: to describe how to make objects persistent, i.e., how to convert the class diagram into the relational database schema, and to assess the effectiveness of using the class diagram notation to draw the ER diagram. Throughout the chapter we use a real example of a systems design for an extranet-based retail pharmacy drug dispensing system. We briefly describe this system in the next section, then continue with our discussion of mapping from class diagrams to relational database schemas.

EXAMPLE – RETAIL PHARMACY (DRUG DISPENSING) SYSTEM

There are a number of actors in the retail pharmacy (drug dispensing) system. A central actor is the Pharmacy Broker Manager (PBM). The PBM sets up a contract with a retail Pharmacist. The Employer buys healthcare benefits plans from the PBM. The PBM issues a healthcare insurance card to the Employer's Employee. The Employee (Patient) becomes ill and goes to the Doctor.

The Doctor diagnoses the Patient's condition. The Doctor asks the Patient about prior health conditions, existing prescriptions and any preferred formularies. Based upon this information and the diagnosis, the Doctor writes out a prescription for the Patient.

The Patient goes to a retail pharmacy and gives the prescription to the Pharmacist. The Pharmacist gives the Patient the prescribed brand drug or makes a generic substitution. The Patient can pay a co-payment and also a penalty for brand drugs not on the preferred formulary. The Pharmacist and PBM submit the insurance claim. The PBM receives payment from the Employer for the Patient's prescription costs and passes on payment to the Pharmacist.

Drug Manufacturers market and sell their brand drugs to the Pharmacists. They also "detail" (advertise) the benefits of their drugs to Doctors in hopes of getting their brand drugs prescribed. Figure 1 illustrates the class diagram representing the design of the retail pharmacy system.

EXTENDING THE UML METAMODEL[3]

The UML meta-model specifies constructs for classes (which also include attributes, and operations) and for the relationships between classes (which include binary and n-ary associations, inheritance, dependency and instanceOf). In addition to this, various

Figure 1. Class Diagram for Retail Pharmacy System

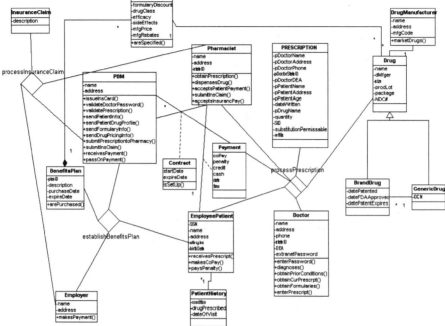

Drug Dispensing System: Extranet-Based

adornments can also be specified at the class, attribute, operations and association level. On the other hand, the UML meta-model is not semantically rich when it comes to specifying constraints. It offers some mechanisms for specifying integrity constraints. For example, the properties of an AssociationEnd, such as aggregation, isNavigable, multiplicity and qualifier, can be used to specify integrity constraints. However, the core UML meta-model does not include specification of integrity constraints. For example, the uniqueness constraint or primary key field constraint is not included (Ou, 1998).

The OCL can be used to specify the constraints at the model level; however, it is semi-formal. The Rational Data Modeler uses new stereotypes and tag values to extend the metamodel and achieve the goal of specifying integrity constraints during UML modeling; however, it may be argued that this is not the best way to denote the constraints as it violates the standard UML constraint notation (which is, specifying constraints within braces). On the other hand, some authors (e.g., Ou, 1998) have added compartments in the class diagram, and have introduced new model elements and some attributes to the core package of the UML meta-model. In this chapter, we show the primary key and foreign key constraints using {PK} and {FK} notations, respectively. We now describe the steps for converting class diagrams into logical database schemas, using our example of the retail pharmacy system to illustrate the process.

STEPS FOR CONVERTING CLASS DIAGRAM INTO A LOGICAL SCHEMA

The UML class diagram forms the conceptual view of the system that needs to be converted into the logical view to design the relational database schema. This section reviews different UML/Class Diagram constructs and discusses a process that can be used for translating these constructs into the logical view.

Mapping Classes

A class is a descriptor for a set of objects with similar structure, behavior and relationships. It represents a concept within the system being modeled. Classes have data structure and behavior as well as relationships to other elements. Graphically, a class is drawn as a solid-outline rectangle with three compartments separated by horizontal lines, and the top compartment holds the class name.

One table can be created for each persistent class of the conceptual view. However things can become complicated when considering generalization and associations with other classes of the schema. Generalization and associations (binary and n-ary associations along with different types of association adornments) are discussed in more detail later in this section.

Mapping Attributes

An attribute displays the various properties of the class. It is shown as a text string within the second compartment of the class.

When mapping attributes into columns, an attribute can be mapped to zero or more columns. Attributes that can be derived from other attributes can be left unconverted. In the UML diagram, one can also specify different attribute properties at the attribute level.

Visibility: At the database level, all the columns of a table are public. Hence, while mapping an attribute into columns, this property can be ignored.

Multiplicity: Multiplicity is of the form: "lower-bound .. upper-bound." For example, a multiplicity of 0..1 denotes an attribute as not-mandatory, single-valued attribute; whereas a multiplicity of 1..* denotes an attribute as mandatory, multi-valued attribute. A mandatory/non-mandatory property of an attribute could be translated as a null/not-null property at the database level. However, translating a multi-valued attribute is not a straight forward task, because in relational databases, it is not possible to store multiple values in one column. If the number of values that a multi-valued attribute can take is fixed (for example, days of the week), then a column can be created for each value of an attribute (i.e., one column for each day of the week). However, if the number of values that an attribute can take is not fixed, then the best way will be to create a separate table to store the values and link it with the original table using a foreign key reference.

Property-string: The UML syntax uses property-string to denote a type (domain) of an attribute. Translating an attribute type into a corresponding column type at the database level will depend on the set of types supported by a particular DBMS. There could be some differences. For example, an attribute of type 'String' in C++ can occupy n-number of characters, whereas a corresponding VARCHAR2 column at the Oracle database level restricts column size to 255 characters only. The problem could be alleviated by identifying such differences beforehand and implementing constraints at the code level.

Mapping Associations

Mapping Binary Associations

An association is a relation between two or more classifiers. Binary associations are shown as lines connecting two classifier symbols. Note that a binary association includes the possibility of an association from a classifier to itself. Ternary and higher-order associations are shown as diamonds connected to class symbols by lines. A binary association is drawn as a solid path connecting two classifier symbols.

A multiplicity item specifies the range of allowable cardinalities that a set may assume. It may be given for roles within associations, parts within composition, repetitions and other purposes. Multiplicity is often shown in the format: "lower-bound .. upper-bound," where lower-bound and upper-bound are literal integer values, specifying the closed range of integers from the lower bound to the upper bound. The symbol '*' is used to denote the unlimited nonnegative integer range. Note that UML combines the concepts of Multiplicity and Modality, whereas in the ER diagrams both of these concepts are orthogonal.

Mapping One-to-One Associations

Either separate tables can be created for each class involved in the association or classes can be combined to form one table. The decision usually depends on the application domain and the degree of coupling that exists between the two tables. To illustrate this point further, consider the scenario where the designer has created two classes to represent patient information: the first one includes the patient's name, age and other personal information;,whereas the second class contains address information. However, at the database level, it may be inefficient to store this information in two separate tables, and hence information can be combined and stored into one table.

Mapping One-to-Many Associations

A separate table can be created for each class involved in the association. An association is realized by storing the primary key of the class (the class whose one instance participates in the relationship) as a foreign key into the second class (the class whose 'n' instance participates in the relationship).

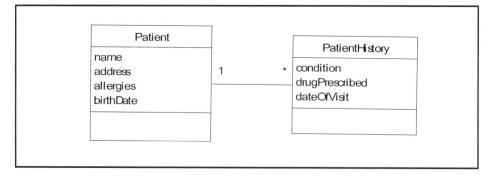

Example: A patient can have a history of multiple visits:

The above diagram can be converted into the following logical schema. The relationship between the two classes is stored into the 'Patient History' table as a foreign key.

Mapping Many-to-Many Associations

A separate table can be allocated for each class involved in the association, and in addition to that, one table can be created to store the association itself. This table will also

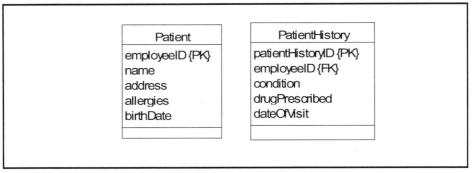

maintain the primary key of both the associated tables in addition to the associated attributes.

Example: Drugs can be included on many formularies, and formularies include many drugs...

can be converted into the following logical schema:

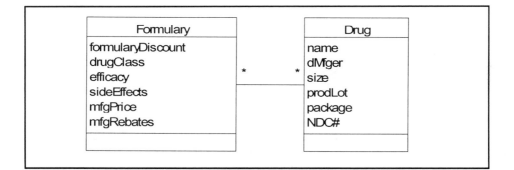

Mapping n-ary Associations

An n-ary notation is an association among three or more classifiers (a single classifier may appear more than once). Each instance of an association is an n-tuple of values from the respective classifier. A binary association is a special case with its own notation. The multiplicity of a role represents the potential number of instance tuples in the association when the other n-1 values are fixed. An association can also have an association class. An association class may be attached to the diamond by a dashed line. This indicates an n-ary association that has attributes, operations and/or associations.

While converting the class diagram into the logical schema, n-ary relationships can be broken down into a series of binary relationships, and depending on the cardinality of the relationship, each relationship can be further divided as per rules mentioned later in this section.

Example: The Pharmacist and the PBM submit the insurance claim. The PBM receives payment from the Employer for the patient's prescription costs and passes on payment to the pharmacists. In the class diagram, this is modeled as an n-ary association between 'Insurance Claim,' 'Employer,' 'Pharmacist' and 'PBM'. While converting the class diagram into the logical schema, this n-ary relationship can be broken down into following sets of binary relationships:

Relationship between 'Pharmacist' and 'Insurance Claim' (One-to-Many)
Relationship between 'PBM' and 'Insurance Claim' (One-to-Many)
Relationship between 'Employer' and 'Insurance Claim' (One-to-Many)
The logical schema is shown in the figure below.

Another approach to mapping an n-ary association is to create a separate table to store the relationship. In the above example, such a conversion will create following tables:

However, it is not always possible to break down an n-ary associations into a series

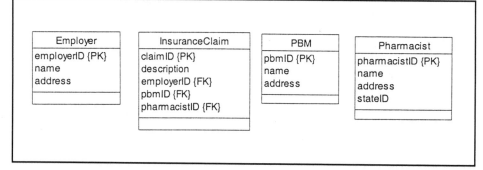

of binary associations, without adding additional implementation concerns (Jones & Song, 1995). Whether or not an n-ary association can be decomposed without loss into binary

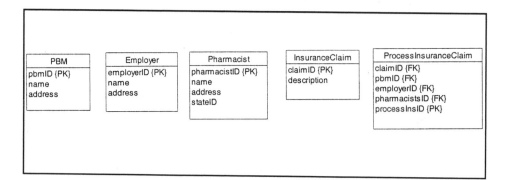

forms depends on the association's application domain. Also, loss-less decomposition does not always provide a complete basis on which to judge equivalent modeling capabilities. N-ary associations are usually difficult to implement, and the resultant schema should always be verified against database normalization principles.

Mapping Aggregation and Composition

When placed on the target end, the relationship specifies whether the target end is an aggregation with respect to the source end. Only one end can be an aggregation.

Aggregate: The end is an aggregate; therefore, the other end is a part and must have the aggregation value of none. The part may be contained in other aggregates.

Composite: The end is a composite; therefore, the other end is a part and must have the aggregation value of none. The part is strongly owned by the composite and may not be part of any other composite.

Composition is a form of aggregation with strong ownership and coincident lifetime of part with the whole. The multiplicity of the aggregate end may not exceed one (it is unshared). Composition may be shown by a solid filled diamond as an association end adornment. Alternatively, UML provides a graphically nested form that is more convenient for showing composition in many cases.

Depending on the multiplicity of the association, classes can be converted into tables. For example, if there is a 1:M relationship between Aggregate and Part, then two tables can be allocated: one for aggregate and one for part, and relationship can be stored in the part table as a foreign key. If there is an M:N relationship between aggregate and part (note that this case is not possible for composition, as with the composition, one instance of a part cannot be shared by more than one instance of the aggregate), then three tables can be allocated: one for each class and one to store relationship. However, care must be taken while designing the physical schema, as usually with the composition and aggregation relationship, one would prefer to retrieve part along with the aggregate and similarly for the insert, delete and update operations.

Example: Benefit Plans are composed of one or more drug formularies.

This can be converted into the following logical schema:

Association End - Adornments

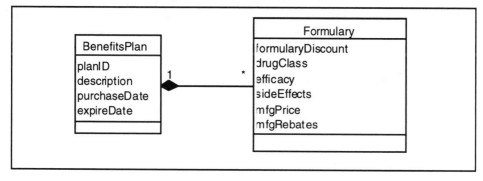

At the Association End, different adornments can be specified, such as multiplicity, ordering, qualifier, navigability, aggregation indicator, role name and changeability.

BenefitsPlan
planID {PK} description purchaseDate expireDate

Formulary
formularyID {PK} planID {FK} formularyDiscount drugClass efficacy sideEffects mfgPrice mfgRebates

Ordering: If the multiplicity is greater than zero, then the set of related elements can be ordered or unordered. While translating such associations, one solution could be to write triggers at the database level.

Navigability: UML supports the concept of either one-direction or bi-direction relationships; however at the database level, the relationship is stored in the tables, and it does not support the concept of uni-directional relationship.

Role name: UML indicates the role played by the class attached to the end of the path near the role name. It does not have any impact on an implementation, and is used to enhance readability. Some versions of ER diagrams (for example, the Oracle version) provide support for specifying relationship names in both the directions. For these versions, translating role name from the class diagram to the database level ER diagram should not be a problem.

Qualifier: A qualifier is an attribute or list of attributes whose values serve to partition the set of instances associated with an instance across an association. The qualifiers are attributes of the association. A qualified association can be mapped to a relationship just like any other association. However, depending on the multiplicity, the multiplicity and primary key of the resultant relationship can differ (Ou, 1997).

Changeability: This adornment denotes whether the links are changeable or not. The property {frozen} indicates that no links may be added, deleted or moved from an object after the object is created and initialized. The property {addOnly} indicates that additional links may be added; however, links may not be modified or deleted. One way to map these two ({frozen} and {addOnly}) constraints, is to control insert , update and delete operations via a trigger at the database level.

Mapping Generalizations

Generalization refers to the relationship between a more general element (the parent) and a more specific element (the child) that is fully consistent with the first element and that adds additional information. In UML, it is shown as a solid-line path from the child (the more specific element, such as a subclass) to the parent (the more general element, such as a superclass), with a large hollow triangle at the end of the path where it meets the more general element.

Implementing the generalization hierarchy is one of the difficult tasks when converting the conceptual view into the logical view. Usually there are three possible alternatives: the first alternative is to allocate a table for each class, including the parent class; whereas the second alternative is to copy the attributes of the parent class into the child classes while converting concrete classes into tables. A third alternative is to allocate a single composite table, containing attributes of the parent class, as well as all the child classes. Note that none of the above three options is a perfect option; however, each option offers some advantages as well as disadvantages over other options, and the choice will be governed by the application domain.

Example: There are two types of drugs: Branded Drug and Generic Drug. Branded Drugs are developed by Drug Manufacturers, whereas Generic Drugs are copies of the Original Drug.

Solution 1 – Allocate a separate table for each class.

One solution could be to create one table for each class, including the abstract class.

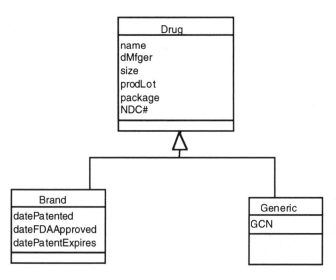

For example, in the above case, three tables can be created: one for the 'Drug' class, one for the 'Brand' class and one for the 'Generic' class. Advantages of this approach would be the ease of modification. For example, if in the future, the need arises to add some more attributes into the abstract class, then changes will be relatively easy to accommodate. Also, this approach is preferable when there exists a relationship between an abstract class and some other class. For example, in the above scenario, if there exists a relationship between a 'Drug' and a 'Formulary,' then it will be beneficial to have a separate class for 'Drug' rather than copying down its attributes into its child classes.

An apparent disadvantage of the above approach is in terms of performance. Now every access to the child class will result in two accesses: one for the child class itself and another one for the parent class. The same would be true for the insert and delete operations.

Solution 2 – Create one table for each child class.

A second solution is to create a table for each child class, duplicating the parent class attributes into the child class. An apparent advantage of this approach would be a

Brand
drugID {PK}
datePatented
dateFDAApproved
datePatentExpires
genericDrugID {FK}

Drug
drugID {PK}
name
dMfger
size
prodLot
package
NDC#
drugMfgerID {FK}
type

Generic
drugID {PK}
GCN

performance gain. Since there will not be any access overhead for getting the information from the super-class, better performance can be realized. A disadvantage of this approach is that the solution is not flexible enough to accommodate future changes with respect to the parent class.

Solution 3 – Create one table for entire hierarchy

A third solution is to create one single table for the entire hierarchy. The table would contain the attributes of the parent class as well as of child classes. An advantage of this

Brand
drugID {PK}
datePatented
dateFDAApproved
datePatentExpire
genericDrugId {FK}
drugMfgerID {FK}
type
name
size
prodLot
package
NDC#

Generic
drugID {PK}
GCN
drugMfgerID {FK}
type
name
size
prodLot
package
NDC#

approach would be the performance gain. Only one access to the table would be needed to access any type of drug information. However, this approach would offer less flexibility, as any modifications like the addition of an extra child would be difficult to achieve. Another disadvantage would be the data redundancy, as in the Brand table, fields like 'GCN' and brand 'drugID' would be null for the branded drugs, and the fields 'datePatented,' 'datePatentExpire' and 'dateFDAApproved' would be null for the generic drugs.

Selecting Primary Keys

In a relational database, a unique identifier is needed in order to identify each distinct row in the table, as well as to store the relationships. An identifier should be assigned to each object (or to each 'row' in relational database terminology) in order to uniquely identify it.

There are several options for selecting primary keys:

Selecting an attribute that has a functional meaning as a primary key: One of the attributes having a business or functional meaning can be selected as a primary key; for example, the 'Order Number' attribute in the 'Order' class, or the 'Invoice Number' attribute for the 'Invoice' class. An advantage of this approach would be that the users of the system are familiar with the key. A disadvantage would be that if a business domain changes, then the key having a functional meaning changes its definition as well. For example, consider the case where Invoice Number is used as a primary key in the table 'Invoice' and is used as a foreign key in the tables 'Invoice Line,' and 'Payment.' Changing the size of the 'Invoice Number' field will require changes in the base table, as well as all the dependent tables.

Drug
drugID {PK}
drugMfgerID {FK}
type
name
size
prodLot
package
NDC#
datePatented
dateFDAApproved
datePatentExpire
genericDrugID {FK}
GCN

Assigning a separate attribute to store the object identifier: A separate attribute can be added in the class definition to store unique key identifiers; for example, the 'Order Id' attribute for the 'Order' class, or the 'Invoice Id' attribute for the 'Invoice' class. These separate attributes can be automatically generated by the system. A disadvantage of this approach would be that since the primary key will not have a functional meaning, a table will still need one more field to serve as a unique key. For example, in the Invoice table, apart from Invoice ID, the Invoice Number column will still be necessary. Invoice ID can be assigned as a primary key field and used in joins with other tables, whereas Invoice Number will serve as a unique functional key on the table.

Example

Figure 2 represents the resultant logical schema of the Retail Pharmacy Drug Dispensing System, obtained after applying the different methods mentioned in this section to the conceptual view (the class diagram, shown in Figure 1) of the Drug Dispensing System. The logical schema does not show the relationship between different tables explicitly because in the relational database, the relation between two tables is defined implicitly (via foreign key constraints) and not explicitly.

We encountered some additional issues in mapping the class diagram to the logical schema.

Selecting a Primary Key

We decided to assign a separate attribute, i.e., to create separate fields in the table to store object identifiers of the class diagram. The key selected as a primary key does not have any functional meaning associated with it. A separate 'Id' column has been added in all the tables.

Mapping Classes into Tables

In this step, we considered only those classes that are related via one-to-one relationships. In later steps, we mapped generalizations and associations.

Mapping Attributes into Columns

This was a straight-forward task as none of the columns were multi-valued columns; however, some of the attributes that we could have computed from the other attributes were left unconverted.

Realizing Generalization

In this step, we considered the generalization between the classes 'Brand,' 'Generic' and 'Drug.' 'Brand' and 'Generic' are inherited from 'Drug.' We decided to assign a separate persistent table to each class ('Brand' and 'Generic') as well as to the parent class ('Drug'), because of the association between the 'Drug' class and other three classes: 'Formulary,' 'Doctor' and 'Drug Manufacturer.'

Mapping Binary Associations

In this step, we considered 1:M and M:N associations present in the class diagram. In all the cases, 1:M association was replaced by storing the primary key of the class (whose one instance participates in the association) as a foreign key into the second class (whose multiple instances participate in the association), and M:N association was replaced by a separate table to store the relationship.

Mapping n-ary Associations

This was a particularly interesting problem, and the solution was driven by domain knowledge. The n-ary relationship between 'Doctor,' 'Prescription,' 'Pharmacist,' 'Drug,' 'Employee/Patient' and 'PBM' was broken into following multiple binary associations:

Relationship between 'Prescription' and 'Doctor' (M:1 relationship).
Relationship between 'Prescription' and 'Employee/Patient' (M:1 relationship)
Relationship between 'Prescription' and 'Drug' (M:1 relationship)
Relationship between 'Prescription' and 'Pharmacist' (M:1 relationship).

Binary association mapping rules, discussed earlier in this section, were applied to each of the above relationships.

The n-ary relationship between the classes 'Employer,' 'Benefits Plan,' 'PBM' and 'Employee/Patient' was broken down further into the following binary relationships:

The relationship between 'PBM' and 'Benefits Plan.'

The relationship between 'PBM,' 'Employee/Patient,' and 'Employer' was broken down further by adding one more table 'Insurance Card' ('PBM' issues an Insurance Card to an Employer and eventually gets assigned to the Employee).

Mapping Aggregation and Composition

The relationship between 'Benefits Plan' and 'Formulary' was converted by considering the relationship as a 1:M relationship.

Figure 2 represents the final logical schema derived after applying the above-mentioned process.

Figure 2. Logical Schema for Retail Pharmacy System

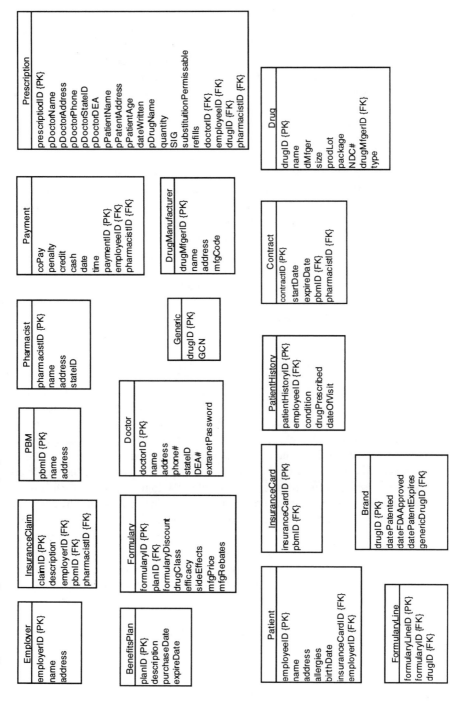

FUTURE DIRECTIONS

In this chapter, we have discussed the step-by-step process of converting the class diagram into the ER diagram, which can be used to make objects persistent. We have also shown the possibility of using the UML notation to draw the ER diagrams. We admit that the chapter does not address all conversion issues. We have concentrated only on the static behavior of the class diagram, and during the process we have ignored the dynamic aspect of the UML/Class diagrams. Also, some of the qualifiers such as Dependency and instanceOf are not addressed in this chapter.

One potential area where further study can be conducted is how to implement the class operations at the database level. Muller has discussed this issue in some detail in his book (Muller, 1999). The work could also be enhanced to draw the similarity and differences between dynamic aspects of the UML (sequence diagrams, activity diagrams, etc.) and the Structured Systems Analysis and Design Data Flow Diagrams and the other notations.

Another interesting topic for future research could be how to map access information to the ER model level. For example, one can mark the attribute private/public/protected at the class model level; however, at the relational database level, all the columns are public. Also the class diagrams are often decomposed into packages (or a hierarchy of packages), whereas this concept does not exist at the relational database level. Mapping access information and other constraints from the class diagram to the ER diagrams could also be an interesting topic for further research. Finally, formalizing the base of the UML model could also be a very challenging research topic.

CONCLUSION

Making objects persistent is one of the most challenging tasks the developer of an object-oriented system is facing today. Although application development using object-oriented methodologies is widespread, the relational database has become a norm to store the persistent objects. In this chapter, we have tried to bridge the gap between the two methods. We have specified the steps that can be followed to convert the conceptual schema, designed using the UML class diagram notation into a logical schema. Relational database normalization principles can be applied to the logical schema to ensure that the schema is in the intended normal form before converting it into the physical schema. Converting the class diagram into the logical schema is a difficult task as even though both of them share some of the same concepts, their underlying principles can be very different. While the class diagram enjoys success for being more realistic and closer to the user, ER diagrams are based on sound formal notations and design rules such as normalization.

Another purpose of this chapter was to show that the syntax of the class diagram can also be used to draw the ER diagrams. The logical schema represented in this chapter has been drawn using the UML class diagram notation. Based upon our experience, we believe that if the syntax of the UML class diagram can be extended, it can also be used as a basis to draw the logical schema. Systems built using Object-Oriented programming languages and databases like Oracle, SQL*Server as a backend (for example) are ubiquitous. Having two different sets of tools, one to maintain the schema and another to maintain the use cases/ class diagrams/etc. results in two different sets of documentation that are independent of each other, and could often be out of sync. UML has the potential to become a standard modeling notation that can be used across applications. However, to achieve this, the underlying syntax and semantics of UML need to be enhanced to incorporate ER diagram notations such as Primary Key, Foreign Key and Uniqueness.

REFERENCES

Bahrami, A. (1999). *Object Oriented System Design Using the Unified Modeling Language*. New York: Irwin/McGraw-Hill.

Banerjee, J. (1987). Data model issues for object-oriented applications. *ACM Transactions on Office Information System, 5(1), 3-26*.

Batini, C., Ceri, S. & Navathe, S. (1992). *Conceptual Database Design: An Entity-Relationship Approach*. New York: The Benjamin/Cummings Publishing Company, Inc.

Booch, G., Rumbaugh, J. & Jacobson, I. (1999). *The Unified Modeling Language User Guide*. New York: Addison-Wesley.

Chen, P. (1976). The entity-relationship model toward a unified view of data. *ACM Transactions on Database Systems, 1(1), 9-36*.

Chen, P. (1977). *The Entity-Relationship Approach to Logical Data Base Design*. New York: Q.E.D. Information Sciences, Inc.

Dewitz, S. (1995). *Systems Analysis and Design and the Transition to Objects*. New York: McGraw-Hill.

Date, C.J. (2000). *An Introduction to Database Systems*. New York: Addison-Wesley.

Elmasri, R. & Navathe, S. (1994). *Fundamentals of Database Systems (2nd ed.)*. New York: The Benjamin/Cummings Publishing, Inc.

Gogolla, M. & Richters, M. (1998). Transformation rules for UML class diagram. *The Unified Modeling Language <<UML>>'98: Beyond the Notation*.

Jones, T. & Song, I. (1995). Binary representation of ternary relationships in ER conceptual modeling. *OOER'95 – Object-Oriented and Entity-Relationship Modeling, 14th International Conference*.

Ling, T. & Teo, P. (1994). *A Normal Form Object-Oriented Entity Relationship Diagram*. Technical Report, Department of Information Systems and Computer Science, National University of Singapore.

Muller, R. (1999). *Database Design for Smarties Using UML for Data Modeling*. New York: Morgan Kaufman Publishers.

Ou, Y. (1997). *On Mapping Between UML and Entity-Relationship Model*.

Ou, Y. (1998). On using UML class diagrams for object-oriented database design specification of integrity constraints. *The Unified Modeling Language <<UML>>'98: Beyond the Notation*.

Pressman, R. (1997). *Software Engineering: A Practitioner's Approach*. New York: McGraw-Hill.

Rumbaugh, J., Blaha, M., Premerlani, W., Eddy, F. & Lorensen, W. (1991). *Object-Oriented Modeling and Design*: Englewood Cliffs, NJ: Prentice Hall.

Rumbaugh, J., Jacobson, I. & Booch, G. (1999). *The Unified Modeling Language Reference*

Manual. New York: John Wiley & Sons.

ENDNOTES

1 Having said that, there are a few occasions where corresponding notation does not exist in the UML model, for example, for specifying unique keys.

2 Some versions of the ER diagram, including Chen's original notation (see Chen, 1976; 1977), do include support for n-ary notation; however the concept is not supported at the logical schema level, as none of the currently available relational databases supports the concept of n-ary associations at the implementation level.

3 Here, our discussion is limited to the class diagrams and the static behavior part of object modeling.

Chapter IV

RUP: A Process Model
for Working with UML?

Wolfgang Hesse
Philipps-University Marburg, Germany

Recently, the Rational Unified Process (RUP) has been published as the second part of Rational's Unified Method project. The RUP is advertised as an "iterative and incremental, use case-driven, architecture-centric" process model and aims to support system designers, builders and managers working with the Unified Modeling Language (UML) by a procedural guideline.

In this chapter, a brief review and a critical analysis of the RUP is attempted. Its general aim and its contribution towards more harmonisation in the software process field are acknowledged. However, its ability to reduce the complexity of software development and to clarify its interlaced structure and terminology is doubted. Major problems may result from concepts not clearly specified like workflow or architecture. In particular, RUP core concepts like phase, iteration, workflow and milestone are debated. It is argued that RUP phases and milestones do not support the requirements of modern object-oriented (and, in particular, component-based) software projects. Iteration cycles should be based on software building blocks rather than on phases and activities. As one possible alternative to the RUP, a component-based (and truly architecture-centric) process model is sketched, and a multi-variant approach to software process modelling is recommended.

INTRODUCTION: THE "UNIFIED PROCESS," ITS HISTORY AND AIMS

In the mid-'90s Rational company has started a project trying to merge some existing methodologies for object-oriented analysis and design into a common "Unified Method." For this purpose their chief methodologist G. Booch, joined by J. Rumbaugh and (later) by I. Jacobson, tried to combine their methods which became popular at that time. Realizing that this goal was not to be achieved, within one single step the authors reduced their ambitions and started with a common metamodel and notation, an approach which resulted in the "Unified Modeling Language" (UML) disseminated since 1997 and now available in its version 1.3 from June 1999 (UML 1999).

In early 1999, the UML which deliberately had left aside any process aspects was complemented by the so-called "Rational Unified Process" (RUP), now documented by two books (Kruchten, 1999; Jacobson et al., 1999), in the Web (RUP, 1999) and by further presentations of its authors. With this generalised process description, the authors claim to "enhance team productivity" and to "give project managers control over schedules and deliverables."

The RUP has various sources like Boehm's spiral model (Boehm, 1988), Booch's macro and micro process approach (Booch 1994) or Rumbaugh's OMT (Rumbaugh et al., 1991). However, there is no doubt that its most important source is Ivar Jacobson's Objectory process (Jacobson, 1993). Some of the outstanding RUP features, like the focus on use cases and on iterations or the intertwined phase and workflow structures, have been very much influenced by this predecessor process.

According to its own advertisements, the RUP has been designed with the following aims (Jacobson et al., 1999):

- Provide guidance to the order of a team's activities.
- Direct the tasks of individual developers and the team as a whole.
- Specify what artifacts should be developed.
- Offer criteria for monitoring and measuring a project's products and activities.

Of course, these are aims nobody would object to, at least when a process definition *for a specific project* is required. For a *reference process model* like the RUP, there are surely broader goals as, for example:

- Provide a general structure and terminology covering the ingredients of software processes like its phases, artifacts, roles of people concerned, milestones, etc.
- Define the purpose, properties and relationships of these ingredients and establish a consistent and ready-to-use terminology.
- Provide a framework of common understanding for people working at different projects to support their cooperation, exchange of experiences, comparison of results, qualification of staff, etc.

There is no doubt that the RUP, although not explicitly claimed by its authors, stands for the first serious attempt to set up a standard for such a reference model in the "object-oriented world."

- It has set up definitions and given examples for central concepts of process technology such as *phases, activities, artefacts, workflows, actors* and *roles*.
- It is based on the experience of various software development teams that have worked in large and diversified projects.
- It is clearly oriented towards and closely connected with UML as a modeling language, and it supports working with this language and its tools.

Regarding the so far rather chaotic landscape of software life-cycles and process models, such an attempt has to be acknowledged. Surely it will influence the way of carrying out and managing software projects in the next decade.

Nevertheless, I think that a critical analysis is required covering the goals cited above (Where and to what degree is standardisation of software processes useful?) as well as the RUP way to achieve these goals (Are the concepts and guidelines offered by the RUP appropriate to match the goals?).

Concerning the goals, some of them already seem to be too specific, e.g., *"Provide guidance to the order of a team's activities"* or *"Specify what artefacts should be developed.*" We would not expect a *reference model* to give any concrete answers to such questions but rather a toolbox which supports *building an order of a team's activities* or *selecting from a variety of possible artefacts.* Some general limitations of standardisation (and a possible alternative to the RUP approach) will be discussed in the concluding section of this chapter.

Some RUP concepts and their appropriateness to support software processes will be addressed in the following sections. The characteristic properties of the RUP are summarised by its authors in the following four keywords:

- iterative,
- incremental,
- use case-driven,
- architecture-centric.

This sounds like a list of reasonable goals which should be supported by any modern software process model. However, a closer analysis raises questions like (for example)

- whether "use case-driven" or "architecture-centric" are really *unique options* to become part of a standard,
- which are the *subjects of iterations*,
- what terms like *architecture* or *workflow* really mean and
- what their *role* is within the software process.

It is too early for an encompassing evaluation of the benefits and failures of the RUP approach based on representative experience reports. However, comparing the requirements on modern software processes with the RUP publications now available, a first review of its overall approach and its core concepts is possible. In the subsequent sections, such an attempt is undertaken without going too far into any particular details. A more detailed critique (in German) can be found in Hesse (2000).

In this review, I shall concentrate on three major subject areas which I consider central and characteristic for the whole RUP approach:

- the way of dealing with the increasingly growing complexity of software projects, in particular the role of the *software architecture*,
- the RUP concepts for *software process modeling*, in particular its *phases, milestones, activities and core workflows*, and their relation to each other,
- the way of integrating the different *perspectives* on the software process to a *common, uniform process model.*

UML AND RUP—DINOSAUR MEETS ARCHAEOPTERYX?

For an uninitiated reader not familiar with the RUP history, this new approach raises quite a few questions and puts up some considerable intellectual hurdles. Similar or parallel concepts like *activity, phase, iteration and workflow* compete with each other and are difficult to separate. The role of a repeatedly addressed but never clearly specified *architecture* is rather nebulous, e.g., in connection with the overall incremental approach. A lot of new vocabulary (like the new, rather uncommon phase names) is introduced, the benefits of which are difficult to grasp.

Readers who are looking for simple and transparent but powerful concepts to master the increasing complexity of software processes might be rather disappointed by a process description which offers a vast variety of competing, complicated and intertwined terms, structures and relationships. In a recent paper criticising UML, K.D. Schewe has called

UML a "modern dinosaur" (Schewe, 2000). Having struggled through the RUP documents, readers might conclude that the dinosaur UML is being married to another hypertrophied entity, let us call it *archaeopteryx*, where a slim, efficient and powerful tiger or eagle would have been their favourite choice.

In particular, it will be argued that:

- in contrast to what its authors claim, the RUP is a *phase- and activity-centred* rather than *an architecture-centric* process;
- traditional concepts like *phases* and *milestones* still playing a prominent role in the RUP should be replaced by newer and more refined concepts, which are better suited to cope with current development paradigms like object orientation, component-based or evolutionary development;
- *iterations* should indeed be addressed by a modern process model like the RUP, but be linked to software *architectural units* rather than to *phases*;
- the so-called RUP *workflows* led an over-complicated and blurred overall process structure and some of the *core workflows* are mistaken *activity types;*
- the RUP favours a *monolithic view* on the software process, ignoring its *recursive structure* and its possible decomposition into subprocesses which are associated with the involved *roles* (stakeholders) and, in particular, include the *user's process(es)* and their feedback;
- by under-estimating important architectural issues, the RUP misses the chance of mastering the complexity of software processes by powerful concepts like *recursion* and *orthogonality*.

Summarising the RUP achievements and failures, the chances for *unifying* software processes and possible alternatives will be discussed in general.

THE ROLE OF SOFTWARE ARCHITECTURE

One of the outstanding and repeatedly claimed characteristics of the RUP is to be "architecture-centric." Moreover, Kruchten lists *"use component-based architectures"* among the six "best practices" the RUP is going to disseminate (Kruchten, 1999, p. 9 ff). If we try to learn what an architecture is, we get the laconic (and not much useful, since self-referential) answer: *"It is what the architect specifies in an architecture description"* (Jacobson et al., 1999, p. 83). More seriously taken, we are led to Kruchten's "4+1 view model of architecture" (Kruchten, 1995). But there we learn more about the various *views* on the architecture (which indeed play a major role in the RUP as *use case model, analysis model, design model, implementation model,* etc.) than on the architecture itself.

Also the glossary (Kruchten, 1999, p. 239) does not give much more support, culminating in the sentence: *"Software architecture is concerned not only with structure and behaviour but also with usage, functionality, performance, resilience, reuse, comprehensibility, economic and technology constraints and trade-offs, and aesthetic issues."* Taking this seriously the reader might conclude that "architecture-centric" means "everywhere centred," which does not give him any orientation at all.

If we try to find a more helpful (i.e., better focussed) interpretation of "architecture," we might come up with *"The structural elements and their interfaces that will comprise the system"* (Jacobson et al., 1999, p.61). Although this is just one aspect listed by the authors among many others (see above), I believe it might be a good basis for an "architecture-centric" process. However, this would mean that the process (or at least its parts) is indeed *based on the architecture*, i.e., on its structural elements. With his *cluster*

Figure 1. Two Approaches to Structure the Software Process

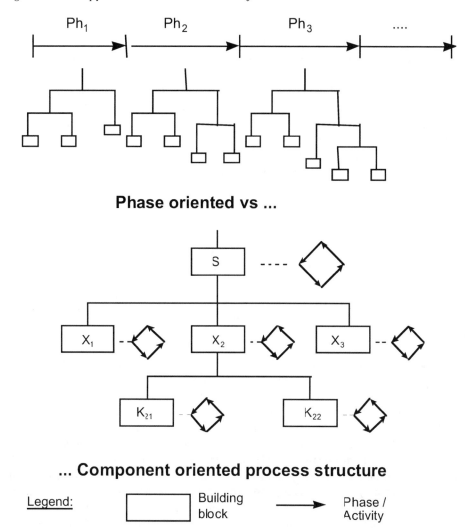

Phase oriented vs ...

... Component oriented process structure

Legend:　□ Building block　　→ Phase / Activity

model B, Meyer has already shown in 1989 a simple but very powerful way to associate activities with *clusters,* the structural elements of his architecture (Meyer, 1989): a system is decomposed into several clusters, each of which has its own process comprising stereotype activities like specification, design, implementation and validation.

In Figure 1 the traditional phase-oriented approach (in the upper part of the diagram) is contrasted with a component-oriented or cluster-centred approach (in its lower part):

In the first approach (often called the "waterfall approach"), priority is given to *phases* which comprise *activities* aiming to build, enhance and refine *models* which eventually represent the software architecture. In the second approach, priority is given to the *architecture* and its *structural units.* Phases are replaced by *development cycles* which are not only global, i.e., bound to the system development level, but local, i.e. bound to each structural unit on any level (cf. also Hesse 1996, 1997).

Although it is claimed to be "iterative" and "architecture centric," the RUP sticks to a phase-oriented structure (and in this respect it follows good old waterfall tradition) insofar as:

- it starts with *phases* on top of the process hierarchy;
- it links processes, activities and iterations to *phases* instead of linking them to *structural elements* of the architecture and
- it treats architectural elements rather at a marginal than at a central position. For example, *models* grow as results of certain activities. Since (according to the RUP authors) models are *vehicles for visualising, specifying, constructing and documenting architecture,* rather seems to move the "architecture" into a subordinate rather than into a "central" position of the process.

The five or six models produced during the first RUP phases led to further questions. Different names (*use case model, analysis model, design model, deployment model, implementation model, test model*) and their parallel construction from the use cases suggest that all these models coexist next to each other and are to provide different complementary views on the architecture. But wasn't it one of the central messages of object orientation that we no longer need many models but just one model, *the unique OO-model?* Its architecture should be established in the analysis stage and then *refined* to its design and implementation stages in a stepwise manner. Such an approach would clearly strengthen the role of the architecture and clarify what the "models" really are: different *states of one persistent model* which represents the evolving software architecture in each stage of the development.

To summarize this section: *software architecture* is now a very widely used notion being associated with many different interpretations. Obviously, the RUP interpretation (through a collection of complementary models) is not the only possible one. An alternative approach would call the *overall system structure* (showing its components, subsystems, classes, etc. according to the lower part of Figure 1) an architecture.

With this interpretation, *architecture-centric* would mean to associate activities, iterations (cycles), revisions, quality checks, management actions, etc. with *architectural elements* rather than with phases (cf. Hesse 1996, 1997). Such a truly "object-oriented" approach (based on the *objects of software development*) would help to avoid the well-known management problems with phases (phase overlaps, iterations, milestone dependence on phases, etc.). It would further encourage the developers to identify themselves with their (sub-) product(s) and thus support a product-oriented (rather than an activity-oriented) project management.

PROCESS MODELLING CONCEPTS: PHASES, MILESTONES, ACTIVITIES AND WORKFLOWS

According to the RUP, the software lifecycle is decomposed into:

- *phases* and *activities*, which may be subject to several
- *iterations,* which are associated with
- *workers (roles),* which are overlapped by and intertwined with
- *workflows*, and terminated by
- *milestones.*

In the following subsections these concepts and their role in the RUP will be discussed.

PHASES: STILL TOO DOMINANT IN THE RUP

Phase-structured lifecycle models (mostly known as waterfall models) have a long tradition within Software Engineering and have proven successful in many practical projects. Their success was due to their simplicity, their transparency (in particular for project managers) and their compatibility with traditional engineering paradigms. This still holds true for their modifications and enhancements such as the spiral, incremental, prototyping and V-shaped models (Hesse, 1996).

However, since new development methods have been introduced, the requirements on corresponding software processes have changed as well. The new approaches (like iterative, evolutionary, object-oriented or component-based development) all favour the co-evolution of several sub-products or components in an independent way. Thus phases will no longer play the dominant role they had played in the first decades of Software Engineering.

For example, object-oriented development and, even more so, component-based development encourage parallel and iterative work on independent components or subsystems. This is particularly important for projects where so-called "virtual teams" are involved, i.e., groups distributed over several locations maybe in different countries or even continents. A traditional phase model would be insufficient to coordinate parallel development processes concerned with such components and would unnecessarily force them into a rigid time scheme of phases and milestones. Therefore, several alternatives have been proposed which are better suited to cope with the new development paradigms (e.g. Floyd et al., 1989; Henderson-Sellers & Edwards, 1990; Booch, 1994; Hesse, 1996). Of course, milestones are not completely abandoned in these alternatives but have to be replaced by more refined concepts (see next section).

According to the RUP documents, each software development process is decomposed into four phases. Even the invention of new names *(inception, elaboration, construction* and *transition)* cannot camouflage their acquaintance to the waterfall model, i.e., the idea of synchronised work guided by a project-wide phase schedule. However, this idea will prove unrealistic as soon as concurrent processes are enacted for developing several independent components in parallel. There is no reason to synchronise their inception, elaboration and construction steps, and even their transition might take place at different points in time in particular in case of incremental development much favoured by the RUP. Similar arguments apply to iterations: Why should they be forced into a phase schedule as suggested by the RUP "panorama" figure (Figure 2)?

MILESTONES: TO BE REPLACED BY MORE REFINED CHECKPOINTS

The phase concept is strongly connected to the *milestone* concept. The RUP offers four standard milestones corresponding to the termination of phases but further milestones can be defined for project-specific purposes. In contrast to phases, we consider milestones most important since project managers need certain checkpoints in order to control the project's progress and to check conformance to budget and time planning. However, such checks will hardly be meaningful and effective if they are based on criteria like *"use case model 10%-20% complete"* or *"use case model at least 80% complete"* (Kruchten, 1999, pp. 65/68).

Problems which are inevitably provoked by these kind of statements could be avoided

Figure 2: The RUP "panorama" of phases and core workflows

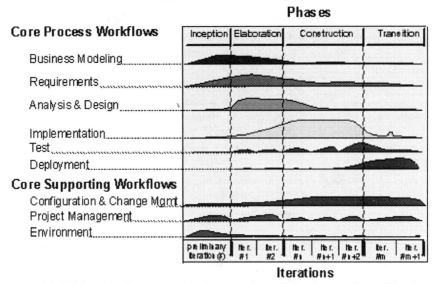

by a refined definition of milestones - then better to be called *reference lines* (Floyd et al., 1989) or *revision points* (Hesse, 1996, 1997). Such a definition lists the termination or scheduled state *of all ongoing activities* which are *individually* stated for *each component* under development. For example, a *revision point* defines a certain *state* for each (sub-) product (= component) under development to be reached at that point of time. These states need not be the same for all involved components, e.g., revision point R1 may imply component A to be in the state "design completed," component B to be in the state "analysis completed," etc. Thus a revision point is some sort of "refined milestone." Some consequences for project management are discussed below.

ITERATIONS: NECESSARY BUT WHERE TO BE ANCHORED?

One of the key characteristics of the RUP is its *iterative* structure. The RUP authors have decided to maintain phases as the overall process structuring principle but they were aware of the problems involved in a purely sequential approach. Iterations are necessary since (among other reasons) user requirements tend to be unstable and innovative software products need exploration, i.e. tentative steps prior to the final development (cf. Kruchten, 1999, pp. 51 ff). The RUP solution is to embed iteration cycles into *phases*, i.e., to foresee a (varying) number of iterations for each of the four phases (Kruchten 1999, p 62).

However, before setting up such a structure, one should analyse what the reason and purpose of an iteration is: is it just the desire to repeat a particular phase or activity? In this case it could simply be managed by prolonging that phase or activity. This might cause enough trouble to the responsible manager and developer(s) but would not affect the process structure as a whole.

According to Kruchten's Figure 4-2 (Kruchten, 1999, p. 58), an iteration is structured by *analysis, design, implementation, test and integration* activities. Looking to possible subjects of such activities we end up again with the *structural elements* of the architecture components or any other building blocks of the system. If such an element needs an iteration (for example due to severe defects), this will require a *re-development cycle*—consisting of an analysis (of the defects and their reasons), a re-design, re-implementation as well as regression test and integration activities. In particular cases, such a cycle might be abbreviated by skipping those activities that do not need any improvement.

As we have seen, iterations are one more reason for demanding an alternative architecture-centric process based on structural units like components, subsystems or even modules and classes. Such an approach would not only cover the iterated re-development of those units but also the *re-use* of components in a natural way: to adapt a class or component for re-use just requires a new development cycle on that product. Such a cycle would start with an analysis to which extent the present product can be re-used, what has to be modified or added, etc., and would be followed by the (re-) design, implementation and test activities in analogy to any other development cycle (cf. Hesse, 1996).

WORKFLOWS: A MIX OF VARIOUS KINDS OF ACTIVITY SEQUENCES

Another key concept of the RUP is that of *workflows*. According to Kruchten's glossary (Kruchten, 1999, p. 239 ff), a workflow is a *"sequence of activities performed in a business that produces a result of observable value to an individual actor of the business."* This definition offers many possibilities of grouping activities to "sequences": Possible criteria for tying activities together are:

    a) the same or similar kind of activities,
    b) the same actor who performs several activities in sequence or in parallel,
    c) the immediate temporal subsequence,
    d) the same object which is subjected to several activities.

In the RUP documentation we find "workflows" of various kinds: the *core workflows* mostly belonging to kind (a), the *core supporting workflows* belonging to kind (b) and the *iteration workflows* belonging to kind (c). Only option (d) which would correspond to our alternative "architecture-centric" view is hardly represented in the RUP.

Figure 2 shows the "RUP panorama" one of the most prominent visualisations of the RUP, taken from Kruchten (1999, p.45). This figure depicts the first two mentioned groups of workflows and their relation to the RUP phases. There are six so-called *core workflows* (formerly called process components): all but the first one (*"business modelling"*) are of type (a), i.e., grouping of activities of the same kind, namely *requirements caption* (formerly misnamed as "requirements" which is no activity at all!) *analysis, design, implementation* and *test*. To call them *workflows* suggests that there is a "flow" of analysis activities (crossing the phase boundaries) concerned with the repeated refinement of the *analysis model* and correspondingly for *design, implementation* and *test* "flows."

However, this view obscures the true reason for multiple analysis, design, etc. activities since it disregards their *involved objects*: *each* component, subsystem, module needs an analysis, needs a design, needs an implementation, etc. An alternative approach, according to the above "object-oriented" option (d) would associate sequences of activities with software building blocks making the RUP-like (pseudo-) core workflows obsolete.

In their panorama picture the RUP authors suggest a two-dimensional structure spanned by the axes called *phases* and *workflows*. However, for the first group of *core workflows,* the relation proves to be almost one-dimensional. Not surprisingly, most requirement-capturing activities occur in the inception and elaboration phase, most analysis and design activities occur in the elaboration phase, etc. (or in other words the upper part of Figure 2 resembles a *diagonal matrix*). Is it reasonable to give away a second dimension and a full set of new phase names for this simple relationship?

On the other hand, if sequences of activities were associated with the objects of development (software products and components), a truly orthogonal relationship between these two categories would arise justifying a proper two-dimensional schema as sketched in Figure 3.

This schema might be taken as:

1) a *development plan* comprising all activities belonging to the cycles shown in the lower part of Figure 1 as well as
2) a *repository structure* for the corresponding results: all documents belonging to the structural units *system, component XA, component XB, class CA,* etc. are gathered in the corresponding repository sections.

Last, but not least, such an approach would open the eyes for a different view of true workflows: there is no natural "workflow" through the *columns* of Figure 3 as suggested by the RUP authors—for example leading from the analysis of one component to that of another. But there are *very important workflows* along the *lines* of Figure 3: the development cycles combining all necessary activities for each structural unit.

PERSPECTIVES AND SUBPROCESS INTEGRATION

There is a second group of workflows, the *core supporting* ones, which are formed according to the actor/role criterion (b) of the above list. Project management, configuration/change management and support management (called "environment" in Figure 2) stand for groups of activities which are associated to particular *actors* or *roles* in the software process. Due to their importance at least two further groups should be added: *quality management* and *use*.

Without any doubt *quality management* is most important and should be reflected in

Figure 3: Architectural Units and Activity Types

Activity type Product or component	Analysis (.A)	Design (.D)	Implementation (I)	Operational Use (.O)
System (S.)	S.A	S.D	S.I	SO
Components XA. XB.	XA.A XB.A	XA.D XB.D	XA.I XB.I	XA.O XB.O
Classes CA. CB.	CA.A CB.A	CA.D CB.D	CA.I CB.I	CA.O CB.O

a process model and in particular in an overview diagram like Figure 2. The German *V-model* standard is an example of a process model structured by so-called *submodels* which describe the perspectives of certain actors like project managers, supporters or quality managers (Bröhl & Dröschel, 1995).

Furthermore, the *user* role deserves particular attention. The RUP offers use cases as a guiding technique to deal with the user requirements. However, following use cases as an analysis technique does not make *user participation throughout the development process* obsolete. In her STEPS model, Ch. Floyd has already shown, in 1989, how an evolving software process is paralleled by *use processes* for testing (sub-) products, prototypes or other intermediate results and giving the necessary feedback to the main development process (Floyd et al., 1989). RUP's use-case driven process is not sufficient to replace such a cooperation of development and use processes.

As an alternative to the RUP panorama of workflows, I recommend an encompassing software process model consisting of concurrent (sub-) processes for development, management, quality assurance, support and, in particular, for use and evaluation of the results developed so far (Hesse, 1997). Figure 4 shows the five subprocesses and their coordination by revision points (cf. the above discussion on milestones). This model addresses the users' role even twice: by including a "use and revision" activity in all development cycles and by a particular use and evaluation subprocess.

Summarising our analysis of the RUP workflow concept, we have found four different

Figure 4. The Overall Structure of the Software Process - (cf. Hesse, 1997)

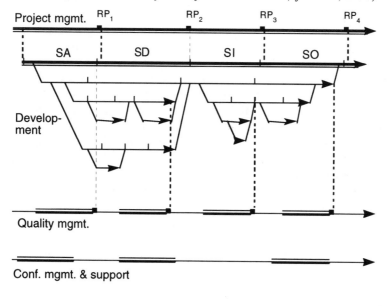

SA: System analysis
SD: System design
SI: System implementation
SO: System operational use

Rp_i: Revision point no. i

kinds of activity clusters which we recommend to treat (and name) as separate concepts: (a) activity types, (b) concurrent subprocesses, (c) purely temporal sequences, (d) development cycles.

MASTERING THE COMPLEXITY OF THE SOFTWARE PROCESS: ALTERNATIVES TO THE RUP

Many traditional lifecycle models worked satisfactorily with normal-size projects but did not offer much help for very large and complex projects. One of their major shortcomings was their *monolithic view* on the software process: "phases" like analysis, design, implementation, test always concerned *the one, unique product* the software system taken as a whole. With its phase, iteration and workflow structures, the RUP has added different *perspectives* on the software process but has not shown an efficient way of *breaking it down* to smaller, better manageable units.

On the other hand, software *modularisation techniques* have been developed and used for many years in order to master very large and/or complex systems by decomposing them into smaller and better manageable units. By following one of the most fundamental engineering principles, they led to a *recursive component structure* of systems which we all consider quite natural and straightforward. Modern programming languages like Ada, Modula or Java include particular constructs for modularisation such as *modules* or *packages*. UML does not stress the modularisation of models but at least offers *packages* and *component diagrams* as structuring constructs.

Why should a process model dedicated for not working with this kind of languages not use similar principles to structure software development processes as well? The component-oriented view sketched in Figure 1 leads to a *recursive process structure*: complex software development processes are decomposed into sub-processes according to the (sub-) products they belong to. As soon as a component (or a "package" in UML terms) is identified to be a possible carrier of future system functionality, its own development process is created starting with *requirements capture* (for that component), followed by *analysis, design, etc.* The same schema applies to any further component, possible sub-components, modules, etc. In Hesse (1996) a process model of this kind (called the EOS model) has been described in more detail.

Of course, such an approach would not free project managers from their challenging task of coordinating a very complex, multi-dimensional and interwoven process. To manage a collection of recursively decomposed, concurrent development tasks might even look more complicated than dealing with just one monolithic process stream. But it would offer managers much more support for structuring development processes and for setting up clear evaluation criteria. In such a model, milestone criteria like *"use-case model 10%-20% complete"* (cf. above) are replaced by clear and unambiguous statements like *"system analysis terminated"* or *"component design for component X terminated."*

CONCLUSIONS

In the previous sections, the overall structure and some central concepts of Rational's Unified Process were subjected to a critical review. In particular, the RUP concepts of phase, iteration, workflow, milestone and its treatment of the software architecture and user involvement have been addressed. Possible critical points were:

- the general RUP structure still dominated by *phases*;
- the underestimated and rather nebulous role of the *software architecture* and its structuring units;
- the embedding of *iterations* in the phase structure;
- the overloaded concept of *workflows* that should better be split into independent concepts like activity types, subprocesses or development cycles;
- the lost chance of mastering the complexity of software processes by powerful concepts like recursion or orthogonality.

The general approach of the RUP towards harmonisation of software processes, their structure and terminology is acknowledged. However, such a harmonisation involves many problems and it is still an open question whether and to what degree it will really be possible. There are many factors (e.g., project size, application area, available methods and tools, team qualification, enterprise "culture") which influence the applicability and efficiency of a software process model. The existing (and unavoidable) diversity of "project configurations" justifies a diversity of process models at least up to a certain degree.

For these reasons we see good chances for a "multi-variant" or "toolbox" approach supporting software processes with a variety of tailorable processes rather than with a pre-fabricated "process model" (Hesse & Noack, 1999). The base material of such a toolbox consists of descriptions of activities, artefacts (documents), roles, techniques, etc. which might be given, for example, in a RUP-like manner. It offers several ways for building so-called "variants" from these basic process elements. Each variant acts as a *guided tour*, showing one possible way of forming a practicable process model from the base material. Having chosen one of these variants, the project team managers and members can cast it to the specific project goals and to their individual requirements.

REFERENCES

Bröhl, A.-P. & Dröschel, W. (Hrsg.) (1995). *Das V-Modell. Der Standard für die Software-entwicklung mit Praxisleitfaden.* 2. Auflage. München: Oldenbourg.

Boehm, B.W. (1988). A spiral model of software development and enhancement. *IEEE Computer* May, 61-72.

Booch, G. (1994). *Object-Oriented Analysis and Design with Applications.* Second Edition, Redwood City, CA: Benjamin/Cummings Publ. Comp.

Floyd, C., Reisin, F.-M., Schmidt, G. (1989). STEPS to software development with users. In C. Ghezzi, J. McDermid (Eds.); *ESEC '89, Second European Software English Conference, LNCS 387*, pp. 48-64. Berlin, Heidelberg, New York: Springer.

Henderson-Sellers, B. and Edwards, J.M. (1990). Objects-oriented software systems lifecycle. *Communications of the ACM, 33(9).*

Hesse, W. (1996). Theory and practice of the software process: a field study and its implications for project management, In C. Montangero (Ed.), *Software Process Technology, 5th European Workshop, EWSPT 96. LNCS 1149*, pp. 241-256. Berlin, Heidelberg, New York: Springer.

Hesse, W. (1997). From WOON to EOS: New development methods require a new software process model. *Bericht Nr. 12, Fachbereich Mathematik, Univ. Marburg* (1996); and pp. 88-101.

Hesse, W. (1997b). Improving the software process guided by the EOS model. In *Proc. SPI '97 European Conference on Software Process Improvement.* Barcelona.

Hesse, W. & Noack, J. (1999). A multi-variant approach to software process modeling. In: M. Jarke, A. Oberweis (Eds.): *CAiSE'99, LNCS 1666*, pp. 210-224. Berlin, Heidelberg, New York: Springer.

Hesse, W. (2000). Software-projektmanagement braucht klare strukturen kritische anmerkungen zum "rational unified process." In Ebert, J. & Frank, U. (Hrsg.): *Modelle und Modellierungsprachen in Informatik und Wirtschaftsinformatik. Proc. "Modellierung 2000,"* pp. 143-150, Koblenz: Fölbach-Verlag.

Jacobson, I. (1993) *Object-Oriented Software Engineering: A Use-Case Driven Approach*. Revised Printing, Reading, MA: Addison-Wesley.

Jacobson, I., Booch, G. & Rumbaugh, J. (1999). *The Unified Software Development Process*. Reading, MA: Addison-Wesley.

Meyer, B. (1989). From structured programming to object-oriented design: the road to Eiffel. *Structured Programming, 1*, 19-39.

Kruchten, P.B. (1995). The 4+1 view model of architecture. *IEEE Software* 12(6), 42-50.

Kruchten, Ph. (1999). *The Rational Unified Process (An Introduction)*. Reading, MA: Addison-Wesley

Rumbaugh, J., Blaha, M., Premerlani, W., Eddy, F. & Lorensen, W. (1991). *Object-Oriented Modelling and Design*. Englewood Cliffs, NJ: Prentice Hall.

RUP. (1999). *Rational Unified Process Product Overview*. Rational Software Corporation, Santa Clara, CA. http://www.rational.com/products/rup as of 24 May 2000.

K.D. Schewe. (2000). UML: A modern dinosaur? A critical analysis of the unified modeling language. *Proc. 10th European-Japanese Conference on Information Modelling and Knowledge Bases*. Saariselkä/Finland.

UML. (1999). *Unified Modeling Language (UML) 1.3 Documentation*. Rational Software Corporation, Santa Clara, CA. http://www.rational.com/uml/resources/ documentation as of 24 May 2000.

Chapter V

UML Modeling Support for Early Reuse Decisions in Component-Based Development

J. A. Sykes
Swinburne University of Technology, Melbourne, Australia

P. Gupta
Central Queensland University, Melbourne, Australia

Component-based development is the software industry's latest answer to some long-standing problems in software development. Its aim is to make actual reuse of existing software units (components) a widespread reality. We argue that significant reuse decisions can occur in the early stages of system development. Using a theory of the modeling process, we show that choice of abstractions and notations is critical. We investigate the kinds of models that would support early reuse decisions. We show that easily composable, business-oriented abstractions about software behaviour and a functional mental model are necessary. Evaluation of the UML in these terms emphasizes its bias towards structural mental models and abstractions derived from the software domain.

INTRODUCTION

Component-based development (CBD) is the software industry's latest answer to some long-standing problems in software development (Allen & Frost, 1998; Szyperski, 1998). Building on lessons learned from earlier software-engineering innovations, CBD focuses on the goal of actual reuse of software (rather than reusability, which is simply the potential for reuse). This is seen as the key to a number of desirable economic outcomes, such as rapid development, clarification of developer roles and amortization of software development costs.

If components are thought of simply as units of software, it might be concluded that reuse is mainly a matter for the design and construction phases of development, but we argue that significant reuse decisions can, and must, occur earlier in the development process. This means that modelling has an important role to play in enabling developers to evaluate different reuse decisions prior to actual implementation.

Software development is a human-activity system that involves many people with different backgrounds, interests and skills. Effective communication between the participants is essential for success. Increasingly, software development is seen as a model-based activity, which means that various kinds of models are used as the chief formal technique for communication during the development process. As a result, the process of modelling has now itself become an important subject for research.

Some of the participants in the early stages of development of software for business and information systems are not software experts. The ways that they think about business systems and software systems can differ in significant respects from those preferred by software designers and programmers. Therefore modelling languages that are based predominantly on concepts appropriate to the software domain, as is the case with the Unified Modelling Language (UML), present obstacles to effective communication.

In this chapter we investigate the modelling process and the kinds of thinking it involves. We do so using a theoretical framework for models and modelling based on the semiotic (meaning) triangle and some ideas about mental models from the field of human-computer interaction.

We examine the interactions between the typical developer roles of Client and Analyst in an assumed component-based modelling context. The framework enables us to identify the characteristics of abstractions and notations suitable for supporting the modelling process. Several UML diagrams that have been put forward as suitable for CBD are evaluated against these characteristics.

CHARACTERIZING MODELS AND MODELLING

The process of modelling is a purposeful, subjective human activity. It involves perception (of the thing to be modelled), conceptualization (thinking about the thing to be modelled in a particular way) and action (actual creation of the model).

One way to study the modelling process is via the semiotic triangle. Based on this, a so-called modelling triangle was used by Brinkkemper (1990) to study formalization of information system modelling. More recently, it was used to investigate the conceptual modelling process (Gupta & Sykes, in press). This approach has now been extended with ideas about mental models and the system development notion of modelling purpose, to create a general theoretical framework for analyzing information systems modelling and development processes.

Figure 1: Meaning Triangle

The Semiotic Triangle

The semiotic triangle (also called the meaning triangle) deals with the process by which a human observer is able to claim that some sign or symbol

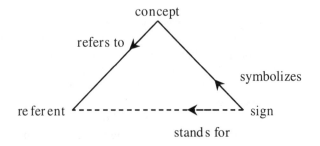

Figure 2: Two Meaning Triangles Representing Communication Between Two Observers

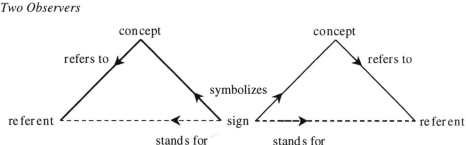

stands for (means) some perceived thing (Figure 1). Its importance lies in the fact that it shows how meaning relies on a two-stage process involving human perception and conceptualization, and is therefore subjective. The meaning of a sign is determined by the observer and not by the thing being observed (referent) or by the sign itself.

When two observers communicate, they do so by using signs. In this sense, natural language is considered to be a system of signs. The semiotic triangle shows that it is only the sign that is indisputably common to both observers. The other elements (referent, concept) could be different for each observer (Figure 2).

Mental Models

The notion of mental models aims to account for the different ways that humans attempt to understand complex systems (Preece, Rogers, Sharp & Benyon , 1994). People who have a notion about how a system is internally structured may be able to explain the behaviour of that system by mentally "executing" their mental model of it. This kind of mental model is called a *structural mental model* (or a "how-it-works" model). Other people may have no idea how the system is structured internally, but instead understand its use in terms of how it responds when operated. This kind of mental model is called a *functional mental model* (or a "how-to-use-it" model).

These ideas are relevant for system development because it appears that software experts tend to prefer structural mental models, while application users are more likely to have a functional mental model of a software application.

Mental models can also be characterized as either normative or descriptive. A normative mental model represents a person's ideas about how a system ought to behave, while a descriptive mental model represents its actual behaviour.

These distinctions are also relevant for system development work. A normative model represents a system yet to be built (a so-called "to-be" model) and a descriptive model represents an existing system (a so-called "as-is" model).

The Modelling Triangle

The modelling triangle is a form of the semiotic triangle in which the sign, the conceptualization and the referent are systems rather than simple signs or icons (Figure 3). In the form of the modelling triangle presented in Brinkkemper (1990), the term *concrete system* is used for the system to be modelled. We prefer the term *perceived system*, because it reflects the fact that conceptualization is preceded by perception, and it avoids the connotation that the system being modelled is a tangible thing existing in the real world. It

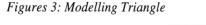

Figures 3: Modelling Triangle

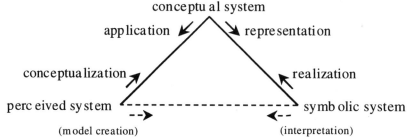

can be a system that the observer imagines, one that exists only in the observer's "mind's eye," as it were. This is the situation that must exist during requirements specification for a new system.

Figure 3 names four of the relationships that can exist between pairs of models (systems). In Brinkkemper's version of the triangle, two relationships for the lower (dashed) side of the triangle are given, and relationships between systems of the same kind are also named. We prefer not to name the dashed side in terms of relationships, but to regard it as representing the results of applying the other relationships. Thus conceptualization followed by representation we call *model creation*, and realization followed by application we call *model interpretation*. Relationships between systems of the same kind are called *translation* (between symbolic systems), *mapping* (between conceptual systems) and *empirical model* (between perceived systems).

The modelling triangle shows that two sets of ideas need to be clearly established for a modelling activity to be successful, namely:

- the notation (corresponding to the representation side of the triangle) and
- the abstractions (corresponding to the conceptualization side).

If the model is to serve as a means of communication between developers, they need to agree about the abstractions and notations, and to have a clear understanding about which notations represent which abstractions.

The Modelling Framework

A summary of the factors that should be considered for any shared modelling activity is as follows:

- *Participants.* Who is involved in the modelling activity? What are their preferred styles of mental models?
- *Purpose.* What is the purpose of the modelling activity? Is it descriptive or normative? Is it to create a specification, or a model that can be implemented as executable software (*a translation*)?
- *Perceived system.* What is the perceived system? If the modelling is normative in purpose, how will agreement about the perceived (imaginary) system be reached?
- *Abstractions.* Which sets of abstractions best suit the purpose of the modelling activity, the knowledge, skills and interests of the participants, and the kinds of mental models they prefer?
- *Symbols.* Which sets of symbols will be used to represent the conceptualized system? Do all participants understand the notations, and can they relate them to the set of abstractions?

APPLICATION OF THE MODELLING THEORY TO CBD

We now apply the modelling framework to investigate what kinds of models are needed to support the making of good reuse decisions as early as possible in the component-based development process.

The characteristics of the framework are considered in the following order: purpose, participants, perceived system, abstractions, symbols. This is done so that we can work from the reuse goal towards a discussion of who will be doing the modelling, followed by an analysis of the modelling support they will need. The analysis will focus on the abstractions and notations that will be required.

Purpose of the Modelling Activity

Broadly, the goal of the modelling activity in CBD is no different than in other kinds of development. Models are used for communication between participants in the process, and to represent the various kinds of artifacts they want to communicate about. Eventually a model is created that can be converted into the executable software for the system (the implementation model).

Because our focus in this chapter is on the reuse decision aspect of CBD, we will restrict our attention to models that can support that activity.

What Is a Reuse Decision?

Actual reuse of a component occurs as the result of a *reuse decision*. A reuse decision is one that can occur at any stage of the development process prior to or during construction, and that eventually causes some part of the construction phase to be handled as a "buy" instead of a "build." For example, under this definition, a decision to specify a use-case in such a way that some or all of its steps could be handled by an existing component would be a reuse decision.

When Can Reuse Decisions Be Made?

A decision to reuse a piece of existing software is clearly one that can be made during the construction phase of software development. However, in this chapter we are interested in reuse decisions that can be made earlier in development.

Allen and Frost (1998), in their component-based "solution process" propose the use of a "service package" (a logical representation of an interface) as a way of deferring implementation considerations, i.e., of dealing with reuse during requirements specification.

Herzum and Sims (2000) argue that component-based development radically changes the concept of information systems and applications. This is related to the idea that reuse-oriented decisions could occur even during the inception phase of software development, because knowledge that certain components are available could influence the assessment of feasibility and risk.

During the elaboration phase of the Unified Software Development Process (USDP), a project plan to guide the construction phase, and estimates of time and cost accurate enough to justify a business bid, are made (Jacobson, Booch & Rumbaugh, 1999). This implies that any reuse decisions capable of affecting these estimates have already been made.

Partitioning a system into sub-system modules, in order to organize which parts will be built first, also occurs during the elaboration phase, in the project-planning step. Close correspondence between a sub-system specification and an existing component reflects a reuse decision.

We conclude that the making of reuse decisions can, and should be, a requirements-focussed activity, occurring during inception and elaboration phases. By making reuse decisions as early as possible in the development cycle, the amount of actual reuse can be increased. But for this to happen, it must be possible to evaluate the choice of components and the way they are to be assembled before the construction phase begins. Models provide the means for doing this.

Participants

We now turn to a discussion about the kinds of knowledge and skills that people involved in making reuse decisions will have, and the effects of these on their communication interactions.

One approach would be to consider the nature of the actual participant roles that occur in particular methodologies. For example the USDP describes workflows in which various *worker types* occur. Steps in the solution process described by Allen and Frost (1998) suggest interaction between participants with differing skills. The Enterprise JavaBeans Specification describes a number of *developer roles* (Sun Microsystems, Inc., 2000).

A more general approach is used here, based on the fact that individual developers, whatever their particular role might be, must communicate with others. Whenever two participants in a software development project are communicating via a model, there are (in terms of our analysis) four steps in each communication act. The communication acts are steps in a process aimed at bringing the developers' understandings about the model into alignment.

The success of their communication depends on their knowledge of, and ability to use effectively, sets of concepts and notations to express those concepts (representing two sides of the semiotic triangle).

We use the term "mindset" to refer to the combined effects of:
- the person's available abstractions (the conceptualizations they know about and can use),
- the person's available notations (the symbolic systems they are able to use effectively),
- their preference for a structural or a functional style of mental model.

Modelling is likely to be least problematic when the participants share (understand and agree on):
- the perceived system,
- the set of abstractions to be used in conceptualizing that system,
- the notation to be used to represent the conceptual system.

Modelling will be more difficult the more we depart from these conditions. A critical or "worst-case" situation occurs when the two participants have significantly different mindsets.

For the discussion here, which is focussed on the requirements elicitation and specification aspects of development, we will use two participant roles that are likely to have quite different mindsets. We will refer to these as the Client and the Analyst roles.

We assume that the mindset of the Client involves detailed business domain knowledge, and a preference for functional mental models of software systems, whereas the mindset of the Analyst involves detailed knowledge of software systems, some business domain knowledge, and a preference for structural mental models of software systems.

Perceived Systems

The Client and Analyst are dealing with two software systems. One is the "to-be" software system being specified. The other is the "system" of existing components available for reuse. The goal is to produce a specification that incorporates an acceptable, agreed level of reuse. Following Allen and Frost (1998) we call the "to-be" system the *perceived solution system*, and the "as-is" system of components, the *perceived component system*.

The two systems are related via the *specification* for the perceived solution system. Some of the requirements expressed therein will be specified in ways that match behaviours offered by components in the perceived component system. That is, the perceived component system provides the raw material on which reuse decisions are based, and the effect that this has on the modelling process needs to be considered.

In order to make a reuse decision, the Analyst and Client must match the behaviour of some combination of existing components with some part of the behaviour required for the perceived solution system. They therefore need to be able to reason about the behaviours of various combinations of available components. This means that the representations of component behaviour must be *composable*, i.e., it must be possible to take the behavioural representations of two components and combine them in a straightforward way to obtain a combined description of behaviour that is expressed in the same way as the separate behaviours.

Since at least part of the matching process will occur at the level of a conceptual system (in modelling terms), it follows that there is a requirement that abstractions of behaviour also be composable.

Finally, the need to compare behaviours of the perceived solution system with the perceived component system means that the same set of modelling constructs (abstractions and notations) should be used for both perceived systems (or suitable transformations should be available).

Abstractions

The purpose of the modelling process has been established and the roles of Client and Analyst have been identified as the participants. The kinds of abstractions that will be suitable can be determined by considering the nature of the interactions between the participants. As a basis for this discussion, we use the setup shown in Figure 4.

The diagram, which is based on two modelling triangles joined via common symbolic systems, shows the modelling transitions and communications that occur as Client and Analyst collaborate on the preparation of a symbolic system that they want to agree "stands for" the perceived system. The diagram is applicable to both kinds of perceived system (*solution* and *component*) mentioned in the previous section. In this section we will consider its application to the perceived solution system only.

Interactions between the Client and the Analyst are aimed at accomplishing the following tasks:

1. bringing their respective perceived solutions systems into alignment,
2. preparation of a specification (model) of the behaviour of the perceived solution system,

Figure 4. Transitions between perceived, conceptual and symbolic systems, and communication between Client and Analyst roles, during requirements elicitation

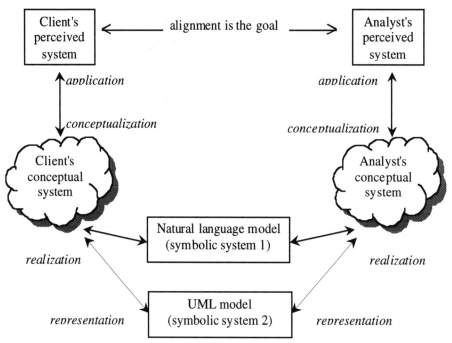

3. deciding which parts of that behaviour will be implemented by means of existing components (which also requires a shared understanding of the behaviours of those components).

For the first two of these tasks, Client and Analyst must share a set of abstractions (and notations) that are relevant for the perceived solution system. For the third task, it will be useful if the abstractions (in particular) and the notations are easily composable, as noted in the previous section.

Abstractions for Specifying the Perceived Solution System

The Client and the Analyst share a common goal that a software system is to be built, and are collaborating in the creation of a normative ("to be") model of that system. But because the system does not yet exist, they cannot perceive it directly. They must each imagine it. How do they know they are imagining the same thing? Presumably they agree that there is just one solution system. In terms of the modelling theory, however, we must say that there are two separately perceived solution systems at the outset.

Any agreement the Client and Analyst might reach about the correctness of the model is likely to be invalid unless they are each perceiving the "same" system. The negotiation process via which they bring their respective perceptions of the two imagined systems into alignment will normally comprise a number of iterations, each consisting of *model creation* by one participant followed by *model interpretation* by the other. We assume that either the Client or the Analyst can originate a model.

Essentially what is being sought is agreement about correspondence between elements of the symbolic system and elements of the perceived system, i.e., the *meaning* of the symbolic system (model) in terms of the proposed software system. As the meaning triangle shows, the association between sign and referent has two parts. An association between referent and concept results from the observer's scheme of abstraction. An association between concept and sign results from the observer's scheme of notation. Thus an agreement between Client and Analyst that a certain model element "stands for" a certain element in the perceived solution system can have validity only if there is already agreement about their respective schemes of abstraction and their respective schemes of notation. For an informal specification expressed in natural language, agreement about notation is implicit, but if the specification is to be expressed formally, Client and Analyst must explicitly agree on a scheme of formal notation.

What abstractions and notations are likely to be familiar to both the Client and the Analyst? We will assume that both are familiar with abstractions about the real world, and that a natural language provides one shared notational scheme. We will also assume that the Client is familiar with abstractions about the business domain that might not yet be shared by the Analyst, and that the Analyst's familiarity with a formal notation such as the UML is not yet shared by the Client.

For the negotiation about the perceived solution system to succeed, the Analyst must learn enough about the Client's business domain to agree on a shared set of abstractions for discussing the context in which the proposed system will function, and the Client must learn some abstractions suitable for discussing software systems. Furthermore, if the Client is to be able to validate the model, he or she must also learn some part of the formal modelling language to be used for representing the model.

Initially, the only notation suitable for a symbolic system available to both Client and Analyst is natural language. It provides the necessary "common ground" for discussion and explication of a relevant, shared scheme of composable abstractions.

As an example of the kinds of abstractions in the business domain likely to be understood by the Client we take those used by Herzum and Sims (2000) in a discussion of component-based business modelling. A *business process* creates an output of value to the customer from one or more inputs. A *business entity* is a part of the business required by a business process for its successful operation. A *business event* triggers one or more business processes. A *business rule* governs the behaviour of one or more business processes. The Analyst should have no difficulty in understanding these kinds of abstractions in a general sense, but has to become familiar with the instances of their use that characterize the particular business domain, i.e., become a domain expert.

The shared abstractions for the business domain (process, entity, event and rule) are relevant for discussing the business *context*, but less useful for discussing the *interaction* between the software and the context. For example, the abstraction *business event* is sufficient for conceptualizing the occurrence of an event in the business context, but to conceptualize the interaction, abstractions such as the event as a *stimulus* to the software and the software's *response* to the stimulus are more relevant.

Care is needed in choosing such abstractions. Behavioural abstractions for interaction found in software modelling techniques often require specialist knowledge and training for their effective use, e.g., interaction diagrams in the UML, and are not easily accessible to the Client. Furthermore, the Client's understanding of the perceived solution system, which is a software system, is likely to take the form of a functional ("how to use it") mental model, although for the business enterprise itself, the Client might have a structural ("how-it-works") mental model. The Analyst, on the other hand, will often have a preference for structural mental models of software systems. Such an understanding of the system will be required eventually (e.g., in the construction phase of the Unified Software Development

Process). However, in order to facilitate communication during requirements specification, the Analyst should strive to adopt a functional outlook compatible with the Client's and to conduct the modelling activity in terms of abstractions familiar to the Client.

Consequently, the most suitable abstractions for behaviour will be those that conceptualize behaviour that is perceivable at the user interface, and that have a stimulus-response style, so that the Client can reason as follows: "If I do this, the system responds by doing that ...." This form is, of course, the basis of use-cases. We regard this as an explanation for the growing acceptance of use-cases for requirements specification.

In short, what is needed is a set of abstractions for the interaction between software system and context that will be more meaningful (or "natural") for the Client than those based on a structural model of software. Table 1 proposes a set of abstractions about software behavior based on the business context abstraction categories named in the previous section. These *might* be suitable as the basis for a conceptualization about interaction that is shareable by both Client and Analyst, but they can only be suggestions at this stage. There must be evidence that the Client will find them suitable. Only after this is established would it be appropriate to devise suitable notations, such as stereotypes to extend the UML.

Symbols

After the Client and Analyst have reached agreement on a set of abstractions about system behaviour and have developed a common (functional model) perception of the behaviour of the "to-be" system, they need to specify the system more precisely than is possible using natural language alone. In terms of the modelling triangle, the focus now shifts from conceptualization to representation. It becomes necessary to use a modelling language (notation) such as the UML. At the conclusion of this step, the natural language representation of the perceived solution system (symbolic system 1 in Figure 4) will have been replaced, or complemented by, a more formal representation (symbolic system 2 in Figure 4).

As already noted, if it is necessary for the Client to participate in validation of the more formal representation, he or she must be familiar with the modelling notation. Once again, the success of the process depends on there being a shared understanding. The client and Analyst should work to explicate their understandings of the formal system to be used. The emphasis should be on notations for "black-box" representations of behaviour, as a result of the Client's assumed preference for a functional mental model.

Table 1. Related Business and Software Abstractions

Business Context Abstraction	Related Software Behaviour Abstraction
Business process	Participation in a process.
Business entity	Representation of data about an entity.
Business event	Response to a stimulus. Generation of an event.
Business rule	Documentation of a rule. Notification of infringement of a rule. Enforcement of a rule.

Summary of CBD Modelling Requirements

The Analyst and Client will use natural language to establish a shared set of abstractions for negotiating agreement about the perceived solution system, the perceived component system and the separate components in it.

Suitable abstractions will:

- allow the Client and Analyst to communicate about system behaviour as it appears at the interface between the software application and the business system;
- be compatible with the Client's functional mental model of the software, i.e., not require an "inside" or "white-box" understanding of the proposed software;
- be composable, so that the Client and Analyst can reason about composition of components that provide some of the behaviour.

Analyst and Client will establish a shared set of notations which they will use to represent their shared conceptualization of the perceived solution system and the perceived component system.

Suitable notations will:

- have clear associations with particular abstractions, to facilitate interpretation of the model in terms of the perceived solution system;
- be readily understandable by the Client, to support validation of the model;
- be composable, to facilitate evaluation of alternative solutions.

EVALUATION OF THE UML FOR CBD

One of the stated goals of the UML is to "support higher-level development concepts such as components, collaborations, frameworks and patterns" (Object Management Group, Inc., 2000). It is therefore relevant to evaluate the UML in terms of the modelling requirements for CBD discussed in the preceding section.

UML Terminology

In the UML, a diagram is a visual rendering of an underlying model. There can be many diagrams of the same model, each presenting a different aspect. When a software tool is used to prepare UML models and diagrams, the underlying model integrates the various diagrams associated with it. When UML diagrams are prepared manually, the model is normally implicit (the modeller could write it down in some symbolic form, but usually does not do so).

Although the terms model and diagram are regarded as different things in the UML, in the modelling framework used here they are both models. In fact, both are symbolic models, and the modelling relationship between them is thus a *translation*. The perceived system in the modelling triangle corresponds to the "system under analysis or development" in UML terminology. The conceptual system of the modelling triangle corresponds to the modeller's conceptualization of the perceived system formulated using the UML semantics.

According to the UML specification, a modelling language must include model elements ("fundamental modelling concepts and semantics"), notation ("visual rendering of model elements") and guidelines ("idioms of usage within the trade"). Model elements thus provide the abstractions that link the perceived and conceptual systems in the modelling triangle, and notations link the conceptual and symbolic systems. UML abstractions are based on ways of thinking about the structure of software systems.

The UML has extensibility mechanisms (e.g., stereotypes) that can be used to extend the range of available abstractions. It is also permissible to define new symbols to represent such extensions. However, the introduced abstractions are of lesser standing compared with other elements of the UML semantics, and excessive use of the extensibility constructs can lead to UML "dialects" of limited comprehensibility, which therefore become less effective as a standardized means of communication.

UML Diagrams for CBD

The UML as a whole is intended to facilitate component-based development, but we have selected only some parts of it for evaluation here. In keeping with the topic of this chapter, we have chosen those parts of the UML that have been proposed for use in the early stages of component-based development, namely use-cases, packages and activity diagrams. Due to its specific nature, the UML component diagram was also included. We think it is significant that all of these are well-suited to representing an external view of software, and that they are not strongly object-oriented. The more object-oriented diagrams in the UML use software-based abstractions and adopt a structural mental model of software.

UML Component Diagram

The UML provides a component diagram for representing components, interfaces and the dependency relationships between them. The symbol for a component is a specialized iconic representation of a UML package, and that for an interface is simply a named circle (a so-called "lollipop"). A component may have more than one interface via which its services (operations) are obtained. An arrow from a component to an interface shows how the component depends on operations offered by another.

In the UML, the component diagram is categorized as one of two *implementation diagrams* (the other being the deployment diagram). Fowler & Scott (2000) advocate combining component diagrams and UML deployment diagrams to show the physical deployment of components to system nodes as well as the dependencies between components.

Our evaluation of the component diagram is:
- as an implementation diagram, it does not address the requirements specification that is our focus;
- it provides no details of the actual operations offered by component interfaces;
- its composability is hierarchical, thus encouraging a structural view of the application software.

UML Packages

The package concept in the UML is a general way of representing collections of modelling elements of various kinds. Packages can be nested to provide a hierarchical representation of modelling elements.

Packages are used to represent interfaces (collections of operations). They have been used in this way to represent component interfaces. Dependencies between interfaces are depicted by means of a directed arrow.

As an example of this approach, we refer to Allen and Frost (1998). Components are classified according to the kinds of services they offer. The categories reflect a layered architectural approach to information systems analysis. Thus there are *user services*, *business services* and *data services*. A user service will normally depend on services in the same layer or one of the "lower" layers, but dependencies in an upward direction are not allowed. A user of the business system interacts directly only with the user services. In order to defer consideration of implementation details, Allen and Frost use the idea of a "service package." It takes the form of a UML interface and is intended as a logical representation of services offered by a component.

Our evaluation of this approach is:

- the use of interfaces as the basic construct, which allow individual services (operations) to be named, is an improvement compared with the component diagram's lack of detail on this point;
- merely naming operations, however, is not likely to be sufficiently informative to either the Analyst or the Client;
- the allocation of components to layers, and the hierarchical arrangement of dependencies between components, both encourage a conceptualization of the system in physical terms and a correspondingly structural mental model.

Use-Cases and Activity Diagrams

Use-case diagrams are part of the UML notation, but use-cases themselves are incompletely defined. A use-case is a legal model element, but the form used to represent it is not specified. In practice, various textual formats are to be found, and activity diagrams are also used (Fowler & Scott, 2000; Schneider & Winters, 1998).

Use-cases have become popular as a means of specifying system behaviour. As mentioned earlier, we believe this is due to the following characteristics: they use abstractions about system interaction that are likely to be familiar to the Client, they are compatible with a functional mental model of the system and they are often expressed in natural language.

Activity diagrams offer a more formal way to represent use-cases. Many of their underlying abstractions are similar to those of flowcharts and data flow diagrams, which have a long history of use in business modelling. This suggests that activity diagrams can be meaningful to the Client as well as to the Analyst.

However, we consider that the composability of use-cases, whether expressed as text or as activity diagrams, is too unwieldy to provide the compositional reasoning ability that is needed. Nevertheless, in text form particularly, use-cases do offer an approach to composability that is compatible with a functional mental model.

CONCLUSION

The analysis presented in this chapter is based on the idea that reuse decisions in CBD can occur prior to construction, and that they emerge from interaction between participants with quite different mindsets (characterized here as the Client and Analyst roles). This interaction was analyzed using a theoretical framework based on the semiotic (meaning) triangle, adapted for systems work, and extended with classifications of mental models from the field of human-computer interaction.

The analysis suggested that the kinds of models needed to support early reuse decisions should be based on composable, functional abstractions about the interactions between a software system and the business context that it is intended to support. To foster interaction between Client and Analyst, and to permit validation of models by the Client, the modelling must make use of both natural language and a modelling formalism that is comprehensible to the Client.

Some UML diagrams that have been proposed for CBD work were evaluated for their ability to support early reuse decisions. It was found that the component diagram is unsuitable, due to its focus on implementation and its lack of detail about component behaviour. Packages representing component interfaces, which have been proposed in various forms as suitable for CBD modelling, were found to be better than the component diagram because they can provide more detail about behaviour. However, when used in conjunction with a layered architectural view of the software system, they invite a structural view of the system that is likely to be incompatible with the Client's preference for a functional mental model. Use-cases do offer a functional view of the system, but were considered too detailed and unwieldy to be easily composable.

The research has suggested a promising avenue for further work. We believe the approach of using UML-style interfaces is sound, but they should represent a single layer of logical abstractions familiar to the Client rather than abstractions of a layered architectural view of the system. This would mean, for example, that the business services layer of the layered architecture would be replaced (at the interface) by three abstract categories for processes, events and rules, respectively. The data services layer would be regarded not so much as a physical part of the system (e.g., the database) but more as an abstract behavioural category for persistence behaviours that are apparent to the Client at the user interface. The hierarchical structuring of dependencies between interfaces would have to be avoided, being incompatible with the required functional mental model. In other words, the means by which such abstractions could be composed remains as the main problem to be solved.

REFERENCES

Allen, P. & Frost, S. (1998). *Component-Based Development for Enterprise Systems: Applying the Select Perspective.* New York: Cambridge University Press.

Brinkkemper, S. (1990). *Formalisation of Information Systems Modeling.* (PhD thesis). Nijmegen, The Netherlands: University of Nijmegen.

Brown, A. W. & Wallnau, K. C. (1998). The current state of CBSE. *IEEE Software, 15*(5), 37-46.

Fowler, M. & Scott, K. (2000). *UML distilled: A Brief Guide to the Standard Object Modeling Language* (2nd ed.). Reading, MA: Addison-Wesley.

Gupta, P. & Sykes, J. A. (in press). The conceptual modelling process and the notion of a concept. In Rossi, M. & Siau, K. (Eds.), *Information Modelling for the New Millennium.* Hershey, PA: Idea Group Publishing.

Herzum, P. & Sims, O. (2000). *Business Component Factory: A Comprehensive Overview of Component-Based Development for the Enterprise.* New York: Wiley.

Jacobson, I., Booch, G. & Rumbaugh, J. (1999). *The Unified Software Development Process.* Reading, MA: Addison-Wesley.

Object Management Group, Inc. (2000). *OMG Unified Modeling Language Specification.* (Version 1.3). Framington, MA: Author.

Preece, J., Rogers, Y., Sharp, H. & Benyon, D. (1994). *Human-Computer Interaction.* Reading, MA: Addison-Wesley.

Schneider, G. & Winters, J. P. (1998). *Applying use-cases: A practical guide.* Reading, MA: Addison-Wesley.

Sun Microsystems, Inc. (2000). *Enterprise Java Beans specification.* (Version 2.0). Palo Alto, CA.

Szyperski, C. (1998). *Component software: Beyond object-oriented programming.* Reading, MA: Addison-Wesley.

Chapter VI

Using a Semiotic Framework to Evaluate UML for the Development of Models of High Quality

John Krogstie
SINTEF Telecom and Informatics
and IDI, NTNU,
Oslo, Norway

Many researchers have evaluated different parts of UML and have come up with suggestions for improvements to different parts of the language. This chapter looks at UML (version 1.3) as a whole, and contains an overview evaluation of UML and how it is supported in the modeling tool Rational Rose as a basis for creating models of high quality.

The evaluation is done using a general framework for understanding quality of models and modeling languages in the information systems field. The evaluation is based on both practical experiences and evaluations of UML and Rational Rose made by others.

Based on the evaluation, we conclude that, although being an improvement over its predecessors, UML still has many limitations and deficiencies. Also Rational Rose only partly supports the development of information system models of high quality, and provides too limited support for using different modeling techniques in concert within a larger methodological framework.

INTRODUCTION

According to Booch, Rumbaugh & Jacobson (1999), developing a model for an industrial strength software system before its construction is regarded increasingly as a necessary activity in information systems development. Good models are essential for communication among the members of project teams and to assure that it is possible to implement the system.

Modeling has been a cornerstone in many traditional software development method-ologies for decades. The use of object-oriented modeling in analysis and design started to become popular in the late '80s, producing a large number of different languages and approaches. Lately, UML has taken a leading position in this area, partly through the standardization of the language within the Object Management Group (OMG).

In this chapter, I give an assessment of UML (version 1.3) and accompanying tools highlighting both the positive aspects and the areas where improvement is needed. I will first present the evaluation framework. I will then evaluate both the language quality of UML, and how this in combination with the modeling techniques found in one UML-tool, Rational Rose, can support the development of models of high quality. Evaluations of this kind usually only deal with language quality, but since this is only one of the factors influencing the creation of high-quality models (modeler characteristics, methodology and tools being other factors), I have included a tool evaluation to illustrate how the framework can be applied in a more general evaluation.

BACKGROUND ON THE EVALUATION FRAMEWORK

Most existing UML evaluations focus narrowly on what we call language quality, either by:

- evaluating UML relative to an existing approach (e.g., Henderson-Sellars, 1998; Paige & Ostroff, 1999), and highlighting those areas where the other approach is better than UML;
- looking upon detailed aspects of the language and presenting improvements for these areas (e.g., Hitz & Kappel, 1998);
- using a developed framework for assessing different aspects of language quality in a certain context (Hommes & van Reijswoud, 1999; Prasse, 1998) or only parts of language quality such as expressiveness.

Even those using a general evaluation framework look upon the language quality features as the goals to achieve. Contrary to this, Krogstie et. al. (Krogstie, 1995; Krogstie, Lindland & Sindre 1995; Krogstie & Sølvberg, 2000) have developed a framework for discussing the quality of models in general.

The framework;

- *distinguishes between quality goals and means to achieve these goals.* Language quality goals are one type of means, but means can also be related to modeling process, techniques and tools. Even if it can be argued from both activity theory and decision theory that the interrelationships between goals and means are being determined through the preference function of the modeler, we have found that most modeling techniques in practice primarily contribute to a specific model quality goal.
- *is closely linked to linguistic and semiotic theory.* In particular, the core of the framework including the discussion on syntax, semantics and pragmatics is parallel to the use of these terms in the semiotic theory of Morris. It is further based on the use of semiotic theory within the information systems field by Stamper (1998).
- *is based on a constructivistic world-view, recognizing that models are usually created as part of a dialogue between the participants involved in modeling.*

Further details on the framework can be found in Carlsen, Krogstie, Sølvberg and Lindland, (1997), Krogstie (1995, 1999b) and Krogstie and Sølvberg (2000), where several modeling approaches including OMT and approaches for workflow modeling have been evaluated. What one is able to evaluate using the framework is the *potential* of a modeling approach to support the creation of models of high quality. Used in this way we only utilize parts of the total framework as will be illustrated below. How the framework can be specialized for requirements specification models is discussed in Krogstie (1999a).

The main concepts of the framework and their relationships are shown in Figure 1 and are explained below. Quality has been defined referring to the correspondence between statements belonging to the following sets:

- L, the language extension, i.e., the set of all statements that are possible to make according to the graphemes, vocabulary, syntax and structure of the modeling language.
- D, the domain, i.e., the set of all statements which can be stated about the situation at hand.
- M, the externalized model, i.e., the set of all statements in someone's model of part of the perceived reality written in a language.
- K, the relevant explicit knowledge of the audience.
- I, the social actor interpretation, i.e., the set of statements that the audience perceive that the externalized model contains.
- T, the technical actor interpretation, i.e., the model as interpreted by the modeling tools.

The main quality types are indicated by solid lines between the sets, and are described briefly.

- Physical quality: There are two basic quality means on the physical level.

Figure 1. Framework for Discussing the Quality of Models

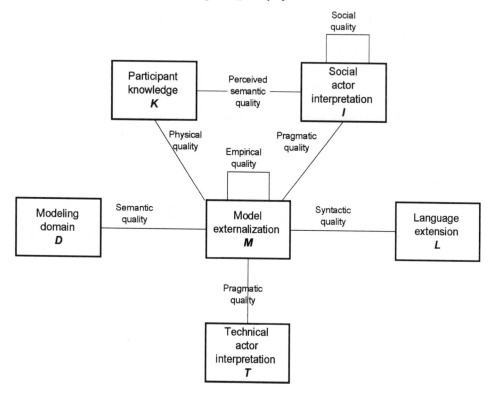

1. Externalization, that the explicit knowledge of some person has been externalized in the model by the use of a modeling language.
2. Internalizeability, that the externalized model is persistent and available, enabling the other persons involved to make sense of it.

- Empirical quality deals with error frequencies when a model is read or written by different users, coding and ergonomics of computer-human interaction for modeling tools.
- Syntactic quality is the correspondence between the model and the language extension of the language in which the model is written.
- Semantic quality is the correspondence between the model and the domain. The framework contains two semantic goals:
  - Validity, which means that all statements made in the model are correct and relevant to the problem.
  - Completeness, which means that the model contains all the statements that are correct and relevant about the domain.

  These goals are made more applicable by introducing the notion of feasibility.
- Perceived semantic quality is the similar correspondence between the participants' interpretation of a model and his or her current explicit knowledge. Whereas the primary goal for semantic quality is a correspondence between the externalized model and the domain, this correspondence can neither be established nor checked directly. To build a model, one has to go through the participants' knowledge regarding the problem at hand, and to check the model one has to compare with the participants' interpretation of the externalized model.
- Pragmatic quality is the correspondence between the model and the audience's interpretation of it.
- Social quality: The goal defined for social quality is agreement among participants' interpretations.

Language quality relates the modeling languages used to the other sets. It is distinguished between two types of criteria:

- Criteria for the underlying (conceptual) basis of the language (i.e., what is represented in the metamodel).
- Criteria for the external (visual) representation of the language (i.e., the notation).

Five quality areas for language quality are identified, with aspects related both to the metamodel and the notation.

Domain Appropriateness

Ideally, the conceptual basis must be powerful enough to express anything in the domain, i.e., not having construct deficit (Wand & Weber, 1993). On the other hand, you should *not* be able to express things that are not in the domain i.e., what is termed construct excess (Wand & Weber, 1993).

There are an infinite number of statements that we might want to make, and these have to be dealt with through a limited number of phenomena classes to support comprehensibility appropriateness, as will be discussed below. This means that:

- The phenomena must be general rather than specialized. This is parallel to what is termed genericity (Oei, 1995).
- The phenomena must be composable, which means that we can group related statements in a natural way. When only domain appropriateness is concerned, it is an advantage if all thinkable combinations are allowed.

- The language must be flexible in precision:

The only requirement to the external representation is that it does not destroy the underlying basis.

One approach to evaluating domain appropriateness, which will be used here, is to look at how the modeling perspectives found useful for the relevant modeling tasks are covered. Seven general modeling perspectives have been identified (Krogstie & Sølvberg, 2000). Structural, functional, behavioral, rule-oriented, object-oriented, language-action-oriented (Winograd & Flores, 1986), and role and actor-oriented. More detailed evaluations of languages within these perspectives can be based on evaluation frameworks such as Embley, Jackson and Woodfield (1995) and Iivari (1995). Another approach is to base an evaluation on an ontological theory, (see e.g., Opdahl, Henderson-Sellers & Barbier, 1999) that uses the ontology presented by Wand & Weber (1993). Domain appropriateness is primarily a means to achieving physical quality, and through this, to achieve semantic quality.

Participant Language Knowledge Appropriateness

This area relates the participant knowledge to the language. The conceptual basis should correspond as much as possible to the way individuals perceive reality. This will differ from person to person according to their previous experience, and thus will initially be directly dependent on the participants in a modeling effort. On the other hand the knowledge of the participants is not static, i.e., it is possible to educate persons in the use of a specific language. In that case, one should base the language on experiences with languages for the relevant types of modeling, and languages that have been used successfully earlier in similar tasks. We will not look into this in the evaluation of UML presented here, but note that for those being familiar with the main OO-modeling concepts and main OO modeling-languages, the core of UML should not represent a too steep learning curve. We should also note that almost all CS and IS degrees now include a course or more where UML is lectured and used. Participant language knowledge appropriateness is primarily a means to achieving physical and pragmatic quality.

Knowledge Externalizability Appropriateness

This area relates the language to the participant knowledge. The goal is that there are no statements in the explicit knowledge of the participant that cannot be expressed in the language. Since this is partly dependent on the participants, we do not look into this aspect of language quality in this chapter. Knowledge externalizeability appropriateness is primarily a means to achieving physical quality.

Comprehensibility Appropriateness

This area relates the language to the social actor interpretation. For the conceptual basis we have:

- The phenomena of the language should be easily distinguishable from each other (vs. construct redundancy (Wand & Weber, 1993)).
- The number of phenomena should be reasonable. If the number has to be large, the phenomena should be organized hierarchically, making it possible to approach the framework at different levels of abstraction or from different perspectives.
- The use of phenomena should be uniform throughout the whole set of statements that can be expressed within the language. Using the same construct for different

phenomena or different constructs for the same function depending on the context will tend to make the language confusing (vs. construct overloading (Wand & Weber, 1993)).

- The language must be flexible in the level of detail. Statements must be easily extendible with other statements providing more details. At the same time, details must be easily hidden.

As for the external representation, the following aspects are important:

- Symbol discrimination should be easy.
- It should be easy to distinguish which of the symbols in a model any graphical mark is part of.
- The use of symbols should be uniform, i.e., a symbol should not represent one phenomenon in one context and another one in a different context. Neither should different symbols be used for the same phenomenon in different contexts.
- One should strive for symbolic simplicity.
- The use of emphasis in the notation should be in accordance with the relative importance of the statements in the given model.
- Composition of symbols can be made in an aesthetically pleasing way. A negated example of this is a process modeling language which mandates that all inflow enters the same side of the process symbol, which can lead to the resulting model having unnecessarily many crossing or long lines.

Comprehensibility appropriateness is primarily a means to achieving empirical and pragmatic quality.

Technical Actor Interpretation Appropriateness

This area relates the language to the technical actor interpretations. For the technical actors, it is especially important that the language lend itself to automatic reasoning. This requires formality (i.e., both formal syntax and semantics. The formal semantics can be operational, logical or both), but formality is not sufficient, since the reasoning must also be efficient to be of practical use. This is covered by what we term analyzability (to exploit the mathematical semantics) and executability (to exploit the operational semantics). The power of a formal semantics lies in three aspects (Wieringa, 1998):

1. The process of making a (more) formal specification may reveal errors and ambiguities at an early stage.
2. Formal and even automated proofs may be available.
3. The remaining (or unprovable) rules may be translated into executable constraints in some imperative language.

Different aspects of technical actor interpretation appropriateness are a means to achieving syntactic, semantic and pragmatic quality (through formal syntax, mathematical semantics and operational semantics).

As already mentioned, many means might be useful on several levels, and we have here positioned them within the area where they are believed to have the most effect. This part of the framework is summarized in Table 1 taken from Krogstie and Sølvberg (2000). The table is an extension of the table originally presented in Krogstie, Lindland and Sindre).

EVALUATION

Before presenting the evaluation, we will position UML in relation to the sets of the

Table 1. Goals and Means in the Quality Framework

Quality type	Goals	Means *Beneficial existing quality*	*Model & language properties*	*Activities & tool-support*
Physical	Externalization		Domain appropriateness Participant language knowledge appropriateness Knowledge externalizeability appropriateness Language extension mechanism	Metamodel adaptation Language extension
	Internalizeability		Persistence Availability	Database activities Repository functionality
Empirical	Minimal error frequency	Physical	Comprehensibility appropriateness Aesthetics	Diagram layout Readability index
Syntactic	Syntactic correctness	Physical	Formal syntax	Error prevention Error detection Error correction
Semantic	Feasible validity Feasible completeness	Physical Syntactic	Formal semantics Modifiability Analyzability	Statement insertion Statement deletion Driving questions Model reuse Model testing and consistency checking
Pragmatic	Feasible comprehension	Physical Empirical Syntactic	Operational semantics Executability	Inspection Visualization Filtering Rephrasing Paraphrasing Explanation Execution Animation Simulation
Perceived semantic	Feasible perceived validity Feasible perceived completeness	Physical Empirical Syntactic Pragmatic	Variety	Participant training
Social	Feasible agreement	Physical Syntactic Pragmatic Perceived semantic	Inconsistency handling	Model integration Conflict resolution

quality framework.

Domain: According to OMG (1999), UML is a language for specifying, visualizing, constructing and documenting the artifacts of software systems, as well as for business modeling and other non-software systems. In other words, UML is meant to be used in analysis of business and information, requirements specification and design. UML is meant to support the modeling of (object-oriented) transaction systems, real-time and safety critical systems. For those areas being directly related to the modeling domain, we will differentiate the discussion according to the different domains.

Language: We have based the evaluation on UML (version 1.3) (OMG, 1999). We have not looked at the defined profiles, but concentrated on the core language. This version has been characterized as the first mature release of UML (Kobryn, 1999).

The sets' Knowledge,' 'Model,' and 'Interpretation' must be judged from case to case in the practical application of the modeling language and tools. Also when it comes to weighting the different criteria against each other, this must be done in light of the specific modeling task, such as has been done by Østbø (2000).

When using the quality framework to do an evaluation like this, we should have the following in mind:

- It is possible to make good models in a poor modeling language.
- It is possible to make poor models in a comparatively good modeling language.
- You will always find some deficiencies in any language and tool support. On the other hand, it is useful to know the weak spots to avoid the related potential problems. Such deficiencies should in general be addressed with the use of modeling techniques and an overall methodology. None of these areas are addressed in UML.

The primary aim of this evaluation is to help people using UML to recognize the existing weaknesses. On a longer term, it is also meant to give input to areas that should be addressed in later versions of the standard.

The basis for the evaluation is in addition to the framework:

- UML 1.3 language specification (OMG, 1999).
- Practical experience using Rational Rose both by the author and by other people interviewed by the author in both an industrial and an academic setting. This includes;
- Experiences by consultants in the use of UML for analysis and requirements specification of applications within the financial services sector. The consultants were interviewed after the project was finished.
- Experiences from the design of an object-oriented groupware system. Developers of this system were interviewed during the development of the third release of the system, parts of UML being used also on earlier releases.
- Experiences from the use of UML for the documentation of generic frameworks (Østbø, 2000).
- Experiences from students on larger assignments and project work where they were using the framework specifically for the evaluation.
- Additional evaluations found in the literature (Bergner, Rausch & Sihling, 1998; Bézivin & Muller, 1998; Castellani, 1999; France & Rumpe, 1999; Ovum, 1998, 2000; Prasse, 1998).

Due to the limitation on the length of a chapter of this kind and the breadth of the evaluation, we will only have room for presenting the major results. See Østbø (2000) for a more detailed description of using the framework for evaluating UML.

Language Quality of UML

The UML semantics (based on the metamodel) is the basis for evaluating the conceptual basis, whereas the notation guide is used as a basis for the evaluation of the external representation.

Domain Appropriateness

Looking briefly on the coverage of the seven modeling perspectives, we find:

- The object-oriented perspective is primarily relevant during analysis of information and design (Davis, 1995). UML has (not surprisingly) a very good support for modeling according to an object-oriented perspective, although with a limited modeling capability regarding responsibilities.
- The structural perspective is primarily relevant during analysis of information and design. This perspective is also well supported, although not as well as in languages made specifically for this purpose (Halpin & Bloesch, 1999). Traditional abstraction-mechanisms such as aggregation, classification and generalization are provided, but other modeling languages such as OML (Henderson-Sellars, 1998) and different languages for semantic data modeling have a more precise representation of these abstraction mechanisms. The area of volumetrics is only partly supported.
- The behavioral perspective can be useful in all domains, but is particularly used within design. UML supports the behavioral perspective using Statecharts, but does not support the refinement of Statecharts in a satisfactory way (Hitz & Kappel, 1998).
- The functional (process) perspective is supported on a high level through Use Case modeling (a.k.a. 0-level DFD), for requirements modeling and activity diagrams, which can be used to show control flow and the production of data or objects in a process flow. This is useful for design. Many have also attempted using activity diagrams for business models. Hommes and van Reijswoud (1999) argue that the modeling concepts in the business process domain are not easily mapped to UML. Software processes can be modeled using the interaction diagrams.
- The actor-role perspective can be relevant in analysis of business and design. It is partly covered using the Collaboration Diagrams. Using roles in Sequence Diagrams or 'swimlanes' in Activity Diagrams, we also get a role-oriented view, but there is no intuitive way to represent organizational and group-structures in UML, something which is very useful for the analysis of businesses.
- Single rules can be used in all domains. It is possible to formulate single static rules in OCL. There are some general problems with constraints expressed in an OO modeling framework (Høydalsvik & Sindre, 1993). Temporal and deontic constraints are hard to express. The same problem applies to non-functional requirements, such as performance, reliability or security requirements. There are also technical problems with visibility of, e.g., private attributes used in constraints. There is no support for goal-hierarchies (Mylopoulos, Chung & Tu, 1999), a technique primarily used in analysis of businesses and requirements specification.
- The language-action perspective, which is most useful for the analysis of businesses, is not supported.

A metamodel of UML is defined (using UML), and there exist extension mechanisms to make the language more applicable in specific domains. UML contains only lightweight extension mechanisms, such as stereotypes, constraints and tagged values (compared to metaclasses, which is regarded as a heavyweight extension mechanism).

UML contains several language elements that are first useful during design. These language mechanisms should not be used in analysis and requirements specification, even in areas where the transition from analysis to design is 'seamless.' (There exists quite some evidence that especially for business systems, this transition is far from seamless even when using object-oriented modeling in both domains (Davis, 1995; Høydalsvik & Sindre, 1993; Lauesen, 1998)). Proper guidelines for avoiding this are not consistently provided, and there is no support for avoiding using analysis and design concepts in the same model. It is generally believed that a good method should help you to keep information about what a system should do separated from how that functionality should be implemented in a specific implementation environment. The connections between such models should also be possible to express (Ovum, 1998). UML gives limited support in this regard.

Although comprehensive, UML cannot be used to specify complete applications. The limitations are both that it does not provide an action language (Mellor, Tockey, Arthaud & LeBlanc, 1998) to support the analysis of complete specifications, and that it lacks some constructs for, e.g., architecture (Hilliard, 1999), user-interfaces (Kovacevic, 1998) and hypermedia (Baumeister, Koch & Mandel, 1998) to support more complete code-generation.

Comprehensibility Appropriateness

Some main observations on this area:
- Several inconsistencies exist, partly because the metamodel has resulted in the inheritance of sometimes meaningless (or at least undefined) properties. As an example, a Constraint is a model element that constraints other model-elements (including potentially a constraint), and any model element (including a constraint) might have a state model. Circularities in the definitions are also found (Castellani, 1999).
- UML has 233 different concepts (Castellani, 1999), and it is not surprising that some redundancy and overlap is witnessed. Some examples:
- The concepts Signal and Operation call are almost identical.
- How to differentiate between the use of types and the use of classes is poorly defined.
- Guards, Preconditions, Postconditions, Constraints, Multiplicity and Invariants are all different types of rules. On the other hand, these terms might be so well established that it causes few problems in practice.
- Symbol differentiation:
- Both classes and objects are shown using rectangles.
- Use-cases, States in Statecharts and Activities in Activity Diagrams are all shaped more or less like an ellipse.
- The same symbol is used for choice in Activity diagram, aggregation and n-ary associations.

It is difficult to avoid some overlaps of this kind in a complex language like UML.
- Uniform use of symbols. The predecessor of the structural model in UML, OMT had quite a few deficiencies in this area, some of which have been addressed.
- Contrary to OMT, there is in UML a uniform way of showing cardinality (multiplicity).

Associations are shown in two ways, compared to the four ways of showing associations in OMT.
- Different symbols are used for a role if it is external to the system (pin-man) or

internal (rectangle).

- An interface is shown in two different ways (as a circle or as a class-symbol).

Many of these deficiencies are relatively unproblematic, since different aspects are focussed on in the different models. On the other hand, having too many issues like this makes it more difficult to learn the language and comprehend models made using the language. This is specifically important in models used to analyze business and information, and requirements specification, which are meant to be comprehended by many people with different backgrounds.

- In the structural model, emphasis is set on classes and objects through the size of the symbols, which is sensible. Most of the usage of filled symbols found in OMT is removed, with the exception of full aggregation, which is an intuitive use of this effect. That the class-symbols get different size and shape dependant on the number of attributes and operations that are defined makes these potentially visually complex. This is outweighted by the fact that the diagrams get much simpler than if these concepts should be represented separately as done in many other languages for structural modeling. The same positive remark can be made on the onion-notation inherited through adopting the use of Statecharts. The possibility of grouping classes/ objects in packages and composite classes and objects is also potentially a positive aspect in this connection, which is an improvement over its predecessors.
- Some symbols are unnecessarily complex, e.g., the components in Components Diagrams. There are historical reasons for this, to make it easier for people used to the Booch notation to recognize these.

Technical Actor Interpretation Appropriateness

The UML-syntax is rigorously defined, and the language is described through a metamodel made in the structural model of UML with accompanying OCL-rules and natural language description. Using UML to model UML means that some of the definitions are circular, and this leaves UML (formally speaking) undefined. This would be unproblematic if most practitioners already understood the meaning of the concepts (classes, inheritance and associations) that are involved. To illustrate that this can be problematic, we can point to that the concept 'inheritance' is used in three different ways in the literature (Taivalsaari, 1996). UML supports one of these. There are significant improvements in the metamodel of UML 1.3, although it falls short of a strict metamodeling approach (Kobryn, 1999). UML neither has a formal mathematical nor an operational semantics, and there is no support for the generation of design models from analysis models, or implementation models from design models. OCL also gives the potential for some of the analysis and consistency checking that a formally defined mathematical semantics would. On the other hand, it is unclear what tool support will be developed. Other groups have proposed extending Z to provide a formal semantics to UML (Evans, 1998). A formal (operational) action language would also be useful to be able to support a wider repertoire of modeling techniques (Mellor, Tockey, Arthaud & LeBlanc, 1998).

Tool Support in Rational Rose as Means for Model Quality

Regarding tool support for model quality, we have originally evaluated the support given by Rational Rose 98 Professional. We have also included improvements presented in Rational Rose 2000, but our main practical experiences are from the use of Rational Rose

98 Professional. We have not looked at Rational Rose for Real Time. Many other tools also exist that support the development of UML models such as Select Enterprise, Together, System Architect, Tau UML Suite, Paradigm Plus and Objecteering. The choice of Rational Rose can here be looked upon as a pragmatic one to illustrate how to use the framework for this kind of evaluation. In Østbø (2000) both Rational Rose and Select Enterprise are evaluated.

Physical Quality

This is partly dependent on language quality aspects covered by Knowledge Externalizability Appropriateness and Domain Appropriateness. A discussion on domain appropriateness was given above and is not repeated in full. Briefly, Rational Rose has the same strengths and weaknesses in this respect as UML. In addition, Rational Rose does not support several areas of UML. The implementation of UML in Rational Rose 2000 uses a mix of UML 1.0-1.3. Looking at the different diagram-types, we have the following limitations:

- Class models:
    - signal receptions are not supported
    - Rose supports operations, but requires you to define (single) methods as select free text
    - there is no specific provision for defining responsibilities of classes, attributes or operations
    - you can define pre and post-conditions for operations, but not general ized invariants
    - you cannot define UML power-types
    - you cannot define incomplete, non-disjoint or ordered sub-types
    - the tool does not provide a standard constraint to implement exclusive relationships
    - there is no way to distinguish between classes and types

Some of the deficiencies in the area, which make it impossible to generate complete DDLs, are addressed through a two-way link to the data modeling tool ERWIN.

- Collaboration diagrams and sequence diagrams:
    - the tool does not make a proper provision for the specification of conditional and iterative messages
    - the ability to group messages into transactions is not supported
    - semantics for parallel execution is not supported
    - 'vote' constraints are not supported
    - explicit indication of the creation and destruction of instances is not supported
    - specifically for sequence diagrams, no distinction is made between messages that constitute operation calls and those that constitute signals; Messages that take time to transmit are not represented by slanting arrows
- The Statecharts are not yet fully integrated with the other models:
    - there is no special variable that holds the current state of the machine
    - neither signal events nor time events are supported
    - no support is provided for the definition of UML actions
    - provision for parallel execution semantics is a little weak; for example,

     the concurrent sub-state notation is not supported
-     the full UML syntax for concurrent nested states is not implemented
- For deployment diagrams in Rational Rose:
  - you cannot say that a component is to be deployed on a node by linking the component to the node
  - no distinction is made between nodes and node instances, or components and component instances
  - processes must be tied to a given node, the concept of mobile processing is not supported
  - nodes do not inherit all the characteristics
  - the information that can be recorded against a node is largely free text

Rational Rose does not have metamodel architecture. The standard extension-mechanisms provided in UML are supported, with the exception of Constraints on other concepts than associations.

Rational Rose enables the modeling of many aspects during analysis that are first relevant in design. Some filtering-mechanisms and ways to constrain or extend the available modeling-palette are included.

As for persistence and availability, on the version we have worked with, it is only possible to store complete models on a file-format. The repository support on a detailed level is thus limited. There is limited multi-user support. The model can be partitioned into units that can be checked out by individual developers. Later versions of the tool can be integrated with Microsoft Repository. Configuration management and versioning are meant to be supported by the use of other products (e.g., ClearCase). Printing of models is supported, including set-up for choosing which part of the model to print. The last version of the tool also has the possibility to make project design and analysis information available on the web.

Empirical Quality

A Diagram Layout function is provided, but our experience is that it has limited usefulness. It is most useful when providing a starting point for automatically generated models, see the description of this as part of semantic quality. The tool has a grid-functionality, but the support for alignment and spacing to help in the semi-automatic creation of 'nice' models is limited compared to more traditional drawing-tools such as Visio. The automatic resizing of model elements as they are filled with more information is useful to avoid text crossing symbol-borders.

This area also covers the aspects related to Comprehensibility Appropriateness. Some improvements are provided in Rose in this area to address problems in UML. It is possible to remove attributes and operations from the graphical model, making the class-symbols more equally sized. On the other hand, we have not found an easy way to indicate that this should be done for all classes on a diagram, thus potentially getting class diagrams where classes are depicted very differently. On the other hand, the use of icons for, e.g., attributes and operations clutters these diagrams unnecessarily, especially when being used for analysis purposes.

Methods are not supported (covered by Operations) and neither are Signals (covered by Operation calls). This is looked upon as good in light of our discussion on language complexity above. The mix of actors and classes, on the other hand, is unfortunate and makes the actor-concept superfluous.

It is possible to freely change fonts, font-size, color, etc., which if done in an undisciplined manner can lead to the creation of very messy models.

Syntactic Quality

Good facilities exist for error prevention, e.g., forcing that an association needs to be between two classes, and that there are no cycles in the inheritance hierarchy.

Only limited error detection functionality is implemented, since a lot of the information that can be provided is only entered as free text. The check does not cover all the rules of UML in this area. It is possible to create one's own check-scripts.

Semantic Quality

Several mechanisms to make it easier to create, change and update the models are provided (e.g., framework wizard, class wizard, automatic generation of Collaboration Diagrams from Sequence Diagrams and vice versa, change into and reassign functionality). It is possible to enter several model-elements without giving them a description, and 'stamping' functionality is provided to, e.g., enter several classes at once. Pick-lists are supported wherever possible. The undo-functionality is very limited.

The reverse engineering facilities into Class and Component diagrams can be used to support model-reuse when an explicit model is not available. Links between Class, Collaboration and Sequence diagrams are maintained to keep these consistent.

There is only limited support for consistency-checking and other types of (semantic) model checking.

The above aspects are quite general across domains. Looking in more detail on the support of different domains, we note that there is no specific support of creating good business models (good in the sense that they provide a model of a better business process than what currently exists). As an example of tool support for this, a variant of the driving question technique could be used, where based on the existing model and standard BPR-heuristics, the tool could suggest improvements of the models. Another domain with many specific means is requirements specifications (Krogstie, 1999a). Rational Rose does not provide support for requirement definition. However, requirements in RequisitePro can be imported into Rose, where they are represented as use cases or classes. Use cases can be exported to RequisitePro as requirements. Alternatively, RequisitePro requirements of type 'use case' can be hot-linked to Rose use cases. The link is constrained to be one-to-one, and no other Rose item type can be linked in this way. The links cannot be annotated or classified.

Pragmatic Quality

A good filtering-mechanism is provided for some of the models.

It is possible to rephrase the relevant models in the OMT or the Booch notation, which can be useful for those more familiar with those notations.

The use of flyover text on the models can also be useful for comprehending the models, together with the (context-sensitive and traditional) help-text and tutorials, which visualizes the modeling-sequence. There are also several simple ways of getting to the description of the model element. Traditional functionality for zooming, fit in window, etc., is provided.

Some simple reporting and query-functionality is provided. If the tool SoDA is used, the possibilities for reporting are improved significantly. It is also possible to create one's own reporting-scripts.

No complete code-generation from the models is provided, which makes the support of creating functional prototypes for comprehension and validation purposes limited. No model execution mechanisms are thus supported. More advanced comprehension techniques such as simulation, animation or explanation generation are not supported.

Social Quality

Model matching is supported through an additional tool called Visual Differencing. We are uncertain of the usefulness of this tool, as an attempt to match two identical models resulted in many differences being reported.

Rose itself provides the ability to compare and merge the contents of Rose units, but cannot conduct a merge with a sub-package within a unit as the input item. The merge facility presents conflicts to the user for decision.

CONCLUSION AND FURTHER WORK

Many improvements can be found in UML compared to its predecessors. Due to its strong support, UML is probably the best general modeling language to adopt as a basis for object-oriented development if one is not already using another language with good tool support that one is satisfied with. Another positive aspect is the inclusion of use-cases (Hitz & Kappel, 1998). Thanks to this, the very first step in object-oriented development does not encompass finding objects in the problem domain, but the identification of the system functionality as required by the users. Most of the accidental problems, such as inconsistencies in the language-descriptions found in earlier versions of UML, seem to be addressed in UML 1.3, but there are still major concerns.

A major lesson from the introduction of CASE tools based on structured approaches can be summarized with 'No methodology – no hope' (Parkinson, 1990). This is a major point also made by OVUM (1998). Even if it has not been possible to agree on a standard process, outline process guidelines need to be included even if the best that can be done is to describe a number of alternatives. This would have helped users to understand UML. Particularly problematic is the logical/physical confusion. As discussed by Davis (1995), there are fundamental differences between the models related to analysis, design and requirement specification. What our investigation has also illustrated is that although there is a perceived need to extend the expressiveness and formality of the language, the language has several weaknesses regarding comprehensibility appropriateness, and is already looked upon as difficult to comprehend, with a steep learning curve (France & Rumpe, 1999). It has been suggested that a successful response to these challenges will require the OMG to adopt a sculpting approach (where "less is more"), rather than a mudpacking approach. It is then an open question what should be kept in the core of UML, and what should be kept as part of internally consistent, but separate profiles or in standard model libraries. In our opinion, UML currently has its main strengths in the creation of design models for traditional object-oriented systems, and this domain (with the extension and necessary elaboration of use cases to be able to say something sensible about requirements) should probably define the scope for the core language. Profiles should then be developed just as rigorously for extensions using a full meta-modeling approach, and tools should enable the use of those extra profiles than are deemed necessary for the modeling activity at hand.

This work will be followed up and updated as new versions of UML and tools supporting modeling with UML are made available. We will in the future also look upon how different UML-based methodologies help in addressing the problematic areas still found in UML.

ACKNOWLEDGMENTS

We would like to thank Reidar Conradi for input to an earlier version of this work, and the anonymous referees, whose comments have helped to improve the quality of this chapter.

REFERENCES

Baumeister, H., Koch, N. & Mandel, L. (1999). Towards a UML extension for hypermedia design. In France and Rumpe (1999), pp. 614-629.

Bergner, K., Rausch, A., & Sihling, M. (1998). Critical look upon UML 1.0. In Schader, M. and Korthaus, A. (Eds.), *The Unified Modeling Language – Technical Aspects and Applications*. Heidelberg. Physica-Verlag.

Bézivin, J. & Muller, P.-A. (Eds.) (1998). *UML'98- Beyond the Notation*. June 3-4 Mulhouse, France. Springer-Verlag.

Booch, G., Rumbaugh, J. & Jacobson, I (1999). *The Unified Modeling Language: User Guide*. Addison-Wesley.

Carlsen, S., Krogstie, J., Sølvberg, A. & Lindland, O.I. (1997). Evaluating flexible workflow systems. In Nunamaker, J. F. & Sprague, R. H. (Eds.), *Proceedings of the Thirtieth Annual Hawaii International Conference on System Sciences (HICCS'97). Volume II Information Systems Collaboration Systems and Technology*. January, pp. 230-239.

Castellani, X. (1999). Overview of models defined with charts of concepts. In E. Falkenberg, K. Lyytinen & A. Verrijn-Stuart (Eds.), *Proceedings of the IFIP8.1 working conference on Information Systems Concepts (ISCO4); An Integrated Discipline Emerging*. September 20-22, Leiden, The Netherlands, pp. 235-256.

Davis, A. (1995). Object-oriented requirements to object-oriented design: An easy transition? *Journal of Systems and Software* 30(1/2), 151-159.

Embley, D. W., Jackson, R. B. & Woodfield, S. N. (1995). OO system analysis: Is it or Isn't it? *IEEE Software 12* (3) July 19-33.

Evans, A., France, R., Lano, K. & Rumpe, B. (1998) Developing the UML as a Formal Modeling Language. In (Bézivin & Muller, 1998) (pp. 346-348).

France, R. & Rumpe, B. (Eds.) (1999). *UML'99 – The Unified Modeling Language – Beyond the Standard*. Springer Verlag.

Halpin, T. & Bloesch, A. (1999) A. Data Modeling in UML and ORM: A comparison. *Journal of Database Management 10*(4) oct-dec, 4-13.

Henderson-Sellars, B. (1998). OML – Proposals to Enhance UML. In (Bézivin & Muller, 1998), (pp. 349-364).

Hilliard, R. (1999). Using the UML for Architectural Description. In (France & Rumpe, 1999). (pp. 32-48).

Hitz, M. & Kappel, G. (1998). Developing with UML – Some Pitfalls and Workarounds. In (Bézivin & Muller, 1998), (pp. 9-20).

Hommes, B-J. & van Reijswoud, V. (1999). The quality of Business Process Modeling Techniques. In E. Falkenberg, K. Lyytinen, & A. Verrijn-Stuart (Eds.), *Proceedings of the IFIP8.1 Working Conference on Information Systems Concepts (ISCO4); An Integrated Discipline Emerging*. September 20-22, Leiden, The Netherlands, (pp. 117-126).

Høydalsvik, G. M. & Sindre, G. (1993). On the Purpose of Object-Oriented Analysis. In A. Paepcke (Ed.), *Proceedings of the Conference on Object-Oriented Programming Systems, Languages and Applications (OOPSLA'93) September* (pp. 240-255) ACM Press.

Iivari, J. (1995). Object-orientation as structural, functional and behavioral modeling: A comparison of six methods for object-oriented analysis. *Information and Software Technology 37* (3) , 155-163.

Lauesen, S. (1998). Real-life Object-oriented Systems. *IEEE Software 15*(2), 76-83.

Kobryn, C. (1999). UML 2001. A standardization Odyssey. *Communication of the ACM 42* (10) October, 29-37.

Kovacevic, S. (1998). UML and User Interface Modeling. In (Bézivin & Muller, 1998), (pp. 253-266).

Krogstie, J. (1995). *Conceptual Modeling for Computerized Information System Support in Organization*. Doctoral Thesis, NTH, Trondheim, Norway.

Krogstie, J., Lindland, O.I. & Sindre, G. (1995). Defining Quality Aspects for Conceptual Models. In E. D. Falkenberg, W. Hesse, & A. Olive (Eds.). *Proceedings of the IFIP8.1 Working Conference on Information Systems Concepts (ISCO3); Towards a Consolidation of Views,* March 28-30 pp. 216-231, Marburg, Germany.

Krogstie, J. (1999a). Pulling together the understanding of quality in requirements specifications and modeling. In *Proceedings of Norsk Informatikkonferanse (NIK'99).* November 15-17 pp. 315-326, Trondheim, Norway.

Krogstie, J. (1999b). Using Quality Function Deployment in Software Requirements Specification. In A. L. Opdahl, K. Pohl, & E. Dubois. *Proceedings of the Fifth International Workshop on Requirements Engineering: Foundations for Software Quality (REFSQ'99), June 14-15,* (pp. 171-185), Heidelberg, Germany.

Krogstie, J. & Sølvberg, A. (2000) *Information Systems Engineering: Conceptual Modeling in a Quality Perspective.* Draft of Book, Information Systems Groups, NTNU, Trondheim, Norway.

Mellor, S. J., Tockey, S. R., Arthaud, P. & LeBlanc, P. (1998). An Action Language for UML. In (Bézivin & Muller, 1998), pp. 307-318.

Mylopoulos, J., Chung, L. & Tu, E. (1999). From Object-oriented to Goal-oriented Requirements Analysis. *Communications of the ACM. 42* (1), January , 31-37.

Oei, J. L. H. (1995). A meta model transformation approach towards harmonization in information system modeling. In E. D. Falkenberg, W. Hesse, & A. Olive (Eds.). *Proceedings of the IFIP8.1 working conference on Information Systems Concepts (ISCO3); Towards a Consolidation of Views,* March 28-30 pp. 216-231, Marburg, Germany.

Opdahl, A., Henderson-Sellers, B. & Barbier, F. (1999). An Ontological Evaluation of the OML Metamodel. In E. Falkenberg, K. Lyytinen, & A. Verrijn-Stuart (Eds.), *Proceedings of the IFIP8.1 Working Conference on Information Systems Concepts (ISCO4); An Integrated Discipline Emerging* September 20-22, Leiden, pp. 217-232. The Netherlands.

Ovum. (1998). Ovum evaluates: CASE products. *Guide to UML.*

Ovum. (2000). Ovum evaluates: CASE products. Rational Rose 2000.

Paige, R. F. & Ostroff, J. S. (1999). A comparison of the Business Object Notation and the Unified Modeling Language. In (France & Rumpe, 1999) (pp. 67-82).

Parkinson, J. (1990). Making CASE Work. In K. Spurr and P. Layzell (Eds.) *CASE on Trial* (pp. 213-242). John Wiley & Sons.

Prasse, M. (1998). Evaluation of Object-oriented Modeling Languages. A Comparison between OML and UML. In M. Schader, & A. Korthaus (Eds.), *The Unified Modeling Language – Technical Aspects and Applications.* pp. 58-78. Physica-Verlag, Heidelberg.

Stamper, R. K. (1998). Organizational semiotics. In J. Minger & F. Stowell (Eds.): *Information Systems: An Emerging Discipline?* (pp. 267-283). McGraw-Hill.

Taivalsaari, A. (1996). On the Notion of Inheritance. *ACM Computing Survey 28* (3) September, 438-479.

Wand, Y. & Weber, R. (1993). On the Ontological Expressiveness of Information Systems Analysis and Design Grammars. *Journal of Information Systems 3*(4), 217-237.

Wieringa, R. (1998). A Survey of Structured and Object-Oriented Software Specification Methods and Techniques. *ACM Computing Surveys 30* (4) December, 459-527.

Winograd, T. & Flores F. (1986): *Understanding Computers and Cognition. A New Foundation for Design.* Reading, MA: Addison-Wesley.

Østbø, M. (2000). *Anvendelse av UML til Dokumentering av Generiske Systemer (In Norwegian).* Unpublished Masters thesis, Høgskolen i Stavanger, Norway, 20 June.

Chapter VII

Rational Unified Process and Unified Modeling Language A GOMS Analysis

Keng Siau
University of Nebraska-Lincoln, USA

GOMS is a model that analyzes knowledge of how to do a task in terms of Goals, Operators, Methods and Selection rules. GOMS is one of the most popular theoretical models in the field of human-computer interaction. Since its introduction, the GOMS model has been extended, enhanced and applied to areas outside human-computer interaction. The goal of this chapter is to discuss the use of the GOMS model for the design and evaluation of modeling techniques. In this chapter, we introduce the GOMS concepts, discuss the applicability of GOMS for modeling and describe how GOMS can be used to analyze Rational Unified Process and Unified Modeling Language.

INTRODUCTION

The Unified Modeling Language (UML) is a visual modeling language for modeling system requirements, describing designs and depicting implementation details. Grady Booch, Jim Rumbaugh and Ivars Jacobson, known collectively as the "three Amigos" at Rational Software Corp, spearheaded development of UML in the mid-1990s. Unified Modeling Language (UML) borrows concepts from a large number of different methodologies, and is tailored specifically for object-oriented design. Since its inception, UML has emerged as the software industry's dominant modeling language. UML is not only the *de facto* modeling language standard for specifying, visualizing, constructing and documenting the components of software systems but it is also fast becoming a *de jure* standard (Booch, 1999).

By offering a common blueprint language, UML relieves developers of the proprietary ties that are so common in this industry. Major vendors, including IBM, Microsoft and Oracle, are brought together under the UML umbrella. Many of the language's supporters claim that UML's simplicity is its chief benefit (Kobryn, 1999) and argue that UML uses simple, intuitive notations that are understandable by nonprogrammers. If developers, customers and implementers can all understand a single modeling language instead of a few dozen (Siau, 1999; Siau and Cao, 2001), they are more likely to agree on the intended functionality, thereby improving the communication process among the stakeholders and enhancing their chances of creating an application that truly addresses business problems.

Rational Unified Process

The Rational Unified Process is a software engineering process developed and marketed by Rational Software. It uses UML when preparing all blueprints of the software system (Jacobson et al., 1999). UML is considered to be an integral part of the Rational Unified Process and the two were developed hand in hand. The Rational Unified Process, in a nutshell, consists of four main concepts it is use-case driven, architecture-centric, iterative and incremental. Major goals of the Rational Unified Process are model development and maintenance for systems under development (Krutchen, 2000).

Unified Modeling Language

The Unified Modeling Language (UML) defines a number of graphical views that provide different perspectives of the system under development. Each diagram shows a different aspect of the full model, and is by design incomplete. UML encompasses a total of nine views, which taken together, form a comprehensive model of the system. Some of the views depict the static aspect of the system whereas others show the dynamic aspect. The views include class diagrams, use-case diagrams, statechart diagrams, activity diagrams, sequence diagrams, collaboration diagrams, object diagrams, components diagrams and deployment diagrams (Booch et al., 1999). A class diagram shows a set of classes, interfaces, and collaborations and their relationships. An object diagram depicts static "snapshots" of the elements within a system, showing objects' structure, attributes and relationships to one another. An activity diagram shows the flow of control from one activity to the next, and a use-case diagram illustrates how elements outside the system use the system. For instance, the internal workings of a new payroll system would be shown in an activity diagram, whereas external actors, such as the mail order department, would appear in a use-case diagram. Sequence and collaboration diagrams show interactive processes: developers see not only objects and classes, but also the messages that pass between them. Thus, developers can simulate passes through the system using a conventional "what if" approach. A statechart diagram shows a state machine, consisting of states, transitions, events and activities. Finally, component and deployment diagrams show the physical or implementation view of the system (including executables, libraries and interfaces).

In this research, we are interested in analyzing the Rational Unified Process and UML using GOMS. The rest of the chapter is organized as follows: the next section discusses the GOMS model and the components in the model. The applicability of GOMS to studying modeling techniques is then discussed. Finally, we apply GOMS to analyze the Rational Unified Process and UML.

THE GOMS MODEL

The GOMS model was introduced in the seminal book, *The Psychology of Human-Computer Interaction* by Card, Moran and Newell (1983). They suggested that, when designing user interfaces, it is helpful to analyze operations on how to perform a task in terms of four components: a set of goals, a set of operators, a set of methods[1] for achieving the goals and a set of selection rules for choosing among competing methods for a goal. The idea of looking at the user interface design in terms of goals, operators, methods, and selection rules has spawned much interest in the research community. Over the years, several variants of the GOMS model were proposed and the GOMS approach was also applied to areas outside human-computer interaction. In this research, we are interested in applying GOMS to the modeling field and in the evaluation of the Rational Unified Process and UML. The next few subsections will discuss the components of the GOMS model in the context of modeling.

Goals

Goals are what the analyst wants to accomplish by using the modeling technique. It is a symbolic structure that defines a state to be achieved, and determines a set of possible methods by which it may be accomplished. For example, in the context of modeling, the Goals may be DRAW-MODEL, INTERPRET-MODEL, MODIFY-MODEL or EDIT-MODEL. The higher-level goal can be further divided into a number of subgoals. For example, to accomplish the goal of drawing a use case diagram, the analyst may set subgoals to extract information from the problem domain and project documentation — to identify the use cases involved, the actors, and their relationships. The following illustrates the goal hierarchy:

```
GOAL: DRAW USE CASE DIAGRAM
    GOAL: FIND INFORMATION
        GOAL: FIND USE CASES
        GOAL: FIND ACTORS
        GOAL: ESTABLISH RELATIONSHIPS BETWEEN ACTORS
            AND USE CASES
```

Operators

Operators are elementary perceptual, motor or cognitive acts, whose execution is necessary to change any aspect of the analyst's mental state or to affect the task environment. In the context of modeling, operators are the modeling constructs that the modeling technique provides. Examples of operators in drawing a class diagram are: USE-CLASS-CONSTRUCT, USE-INTERFACE-CONSTRUCT, USE-COLLABORATION-CON-STRUCT and USE-RELATIONSHIP-CONSTRUCT. The behavior of the analyst drawing a use case diagram or a class diagram can be captured as a sequence of these operations. Operators can be defined at many different levels of abstraction. In general, they embody a mixture of basic psychological mechanisms and learned skill, the mixture depending on the level at which the model is cast. The finer the grain of analysis, the more the operators reflect basic psychological mechanisms. The coarser the grain of analysis, the more the operators reflect the specifics of the task environment (Card et al., 1983). The selection of operators for any specific GOMS model defines its grain of analysis. Take the example of class diagrams; at a high-level, the operators available are classes, interfaces, collaborations and relationships. Relationships, however, can be further classified into dependency, generalization and association relationships. An association relationship, in turn, can be divided into a few smaller operators name, role, multiplicity and aggregation.

Methods

Methods are well-learned sequences of subgoals and operators that can be used to accomplish a modeling task. The description of a method is cast in a GOMS model as a conditional sequence of goals and operators, with conditional tests on the content of the analyst's immediate memory and on the state of the modeling task environment. For example, assuming the goal is to interpret a simple use case diagram, one of the possible subgoals is to identify chunks of information (each consisting of a use case and an actor) in the diagram.

> GOAL: INTERPRET USE CASE DIAGRAM
>   GOAL: IDENTIFY CHUNK   *repeat until there are no more chunks*
>   FIND USE CASE
>   FIND ASSOCIATED ACTOR

If the goals have a hierarchical structure, then there is a corresponding hierarchy of methods. The content of the methods depends on the set of possible operators and on the nature of the modeling tasks represented. If there is more than one method to accomplish the same goal, then selection rules, the last component of the GOMS model, are required.

Selection Rules

When a goal is attempted, there may be more than one approach available to the analyst to accomplish the goal. In the GOMS model, method selection is handled by a set of selection rules. Each selection rule is of the form "if such-and-such is true in the current task situation, then use approach M." Typically such rules are based on the specific properties of the modeling task instance. Selection rules can arise through an analyst's personal experience with the modeling technique or from explicit training. The following are examples of selection rules for interaction diagrams:

> IF TIME ORDERING OF MESSAGES IS IMPORTANT
>   THEN USE SEQUENCE DIAGRAM

> IF STRUCTURAL ORGANIZATION OF OBJECTS SENDING AND RECEIVING
>   MESSAGES IS IMPORTANT
>   THEN USE COLLABORATION DIAGRAM

The GOMS Family

Four different versions of GOMS are in use today. John and Kieras (1996) provided a good review of the different versions. The original version of GOMS (Card et al., 1983), known widely as CMN-GOMS, is a loosely defined demonstration of how to express a goal and subgoals in a hierarchy using methods and operators, and how to formulate selection rules. A simplified version of CMN, called the Keystroke-Level Model, uses only keystroke-level operators with no goals, methods or selection rules. A more rigorously defined version of GOMS called NGOMSL (Kieras, 1988) presents a procedure for identifying all the GOMS components, expressed in a form similar to an ordinary computer programming language. A parallel-activity version of GOMS, known as CPM-GOMS (John, 1990), uses cognitive, perceptual and motor operators in a critical path method schedule chart (PERT chart) to show how activities can be performed in parallel.

APPROPRIATENESS OF GOMS FOR RATIONAL UNIFIED PROCESS AND UML

Although modeling tasks can be characterized in many different ways, four dimensions are important in deciding whether the GOMS analysis technique is applicable (adapted from John & Kieras, 1996): (1) the degree of goal-directedness, (2) the degree of routinized skill involved in the modeling task, (3) the degree to which the modeling task is under the control of the analyst, and (4) the sequentiality of the modeling tasks.

Goal-Directedness

GOMS is appropriate only for analyzing the goal-directed portion of modeling. The Rational Unified Process and UML are, in a way, attempts to support goal-directedness in software development. The goal of the Rational Unified Process is to ensure the production of high-quality software that meets the needs of its end users within a predictable schedule and budget (Kruchten, 2000). In the Rational Unified Process, a disciplined approach to assigning tasks and responsibilities within a development organization is suggested. UML, on the other hand, is an integrated part of the Rational Unified Process.

Although GOMS analyses must start with a list of high-level goals, GOMS analyses and techniques do not provide this list. The list must come from sources external to GOMS. In software development, high-level goals can be obtained using several approaches, such as interviewing potential users, observing end users, reading minutes of meetings, prototyping, etc. The quality of GOMS analyses depends heavily on the success of such a high-level task analysis. This is particularly important in software development because inaccurate understanding of end user's needs is the most significant factor that leads to software project failure (Siau *et al.*, 1996, 1997; Siau, 1999; Kruchten, 2000). In UML, high-level goals can be specified using use case diagrams. Once the list of high-level goals is assembled, GOMS analyses can help identify the lower level goals quickly. The GOMS analyses will not identify any new high-level goals or tasks that the analyst may have overlooked, and will not correct misformulations of goals. The analyses, however, may stimulate the analyst's intuition, and thus lead to a correction in the list of goals.

Routine versus Non-Routine Skill

Skill for performing modeling tasks falls into a continuum with routine skill on one end and non-routine skill on the other end. When the analyst does not know how to perform a task and must search for a solution, s/he will require non-routine skill (similar to the notion of general problem-solving skill). On the other hand, when the analyst knows exactly what to do in the task situation and simply has to recognize that situation and execute the appropriate actions, routine skill is utilized. GOMS can only be used to analyze tasks that involve routine skill and there is no direct way of using GOMS to represent the non-routine skill required. Having said that, it is important to note that most modeling tasks, even very open-ended and creative ones, have a substantial amount of routine skill involved.

First, skill involved in the use of a particular modeling technique will evolve from non-routine to routine skill after some use. For example, identifying objects when using an object-oriented modeling approach will be challenging in the beginning but will become a routine skill after some training and experience. Second, many tasks require elements of both routine and non-routine skill. An experienced analyst performing a modeling task using UML, for example, will find the use of the modeling technique a routine skill, but the problem domain may be new and therefore requires non-routine skill. It should also be stated that the objective of the Rational Unified Process is to move modeling using UML to as much of a routine skill as possible by attempting to provide a systematic approach to software development.

Locus of Control

Modeling tasks can be categorized into passive and active tasks. For passive tasks, the analyst has control over the pace and timing of the task events. Modeling carried out by an analyst on a familiar problem domain where the requirements are stable and predictable is an example of a passive task. On the other hand, for active tasks, the modeling process can produce spontaneous, asynchronous events outside the analyst's control and the analyst must be prepared to deal with the situations. Modeling in an environment where the requirements change frequently and unpredictably (the most commonly cited problem of modeling) is an example of active tasks. GOMS is useful for both passive and active modeling tasks. Compared to passive tasks, active tasks are harder to model and require different approaches. One approach to active tasks is to assume that the interruptions can be handled by the analyst. That is, the analyst provides a particular sequence of activities that includes interruptions and goal rescheduling to account for the interruptions represented in the GOMS model. Another approach is to assume that the active system produces events that can be responded to with methods that either will not be interrupted, or do not conflict with each other. Typically the top-level method simply waits for an event, and then invokes lower level methods that are appropriate for responding to the event.

Sequential Versus Parallel Activity

CPM-GOMS can handle parallel cases. The other variants of GOMS support only sequential tasks. This is not a severe limitation as many modeling tasks can be approximated as a series of sequential activities. If necessary, parallel operations can be represented as a simple modification to the sequential model. For example, in interpreting a use case diagram, an analyst may visually locate an actor before s/he forms a chunk of information (with an associating use case). In a sequential analysis, there would be an operator such as FIND-ACTOR followed by a FIND-ASSOCIATED-USE CASE operator. But for an expert analyst, s/he can locate the whole chunk of information almost instantaneously it has become an automated skill. To account for this "parallelism," we can simply set the time for the FIND-ASSOCIATED-USE CASE operator to zero.

HOW CAN GOMS BE USED TO ANALYZE RATIONAL UNIFIED PROCESS AND UML?

As can be seen from earlier discussions, the GOMS analysis is potentially applicable to many instances of goal-directed routine modeling tasks, even when the modeling tasks involve problem-solving activities, creative interactions or unstructured explorations. The tasks can be both passive and active, and can either be approximated as sequential operators or as truly parallel.

In this research, we are interested in applying the GOMS model to evaluate the Rational Unified Process and UML. GOMS can be used to obtain the sequence of operators required to accomplish a task using the Rational Unified Process and UML. It enables evaluation without actually applying the modeling techniques to a problem domain. The following subsections discuss how GOMS can be used for analyzing the Rational Unified Process and UML.

Evaluation of Diagramming Techniques

Evaluating the diagramming techniques in UML is the most obvious use of GOMS. GOMS can be used to evaluate the diagramming techniques without actually trying out the techniques on some problem domains. Comparisons can be made with summative predictions, i.e., diagramming technique A takes half the time of diagramming technique B to carry out the analysis, or diagramming technique C requires one-third of the learning time of diagramming technique D. Also, we can compare the procedures of one technique with those of another technique to discover the merits and deficits of each. Although the effort required to perform the comparison may be huge, once the first model is constructed, it can serve as a basis for similar designs. So the effort put into modeling the first technique can be amortized over the number of other techniques evaluated.

Coverage of UML Diagramming Techniques

One primary question about functionality is whether the diagramming techniques in UML provide the means to satisfy every possible goal. In other words, can the analyst model a certain real-world phenomenon using UML? One of the strengths of UML is that it provides extensibility and specialization mechanisms to extend the core constructs of UML. Under most circumstances, users should be able to build applications without extra constructs. However, when there is a need, users are able to add new concepts and notations (e.g., stereotypes). These newly created stereotypes can in turn be tested by GOMS for coverage. It should be noted that the GOMS model cannot generate or predict the range of goals an analyst may bring to the modeling task (as discussed earlier), however, once a list of likely goals is generated, GOMS can be used to check whether a diagramming technique exists in UML to satisfy each goal. GOMS also goes beyond other methods of analyzing functionality by looking at the procedures to accomplish the function.

Sequence of Operators

CMN-GOMS and NGOMSL can predict the sequence of operators an analyst needs to invoke when using the Rational Unified Process or the UML diagramming techniques. For example, the methods and selection rules can specify which constructs the analyst will select, how the constructs will be associated and so forth to accomplish the goals. This prediction can be used to decide whether to add a new construct or stereotype to a diagramming technique, and how best to conduct training for the technique.

Understandability of Rational Unified Process and UML

A GOMS model can have purely heuristic value since it makes explicit what the analyst is required to do in constructing or understanding a UML diagram. This is useful as the language specification of UML includes many standard elements (stereotypes, tagged values and constraints) that were hastily added to address the requirements of various competing methods groups. Although it may be argued that the size and complexity of UML is inevitable because it is a general-purpose modeling language, the language also includes a large number of standard elements with vague or sparse semantics. Constructing a GOMS model will force the designer/developer to become more aware of the implications of each UML diagramming technique and the modeling construct. Any exercise that requires the designer to think carefully about the procedures entailed by the Rational Unified Process or a UML diagram can help in a purely intuitive way to identify usability problems and clarify the nature of the modeling task.

Learning and Modeling Time

One of the criticisms of UML is that it is monolithic and difficult to learn. The learning time and the modeling time are of great concern to software developers. GOMS is useful in these aspects. Some variants of GOMS can be used to predict the required modeling time, under the restrictions that the analyst must be well practiced and make no errors during the modeling task. Visual-search tasks (e.g., scanning the information model to locate information) can also be modeled with GOMS, allowing different display layouts to be evaluated. For example, GOMS can be used to evaluate whether a sequence diagram or a collaboration diagram is easier to comprehend. A benefit of UML is that it is independent of any particular programming language or development platform. This simplifies the studying of execution and learning time, as we need not be concerned about implementation alternatives.

Selection of Stereotypes

A common issue involved in UML is the design of new stereotypes. GOMS can make substantial contributions to the problem. Since GOMS analyses do not require fully developed and fully designed modeling techniques but can make *a priori* predictions of performance, they can be used early in the design process to evaluate different approaches (e.g., choice of stereotypes) before they are actually incorporated into the modeling techniques. For example, a researcher may need to know which stereotype facilitates interpretation of the model. GOMS can be used to profile the analyst's overall interpretation process in order to determine which representations will take significantly more time to interpret or are more error prone. Profiling is, however, time-consuming and effort-intensive. Nevertheless, the payoff can be substantial because analyses can be done early in the design process.

DISCUSSION AND FUTURE RESEARCH

This chapter investigates the use of GOMS for the evaluation of modeling techniques. GOMS has the potential to provide information on many parts of the design and evaluation processes, both qualitatively and quantitatively. As an aid for the development of new modeling techniques, its flexibility and versatility allow the designer to choose the right GOMS model for the required level of detail in the design problem. As a tool for evaluating existing modeling techniques, it provides a systematic, theory-based and empirically validated approach to evaluating modeling techniques.

There is, however, some relevant information not provided by GOMS. For example, the goals have to be solicited using techniques other than GOMS. Problem-solving skill, creative skill and domain knowledge required for the modeling task also cannot be adequately modeled using GOMS. Performing GOMS analyses can be tedious and time-consuming. Also, GOMS was originally designed for analyzing human-computer interaction. Its uses in modeling require further investigation and refinement. Nevertheless, the benefits provided by GOMS analyses are potentially substantial and in many cases may outweigh the costs involved.

The next phase of the research is to derive a few basic GOMS models for the various diagramming techniques in UML. These GOMS models can then be validated, modified and enhanced using verbal protocol data. Once the GOMS models are fairly reliable and accurate, we will be able to investigate the pros and cons of each diagramming technique in UML. Recommendations and refinement to the Rational Unified Process and UML can then be suggested.

ACKNOWLEDGMENT

This research is partly supported by research funding from the University of Nebraska-Lincoln (LWT/06-185-92501).

REFERENCES

Booch, G. (1999). UML in action. *Communications of the ACM*, 42(10), 26-30.

Booch, G., Rumbaugh, J. & Jacobson, I. (1999). *The Unified Modeling Language: User Guide*. Addison-Wesley.

Card, S.K., Moran, T.P. & Newell, A. (1983). *The Psychology of Human-Computer Interaction*. Hillsdale, NJ: Lawrence Erlbaum Associates.

Jacobson, I. , Booch, G. & Rumbaugh, J. (1999). *The Unified Software Development Process*. Addison-Wesley.

John, B.E. (1990). Extensions of GOMS analyses to expert performance requiring perception of dynamic visual and auditory information. In *Proceedings of CHI*, 1990 (Seattle, Washington, April 30-May 4, 1990) ACM, New York, 107-115.

John, B.E. & Kieras, D.E. (1996). The GOMS family of analysis techniques: Comparison and contrast. *ACM Transactions on Computer-Human Interaction*, 3(4), 287-319.

Kieras, D.E. (1988). Towards a practical GOMS model methodology for user interface design. In M. Helander (Ed.), *The Handbook of Human-Computer Interaction*. Amsterdam: North-Holland, 135-158.

Kobryn, C. (1999). A standardization odyssey. *Communications of the ACM*, 42(10), 29-38.

Kruchten, P. (2000). *The Rational Unified Process – An Introduction*. Addison-Wesley.

Siau, K. (1999). Information modeling and method engineering: A psychological perspective. *Journal of Database Management*, 10(4), 44-50.

Siau, K., Cao, Q. (2001). Unified modeling language: A complexity analysis." *Journal of Database Management*, 12(1), 26-34.

Siau, K., Wand, Y. & Benbasat, I. (1996). "When parents need not have children — cognitive biases in information modeling." *Lecture Notes in Computer Science — Advanced Information Systems Engineering*, 1080, 402-420.

Siau, K., Wand, Y. & Benbasat, I. (1997). "The relative importance of structural constraints and surface semantics in information modeling." *Information Systems*, 22(2&3), 155-170.

ENDNOTE

1 The four components of GOMS are known as Goals, Operators, Methods and Selection Rules. The term method used in GOMS should not be confused with the term method used in the context of UML (e.g., in classes).

Chapter VIII

Extension of the Unified Modeling Language for Mobile Agents

Cornel Klein
Siemens ICN, Munich, Germany

Andreas Rausch, Marc Sihling and Zhaojun Wen
Institut für Informatik, Technische Universität München, Germany

Mobile agents gained immense attraction as a new programming concept for implementing distributed applications. However, up to now mobile agent programming has been mainly technology driven, with a focus on the implementation of mobile agent platforms and only small programming applications. In this chapter, we present an extension of the standard UML that provides language concepts for modeling mobility both in analysis and design phases. This extended version of UML is applied to the modeling of an advanced telecommunication system.

INTRODUCTION

Mobile agents are software entities that can migrate autonomously on a network from host to host. As a result of this intrinsic characteristic, they raise considerable interest as a new concept for networked computing. The often-cited advantages attributed to mobile agents are: reduction of network traffic, load balancing, fault tolerance, asynchronous interaction, data access locality and flexible distribution of intelligence in a network.

In the past, development of mobile agent concepts was mostly technology-driven. In particular since the invention of Java, which allows to easily move an agent's code even in heterogeneous networks, dozens of mobile agent platforms have been developed both within the research community as well as within industrial projects (Bäumer, Breugst, Choy, & Magedanz, 1999; Chess, 1995; Chang, & Lange, 1996; Jul, Levy, Hutchinson, & Black, 1988; Krause, 1997). On the more theoretical side, authors like Luca Cardelli invented formalisms for modeling and reasoning about mobile agent systems. Cardelli and others argue that mobility is not only important as a programming concept, but that it is inherently introduced by the advent of mobile devices such as laptops, mobile phones, PDAs, etc. and hence has to be appropriately represented in corresponding models.

However, in spite of these activities there is yet little evidence of an engineering approach to the development of mobile agent-based applications. At present, the majority of existing agent-based applications are created in an ad-hoc fashion, following little or no rigorous design methodology and producing only limited specifications with respect to requirements or design aspects of mobile agents. That might be because of the vast lack of appropriate modeling concepts in standard languages like the Unified Modeling Language (UML). This pertains even to most basic characteristics, for instance, concepts for mobility or cloning.

In this chapter, we present an extension of the UML with a focus on mobile agents. In the next section we start with a discussion on basic concepts and notions of mobile applications. Then, we introduce a small application example that is used to motivate and illustrate the UML extensions. From those we choose a set of extensions and present them in greater detail. We end up with a table showing all additional language elements for mobile applications for each UML diagram. A discussion about the future trends and a short conclusion ends the chapter.

BACKGROUND

The term "agent" is associated with various expectations and used in many different contexts. Therefore, there is no common understanding of the involved concepts. A good starting point to describe the idea of agents is to find what makes them different from "ordinary" components (e.g. mobility, cooperativity, autonomy, etc.). However, we do not want to discuss the characteristics of agents in detail but believe that "mobility" is the most prominent, promising and advanced feature. Mobility provides clear advantages as a programming concept and thus should be seen as an important concept within the early phases of the development process by modeling languages such as the UML. For this reason, we focus on "mobile agents" in the following.

Mobile agents promise advantages over other existing computing paradigms such as client/server programming or distributed systems. In particular, the ability to move allows mobile agents to bring the computation to the data instead of the data to the computation. In many situations, this reduces network traffic extremely. Hence, some kind of applications may be more efficient utilizing mobile agents. They might also profit from the agents' high degree of autonomy: mobile agents can operate asynchronously and independently from the user or the requesting program. This allows, for instance, a mobile device to dispatch an autonomous diagnostic and search agent into some network and then to disconnect. Some time later, it might reconnect to the network to collect the results of the issued query. A deeper discussion of the benefits of mobile agents can be found in Chess, (1995); Hurst, Cunningham, & Somers, (1997); Krause, (1997); and Chang, & Lange, (1996).

Note that any task that can be performed with mobile agents can also be realized using existing technologies and concepts but the traditional solution might be less flexible, less efficient or much more difficult to deploy.

Some advantages of the mobile agent paradigm have been discussed. They stem from the capability of the involved concepts to reduce network usage, increase asynchrony between clients and servers, to add client-specific functionality to servers and to introduce concurrency. Several application types may exploit these advantages, for instance, workflow applications, groupware systems, electronic commerce applications, personal assistants, monitoring systems or information dissemination applications, just to name a few.

Moreover, agents are a very intuitive concept people are used to, e.g., from the agent in their travel agency. Hence, the technology of mobile agents received a great deal of attention in the last couple of years. However, the notion of a mobile agent and the concepts of applications involving mobility are still not clear at all. The advent of software agents gave rise to much discussion of just how they differ from objects in general. Some developers consider agents to be objects and they tend to define agents beginning with the phrase "An agent is an object that..."—where the definers add their favorite discriminating features. Then there are those who see agents and objects as different even though they share some common concepts. Both approaches envision the usage of objects and agents together in the development of a software system. In the following, we present a specific understanding of mobile agents and their environment that captures most essential concepts.

Mobile agents as well as applications built with mobile agents are developed for and run in a so-called distributed agent environment. It is composed of one or several *regions*, some *agent systems*, *agencies* and different *agents*, as shown in Figure 1.

A *region* is a logical entity that groups a set of agencies, which are associated to the same authority, e.g., a company or administrative domain. But these agencies are not necessarily provided by the same agent system. Associated with each region is a region registry that automatically registers each agent that is currently hosted by an agency associated to an agent system of the region. If an agent moves to another location, the corresponding registry information is correspondingly updated.

An *agent system* is a platform that can create, interpret, execute, transfer and terminate agents. For instance, we used the Grasshopper agent platform (Bäumer, Breugst, Choy, & Magedanz, 1999) in our sample application. Agent systems provide services and an infrastructure necessary for agent-based software development. Examples are communication mechanisms, directory services as well as concepts for distributed transactions, persistency, security and migration of agents between nodes. Moreover, they also intend to provide standards for the interoperation of agents of different vendors.

An *agency* is a runtime environment within an agent system. It provides the functionality required to support the execution of agents. Conceptually each agency is

Figure 1. The Distributed Agent Environment

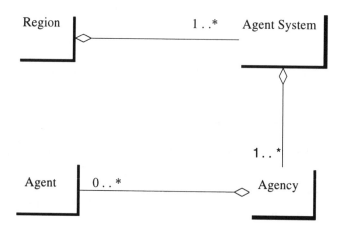

associated with a location. The location might be given, for instance, by the agency name, the address of the agent system and the name of the region.

From our point of view, there is only one significant difference between mobile *agents* and traditional objects. In contrast to the latter, mobile agents exhibit some additional features with respect to their dynamic behavior, namely *move, remote execution, clone* and *role change*.

A *move* specifies the process during which a mobile agent migrates from one agency of the distributed agent environment to another. This allows an agent to continue its task execution at the destination location exactly at the point where it was interrupted before the move. For this purpose, not only the agent's code, but also its execution state is transferred.

The *remote execution* defines in which way the mobile agent itself initiates its own execution on another host. Similar to move, the agent is removed from the current host and recreated on the remote one. However, note that the task execution starts on each new host from the beginning.

A *clone* specifies the procedure during which an agent creates an exact copy of it. The clone comprises the same internal information, e.g., the same execution state, and thus starts its task execution at the very same point where the original agent instance is after cloning. Each agent is able to create a clone of itself. Note that clones are always created within the same agency in which the original agent is currently executing.

A *role change* refers to the different roles an agent might play. Consider, for example, roles like person, employee, spouse, landowner, customer and seller, which might be played by the same agent. When the agent acts as an employee, it has all the state and procedural elements consistent with the role of an employee. If the agent is terminated from his or her job, the employment-related state and procedural elements are no longer available to the agent. Whether employed or not, the agent is still the same entity—it just has a different set of features.

MAIN THRUST OF CHAPTER
Application Example: Negotiation of QoS

In this section we present a sample application from the telecommunications domain. The application serves two purposes. First, during the development of our enhanced version of the UML, it was used to identify system properties, which cannot be modeled with UML's standard language concepts. Second, it now shows the benefits of the introduced model concepts by means of simple example diagrams.

The application has been carefully chosen in order to be able to demonstrate critical aspects of mobile agent systems such as mobility in the scope of multiple domains as well as security. It is a typical example of a networking application where software components from multiple parties (e.g., Customer, Service Provider, Network Operator) work together in order to provide a particular service to end-users.

In the traditional approach for building up networks, the protocols to be used between network elements are standardized by groups such as the IETF, ITU, etc. It is assumed that network components such as routers or switches are assembled by a single vendor and operated by a single operator, and the cooperation between these network components is regulated by protocol standards. With the advent of mobile agents, the situation becomes more flexible but also more complex. Not only are network protocols standardized, but also programming interfaces enabling a more flexible approach for building up network services from software components. Mobile agents freely roaming around in the network can access these interfaces. This is the basic idea of active networks (Stadler, Stiller, 1999) that provide open APIs on network components that can be accessed by mobile agents. These APIs can be used to introduce value-added network services more rapidly in a network.

In this case, a value-added network service is a service, which—beyond pure best-effort IP forwarding—provides additional features on the IP layer supported by the individual network components. In the context of the Internet protocol, best-effort forwarding means that IP packets are only forwarded from a source node to a destination node without changing their contents and that they may be even dropped within the network, e.g., in overload situations. Hence there are no guarantees made by the network concerning the delay or bandwidth.

In contrast to such best-effort network include value-added network services like virtual private networks, transparent web proxies/caches, reliable multicast and quality of service (QoS). The latter refers to the preferred treatment of particular data flows within a network with respect to delay, latency, bandwidth. In the traditional approach, such services are difficult to be integrated in an existing network, since they require software upgrades of all involved routers. The expectation of active networks is that based on a standardized API, a variety of value-added IP network services can be deployed quite easily. This is in particular due to the fact that only the necessary service logic has to be installed on the respective network elements e.g. represented as mobile agents.

In our example, we use mobile agents to introduce quality of service (QoS) in an IP-based network. Figure 2 provides an overview of our sample application. In this application scenario, the following components are involved:

- *Service User*: in our case an Internet user who is connected with the public Internet via a dial-up link to a network access router.
- *Network Provider*: operating several Internet routers handling IP packets within the Internet. In our prototype, we used Linux boxes providing the IP chains package for accessing the IP layer as IP routers (IPC, 2000). In the future, we expect standardized APIs that are supported by routers from different manufacturers (FAIN, 2000).
- *Service Provider*: providing value-added services through mobile agents who roam

Figure 2. The Sample Application

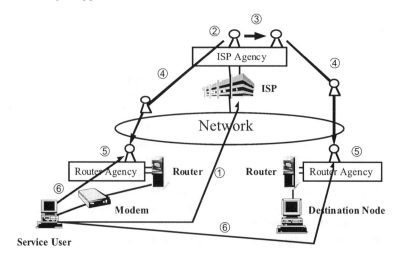

between service user and network routers in order to provide particular value-added network services.

Figure 2 shows the application of mobile agents: Here, the user accesses a service provider host, e.g., via a Web interface. She (resp. he) selects a specific value-added service for one of her (resp. his) applications (1). The service provider creates (2) and clones (3) a mobile agent, which then migrates to the respective routers (4). During the lifetime of these agents, they may be configured by the service user via a remote interface (5) until they terminate (6).

As a sample service to be implemented, we considered QoS for particular IP applications. The user may enter the destination IP address and port name, e.g., telnet, http and ftp, and the desired QoS, e.g., low cost, low delay, high throughput. These settings are communicated to mobile agents residing on the router agencies. The mobile agents in turn call the ipchains API in order to control the routing facilities appropriately. For instance, if the user selects low delay, packets sent to the destination IP address/port name are placed into a dedicated queue, which is dequeued with higher priority.

Development Artifacts of the Sample Application

In the process of modeling the sample application as presented in the previous section, we evaluated the graphical description techniques of the UML with respect to modeling mobile-agent applications. Following our development process, we present the most essential techniques, reason about their deficiencies and motivate and propose sophisticated extensions. Finally, we will build on these results as we present an overview of all UML modeling techniques and their flaws in this scope.

Analysis Use Case Diagram. Figure 3 shows the use case diagram that resulted from a preliminary requirements elicitation. An actor *Service User* utilizes the system to *Request QoS Services* or to *Cancel all QoS Services* that he or she does not need anymore.

The *Request QoS Services* use case represents functionality for configuring routers using service agents provided by the service provider. The use case *Cancel All QoS Services* allows for reset configurations of routers using agents that reside on them. This is especially important as the user is probably paying for the services her or she requests. As shown in the use case diagram above, we used the well-known *«uses»* stereotype to indicate that *Cancel All QoS Services* use case offers additional functionality for the *Request QoS Services* use case.

Analysis Class Diagram. An analysis class diagram captures the static structure of the sample application. In particular, the entities *QoSAgency*, *QoSAgent* and *QoSApplication* have been identified.

QoSAgency offers the runtime environment for mobile agents. It describes various agency objects, for example, the *ISPAgency* object and *RouterAgency* objects. *ISPAgency* represents the Internet service provider. It creates a ser-

Figure 3. Analysis Use Case Diagram

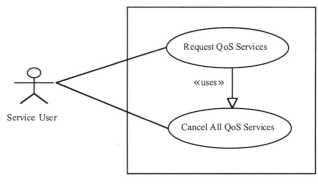

Figure 4. Analysis Class Diagram

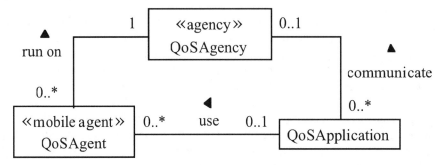

vice agent and sends it to the *RouterAgency* to configure the router on which the *RouterAgency* is started. The next section discusses this aspect in detail.

QoSAgent represents a mobile agent object that is created by the Internet service provider and sent to routers to configure them for supporting the QoS services.

QoSApplication is the main program that service users can utilize to request their demanded QoS services from the Internet service provider.

To be able to model these different kinds of concepts in early stages of the development process, we defined new modeling elements that correspond to the concepts shown in Figure 1: we introduced two stereotypes—*«mobile agent»* and *«agency»*— that are derived from the existing metamodel element class. The stereotype *«mobile agent»* specifies that objects of this class are not bound to the system where they began execution. Thus, they have the unique ability to transport themselves from one system over some network to another. The stereotype *«agency»* specifies a class of agency objects that impose an execution environment for mobile agents. An agency object provides agents with necessary services and functionality to be executed, such as access control.

Design Sequence Diagram. During the analysis phase we refined the use case *Request QoS Service* from Figure 3. Hence, we modeled the interaction among the classes in this use case and the user more concretely. Questions like "How can an agent be sent to routers and configure them?" had to be answered. Figure 5 shows the elaborated version of this use case in a sequence diagram.

In the diagram, there are two routers to be configured, namely the access router (on the user side) and the server router (on the side of the server the user tries to connect to). Both routers are the upstream/downstream routers of an Internet link. Basically, there are two possible solutions to configure these two routers. Either the Internet service provider creates a single agent that moves from one router to another and handles the configuration, or the Internet service provider creates two identical agents and sends each of them to a separate router respectively. Usually, in mobile agent systems, the creation of several identical agents is performed by a special operation called the *clone* operation. Hence we prefer the second solution for the router configuration, not for technical reasons but in order to be able to model this mobile-agent specific programming concept.

The stereotype *«region»* derived from the existing metamodel element *package* specifies a mechanism for organizing agencies into groups. Agencies that have the same authority may be placed in a region, but are not necessarily of the same agent system type. The concept of a region allows more than one agency to represent the same person or organization. An agent may also have the same authority as the region in which it is

Figure 5. Design Sequence Diagram: Request QoS Service

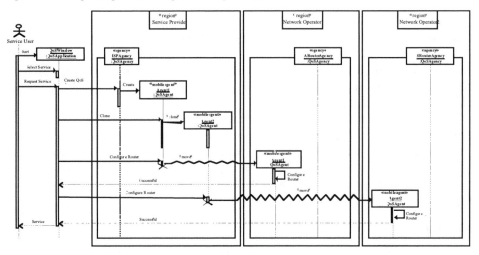

currently residing and executing. Graphically, a region is represented with a large rectangle, with a small one attached inside the large rectangle on the topside, usually including its name and its contents.

In order to express the relation between agency and its agents better, we introduced a notation for the new model element *«agency»* as shown in Figure 5. Graphically, it is represented by a large rectangle with a small one attached on the top of it. Note, the stereotype *«agency»* in the sequence diagram (Figure 5) is the same as in the class diagram (Figure 4) but it is illustrated differently.

The new stereotype *«move»* derived from the metamodel element *dependency* specifies a dependency between a source agent and a target agent. It further states that the source agent object and the target agent object represent the same instance at different agencies and different points in time albeit with the same execution state. Hence, the agent continues its task execution at the destination agency exactly at that point where it has been interrupted prior to the migration. Graphically, a wavering arrow represents a move.

The new stereotype *«clone»* (also derived from the metamodel element *dependency*) defines a dependency between a source agent and a target agent. The dependency specifies that the source agent object creates the target agent object as the exact copy of itself. The target agent object comprises the same internal information, e.g., the same execution state, and thus it starts its task execution exactly at the point the source agent object had reached when the target agent object was created. Graphically, a clone is represented by a double lined arrow.

Design Statechart Diagram. Statechart diagrams are a useful technique to describe the behavior of a system. In our example, we used it with respect to the behavior of our mobile service agent. Figure 6 depicts a statechart diagram for a service agent for both use cases *Request QoS Service* and *Cancel All QoS Services*. The service agent switches between three states: *Waiting, Configure Router* and *Deconfigure Router*. Within the *Waiting* state, there are no activities for this state, so the service agent remains in this state waiting for an event. Within the *Configure Router* state, the service agent configures the router and within the *Deconfigure Router* state it resets the router.

Again, we defined two new stereotypes *«move»* and *«clone»*. They are derived from the metamodel element *action*. The action *«move»* specifies a process in which the service agent migrates from its current agency to the remote one. When a *Request QoS* event occurs and a new destination node has been given, it performs a *move* action and enters the *Configure Router* state if it is not in *Configure Router* state. If it is, the next state is *Deconfigure Router*. After the agent deconfigured the router, it migrates to the new router and enters the *Configure Router* state. The action *«clone»* specifies a process in which the service agent creates an exact copy of itself within the same agency. The clone has the same execution state as the original one.

The service agent changes its state constantly, possibly also changing its location at the same time. It is very difficult and also not necessary to model each state that an agent can get into in each different location. We believe it is more useful to show the relationship in the statechart diagram between the agent state change and agent location change, that is, to express whether an agent will also change its location, when its state is changed. This mainly depends on the agent performing a *move* action or not.

Mobile UML Distilled

In our work we evaluated the description techniques of the UML and discovered their flaws with respect to modeling applications based on mobile agents. The previous section discussed the most important techniques as, for instance, class diagrams. Those and all other kinds of diagrams are now presented in an overall overview of the extensions we made to standard UML.

The extension mechanisms used are those defined by the creators of the UML: *stereotypes*, *tagged values* and *constraints* (D'Souza, Sane, & Birchenough, 1999). Table 1 shows all stereotypes we propose. They either correspond to characteristics of a mobile agent or specify the location hierarchy (agent system, region and agency). While the first column of Table 1 denotes the name of the stereotype, the second column specifies the metamodel element it further refines. Column three gives a textual description of the stereotype's semantics.

Furthermore, some tagged values have been defined in our UML extension to further specify relevant characteristics of agent systems. Table 2 describes these extensions using the same scheme as Table 1.

During their lifecycle, agents can normally be in one of the following sates: active, suspended or deactivated. For the state "active," UML hat already predefined a constraint

Figure 6. Design Statechart Diagram for the Service Agent

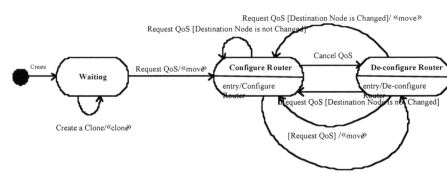

Table 1. UML Stereotypes for Mobile Agent-Based Applications

Name	Application	Semantics
«mobile agent»	Class	This class defines a mobile agent that is not bound to the location where its execution began. It has the unique ability to transport itself from one system over some network to another system.
«region»	Package	This package denotes a logical entity that groups a set of agencies that have the same authority, but are not necessarily of the same agent system type.
«agent system»	Component	This component is an agent platform that can create, interpret, execute, transfer and terminate agents. An agent system is associated with an authority that identifies the person or organization for whom the agent system acts.
«agency»	Class	This class defines an execution environment for mobile agents. An agency represents a context (within an agent system) in which a mobile agent can be executed. This context can provide various functionalities (e.g., access control).
	Package	The package denotes a collection of mobile agents that are executed within the agency. When a client requests the location of an agent, it receives the address of the agency where the agent is executing.
«move»	Dependency	The dependency is between a source agent and a target agent. It specifies that the source agent and target agent represent the same agent at different agencies and different points of time. In particular, a «move» stops the execution of the agent, moves it from its current agency to another one and restarts the execution at exactly the point where it has been interrupted before its migration. For this purpose, not only the agent's code, but also its execution state is transferred.
	Action	The action denotes a process that an agent object enclosing the state machine migrates from an agency to another. During the action, the execution state of the agent object is also transferred.
«remote execution»	Dependency	This dependency is similar to that of «move». However, «remote execution» restricts an agent to restart from the beginning each time it changes its agency.
	Action	This action denotes that an agent object initiates its own execution on another agency. The agent starts its task execution on the new agency from the beginning on.
«clone»	Dependency	Again, this stereotype implies a dependency between a source agent and a target agent. It specifies that the source agent creates the target agent as the exact copy of itself. This clone comprises the same internal information, and particularly the same execution state. Note that the clone is always created within the same agency in which the original agent is currently executing.
	Action	This action denotes a process that an agent object enclosing the state machine creates an exact copy of itself.
«role change»	Dependency	This dependency between two agent representations denotes a role change of a single agent.

Table 2. UML Tagged Values for Mobile Agent-Based Applications

Name	Application	Semantics
Type	Agent system	The type of the agent system. This value indicates whether the agent system is compliant to the MASIF standard.
Language	Agent system	The programming language that is used by the agent system for coding agents.
Version	Agent system	The version of the agent system.
Agent State	Mobile agent	The mode of existence of an agent. An agent can be active, suspended or deactivated.

Table 3. UML Constraints for Mobile Agent-Based Applications

Name	Application	Semantics
Suspended	Mobile agent	The agent object still exists, but its task execution is temporarily interrupted, i.e., the agent thread is stopped.
Deactivated	Mobile agent	The agent object does not exist anymore in the form of a real "living" object. Its code and its execution state are permanently stored, e.g., on a hard disk.

element called "active." Table 3 shows the constraints that we have defined for UML extension for the other agent states.

To sum up, we have introduced some new metamodel elements through defining stereotypes, tagged values and constraints. In order to use these elements efficiently to model mobile agent applications in various UML diagrams, we now come up with the definition of a corresponding notation. For each of the graphical description techniques defined in the UML, we now present extended notations where reasonable. Hence, each UML diagram is represented with a row in Table 4 and defined notations in the rows indicate that the aspect on that column can be expressed using the UML diagram in the row's heading, and its notation can be used in the UML diagram.

FUTURE TRENDS

In order to demonstrate the viability of our concepts, it would of course be necessary to model more applications with them. These applications should also use different mobile agent platforms in order to possibly abstract our concepts to more generic, platform-independent ones. For instance, the notions of *Agency*, *Agent System* and *Region* may be specific to Grasshopper, although other mobile agent platforms use similar but not identical concepts. Standardization activities, e.g., within OMG MASIF should also be taken into account here.

A necessary prerequisite for a successful evaluation in large-scale development projects is the availability of sophisticated tool support. A first step is to use the presented stereotypes with existing tools, such as Rational Rose. Albeit, these tools are rather closed

Table 4. UML Notation and Usage Guide in UML Diagrams

Description Techniques	Mobile Agent	Region	Agent System	Agency	Move	Remote Execution	Clone	Role Change
Class Diagram				√				
Object Diagram								
Use Case Diagram								
Sequence Diagram	Agent Name/Role:Class	▢		▢	∿,	∿,	⟹	----▶
Collaboration Diagram	Agent Name/Role:Class	▢		▢	∿,	∿,	⟹	----▶
Statechart Diagram					√	√	√	√
Activity Diagram		▢		▢	√	√	√	√
Component			√					
Deployment			√					

except to third-party extensions. What would be desirable is a graphical editor that is able to edit graphic descriptions as shown in Figure 5, or to incorporate the presented concepts in algorithms for consistency checks as well as code generation. Open source tools may be more open in this respect.

Another continuation of our work is to elaborate more on process and methodological aspects. The authors are not aware of any systematic investigation for applying mobile agent technology in a structured development process. There is definitely a need for rules which help developers to decide whether mobile agents should be applied in a particular development situation or not and based on which objectives. Patterns could be of great help at this point (Gamma, Helm, Johnson, & Vlissides, 1995).

Agent technology is a diverse field that incorporates "besides mobility" concepts like intelligence, learning capabilities, cooperation and so on. As soon as these concepts have been validated by real-world working examples and thus stabilized, they should also be taken into account for future agent-oriented extensions of the UML.

CONCLUSION

Mobile agent technology is of increasing importance not only for prototyping activities, but also for industrial software development. Up to now, research in mobile agent technology has been mainly technology driven, with a focus on the development of new agent platforms. We have presented a proposal for a sophisticated extension of the UML for mobile agent technology in order to enable modeling of mobile agents in the analysis and design phases of a seamless development process with mobile agents. The proposed language concepts have been developed and demonstrated by means of a prototype implementation of an advanced telecommunication system.

REFERENCES

Bäumer, C., Breugst, M., Choy, S. & Magedanz, T. (1999). Grasshopper A universal agent platform based on OMG MASIF and FIPA standards. In A. Karmouch and R. Impley

(Eds.), *First International Workshop on Mobile Agents for Telecommunication Applications (MATA'99)* (pp. 1-18), Ottawa, Canada: World Scientific Publishing Ltd. Available at http://www.ikv.de/download/grasshopper/ghandstandards.pdf

Cardelli, L. (1999). Abstractions for mobile computation. In J. Vitek and C. Jensen (Eds.), *Secure Internet Programming: Security Issues for Mobile and Distributed Objects. Lecture Notes in Computer Science* (pp. 51-94), 1603, Berlin, Heidelberg, New York: Springer-Verlag.

Chess, D. (1995). *Itinerant Agents for Mobile Computing.* IEEE Personal Communications, 2.

Chang, D. & Lange, D. (1996). Mobile agent : A new paradigm for distributed object computing on the WWW. In *Proceedings of the OOPSLA'96 Workshop.*

D'Souza, D., Sane, A. & Birchenough, A. (1999). First-class extensibility for UML – packaging of profiles, stereotypes, patterns, In *Proceedings of the UML '99, Lecture Notes in Computer Science* (pp. 265-278), 1723, Berlin, Heidelberg, New York: Springer Verlag.

Gamma, E., Helm, R., Johnson, R. & Vlissides, J. (1995). *Design Patterns: Elements of Reusable Object-Oriented Software.* Addison-Wesley.

FAIN. (2000): *FAIN – Future Active IP Networks. Project Description of IST Project FAIN* (to be submitted to IWAN 2000).

Hurst, L., Cunningham, P. & Somers, F. (1997). Mobile agents – Smart messages. In *Proceedings of the First International Workshop on Mobile Agents*, Berlin, Germany.

IPC. (2000). *Linux IP-Chains Description.* Available from the Ipchains homepage, http://www.rustcorp.com/linux/ipchains/.

Jul, E., Levy, H., Hutchinson, H. & Black, A. (1988). Fine-grained mobility in the emerald system. *ACM Transactions on Computer Systems*, 6(1).

Krause, S. (1997). MAGNA-A DPE-bused platform for mobile agents in electronic service markets. *Submission for ISADA'97 – The Third International Symposium on Autonomous Decentralized Systems*, Berlin, Germany.

Stadler, R. & Stiller, B. (Eds.). (1999). Active technologies for network and service management. In *Proceedings of the 10th IFIP/IEEE International Workshop on Distributed Systems Operations and Management DSOM 1999, Springer Lecture Notes in Computer Science*, 1700, Berlin, Heidelberg, New York: Springer Verlag.

Chapter IX

Rendering Distributed Systems in UML

Patricia Lago
Politecnico di Torino, Italy

This chapter is about the use of UML in the design of distributed systems. We have been using UML in the context of both international and local projects, and we continuously face the need for additional constructs that are especially conceived for distributed software components in general, and specifically for software running on middleware such as CORBA.

In particular, it is our opinion that various UML diagrams would need some extensions (or customizations). Also we defined a development methodology supporting UML and a set of conventions that help us in overcoming such needs. Nevertheless, they contribute just to software documentation and communication, and do not provide any help in the low-level design phase as well as in the generation of code for the subsequent implementation phase. The chapter is intended to discuss our requirements and possible solutions.

INTRODUCTION

A software development methodology can be defined as "the overall approach to manage the development of software. It should incorporate an integrated set of processes, architecture rules, standards and practices, and should be supported by tools" (see the ESI dictionary of software). Processes should be the result of the know-how and expertise gained by a company with the development of various projects. *Architecture rules* should help in solving recurring architectural problems common to domain-specific applications, like standards provide stable patterns for different companies to integrate complementary (or similar) software products. At last, *tools* should guide the developer to carry out a production process, according to the supported methodology.

In other words, a software development methodology can be summarized as "a set of techniques supporting a defined development process, and a software product notation": the process guides the developer in the various phases of software engineering, whereas the notation supports the visual description of the resulting software product.

While the development process varies according to at least the type and dimension of the system to be developed, and the dimension and organization of the developing team, UML represents a *de facto* standard notation for object-oriented software modeling (OMG, 1997). Nonetheless, for the development of domain-specific software systems, like distributed systems, it still needs further work. In particular, in this chapter we focus on the specification of those aspects that are critical to distributed software architectures. Our aim is to describe both the experience gained in modeling such systems, and the requirements on a notation suitable for their complete representation.

In particular we based this work on developments carried out in the field of advanced telecommunication services (or service architectures), for which aspects like inter-operability, portability, software distribution and deployment need specific attention. Hence, to describe a service architecture thoroughly, there is the need for a modeling language with constructs describing the various aspects mentioned above, in an integrated and possibly intuitive way.

The work is structured as follows: "Background" discusses related work. "Impact of Distribution on UML Diagrams" describes those aspects that are critical in representing distributed systems: for each aspect, the associated UML diagram is discussed to draw the lacks and possible extensions. "A Development Methodology for Distributed Software" draws a methodology for software development, in which discussed diagrams find context. The chapter ends with some Conclusions and future trends.

BACKGROUND

This work addresses two directions in the development of distributed object-oriented systems: the notation used for modeling and the process followed by software engineers. This Section discusses some related work and makes a comparison with the work presented here.

Notations

UML is the successor of the object-oriented analysis and design notations of the late '80s and the early '90s. In particular it is an evolution of Booch & Rumbaugh's OMT, Jacobson's OOSE, and other object-oriented methods like Harel's statecharts.

In this context we do not want to discuss the benefits and drawbacks of the different modelling notations for which comparisons and surveys already exist in the literature (see for instance Berard, 1995; Wieringa, 1998). We base this on the fact that UML was a standard *de facto* since some years earlier, and since 1997 it is an OMG standard. Rather, we would like to discuss some examples of distributed systems modelling, which face problems in using UML.

Emmerich (2000, pp. 50-51) discusses some differences in the development of non-distributed applications and distributed objects. For instance, in the first case object creation is considered an implementation problem, whereas in distributed systems it is a design problem that needs dedicated modelling. Also, object composition, which represents a critical aspect in distributed systems, can be represented in UML, e.g., by using packages in Class diagrams, even if the notation syntax lacks in expressiveness and communication. Similar conclusions are discussed in our work.

To model software architectures for telecommunication services, both ISO (ISO/IEC,

1993) and TINA-C (see The TINA Consortium [Telecommunications Information Networking Architecture] Homepage) used OMT and afterwards UML to represent distributed systems. Nonetheless, the many auxiliary ACTS European projects carried out in the past years (e.g., Vital, Dolmen, Retina; see The ACTS information window Homepage), aiming at validating standards and baseline architectures, identified the need for a more specific notation modelling distributed components. This work has its roots in these projects, as explained in the rest of the chapter.

At last, various distributed application domains require extensions to UML to model at best their peculiar aspects. A well representative example is given by Web applications (Conallen, 2000), whose design is characterized by "partitioning objects onto the client or the server side, and by defining Web page user interfaces." Conallen (2000) resolves these requirements mainly by using domain-specific stereotypes. For instance, business objects, server pages and client pages are class stereotypes having a different graphical representation, and the latter with no active behavior. Forms are aggregates in a client page, and can only exist in their context. Frames and framesets are associated with targets that are loaded each time a frame is included in a Web page. Constraints are defined on stereotypes, e.g., a server page can have relationships only with objects on the server side.

Compared to general distributed systems, Web applications are very specific, with a rather simple architectural model. Some of the extensions required by our work might be achieved through UML extension mechanisms. Some others, like the definition of new diagrams such as the computational model discussed later on, is still under investigation.

Process-Related Issues

OPEN (Object-oriented Process, Environment and Notation; see the OPEN Consortium Homepage) is a methodology created by merging a large number of existing methodologies and ideas coming from a consortium of internationally recognized researchers. The followed approach is very similar to the work carried out in the software process modeling research community, by defining the so-called OPF (OPEN Process Framework) to define software process models. An analysis of related work can be found in Jaccheri, Picco and Lago, (1998). Nonetheless, OPF approach is different by trying to unify in a single flexible framework valuable contributions coming from various sources.

Compared to our work, OPEN and the OPF could be used to model our software process. Alternatively, in this chapter we used a process modeling language (the E3 language, see Jaccheri, Picco, & Lago, 1998) especially conceived for process model elicitation and communication.

The Unified Process (see Kruchten, 1999) is "iterative and incremental, use-case driven and architecture centric": iterations are carried out on each process phase until a satisfactory result has been achieved, and the whole development process (from requirements analysis to test) is repeated to incrementally release the software system at increasing maturity levels. Each iteration is driven by the Use cases stating the requirements on the system.

The whole Unified process is based on a set of models (represented by UML diagrams) describing the architecture of the system and mapped on processes. For instance, the requirements analysis process yields to the Use case model, which contains Use case diagrams and Sequence diagrams. The design process yields to both the Design model (mainly made of Class diagrams, Sequence diagrams, Statechart diagrams and Activity diagrams), and the Deployment model (mainly made of Deployment diagrams and

Sequence diagrams).

A basic concept of the Unified process itself, is that there is no universal process: the development of different software types may require different processes, and their representations require different diagrams. The work presented here is based on a subset of the UML diagrams, and a subset of processes as defined in the Unified process; similar to the Unified process, ours covers design, implementation and test. Further, we refine the design process into high-level modeling and low-level modeling, the latter more implementation oriented. Additionally, we refine test processes for component and system test. Differently, Deployment is an explicit process, posed after implementation and Integration, and not implicitly included in Design as in the Unified process.

On the other hand, the Unified process starts with Requirements, the first development process aiming at specifying requirements through Use cases. This technique has been widely recognized as a powerful means, especially thanks to its simplicity, and its informal and intuitive notation. As explained in (Fowler, 2000, pages 46-47), use cases represent an external view of the system, without any correlations between use cases and the system internals. In our development processes we used (among others) Use case diagrams, but they are not discussed here, as no extensions are needed for the particular domain of distributed systems. Also, we experienced large-scale systems characterized by high internal complexity and rather simple and limited external aspects, too simple to motivate a dedicated requirements process.

IMPACT OF DISTRIBUTION ON UML DIAGRAMS

In UML the description of a software system is given by a collection of diagrams, each representing a different aspect of the system. If complex, an aspect can require multiple diagrams of the same type, and it is up to the experience of the developer and his/her knowledge of the system's application domain, the optimal distribution of information over multiple diagrams.

This section illustrates the use of UML diagrams for the representation of distributed systems, by focusing on the aspects that in our opinion are peculiar to this important class of software. In particular, we show how distribution aspects can be modeled (or not) in UML, which are the limitations and how they could be overcome through extensions.

Not all UML diagrams are considered, only the ones that we commonly use in our development projects, and that we find fundamental for modeling distributed systems, namely Class diagrams, Component Diagrams, Deployment diagrams and Sequence diagrams. Also, we introduce IDL specifications for the description of interfaces, because we believe that even though not represented as any UML diagram, their description is a *must* in distributed software architecting, therefore requiring dedicated notations and methods.

Throughout the section, a common example will be used, i.e., User Profile management. Its application domain is that of a service provider (e.g., an Internet provider) who stores in a user profile all the information regarding its users, and who manages access to this information for authorization decisions, constraints and customizations (TINA-C, 1997, June).

Static Structure Diagrams

Static Structure diagrams show the static structure of a system, as modules and module relationships. Among diagrams of this type, we consider Class diagrams and Component diagrams, even if other diagrams (less important in the context of this work) belong to the same type, for instance object diagrams.

We concentrate on Class diagrams and Component diagrams, as they present the same architectural viewpoint (i.e., the structural one) but on different granularities: the Class diagram defines lower granularity modules (the classes), compared to the Component diagram that focuses on aggregations of classes and distributed interfaces (the components). As it will become clear throughout the next two sections, these two diagrams are central to understand a distributed system, and to both successfully drive developers through software engineering activities and provide users with detailed system documentation.

Class Diagrams

Class diagrams show the static architecture of a system in terms of classes, internal class structure, class inter-relationships and associations (inheritance and aggregation). A class diagram represents the modules (classes) a system if made of, and the functions it supports, without showing any dynamic information. When sufficiently detailed, a class diagram can be directly translated in the corresponding physical representation, i.e., the code skeleton.

Application

In distributed systems there are two main aspects pertaining class diagrams. First, a class diagram can represent the information maintained and manipulated by the system. This information, represented as collections of objects, offer what in the ODP-RM (Open Distributed Processing Reference Model; see ISO/IEC, 1993) is called Information viewpoint (TINA-C, 1995). The second aspect focuses on the decomposition of the system into a distributed set of interacting objects. In this case, class diagrams offer what in ODP-RM is called Computational viewpoint (TINA-C, 1996).

The mapping between the two viewpoints is of type many-many: an information class can be encapsulated in one corresponding computational class, but it could also be aggregated along with other information classes into a single computational class, or be split in multiple computational classes. This mapping depends on both the information semantics and the logic of the system.

As an example consider Figure 1, in which the left side classes belong to the information viewpoint, and represent the information associated with the User, his/her associated data (the User Profile), the Terminals on which the user can be registered (i.e., traceable on the network in a certain instant) and the Services (s)he has subscribed to and that are capable to be run on certain terminal types. These information classes can be mapped on a set of computational classes, like the ones proposed on the right side of the figure: terminal information can be managed by a single class (modeling a terminal type with its own attributes and capabilities) thus implementing a 1:1 mapping relationship; the information describing a Service, is instead commonly mapped on multiple computational classes (i.e., with a 1:N mapping relationship), depending on the kind of service, its complexity and behavior. In general, service computational classes are at least two, one modeling the user interface and one for the server associated with the global service logics. For instance, a flight reservation service could be composed by two service classes (the client and the

Figure 1. From Information to Computational Viewpoint

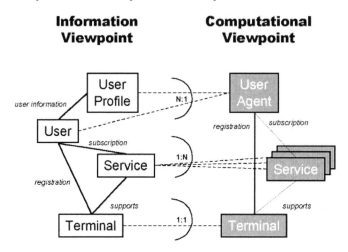

server side managing queries and reservations), whereas an on-line chess service could be composed by at least three service classes: the client for the players, a server managing each match (i.e., chess playing rules and the match status) and a centralized server managing statistics about current on-line matches, classification information, etc.

At last, Figure 1 exemplifies an N:1 mapping relationship with user profile information management: the information associated with users, and the fact that each User Profile regards a single subscribed User, can be modeled by computational class User Agent managing the information of a single subscribed user. In this case, information class User, that was relevant in the Information viewpoint to reason about users and his/her identification and personal information, disappears in the computational model by being implicitly represented by the User Agent.

As UML offers a single type of diagram, the Class Diagram, we must distinguish class diagrams that model the information viewpoint from the ones that model the computational

Figure 2. UML Class Diagram for Information Objects

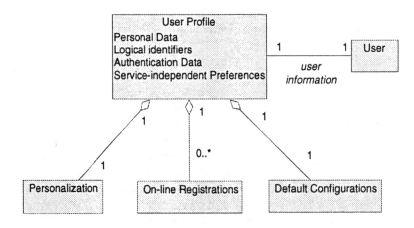
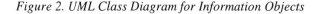

viewpoint. To this aim we call the first information model and the second computational model: the *information model* describes a system in terms of the managed information elements, their semantics and their logical relationships; the *computational model* describes a system as a collection of interacting components that maintain a set of information elements, provide an interface for their manipulation and interact with other components to achieve system functionality.

The information model is usually developed before the computational model, to identify and represent which data are manipulated by the system, and which static associations exist between data. For instance, Figure 2 depicts a UML class diagram representing a fragment of the Information Model for User Profile. In the diagram, class User Profile contains user information classified into four main categories:
- Personal Data (e.g., first name and last name);
- Logical identifiers, representing how the user is logically identified from the external world (e.g., logical name, personal number, email address);
- Authentication Data, representing how the user identifies himself toward the provider (e.g., login/password, personal number/PIN, voiceprint, etc.);
- Service-independent Preferences, representing user preferences that are common to all the services the user is subscribed to (e.g., preferred language, billing information, payment procedures).

Class User Profile also aggregates three information classes that are:
- class Default Configurations, which include the list of terminals of common use;
- class On-line Registrations that dynamically store the terminals where the user is available in a certain moment;
- class Personalization, carrying all customizations defined by the user.

Once information is formalized in the information model, the developer has to define the associated computational model; as introduced earlier in this section, each class in the computational model will encapsulate a set of classes of the information model. Furthermore, each computational class will offer operations that both manipulate the encapsulated information, and realize the properties defined by class associations in the information model.

Four are the properties peculiar to distributed systems and that must be clearly represented in the computational model:

Figure 3. UML Class Diagram for Computational Objects

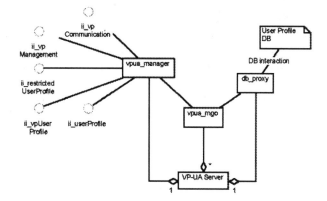

- System components, i.e., the atomic modules aggregating a collection of computational classes. Component representation should identify both the internal and external structure.
- Exported interfaces, i.e., the interfaces that a component offers to external distributed invocations (coming by other components);
- Internal interfaces, i.e., the interfaces that are offered by the classes the component encapsulates, but that are not externally visible;
- Component associations, i.e., relationships between different components and (inside a component) between internal classes.

Figure 3 shows a possible solution for User Profile management, implemented by VP-UA (Virtual Presence[i] - User Agent) Server that is composed of three classes: db_proxy, vpua_mgo (managed object) and vpua_manager.

In this solution, class VP-UA Server is in charge of managing user profile information of all users. All user information is stored in an external database (represented in UML as a note) and accessible via the proxy object db_proxy. Each user is assigned with an object of class vpua_mgo that loads user information from the database and makes this information available for further use or modification. Also, class VP-UA Server aggregates a class called vpua_manager that offers five external interfaces (represented as round icons with prefix "ii_") according to different usage or access rights.

By comparing Figure 3 with Figure 2, information class User Profile and its aggregated classes are encapsulated here in the external database, and will be loaded in vpua_mgo objects at runtime. All other computational classes will implement the system logics.

We can also observe that information class User of Figure 2 is not relevant at computational level: as mentioned earlier in this section, class User represents the logical relationship between a user and his/her data, useful to comprehend the information model, but not part of the computational model.

Discussion

Class diagrams have a twofold interpretation that should be clearly identified: as part of either the information model, or the computational model. This is not a problem concerning just distributed systems, but all software systems in which information modeling can be roughly associated with system analysis or high-level design (in which more focus on information elicitation in given), whereas computational modeling can be roughly associated with detailed design (in which developers start to propose the implementation architecture).

Instead, aspects proper to distributed systems for which a clear representation is crucial start to appear in the computational model. Indeed, Class diagrams are not expressive enough to clearly describe fundamental aspect in distributed systems development, namely components (defined as the atomic modules of distribution), their external (distributed) interfaces, their communication relationships and internal composition. The Class diagram defined in Figure 3 provides the starting point for the computational model: it shows the number of interfaces offered by computation classes, and the usage associations between classes. But it does not further map computational classes on the distributed aspects listed above.

To solve this problem, UML offers the Component Diagram (described and discussed in the following section) that nonetheless does not provide enough expressiveness for a satisfying design.

Also, the use we make of the information model differs from the one originally defined in ODP and typically used in TINA specifications: these really model just information, or in other words data maintained by the system, and few attention (or none) is given to operations. This is a more data-driven than object-oriented approach. In our work, we use the same term to distinguish the modeling of logically related objects with no consideration of distribution concerns, from the computational model transforming the system into a set of interacting distributed modules.

Component Diagrams

Component diagrams, as defined in UML (see OMG, 1999), show the structure of the code itself. We apply them in a broader sense, by showing the structure of the "business modules" to be deployed on a network of computers and that implement distributed communication.

Application

To better draw up the limitations of the UML Component diagram, we start describing what we mean as "complete description of component": Figure 4 (a) shows the computational model of component VP-UA Server, which manages user information structured in a user profile.

First, it is important to outline that, to define the VP-UA Server component we start from the computational viewpoint Class diagram and map classes on components: some classes (e.g., db_proxy) will be local (internal) to a component, some other will also export distributed interfaces (e.g., vpua_manager).

In detail, the Component diagram should define both the internal decomposition of a component and its external interactions. In this respect, Figure 4.(a) focuses on the internal part: it shows the distributed interfaces of the component (and the classes that implement them), and the interactions with the execution environment (e.g., legacy systems or existing software like the database used by class db_proxy to store the User Profile).

The diagram also identifies static classes from dynamic ones: *static classes* (represented as dark boxes) are instantiated at component creation and exist for the complete

Figure 4. (a) Computational Model, (b) UML Component Diagram

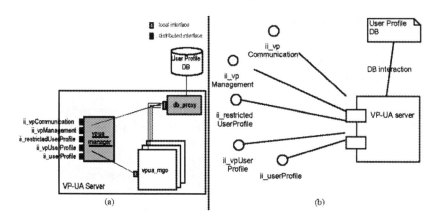

component lifecycle. *Dynamic classes* (represented as white boxes) are instantiated after component creation, in a variable unpredictable number of objects that varies from execution to execution. Also, in a component there always exists a so-called *factory object* (a special kind of static object) exporting the *factory interface*, i.e., the interface implementing component creation and deletion. For instance, the VP-UA Server of Figure 4.(a) is composed of two static classes (the db_proxy and the vpua_manager) and one dynamic class (vpua_mgo) that can be multiply instantiated. Also, vpua_manager is the factory object (identified by underlying its name): in this solution, during component creation it instantiates the db_proxy. Afterwards, whenever a user is created, it creates an associated vpua_mgo instance and maintains a reference to it for later requests.

By comparing the Computational model with its UML equivalent, the Component diagram of Figure 4.(b), we can observe that: (1) the graphical representation of interfaces is less compact, and (2) only the external viewpoint is represented. This implies that we can obtain a view similar to our Computational model, by using two diagrams: the Class diagram of Figure 3 for the component internal structure, and the Component diagram of Figure 4.(a) for the external representation. Also, UML is not enough, lacking in representing:

- distributed/internal interface types;
- static/dynamic class types;
- internal component decomposition.

Discussion

Class diagrams are suitable to describe Informational and Computational viewpoints of a system in terms of classes and class relationships, whereas Component diagrams show the Computational viewpoint in terms of components.

The UML representation of these diagrams in respectively Figure 3 and Figure 4.(b) shows that the expressiveness of its graphical notation is mainly vertical[ii] (as in OMT, see Rumbaugh, Blaha, Premerlani, Eddy & Lorensen, 1991). As composition is an important aspect of distributed systems, this decreases model readability since all the graphical information is at the same plane and there is no pictorial support to zoom into a component.

Figure 4.(a) represents, instead, a more expressive class diagram: relationships like "is_made_of" and "is_supported_by" aggregating managed objects inside a server component and associating interfaces to objects can be deduced at a glance.

In this respect, horizontal notations are better suited for a component-based approach, in which graphical readability is a key requirement for large-scale software systems, characterized by a large number of information and relationships.

Sequence Diagrams

Sequence diagrams (also called Message Sequence Charts) represent detailed interactions among system components for the execution of a specific functionality. In the detailed design of object-oriented systems, a sequence diagram represents a selected scenario (e.g., a use case in UML) in which vertical lines represent the objects involved (see Figure 5), and horizontal directed lines represent the messages exchanged between objects. Time flows from the top of the diagram downwards, and unless specifically annotated, only the sequence order of messages is shown, not the exact time.

Sequence diagramming is a powerful technique, also used for system testing and documentation, and during system execution to trace execution steps, and to understand where bottlenecks will be. This is especially true for distributed systems, in which interactions distributed on a network must be implemented differently from interactions local to a module, and in which module test (i.e., test of a single component) and system test (inter-component) involve different resources and often developers.

Application

As discussed in the section above, crucial aspects of distributed systems regard interfaces and their implementing classes. This is reflected in Sequence diagrams too, which should make clear if for instance an interaction sequence involves multiple components or is internal to a single one, or if it is implemented by distributed or local interfaces.

To highlight these distribution aspects in Sequence diagrams, we adapted the UML sequence diagram notation by substituting objects with the components and the computational objects of the computational model. For instance, Figure 5.(b) shows that component VP-UA Server offers operations through aggregated computational objects, vpua_manager, vpua_mgo and db_proxy. If we want to model the same information in UML, we can adopt a graphical convention shown in Figure 5.(a) in which a note above the group of contained objects shows the name of the component.

Also, the graphical notation for message flows has been enhanced to model different kinds of calls. Major issues are:

Recurring interaction patterns: especially for distributed systems, some scenarios are critical and need to be analyzed. These are at least the ones modeling lifecycle management, i.e., the way objects are created, destroyed and how object references are exchanged between components to operate services. Therefore, sequence diagrams should always model lifecycle management and recurring communication patterns.

Inter-dependencies among different sequence diagrams: the design of realistic software systems yields to large and complex diagrams. For this reason, we need modularization mechanisms to split them in smaller and more readable diagrams, e.g., according to system characteristics or architectural issues. We adopted two modularization conventions:

1. *Vertical modularization*, by organizing diagrams according to two different abstraction levels, inside a component (intra-component) and outside a component (inter-component). Each scenario is implemented by a sequence of interactions: a subset implements interactions between different components; some other implement interactions between objects inside a single component.

   We can then represent two associated diagrams. *Inter-component sequence diagrams* show how components (depicted as black boxes) interact to implement a scenario, without showing internal local calls. In this case, for the same scenario there will be as many *intra-component sequence diagrams* as the number of components involved in the scenario and having a relatively complex internal structure. Each intra-component diagram will explain how the external invocation, activated by the scenario on the component's external interface, is implemented internally by the aggregated computational objects. In other words, each intra-component diagram zooms into each component and shows how the invocation is served internally.

   To give an idea of this mechanism, Figure 5.(b) shows the intra-component sequence diagram for the VP-UA Server, in a scenario representing user subscription. As the diagram focuses on the internal structure of the VP-UA Server,

Figure 5. Interaction Example for the Subscription Scenario

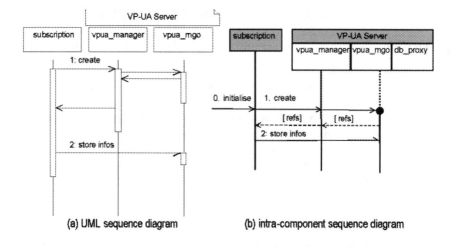

(a) UML sequence diagram   (b) intra-component sequence diagram

component subscription is represented as a black box (just to show where the invocation is originated) whereas component VP-UA Server is decomposed into its computational objects.

2. *Horizontal modularization*, by splitting up diagrams according to groups of invocations. To fragment a scenario into multiple diagrams, and still maintain readability, an invocation can go outside the diagram, and the same invocation can be repeated in the continuing diagram, by coming from nowhere. For instance, the first invocation in Figure 5.(b) comes from outside the diagram by indicating that it belongs to a previous diagram.

Also, often invocation groups are common to multiple scenarios. Instead of repeating them in all of them, they can be represented only once in a separated diagram, and referred to by the multiple scenarios.

At last, another difference in the two diagrams of Figure 5 is the graphical representations of interaction arrows: OMG UML defines a rich variety of interaction types, particularly relevant in distributed systems. These include: object creation (represented in Figure 5.(b) by the arrow ending with a black circle on object vpua_mgo) and object destruction, synchronous or asynchronous invocations, information return due to synchronous invocations (represented in UML by dotted arrows and that we additionally label with the returned information between squared brackets), etc.

Discussion

We described various mechanisms and conventions especially conceived for modeling interactions in distributed systems. While some can be obtained by simply adopting methodological procedures, the need for language support is auspicated to design intra- and inter-component sequence diagrams. This is in fact a powerful instrument for guiding the design process, and to carefully specify and test interactions that pertain to a single machine, rather than interactions that cross distributed domains.

To achieve such two-step representation, it would mainly require in the sequence diagram notation the inclusion of constructs already present in other UML diagrams, like components or aggregation.

DeploymentDiagrams

Deployment diagrams show which software components may reside on which nodes of a distributed computer network, and which dependencies exist among remote components. It is usually developed during detailed design to identify which components must be installed, created and configured to execute the system.

Deployment is commonly foreseen as successive to implementation, and identifies the need to express the information needed for deployment, even though it does not yet specify either how such information should be defined, or the development point where it would be appropriate to pursue this.

Application

The engineering viewpoint of the ODP Reference Model describes distribution-oriented aspects of an ODP system: it identifies distribution concepts like cluster as a set of co-located objects and capsule aggregating clusters. Nonetheless, it does not refer to any particular methodology or diagram.

Experience shows that large-scale development of distributed systems needs to map the computational model (or at least the UML Component diagram) on a Deployment diagram. There are two major deployment aspects important to developers:

1. To highlight *interactions distribution* on the real runtime environment: components defined in the computational model provide both local interfaces (in the native implementation language, e.g., Java) and external interfaces that can be made accessible to remote nodes (e.g., OMG/IDL interfaces, see the example of Figure 4.(a)). In this respect, the deployment diagram should emphasize remotely accessible interfaces, which represent the points of access offered to remote components.
2. To check the system against *standardization* and *security issues*: distributed systems

Figure 6. Business Model Example

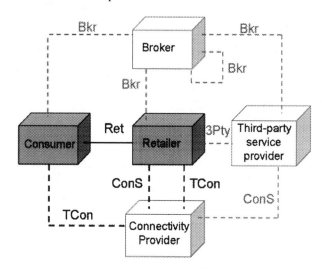

are implicitly mapped on a business model, i.e., on distributed nodes belonging to business domains or playing different industrial roles. An example is provided by the TINA business model (TINA-C, 1997, May), simplified in Figure 6 in which boxes represent business domains and arcs model so-called reference points, i.e., interaction paths between different domains. As domains belong to different companies, nations or entities, they need specific regulation with the objective to ensure both standard interfaces between different domains playing the same business role (e.g., running routers provided by different vendors), and the ability to build up COTS services based on interface specifications.

To give a flavor of the issues associated with deployment and business modeling, let us consider the example of Figure 7, in which some components of our example system have been deployed on part of the business model depicted in Figure 6.

By applying the Deployment diagram to the company business model, we can identify the "real" domains to which nodes belong and observe "on field" operation aspects. For instance:

- We can directly elicit distributed communication implementing reference points. In our example, all interactions between Customer domains and Retailer implement the Ret reference point, and impose a secure connection, especially when customers access and modify personal data. In particular the figure shows Customer A who manipulates his/her User Profile and personalization, through a Personalization client, whereas Customer B (through a generic service client) can communicate with Customer B (via his/her VP-UA, on communication interface) and/or view public information stored in his/her User Profile (via his/her VP-UA, on restricted User Profile interface).
- We can check compliance to standards (whenever applicable). In our example, the four interfaces involved in the Ret reference point should comply with the associated standard. This is an important topic: if for instance, the DB is implemented and

Figure 7. Deployment over a Business Model

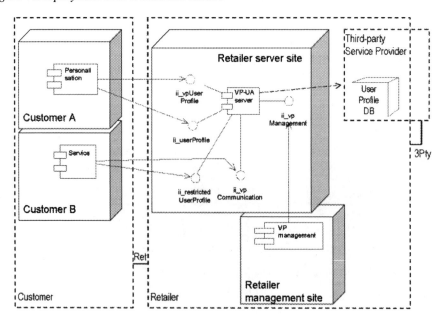

running inside the Retailer domain, DB communication does not imply secure or standard access; if instead we take the DB out of the Retailer domain (as shown in the figure) and outsource DB management to a Third-Party Provider, DB communication must be secure and possibly comply to standard interactions, to be in agreement with the selected company.

• System component analysis. When deployed, we have the instruments to analyze components in details. For instance, Figure 7 shows that interfaces ii_userProfile and ii_vpUserProfile offer full access to authorized customers to respectively change user profile and personalization data, whereas interfaces ii_restrictedUserProfile and ii_vpCommunication permit external customers/users to respectively gain restricted access to customer information and to contact customers.

Discussion

UML defines Deployment diagrams as the mapping of Component diagrams on distributed nodes, like computing devices, mechanical processing resources or even human resources (see OMG, 1999). From the more technical perspective, this represents a good starting point. Nonetheless, more pragmatic issues should also be considered. For instance, the development of domain-specific distributed systems (e.g., telecommunication service architectures; see TINA-C, 1998) is already based on frameworks and specifications based on business models (ISO/IEC, 1993). Unfortunately, these specifications are used during development as documentation input, and there is no automated or formalized procedure to control the compliance of the developed software with such documentation.

In this respect, deployment model mapping components and their interfaces on business domains (as groups of nodes) and reference points (as regulated interactions and public interfaces) would really help in the achievement of a complete architectural design.

Also, general business applications are mainly perceived as involving the two domains (and associated reference points) highlighted in Figure 6, namely the Consumer representing the application client or end-user, and the Retailer, i.e. the provider of the service logic (e.g. an Internet provider or Web-based service provider). However, and especially in the current IT market, the other domains also play a key role in the overall provision of services, even if their involvement is often transparent. Think of on-line shopping applications, in which the consumer is able to buy goods by giving credit card information: (s)he has no idea of the underlying real-time check the seller performs by the consumer's bank, and therefore of the interactions between respectively Retailer and Third-Party Service Provider.

In this scenario, there is the need for diagrams that also model the interactions among the system and other domains' components.

IDL Specifications

The identification of the interfaces in a software system has been often indicated as a crucial software development aspect. Ambler (1997) focuses on human-computer interaction, by recognizing *interface flow diagrams* as one of the fundamental missing techniques in UML. Such diagrams model the relationships between the system and its user, through interface objects, thus explicitly designing the information flow between the user interface and system components. In a similar way, Berard (1995) claims that large-scaled system development requires mechanisms defining interfaces at a higher level than that of a class, and reports IBM and Wirfs-Brock as two methodologies offering user *interface models*.

Our approach puts more emphasis on the interfaces offered by the system (what we call external or distributed interfaces) rather than on *user interfaces* (or GUI). We think that, as stressed for Component and Deployment diagrams, these interfaces are a crucial aspect of distributed systems, and that their correct specification heavily influences overall quality.

In a similar way, the work of Wieringa (1998) defines *communication* as a type of interaction specifying the way functions are ordered in space, and *context diagrams* as the graph showing the external entities a system communicates with. Differently, we explicitly indicate OMG IDL as the medium to represent interfaces, being it language independent and a standard. The Interface Definition Language (IDL) was in fact defined by the OMG Common Object Request Broker Architecture (CORBA) for textually describing the interfaces of different components with a common language. An IDL specification describes the interfaces defined for a class, in terms of interface inheritance and aggregation, and interface definition given by interface name, operation signatures with input and output parameter names and types, operation results and exceptions.

The interface definition specifies what member functions are available to external

Table 1. Example of IDL Specification

```
module VP-UA Server
{
interface ii_restrictedUserProfile

{
void getUserId(
        in commonTypes::t_genericUserId uid,
        in commonTypes::t_authenticationId authenticationId,
        out string userId)
        raises(
                commonTypes::e_operationFailed,
                commonTypes::e_badAuthenticationId,
                commonTypes::e_authenticationIdExpired);
...
};

interface ii_vpUserProfile
{
void getPersonalization(
        in commonTypes::t_genericUserId uid,
        in commonTypes::t_authenticationId authenticationId,
        out vpua::t_personalization personalization)
        raises(
                commonTypes::e_operationFailed,
                commonTypes::e_badAuthenticationId,
                commonTypes::e_authenticationIdExpired);
...
        };
};
```

clients, without making any assumptions about the implementation of the object.

Application

Detailed design of a system includes the IDL specification of the interfaces provided by each system component. For instance Table 1 presents a fragment of the IDL specification of the interfaces provided by class vpua_manager of Figure 4.(a), and exported by the VP-UA Server. We can see that IDL defines all interfaces by listing the signature of each method offered.

Once stable, the IDL specification is compiled to generate the necessary code to port interfaces (and their supporting objects) on a distributed environment, operated by a distributed platform like CORBA (see The Object Management Group Homepage).

IDL specifications provide the starting point for implementation: it starts with the translation of IDL into the source code implementing the components' structure. Therefore, both design and implementation should rely on a stable, possibly frozen IDL, since intuitively the modification of these interfaces would impact both the internal implementation of the server itself, and the way the client component behaves.

At last, the organization of the IDL code is partially subjective. Nonetheless, simple rules help in structuring interfaces and common types in a well-defined form. For instance, it is a good procedure to separate interfaces from the modules that describe common types. Furthermore, types common to the whole system should be separated from those specific to a certain service type or class of services.

Discussion

UML does not include any explicit mechanism to support detailed modeling of neither user interfaces nor system interfaces. Also, UML does not foresee IDL as part of the language, even though most UML-based modeling tools support IDL generation out of class diagrams or component diagrams.

What we think UML lacks for industrial development is support for IDL specification (e.g., for explicit IDL-driven editing), and the integration of IDL specification with static structure diagrams: being IDL is automatically generated out of class diagrams, in theory it pertains to late software engineering phases. In practice, and especially in development in the large or when software has to adhere to existing architectural standards or frameworks, IDL is defined (or specialized) during high-level design already. If development adheres to consolidated standards that already specify interfaces (e.g., The Object Management Group Homepage; TINA-C, 1998), this aspect could be neglected. Otherwise this is fundamental, to achieve overall agreement on distributed interactions specification, and in industrial development this is a requirement to be fulfilled in early stages of development. For this reason, IDL mapping to modeling notations (and not the other way around only) would be of great help.

A DEVELOPMENT METHODOLOGY FOR DISTRIBUTED SOFTWARE

The diagrams discussed in the previous section find their context in different stages of the development process. Their usage and extension (as compared to UML) have been discussed in general for software systems with a relevant distribution factor.

Here we want to sketch out a development methodology that was defined and experimented though the years in the specific field of telecommunication service architectures, but that we think is applicable for the development of any kind of distributed software architecture. Our final objective is to provide the reader with a complete development overview, by showing how the various viewpoints offered by the discussed diagrams over a distributed system fit together during development stages.

Preamble

The evolution of telecommunication market, fostered by the tighter and tighter integration of telecommunications and information technology, have put new requirements on both software engineering disciplines and the related technologies, to guide the development of service architectures. This commonly refers to guidelines given by the TINA-C (see The TINA Consortium Homepage) whose ambition was to give answers coping with these new requirements by providing a series of standards to define the generic architecture of service providers' platforms supporting advanced telecommunication services, and being object-oriented, geographically distributed and heterogeneous.

TINA guidelines have been used, at least as a reference work, by most important industries (e.g., network operators or providers) and research centers in the field of service provisioning. Our starting point was that the TINA approach (see TINA-C, 1997, June) can be adopted as the basis in the definition of a methodology for distributed software architectures in general.

A software architecture can be modeled from at least three different perspectives that usually reflect three successive development steps: the *information model* focuses on the information pertaining to the domain for a certain system and the logical association between them. The *computational model* designs the system as interacting components, which on their own manage the information part of the information model. The *interface specification model* defines the component interfaces through which components interact.

These models are represented in ODP according to pre-existing software engineering object-oriented modeling techniques that have been specialized for the telecommunication application domain. Instead of the considerable effort dedicated to the definition of these models, we think that the field still lacks in a stabilized software engineering methodology guiding the modeler through the development steps. Techniques common to teams are a starting point, but we further need to adopt an engineering approach to the development process.

The Development Process

We defined our development methodology by further elaborating ODP and TINA approaches for distributed service and software architectures, with the following rationale: Information and Computational models can be thoroughly associated with analysis and design, whose border has been for years a very hot topic in object-oriented software engineering (Booch, 1986). We assumed that *analysis* models the problem on an as-is basis, and that design proposes a possible solution to the modeled problem.

Further, object-oriented modeling techniques traditionally belong to either *high-level design* or *detailed design*.

- High-level design gives an abstract view on the overall solution, whereas the latter focuses on specific aspects that pose the foundations to implementation. For instance, Static Structure diagrams describe the overall software system in terms of architectural components[iii] and connectors (according to a general definition of software architecture; see Shaw & Garlan, 1996). Sequence diagrams detail the interactions executing the set of specific functionality that are critical, hence needing further investigation prior to implementation.

- Detailed design is more implementation-oriented by exploiting the features offered by both the specific implementation language, and the execution environment in which the final system will run (e.g., operating system or middleware).

According to the above observations, we formalized development into a process organized in five macro phases as modeled in Figure 8: the upper part shows the chain of phases, and the lower part shows the documents (diagrams discussed in "Impact of Distribution on UML Diagrams") that are either used by each phase (as input arrows) or produced as output.[iv]

Being this work focused on modeling, the following briefly describes the first two phases and their inputs and output, whereas the successive ones are just sketched out. For an extensive report of the complete methodology, the reader can refer to Lago and Canal (2000).

High-Level Modeling: regards requirement analysis and specification, and provides the gross architecture of the overall system. In fact, this phase takes as input System Requirements (e.g., functional requirements, architectural standards, constraints about legacies and programming languages), and it produces as output its architectural description in terms of:

- The information model formalized by a set of class diagrams.
- The computational model making up the overall architecture (as discussed in "Component Diagrams").
- Inter-Component Sequence diagrams designing external interactions among different components.

Detailed Modeling: regards the decomposition of components into internal objects and their associations. Each component is zoomed to detail the computational objects it encapsulates. This permits it to highlight how the overall behavior is actually implemented by each component. To this aim, detailed modeling produces as output at least:

Figure 8. The Development Methodology: Phases, Inputs and Outputs

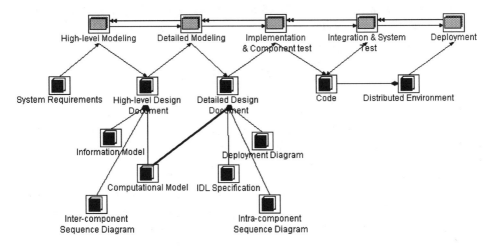

- Intra-Component Sequence diagrams (refining inter-component sequence diagrams), which model how invocations to component operations are implemented internally to each single component.
- The refinement of the computational model showing the internal architecture of every component, i.e., which object implements interfaces exported by the aggregating component.
- The IDL specification of the interfaces exported by components.

At this stage, the developer has a complete, detailed description of the whole system.

Implementation & Component Test: starts with the translation of IDL specifications into the source code skeleton. After their implementation, components are individually tested against their potential servers, to ensure that each component is individually fault free, and its interactions with external components are correct, at least for what concerns their expected behavior.

Integration & System Test: regards the incremental integration of all system components. In this phase, sequence diagrams are used as test suites in order to check the overall dynamics of the system.

Deployment: system components are deployed on distributed sites, according to both site characteristics (e.g. computational power, memory allocation, business domain) and logical cohesion.

FUTURE TRENDS

The immediate way to realize the extensions discussed in this chapter is to apply the extension mechanisms already offered by UML, i.e., stereotypes, constraints and tagged values. In fact, in many cases the extensions required to support the modeling of domain-specific applications can be achieved in this way. By following this approach, future work will focus on the possible application of these UML mechanisms, to identify its potentials and possible limitations.

In particular, in the field of distributed systems, many are the initiatives in this context. Very significant is the initiative of OMG (see OMG Homepage) to open a Request for Proposals specifically addressing distributed component architectures. Also, the OMG UML Revision Task Force and the UML 2.0 Working Group are carrying out multiple tasks concerning the future evolution of UML (see the UML Resource Page), for instance a proposal for a UML profile for CORBA (foreseen by the end of 2001) designed to provide a standard means for expressing the semantics of CORBA IDL using UML notation.

CONCLUSION

This chapter described some aspects that are fundamental to model distributed architectures in a complete and effective way. Conventional extensions applied by the author are based on multiple development projects carried out in the context of both telecommunication services and Internet applications (see Canal & Lago, 1999; Lago & Canal, 2000). Nonetheless, all issues can be applied in general to distributed software architectures as well (Lago & Canal, 2000).

The discussion of each diagram identifies a list of extensions to UML that are desirable when distributed software has to be developed. Our experience shows that our approach provides an helpful design documentation and support. Unfortunately, as soon as a UML-based software tool is adopted, all advantages introduced by tool support, like syntax-oriented editing or cross-diagrams checks, vanish, as conventions are treated as pure pictures with no semantics.

Also, it must be observed that tool adoption often results in a further limitation, because currently available tools just support a subset of UML constructs. Additionally, tools give a partial support to forward engineering (i.e., code generation), whereas the ones supporting reverse engineering (a requirement for successful reuse) are too rigid to be really applicable in real service engineering.

ACKNOWLEDGMENTS

I wish to thank Gianni Canal of CSELT (the Italian Telecom Research Laboratory), whose contribution to many development projects and discussions was essential for the achievements described in this work.

REFERENCES

Ambler, S.W. (1997). What's missing from the UML? *Object Magazine,* October 29-37.

Berard, E.V. (1995). A comparison of object-oriented methodologies. [On-line]. The Object Agency Inc. Available: http://www.mini.net/cetus/oo_ooa_ood_methods.html.

Booch, G. (1986). Object-oriented design. *IEEE Trans. on Software Engineering*, 12(2), 211-221.

Canal, G. & Lago, P. (1999). Integration of commercial Internet applications in a TINA environment. In Sventek, J. (Ed.), *The Application of Distributed Computing Technologies to Telecommunications Solutions. Proceedings of the IEEE Telecommunications Information Networking Architecture Conference, April 12-15*, (pp. 2-13). Oahu, Hawaii, USA.

Conallen, J. (2000). *Building Web Applications with UML*. Addison-Wesley Object Technology Series.

Emmerich, W. (2000). *Engineering Distributed Objects*. John Wiley & Sons, Ltd.

Fowler, M., with Kendall, S. (2000). *UML Distilled: A Brief Guide to the Standard Object Modeling Language*. [2nd edition]. Addison-Wesley Longman Inc.

ISO/IEC. (1993). JTC1/SC21/WG7 Draft recommendation X.902: Basic reference model of Open Distributed Processing Part 1: Overview and guide to use, International Organization for Standardization and International Electro-technical Committee, June.

Jaccheri, M.L., Picco, G.P. & Lago, P. (1998). Eliciting software process models with the E3 language. *ACM Transaction on Software Engineering and Methodology*, 7(4), 368-410.

Kruchten, P. (1999). *The Rational Unified Process An Introduction*. Addison-Wesley Longman Inc.

Lago P. & Canal, G. (2000). Architecture and Platforms I - Toward CORBA-based middleware. In T. Magedanz, A. Mullery, P. Rodier, S. Rao (Eds.), *On the Way to the Information Society*. IOS Press, ISBN 1-58603-007-8.

Lago, P., Canal, G., et al. (2000). Ubiquitous communication over IN and Internet. In *Proceedings of the ITU International Conference on Intelligence in Networks*, January 17-20, (pp. 35-40). Bordeaux, France.

OMG. (1999). UML notation guide. In *OMG Unified Modeling Language Specification*, version 1.3. Available: http://www.omg.org, June.

OMG. (1997). What is OMG-UML and why is it important?. June. Available: http://www.omg.org, on *UML Resource Page* [2000, February 28].

Rumbaugh, J., Blaha, M., Premerlani, W., Eddy F. & Lorensen W. (1991). *Object-Oriented Modeling and Design*. Prentice Hall.

Shaw, M. & Garlan, D. (1996). *Software Architecture: Perspectives on an Emerging Discipline*. Prentice Hall.

Software development methodology. (No date). In *The ESI Dictionary of Software*. Available: http://www.esi.es/Help/dictionary.html [2000, June 5].

The ACTS information window. Homepage. <http://www.infowin.org/ACTS/PROJECTS> [2000, August 21].

The Object Management Group. Homepage. <http://www.omg.org> [2000, August 19].

The OPEN Consortium. Homepage. <http://www.open.org.au> [2000, August 20].

The TINA Consortium (Telecommunications Information Networking Architecture). Homepage. <http://www.tinac.com/> [2000, July 15].

TINA-C (1996). Computational modeling concepts version 3.2. [On-line]. Available: http://www.tinac.com [2000, July 15].

TINA-C (1995). Information modeling concepts version 2.0. [On-line]. Available: http://www.tinac.com [2000, July 15].

TINA-C (1998). Ret reference points specifications version 1.0. [On-line]. Available: http://www.tinac.com [2000, July 15].

TINA-C (1997, June). Service architecture version 5.0. [On-line]. Available: http://www.tinac.com [2000, July 15].

TINA-C (1997, May). TINA business model and reference points, TINA-C Baseline v4.0. [On-line]. Available: http://www.tinac.com [2000, July 15].

The UML Resource Page. Available: http://www.omg.org/technology/uml/index.htm [2000, August 17].

Wieringa, R. (1998). A survey of structured and object-oriented software specification methods and techniques. In *ACM Computing Surveys*, 30(4), 459-527.

ENDNOTES

i Virtual Presence suggests the representation of users in the network as a virtual entity (the User Agent, UA) that maintains user customizations and acts accordingly, hence "in place of the user."

ii From a pictorial point of view, a vertical graphical notation represents composition as arcs that connect the aggregating entity with its aggregates, whereas horizontal notations represent aggregates directly inside the aggregating entity.

iii A component is a generic term representing groups of objects that are logically related. The term is then adapted to the context where it is used. For instance, in a computational model, a component identifies a computational object providing a set of interfaces, whereas in the deployment diagram, it represents a unit of distribution.

iv The model of the development process is given in the E3 process modeling language (see Jaccheri, Picco & Lago, 1998) in which graphical notation is self-explanatory.

Chapter X

Temporal OCL: Meeting Specification Demands for Business Components

Stefan Conrad
Ludwig-Maximilians-University Munich, Germany

Klaus Turowski
Otto-von-Guericke-University Magdeburg, Germany

INTRODUCTION

Compositional plug-and-play-like reuse of black box components requires sophisticated techniques to specify components, especially if we combine third-party components, which are traded on component markets, to customer-individual business application systems. As in established engineering disciplines like mechanical engineering or electrical engineering, we need a formal documentation of business components that becomes part of contractual agreements. Taking this problem as a starting point, we explain the general layered structure of software contracts for business components and show shortcomings of common specification approaches. Furthermore, we introduce a formal notation for the specification of business components that extends the Object Constraint Language (OCL) and that allows a broader use of the Unified Modeling Language (UML) with respect to the layered structure of software contracts for business components.

The remainder of the chapter is as follows. After providing background information in the next section, we discuss the necessity of a multi-level notation standard. Thereafter, we explain how the OCL can be used to specify business components. Taking this as a basis, we proceed to the main thrust of our chapter the temporal extension of OCL. Finally, we present our conclusions and give an outlook.

SOFTWARE CONTRACTS FOR BUSINESS COMPONENTS

Combining off-the-shelf software components offered by different vendors to customer-individual business application systems is a goal that is followed-up for a long time.

By achieving this goal, advantages of individually programmed software with those of standardized off-the-shelf software could come together. In this context, we need compositional reuse techniques. Compositional reuse is a special reuse technique as generative techniques or code and design scavenging (Sametinger, 1997, pp. 25-28). The emphasis on compositional reuse stems from our *guiding model,* which is the compositional plug-and-play-like reuse of black box components that are traded on a component market. In general, a guiding model is an ideal future state that might not completely be reached.

Corresponding to our guiding model, a company, which, e.g., needs new software for stock keeping, could buy a suitable software component on the component market and further integrate it into its business application system with little effort. Brown and Wallnau (1996, pp. 11-14) explain the steps that are generally necessary to do so, e.g., technical and semantic adaptation or composition. Expected improvements, which should come along with using software components, concern cost efficiency, quality, productivity, market penetration, market share, performance, interoperability, reliability or software complexity (cf. e.g., Orfali, Harkey, & Edwards, 1996, S. 29-32).

According to Fellner and Turowski (2000, pp. 3-4), we understand by a *component* a reusable, self-contained and marketable software part, which provides services through a well-defined interface, and which can be deployed in configurations unknown at development time. A *business component* is a component that implements a certain set of services out of a given business domain. Refer to Szyperski (1998, pp. 164-168) and Fellner and Turowski (2000) for an in depth discussion of various other component approaches given in literature.

To use business components according to our guiding model, it is necessary to standardize them (for a detailed discussion on standardizing business components cf. Turowski, 2000). Furthermore, we have to describe their interface and behavior in a consistent and unequivocal way. In short, we have to *specify* them. Specification becomes more and more important with respect to third-party composition of business components, since the specification might be the only available support for a composer who combines business components from different vendors to an application system.

Software contracts offer a good solution to meet the special requirements of specifying business components. Software contracts go back to MEYER, who introduced contracts as a concept in the *Eiffel* programming language. He called it *programming by contract* (Meyer, 1988) and extended it later to the concept of *design by contract* (Meyer, 1992). Furthermore, similar concepts are described in Wilkerson and Wirfs-Brock (1989) or Johnson ad Wirfs-Brock (1990).

Software contracts are obligations to which a service donator (e.g., a business component) and a service client agree.

Figure 1. Software Contract Levels

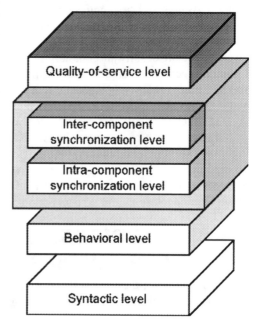

There, the service donator guarantees that:

- a service it offers, e.g., *calculate balance* or *determine demand*,
- under certain conditions, which have to be met by the service client, e.g., the provision of data necessary to process the service,
- is performed in a guaranteed quality, e.g., with a predetermined storage demand or with an agreed response time, and
- that the service has certain external characteristics, e.g., the specified interface.

Beugnard, Jézéquel, Plouzeau and Watkins (1999, pp. 38-40) describe a general model for software contracts for components with four tiers. The authors distinguish between syntactic, behavioral, synchronization and quality-of-service level. Business components need to be specified on each of these levels.

Figure 1 shows contract levels according to Turowski (1999). By subdividing the synchronization level into inter- and intra-component synchronization level, as an extension to Beugnard et al. (1999), this approach allows for an additional specification of a synchronization demand that exists between different business components.

At syntactic level basic agreements are concluded. Typical parts of these agreements concern names of services (offered by a business component); names of public accessible attributes, variables or constant values; specialized data types (in common based upon standardized data types); signatures of services as well as the declaration of error messages or exception signals. To do so, we use, e.g., programming languages or *Interface Definition Languages* (IDL) like the IDL that was proposed by the Object Management Group (OMG, 1998, S. 3.1-3.40). The resulting agreement guarantees that service client and service donator can communicate with each other. However, emphasis is put on enabling communication technically. Semantic aspects remain unconsidered.

Agreements at behavioral level serve as a closer description of a business component's behavior. They enhance the basic agreements of the syntactic level, which mainly describe the syntax of an interface. Agreements at syntactic level do not describe how a given business component acts in general or in borderline cases.

As an example, we could define an invariant condition for a business component *stock keeping* at behavioral level, which says that the reordering quantity for each (stock) account has to be higher than the minimum inventory level. Known approaches to specify behavior are based on approaches to *algebraic specification* of abstract data types (cf. e.g., Ehrig & Mahr, 1985). To describe behavior, the specification of an abstract data type is extended by conditions. These conditions describe the abstract data type's behavior in general (as *invariant conditions*) or at specific times (*pre-conditions* or *post-conditions*). In general, conditions are formulated as equations, and as axioms they become part of the specification of an abstract data type (Ehrig & Mahr, 1985). The *Object Constraint Language* (OCL) (Rational Software et al., 1997a) is an example for a widespread notation to specify facts at the behavioral level. It complements the *Unified Modeling Language* (UML) (Rational Software et al., 1997b).

Agreements at intra-component synchronization level regulate the sequence in which services of a specific business component may be invoked, and synchronization demand between its services. Here, e.g., we may lay down that a minimum inventory level has to be set before it is allowed to book on a (stock) account for the first time, or that it is not allowed to carry through more than one bookkeeping entry at the same time for the same account.

At inter-component synchronization level, we come to agreements that regulate the sequence in which services of *different* business components may be invoked. Here, e.g., we may define that a certain service, which belongs to a business component *shipping*, and which refers to a certain order, may only be processed after a service, which belongs to a business component *sales*, and which refers to the same order, has been processed at any time before. It is to note that the differentiation between intra- or inter-component synchronization level depends on the identification of business components, but not on their granularity. The granularity of a business component depends on the number of services it offers.

There exist various approaches to specify business components at the synchronization levels. These approaches base, e.g., on using *process algebras*, *process calculi* (cf. e.g., Hennessy, 1988) or on using *temporal logics* (cf. e.g., Alagar & Periyasamy, 1998, pp. 79-131). In addition, (semi-formal) graphical notations are in use. These are mostly graphical notations used in the context of business process modeling. Besides extended event-driven process chains (eEPC) (Keller, Nüttgens & Scheer, 1992, pp. 32-35) and approaches that use eEPC as a basis e.g., Rittgen, 1999), Petri net based notations are in use e.g., Jaeschke, Oberweis & Stucky, 1994). In particular, object-oriented software development methods like Rumbaugh, Blaha, Premerlani, Eddy & Lorensen (1991), Coleman (1993) or Booch (1994) provide such modeling means.

As an extension to functional characteristics, we have to describe *non-functional* characteristics of business components. Non-functional characteristics are specified at the quality-of-service level. Examples for these characteristics are the distribution of the response time of a service or its availability. (For further non-functional requirements and their definition cf. e.g., Jalote, 1997, pp. 73-158).

NECESSITY OF A MULTI-LEVEL NOTATION STANDARD

Using software contracts of the type explained in the previous section opens a way to a systematic specification of business components. Therefore, software contracts become a foundation for the third-party composition of business components, which is, conform to our guiding model. In an extreme case, employers of software components must be able to decide just with its specification about the way of its use.

Besides arranging the agreements' contents according to contract levels, in the context of systematic specification of business components, it is helpful to use a well-known and well-accepted formal notation, which can be used on more than one contract level. We call a notation *formal* if syntax and semantics of the notation are unequivocal and consistent. For this reason, formal notations seem to be particularly suited to specify software contracts, which must have these characteristics to be of use for third parties.

The OMG IDL, as part of the *Common Object Request Broker Architecture* (CORBA) (OMG, 1998), gains more and more acceptance as a standardized notation for the syntactic level. It uses a so-called *IDL compiler* to translate the interface's specification into concrete programming languages. UML together with the OCL is the addition (recommended by the OMG) to specify facts that belong to the behavioral level. Furthermore, the UML (together with the OCL) is especially recommended to specify components, e.g., Allen & Frost, 1998; or D'Souza & Wills, 1999). However, the OCL is only conditionally suited to specify facts at the synchronization level(s) as well. Taking this problem as a starting point, we propose a way to extend the OCL with some additional temporal operators to be able to formally specify facts at the synchronization levels as well.

However, we would like to point out that some authors tend to criticize upon the formal specification of (parts of) business application systems. Their main arguments are comparably higher effort and decreased general understandability. As an example for the weaknesses of formal approaches, they often discuss the algebraic specification of abstract data types (cf. e.g., Biethahn, Mucksch & Ruf, 1991, pp. 288-291) and the references given there. It remains to note that these authors also mention the very good separation of inside view and outside view as important advantages of the algebraic specification of abstract data types. This is a fact that is of growing importance with respect to the specification of black box components.

Operational and *verbal* specification are discussed as more practicable alternatives to algebraic specification. For operational specification, specification is done using declarative capabilities of programming languages (Ferstl & Sinz, 1998, pp. 293-294). This way, syntactic and behavioral level may be specified – dependent on the chosen programming language. For verbal specification, natural language is used. Due to its inherent fuzziness, natural languages are only conditionally suited to specify business components. For example, they may be used in addition to a formal specification or together with specialized methods like norm language reconstruction (Ortner, 1997).

USING OCL TO SPECIFY BUSINESS COMPONENTS

In the following, we explain an example to show how to use the OCL to specify business components on the behavioral level. In order to complete the example with respect to the contract levels given in an earlier section, we first explain the agreements necessary of the syntactic level. For the example, we use the OMG IDL as interface definition language (OMG, 1998, pp. 3.1-3.40).

Figure 2 shows examples for the specification of the interface of different business components at the syntactic level. The figure depicts parts of the interfaces of the business components *OrderProcessing*, *ProductionPlanning* and *ProductionControl*. The business components support business tasks from the area of production planning and control (PPC) (cf. e.g., Scheer, 1994).

First, the name of the service donator is defined with the keyword interface. This keyword creates a name space, which allows for an unequivocal definition of contained names. OrderProcessing::PrintInvoice, e.g., indicates that a service *PrintInvoice* should be invoked as part of a business component *OrderProcessing*.

In addition, we need to define data types, structured data types and exceptions, which we will not explain further in the context of our example.

In Figure 3 we extend our example to specify requirements at behavioral level by using the OCL (Rational Software et al., 1997a). The OCL is part of the UML. Furthermore, it was adopted by the OMG as standardized notation. With this, the OCL is the recommended extension of the OMG IDL to specify requirements at behavioral level.

First of all, we fix the context to which the respective specification refers. We mark the context by underlining it. The first condition in Figure 3, e.g., refers to the business component *OrderProcessing* as a whole. Conditions appear either as pre-conditions (keyword pre), as post condition (keyword post) or as invariant condition (no keyword).

For the purposes of our example, order processing encompasses the management of orders. The symbolic term *Order* references orders. Thus, the first invariant condition ensures that all orders, which are held by the business component *OrderProcessing*, are technically practicable.

The other requirements relate to the service *PrintInvoice*. For this reason, :: restricts the conditions' context. In addition, parameters may be enumerated to describe a service's behavior in more detail. Take, e.g., the service *PrintInvoice*. In order to specify it in more detail, we use the typed parameter *at*, which is of type *order*. (The types that we use in the example correspond to those defined in Figure 2.)

We use a pre-condition for the service *PrintInvoice*. It ensures that printing an invoice is allowed, if and only if the corresponding order was delivered before. Furthermore, there

Figure 2: Specification of Business Components at the Syntactic Level

```
interface OrderProcessing {
    ...
    struct OrderPosition {
        double Quantity;
        double PiecePrice;
        double Discount;
        ...
    };

    struct Order {
        ...
        boolean                  TechnicallyPracticable;
        boolean                  Delivered;
        double                   InvoiceAmount;
        double                   Discount;
        ...
        sequence <OrderPosition> OrderPositions;
    };
    ...
    void AcceptCustomerOrder(in Order a);
    void CancelOrder(in Order a);
    void PrintInvoice(in Order a);
    ...
};

interface ProductionPlanning {
    ...
    ProductionPlan RoughPlanning(in Period p);
    ...
};

interface ProductionControl {
    ...
    ProductionsPlan Scheduling(in Period p, in ProductionPlan pp);
    ...
};
```

Figure 3. Examples for the Specification of Business Components at Behavioral Level Using OCL

OrderProcessing
  self.Order->**forAll**(a:Order I a.TechnicallyPracticable = True)

OrderProcessing::PrintInvoice(at:Order)
  pre : **self**.Order->**exists**(a:Order I a = at **and** at.Delivered = True)
  post: at.InvoiceAmount = at.OrderPositions->**iterate**(p:Position; b:Amount = 0 I
                b + p.Quantity * p.PiecePrice * (1 − p.Discount)
) * (1 − at.Discount)

---

is a post-condition that explains in detail how the invoice amount was calculated.

On principle, all requirements of that kind are local to their respective contexts. The context may be the business component that offers the respective service. Therefore, we could suppose, that, e.g., pre-conditions for services, which are part of one single business component, may relate to services or objects of the same business component. However, business components are not isolated, but they collaborate with each other. For that reason, services and properties of other business components are published as interfaces. Thus, all published services and properties of other business components become part of the context of one particular business component. Furthermore, it is possible to refer to other business components while specifying pre-, post- and invariant conditions for a particular business component. Thus, characteristics of one particular business component may influence (or restrict) the behavior of other business components.

The possibility to describe characteristics that spread to different business components raises the question in which business component these kinds of characteristics have to be specified and whether it is necessary to specify these characteristics redundantly. However, these methodic aspects go beyond the concern of our contribution. For this reason we omit a detailed discussion of the mentioned aspects.

TEMPORAL EXTENSION OF OCL

In the previous section, we discussed in which way OCL could be employed for specifying business components. OCL seems to be an ideal approach to describing properties of business components declaratively and independent of specific implementations. Thereby, OCL can be used as an integral part of software contracts. OCL allows describing properties of states (which must hold for each single state of the system or component) and to describe pre- and post-conditions of services offered by a business component. By means of pre- and post-conditions, we can restrict the applicability (or executability) of services. Furthermore, the result of a service (the effect of its execution) can be specified by referring to the state of its invocation (using @pre).

Thus, introducing @pre and @post for explicitly referencing values of the states directly before and after a service execution allows one to specify a certain kind of condition. In the context of database systems, such conditions are usually called transitional integrity constraints (cf. e.g., Lipeck, Gertz & Saake, 1994). Following this comparison with integrity constraints in database systems, OCL, of course, also allows one to specify static integrity constraints (without @pre and @post). In this widely used classification of integrity constraints, the class of temporal constraints remains which cannot be described by means of OCL (except for a few cases where a translation into transitional constraints is possible). Temporal constraints do not only describe state transitions triggered by calling services, but also complete lifespans of objects or large parts of evolution within a business component.

Some restricted kinds of temporal constraints can also be described by means of state charts (being a part of UML for modeling behavior of objects) or other models of state machines, which basically correspond to regular expressions. However, certain temporal constraints cannot be represented by state machines at all, for instance the constraint that after executing a certain service A, another service B cannot be invoked unless a service C has been executed. Of course, we may find a state machine fulfilling this constraint, however, it is always a concrete implementation restricting the behavior of the system more than the temporal constraint requires. For our purposes, we do not want to specify certain implementation, but the general properties business components have to meet.

Temporal constraints are a means to declaratively describe properties of components at the interface level. The required view from outside onto components is essential why state machines are not the adequate level of description for us. A state machine's *operational* character is not appropriate for that level of specification especially in comparison to temporal logic's *descriptive* character that allows for significant reduction of specification effort. In consequence, we focus here on temporal integrity constraints as means of description.

Within the application area introduced before, we may have the following temporal integrity constraints as examples:

- A service *Scheduling* can only provide a result for a certain period of time, if a service *RoughPlanning* was already executed before for the same period.
- The execution of a service *PrintInvoice* for a certain order requires that exactly this order has been entered using a service *AcceptCustomerOrder* and that in-between this order has not been canceled by executing the service *CancelOrder*.

In addition we could require that after executing the service *AcceptCustomerOrder*, an invoice must be written for that order by means of the service *PrintInvoice* or that the order has eventually to be canceled by invoking the service *CancelOrder*.

For specifying such properties, it seems to be a good approach to extend OCL. This is motivated by the fact that OCL is a standardized notation based on a well-known declarative formalism having a clear (and formal) semantics. We do not intend to create an own specification formalism for temporal integrity constraints. Therefore, it is reasonable to look for a minimal but sufficiently expressive extension of OCL being consistent with OCL.

The basic possibilities to describe temporal properties are depicted in Figure 4. On the time axis the different states of an object (which is subject of our description) at different instants of time are given. Starting from the current state of this object, different statements can be made about this object. For instance, we can describe properties of the state directly before or after the current one (by means of the temporal operator *previous* and *next*, resp.). Using the (future tense temporal) operator *always,* we can state properties of all future states. The current state has been reached by executing all state changing operations (services in our context) in their temporal order, starting with the initial state of the object (the initial state is usually given when creating the object). The temporal distances between all pairs of consecutive states need not be the same; in this way, we only use an abstract notion of discrete time representing the order of changes.

A large number of approaches to describing such temporal properties is based on

Figure 4. State Based Specification Using (Linear) Temporal Logics

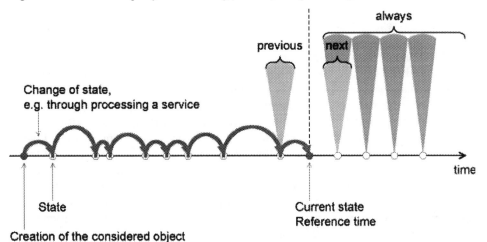

temporal logics (for a survey see, e.g., Manna & Pnueli, 1992, or Emerson, 1990). In Lipeck and Saake (1987) a temporal logic for formulating temporal integrity constraints was developed which then has been adapted and extended for the object-oriented modeling language TROLL (Jungclaus, Saake, Hartmann & Sernadas, 1996). The temporal operators by which we extend OCL and for which all semantic foundations can also be found (in Lipeck & Saake, 1987) are as follows:

Past tense temporal operators:

* sometime_past _
  Starting from the current state (i.e., the state which is currently observed) sometime in the past _ must have been valid (i.e., there is a past state in which _ held).

* always_past _
  Starting from the current state _ was valid always in the past (i.e., in all past states).

* _ always_since_last _
  Starting from the last state in which _ held for the last time, _ held in all states up to the current one.

* _ sometime_since_last _
  Since the state in which _ held for the last time there was a state (before the current state) in which _ held.

Future tense temporal operators:

* sometime _
  Starting from the current state, there will be (at least) one future state in which _ will be valid.

* always _
  Starting from the current state, in all future states _ will hold.

* _ until _
  Starting from the current state, in all future state _ will hold until there is a state in which _ is fulfilled.

* _ before _
  Starting from the current state, there will be a future state in which _ will be valid before a state will be reached in which _ will hold.

Besides these past tense and future tense temporal operators which are always interpreted relative to a current state, we need a special operator for referring to the initial state (of the system or business component):

- initially _

In the initial state _ holds.

By means of this operator, it is possible to specify the initial state of the system (i.e., to provide initial values for some state variables).

Before we consider examples for temporal constraints in our application area using the temporal extension of OCL, the necessity of offering past tense and future tense temporal operators has to be discussed. Taking a puristic view one could claim that one kind of temporal operators (i.e., past tense or future tense) would be sufficient. Although this is already not completely right with regard to expressive power, the main reason for having both kinds of operators is a methodical one. Using each kind of temporal operators in an adequate way essentially improves the readability and, thereby, the comprehensibility of specifications. For instance, pre-conditions for services (i.e., constraints restricting the applicability of services) should be formulated only by using past tense temporal operators. It is obvious that the execution of a service must not depend on future states.

By allowing post-conditions to include future tense temporal operators, we slightly change or extend the notion of post-condition. In the literature, and in particular for object-oriented languages, the notion of post-condition refers usually to a property fulfilled by the state yielded by executing a method. A temporal logic formula as post-condition also refers to other future states. Nevertheless, from a logical point of view, this property formulated in temporal logic can also be considered as a property of that state.

A further important issue is that the grammar of OCL has to be extended corresponding to the temporal operators we add. Considering the grammar for OCL given in Rational Software et al. (1997a, pp. 31-32), we only need very few minor changes and additions, in detail these are as follows:

- An additional alternative temporalExpression is introduced into the rule for relationalExpression.
- For temporalExpression a rule is added in which temporal expressions are constructed in two different ways using either a unary temporal operator (like always) or a binary one (like until).
- In two additional rules the unary and binary temporal operators are defined (unaryTemporalOperator and BinaryTemporalOperator).

The complete extended grammar is given as in the appendix.

Obviously, our extension seamlessly fits into the existing grammar for OCL without requiring significant changes. Thereby, integration into already existing tools supporting OCL should not cause severe problems.

Figure 5 shows formulations of the temporal (integrity) constraints introduced verbally at the beginning of this section. The temporal extension of OCL sketched before is now used to express these constraints. The first statement is a pre-condition for executing the service *Scheduling* for a certain period of time. It is required that for the same period of time a service *RoughPlanning* was already executed sometime before. Here, we assume that the service *RoughPlanning* provided by another business component is known in the component *ProductionPlanning* by declaring its interface description.

The second statement in Figure 5 is a pre-condition for the service *PrintInvoice* in the business component *OrderProcessing*. This pre-condition expresses that before this service can be invoked, the service *AcceptCustomerOrder* must have been executed for the

Figure 5: Specification of Temporal Properties Using the Extended OCL

ProductionPlanning::Scheduling(p:Period)
  pre : **sometime_past**(RoughPlanning(p))

OrderProcessing::PrintInvoice(at:Order)
  pre : **sometime_past**(AcceptCustomerOrder(at)) **and**
      not(CancelOrder(at) **sometime_since_last** AcceptCustomerOrder(at))

OrderProcessing::AcceptCustomerOrder(at:Order)
  post: **sometime**(PrintInvoice(at)) **or sometime**(CancelOrder(at))

---

same order and that since that acceptance of this order, no cancellation of this order has occurred (by executing the service *CancelOrder*).

The third temporal property is a post-condition for the service *AcceptCustomerOrder*. In addition to the previous statement, it is required that after accepting an order by a customer, sometime later an invoice has to be printed for exactly this order by executing the service *PrintInvoice* or that this order must eventually be cancelled by executing the service *CancelOrder*.

The second and third statements express different properties. On the one hand, the pre-condition for *PrintInvoice* does not forbid that the service *AcceptCustomerOrder* can be executed without that an invoice will ever be printed or a cancellation will ever occur for that order. On the other hand, the post-condition for *AcceptCustomerOrder* does not exclude the execution of the service *PrintInvoice* for a certain order although this order was never accepted by means of the service *AcceptCustomerOrder*.

Finally, we have to discuss the issue of formal semantics for this extension of OCL by temporal operators. As already mentioned, the semantic foundations (i.e., a complete definition of the formal semantics for a temporal logic with past tense and future tense temporal operators) are given, for instance in Lipeck and Saake (1987) such that we refrain from repeating those definitions here. In contrast to Lipeck and Saake (1987), we did not introduce the operators *next* (referring to the subsequent state) and *previous* (referring to the previous state). This is due to the well-known semantic problems, which are caused by these two operators in case of composing independently specified systems of components. In general, we implicitly obtain concurrent processes in the composed system where no global synchronization of local states is given. As a consequence, considering a common global state, *next* operators in the specifications of different components may for instance refer to different local states which do not necessarily belong to one global state (cf. also Conrad, 1995, or Mokkedem & Méry, 1994). Although there are several proposals for solving these kind of problems (besides the references mentioned before see also Conrad, 1996; Sørensen, Hansen & Løvengreen, 1994), they all are not yet developed such that a full semantic compositionality of specifications of components is given without causing methodical restrictions in specifying single components.

CONCLUSIONS AND OUTLOOK

The usage of business components offers a possibility to customize business application systems incorporating the advantages of standardized software and individually developed software. However, this requires the standardization of business components and, in consequence, a specification of these components. After having derived basic requirements for specifications of business components from investigating the paradigm of software contracts, we presented a proposal for extending OCL by temporal operators. Based on a widespread notational standard, it is now possible to specify across several software contract levels, avoiding a change of methods and respecting the particular requirements of business components.

It should be noted that our proposal, in contrast to OCL itself, is not standardized and, therefore, it has the same status as other proprietary notations or extension of notations. Considering the fact that such extensions by temporal properties are indispensable for specifying business components, our proposal might be an essential first step towards a later standardization.

We obtain first practical experiences towards practicality and usability of our approach in the context of in-house projects, which concerned the development of business components for the application domain production planning and control. After an introductory tutorial, the notation's extension was well accepted by the project's participants. Problems that arose had their reason basically in a wrong understanding of dependencies of the application domain. Consequently, in some cases we could observe a not adequate specification.

REFERENCES

Alagar, V. S., & Periyasamy, K. (1998). *Specification of Software Systems*. New York: Springer.

Allen, P., & Frost, S. (1998). *Component-Based Development for Enterprise Systems: Applying the Select Perspective*. Cambridge: Cambridge University Press.

Beugnard, A., Jézéquel, J.-M., Plouzeau, N., & Watkins, D. (1999). Making components contract aware. *IEEE Computer, 32*(7), 38-44.

Biethahn, J., Mucksch, H., & Ruf, W. (1991). *Ganzheitliches Informationsmanagement: Daten-und Entwicklungsmanagement*. (Vol. 2). München: Oldenbourg.

Booch, G. (1994). *Object-Oriented Analysis and Design with Applications*. (2 ed.). Reading: Addison-Wesley.

Brown, A. W., & Wallnau, K. C. (1996). Engineering of Component-Based Systems. In A. W. Brown (Ed.), *Component-Based Software Engineering: Selected Papers from the Software Engineering Institute* (pp. 7-15). Los Alamitos, California: IEEE Computer Society Press.

Coleman, D. (1993). *Object-Oriented Development: The Fusion Method*. Upper Saddle River: Prentice Hall.

Conrad, S. (1995). *Compositional Object Specification and Verification*. Paper presented at the International Conference on Software Quality (ICSQ'95), Maribor.

Conrad, S. (1996). A Basic Calculus for Verifying Properties of Interacting Objects. *Data and Knowledge Engineering, 18*(2), 119-146.

D'Souza, D. F., & Wills, A. C. (1999). *Objects, Components, and Frameworks with UML: The Catalysis Approach*. Reading: Addison-Wesley.

Ehrig, H., & Mahr, B. (1985). *Fundamentals of Algebraic Specification 1: Equations and Initial Semantics*. Berlin: Springer.

Emerson, E. A. (1990). Temporal and Modal Logic. In J. V. Leeuwen (Ed.), *Handbook of Theoretical Computer Science* (Vol. B, pp. 995-1072). Amsterdam: Elsevier Science

Publishers, North-Holland.

Fellner, K., & Turowski, K. (2000). *Classification Framework for Business Components.* Paper presented at the 33rd Annual Hawaii International Conference on System Sciences, Maui, Hawaii.

Ferstl, O. K., & Sinz, E. J. (1998). *Grundlagen der Wirtschaftsinformatik.* (3 ed.). (Vol. 1). München: Oldenbourg.

Hennessy, M. (1988). *Algebraic Theory of Processes.* Cambridge: MIT Press.

Jaeschke, P., Oberweis, A., & Stucky, W. (1994). *Deriving Complex Structured Objects for Business Process Modelling.* Paper presented at the Entity-Relationship Approach ER'94, Manchester.

Jalote, P. (1997). *An Integrated Approach to Software Engineering.* New York: Springer.

Johnson, R. E., & Wirfs-Brock, R. J. (1990). Surveying Current Research in Object-Oriented Design. *Communications of the ACM, 33*(9), 104-124.

Jungclaus, R., Saake, G., Hartmann, T., & Sernadas, C. (1996). Troll: A Language for Object-Oriented Specification of Information Systems. *ACM Transactions on Information Systems, 14*(2), 175-211.

Keller, G., Nüttgens, M., & Scheer, A.-W. (1992). Planungsinseln Vom Konzept zum integrierten Informationsmodell. *HMD, 29*(168), 25-39.

Lipeck, U. W., Gertz, M., & Saake, G. (1994). Transitional Monitoring of Dynamic Integrity Contraints. *Bulletin of the IEEE Technical Committee on Data Engineering, 17*(2), 38-42.

Lipeck, U. W., & Saake, G. (1987). Monitoring Dynamic Integrity Constraints Based on Temporal Logic. *Information Systems, 12*(3), 255-269.

Manna, Z., & Pnueli, A. (1992). *The Temporal Logic of Reactive and Concurrent Systems: Specification.* (Vol. 1). Berlin: Springer.

Meyer, B. (1988). *Object-Oriented Software Construction.* Englewood Cliffs, NJ: Prentice Hall.

Meyer, B. (1992). Applying, "Design by Contract." *IEEE Computer, 25*(10), 40-51.

Mokkedem, A., & Méry, D. (1994). *A Stuttering Closed Temporal Logic for Modular Reasoning About Concurrent Programs.* Paper presented at the First International Conference on Temporal Logic (ICTL'94), Bonn.

OMG (Ed.). (1998). *The Common Object Request Broker: Architecture and Specification (Revision 2.2).* OMG.

Orfali, R., Harkey, D., & Edwards, J. (1996). *The Essential Distributed Objects Survival Guide.* New York: John Wiley & Sons.

Ortner, E. (1997). *Methodenneutraler Fachentwurf.* Stuttgart: Teubner.

Rational Software, Microsoft, Hewlett-Packard, Oracle, Sterling Software, MCI Systemhouse, Unisys, ICON Computing, IntelliCorp, i-Logix, IBM, ObjecTime, Platinum Technology, Ptech, Taskon, Reich Technologies, & Softeam. (1997a). *Object Constraint Language Specification: Version 1.1, 1 September 1997.* Available: http://www.rational.com/uml [1999, 04-17].

Rational Software, Microsoft, Hewlett-Packard, Oracle, Sterling Software, MCI Systemhouse, Unisys, ICON Computing, IntelliCorp, i-Logix, IBM, ObjecTime, Platinum Technology, Ptech, Taskon, Reich Technologies, & Softeam. (1997b). *UML Notation Guide: Version 1.1, 1 September 1997.* Available: http://www.rational.com/uml [1999, 04-17].

Rittgen, P. (1999). *Objektorientierte Analyse mit EMK.* Paper presented at the Modellierung betrieblicher Informationssysteme (MobIS'99), Bamberg.

Rumbaugh, J., Blaha, M., Premerlani, W., Eddy, F., & Lorensen, W. (1991). *Object-Oriented Modeling and Design*. Englewood Cliffs, NY: Prentice Hall.

Sametinger, J. (1997). *Software Engineering with Reusable Components*. Berlin: Springer.

Scheer, A.-W. (1994). *Business Process Engineering: Reference Models for Industrial Enterprises*. (2 ed.). Berlin: Springer.

Sørensen, M. U., Hansen, O. E., & Løvengreen, H. H. (1994). *Combining Temporal Specification Techniques*. Paper presented at the First International Conference on Temporal Logic (ICTL'94), Bonn.

Szyperski, C. (1998). *Component Software: Beyond Object-Oriented Programming*. (2 ed.). Harlow: Addison-Wesley.

Turowski, K. (1999). *Standardisierung von Fachkomponenten: Spezifikation und Objekte der Standardisierung*. Paper presented at the 3. Meistersingertreffen, Schloss Thurnau.

Turowski, K. (2000). Establishing Standards for Business Components. In K. Jakobs (Ed.), *Information Technology Standards and Standardisation: A Global Perspective* (pp. 131-151). Hershey, PA: Idea Group Publishing.

Wilkerson, B., & Wirfs-Brock, R. J. (1989). A Responsibility-Driven Approach. *SIGPLAN Notices, 24*(10), 72-76.

APPENDIX (GRAMMAR OF TEMPORAL OCL)

expression	:=	logicalExpression
ifExpression	:=	"**if**" expression
		"**then**" expression
		"**else**" expression
		"**endif**"
logicalExpression	:=	relationalExpression
		(logicalOperator relationalExpression)*
relationalExpression	:=	temporalExpression
		| additiveExpression
		(relationalOperator additiveExpression)?
temporalExpression	:=	unaryTemporalOperator logicalExpression
		| logicalExpression
		binaryTemporalOperator logicalExpression
additiveExpression	:=	multiplicativeExpression
		(addOperator multiplicativeExpression)*
multiplicativeExpression	:=	unaryExpression
		(multiplyOperator unaryExpression)*
unaryExpression	:=	(unaryOperator postfixExpression)
		| postfixExpression
postfixExpression	:=	primaryExpression (("." | "->") featureCall)*
primaryExpression	:=	literalCollection
		| literal
		| pathName timeExpression? qualifier?
		featureCallParameters?
		| "(" expression ")"
		| ifExpression
featureCallParameters	:=	"(" (declarator)? (actualParameterList)? ")"

```
literal                  :=   <STRING> | <number> | "#" <name>
enumerationType          :=   "enum" "{" "#" <name> ( "," "#" <name> )* "}"
simpleTypeSpecifier      :=   pathTypeName
                              | enumerationType
literalCollection        :=   collectionKind "{" expressionListOrRange? "}"
expressionListOrRange    :=   expression
                              ( ( "," expression )+
                              | ( ".." expression )
                              )?
featureCall              :=   pathName timeExpression? qualifiers?
                              featureCallParameters?
qualifiers               :=   "[" actualParameterList "]"
declarator               :=   <name> ( "," <name> )*
                              ( ":" simpleTypeSpecifier )? "|"
pathTypeName             :=   <typeName> ( "::" <typeName> )*
pathName                 :=   ( <typeName> | <name> )
                              ( "::" ( <typeName> | <name> ) )*
timeExpression           :=   "@" <name>
actualParameterList      :=   expression ( "," expression )*
logicalOperator          :=   "and" | "or" | "xor" | "implies"
collectionKind           :=   "Set" | "Bag" | "Sequence" | "Collection"
relationalOperator       :=   "=" | ">" | "<" | ">=" | "<=" | "<>"
addOperator              :=   "+" | "-"
multiplyOperator         :=   "*" | "/"
unaryOperator            :=   "-" | "not"
typeName                 :=   "A"-"Z" ( "a"-"z" | "0"-"9" | "A"-"Z" | "_")*
name                     :=   "a"-"z" ( "a"-"z" | "0"-"9" | "A"-"Z" | "_")*
number                   :=   "0"-"9" ("0"-"9")*
string                   :=   """ ( ( (~["""","\\","\n","\r"])
                                    | ("\\"
                                             ( ["n","t","b","r","f","\\",""","\""]
                                             | ["0"-"7"] ( ["0"-"7"] )?
                                             | ["0"-"3"] ["0"-"7"] ["0"-"7"]
                                    )
                                  )
                                )*
                              """

unaryTemporalOperator    :=   "sometime_past" | "always_past"
                              | "sometime" | "always" | "initially"
binaryTemporalOperator   :=   "sometime_since_last" | "always_since_last"
                              | "until" | "before"
```

Chapter XI

Supplementing UML with Concepts from ORM

Terry Halpin
Microsoft Corporation, USA

The Unified Modeling Language (UML) is useful for designing object-oriented code, but is less suitable for conceptual data analysis. Its process-centric use-cases provide an inadequate basis for specifying data-centric class diagrams, and the UML graphical language suffers from incompleteness, inconsistency and unnecessary complexity. For example, multiplicity constraints can lead to unexpected problems when extended to n-ary associations, the constraint primitives are not optimized for orthogonality or expressibility, and the graphical language does not lend itself readily to verbalization and multiple instantiation for validating models with domain experts. This chapter examines some of these defects, and shows how to compensate for them by augmenting UML with concepts and techniques from the Object Role Modeling (ORM) approach. It highlights the potential of "data use cases" for seeding the data model, using verbalization of facts and rules with positive and negative examples to facilitate validation of business rules. The following approaches are suggested as possible ways to exploit the benefits of fact-orientation: use ORM for the conceptual analysis then map the ORM model to UML; use UML supplemented by informal population diagrams and user-defined constraints; enhance the UML metamodel to better support business rules.

INTRODUCTION

Adopted in 1997 by the Object Management Group (OMG) as a language for object-oriented (OO) analysis and design, the *Unified Modeling Language (UML)* has become popular for designing OO program code. It is well suited for this purpose, covering both data and behavioral aspects, and allowing OO-implementation details to be directly expressed (e.g. attribute visibility and directional navigation across associations). Although not yet widely used for designing database applications, UML can be used for this task also, since

good

its class diagrams effectively provide an extended Entity-Relationship (ER) notation that can be annotated with database constructs (e.g., key declarations).

Late in 1999, UML version 1.3 was approved and work began on version 1.4, with a major revision (2.0) planned for some years later. Though not yet a standard, UML has been proposed for standardization by the International Standards Organization (ISO), and approval seems likely by 2001 (Kobryn, 1999). Further background on UML may be found in its specification (OMG, 1999), a simple introduction (Fowler, 1997) or a detailed treatment (Booch et al., 1999; Rumbaugh et al., 1999). In-depth discussions of UML for database design are provided by Muller (1999) and, with a slightly different notation, by Blaha and Premerlani (1998).

The UML notation includes hundreds of symbols, from which various diagrams may be constructed to model different perspectives of an application (e.g., use case diagrams, class diagrams, object diagrams, statecharts, activity diagrams, sequence diagrams, collaboration diagrams, component diagrams and deployment diagrams). This chapter focuses on conceptual data modeling, so considers only the static structure (class and object) diagrams. Class diagrams are used for the data model, and object diagrams provide a limited means to discuss data populations.

Although useful for designing object-oriented code, UML is less suitable for developing and validating a conceptual data model with domain experts. Its use-cases are process-centric, and in practice the move from use cases to class diagrams is often little more than a black art. Moreover, incompleteness in the UML notation prevents many common business rules from being diagrammed.

It is our belief that these defects are best remedied by using fact-oriented modeling as a precursor to object-oriented modeling in UML. *Object-Role Modeling (ORM)* is the main exemplar of the fact-oriented approach, and though less popular than UML, is used productively in many countries and is supported by CASE tools from a number of companies, including Ascaris and Microsoft. For data modeling purposes, ORM's graphical notation is more expressive and orthogonal than UML's, its models and queries are more semantically stable, and its design procedures fully exploit the potential of data examples using both verbalization and multiple instantiation to help capture and validate business rules with domain experts.

This chapter identifies various flaws in the UML graphical language and discusses how fact-orientation can be used to augment the object-oriented approach of UML. It shows how verbalization of facts and rules, with positive and negative examples, facilitates validation of business rules, and compares rule visualizations in UML and ORM on the basis of specified modeling language criteria. The following three approaches are suggested as possible ways to exploit the benefits of fact-orientation: (1) use ORM for the initial conceptual information analysis and map the ORM model to a UML class diagram; (2) use UML in its current form, supplemented by informal population diagrams and user-defined constraints; (3) correct and extend the UML metamodel to better support the specification and validation of business rules.

The rest of this chapter is structured as follows. The next section provides a comparative overview of UML class diagrams and ORM, based on linguistic design criteria. The following section discusses verbalization issues related to multiplicity constraints on binary associations. The subsequent section illustrates how "data use cases" can be used to guide the data modeling process as a joint activity between modeler and domain expert. In so doing, it also exposes problems with UML multiplicity constraints on *n*-ary associations, and highlights the need for a richer graphical constraint notation. The conclusion summarizes how the lessons learned from fact-orientation can be used to augment UML, identifies areas of future research and lists references for further reading.

ORM, UML AND
CONCEPTUAL LANGUAGE CRITERIA

Object-Role Modeling is a conceptual modeling method, so-called because it views the world as a set of *objects* (entities or values) that play *roles* (parts in relationships, which may be unary, binary or longer). For example, you are now playing the role of being alive (a unary relationship involving just you), and also the role of reading this chapter (a binary relationship between you and this chapter). An entity in ORM corresponds to an object in UML, a value in ORM corresponds to a data value in UML, and a role in ORM corresponds to an association-end in UML, except that ORM allows unary associations.

The main structural difference between ORM and UML is that ORM eschews attributes in its base models whereas UML models typically make extensive use of attributes. Implicitly, attributes may be associated with roles in a relationship. For example, Employee.birthdate is modeled in ORM as the fact type: *Employee was born on Date*. Overviews of ORM may be found in Halpin (1998a, 1998b) and a detailed treatment in Halpin (1995). The ORM notation for information modeling uses only a handful of symbols, readily mastered by UML modelers. Although ORM-based proposals for process/ behavioral modeling exist (e.g., ter Hofstede, 1993), they are ignored here since none are widely adopted.

Drawing upon lessons from linguistics and semiotics, the ORM language was designed from the ground up to meet the following design criteria: expressibility; clarity; learnability (hence orthogonality, parsimony and convenience); semantic stability (minimize the impact of change); semantic relevance (scope views to just the currently relevant task); validation mechanisms; abstraction mechanisms and formal foundation. (Some background and discussion on these principles may be found in Barker, 1990; Bloesch & Halpin, 1996; ter Hofstede et al., 1993; ISO, 1982). Practical trade-offs between design criteria can arise, e.g., expressibility-tractability (Levesque, 1984) and parsimony-convenience (Halpin, 1999). In this chapter, our focus is on validation mechanisms, expressibility and orthogonality.

The feature of ORM that receives the most criticism is its attribute-free nature (i.e., no attributes are used in its base models). This omission was deliberately designed to avoid fuzzy and unstable distinctions about whether a feature should be modeled as an attribute or an association (Falkenberg, 1976). Although this advantage is enjoyed by some other semantic modeling approaches, such as OSM (Embley, 1998), the price paid is that attribute-free diagrams usually consume more space. A detailed argument to justify this expense can be found in Halpin (2000). In short, the main advantages are that all facts and rules can be easily verbalized as sentences, all data structures can be easily populated with multiple instances, the metamodel is simplified, and models and queries are stabler since they are immune to changes that reshape attributes as associations. Finally the compactness of attribute-based models can still be enjoyed when desired, by deriving them as views (tools can automate this).

For reference purposes, Table 1 summarizes the main correspondences between conceptual data constructs in ORM and UML. There is no space here to discuss all of these features, but some examples are given later, and complementary discussions can be found

Table 1. Comparison of the Main Conceptual Data Constructs in ORM and UML

ORM	UML
Data structures:	**Data structures:**
object type: entity type;	object class
value type	data type
— { use association }	*attribute*
unary association	— { use Boolean attribute }
2+-ary association	2+-ary association
objectified association (nesting)	association class
co-reference	qualified association †
Predefined Constraints:	**Predefined Constraints:**
internal uniqueness	multiplicity of ..1 †
external uniqueness	— { use qualified association } †
simple mandatory role	multiplicity of 1+.. †
disjunctive mandatory role	—
frequency: internal; external	multiplicity †; —
value	enumeration, and textual
subset and equality	subset †
exclusion	xor †
subtype link and definition	subclass discriminator etc. †
ring constraints	—
join constraints	—
object cardinality	class multiplicity
— { use uniqueness and ring } †	aggregation/composition
User-defined textual constraints	**User-defined textual constraints**

† = incomplete coverage of corresponding concept

in the references (Halpin, 1995, 1999, 2000; Halpin & Bloesch, 1999). An uncommented "—" indicates no predefined support for the corresponding concept, and "†" indicates incomplete support. This comparison indicates that ORM's built-in symbols provide greater expressive power for capturing conceptual constraints in data models.

Because of its attribute-free nature and its orthogonality, ORM achieves this greater expressibility without adding complexity. For example, ORM includes a disjunctive mandatory role (inclusive-or) constraint to restrict instances of an object type to play at least one of a set of roles (e.g., each Employee must have a SocialSecurityNumber or a TaxFileNumber or both). ORM also includes an exclusion constraint that may apply between compatible role sequences (e.g., no Person who authors a Book may review that Book). In ORM, an exclusion constraint between single roles can be orthogonally combined with an inclusive-or constraint to form an exclusive-or constraint (e.g., each Employee is assigned a TransitPass or a ParkingBay but not both). In contrast, UML has an exclusive-or constraint, but no inclusive-or and no general exclusion constraint.

In contrast to UML, ORM allows constraints to be applied wherever they make sense. For example, subset constraints may apply between compatible role sequences, not just associations (e.g., a Person has a SecondName only if that Person has a FirstName; a

Student obtains a Rating for a Course only if that Student is enrolled in that Course). Ring constraints are logical constraints on ring associations. For example, "no Company acquired itself" and "if $Person_1$ is the father of $Person_2$ then it cannot be that $Person_2$ is the father of $Person_1$," are examples of irreflexive and asymmetric ring constraints respectively. Join constraints apply to roles from different predicates that are conceptually joined (e.g., each Ambassador who is assigned to a Country also speaks a Language that is spoken in that Country).

Even though the additional constraints in ORM often arise in practical applications, our experience suggests that UML modelers typically omit these constraints unless they are very experienced. UML and ORM both permit users to add other constraints and derivation rules in a textual language of their choice. UML suggests OCL (Object Constraint Language) for this purpose (Warmer & Kleppe, 1999), but does not mandate its use. Although OCL is a formal and hence unambiguous language, its mathematical syntax renders it unsuitable for validating rules with non-technical domain experts. ORM's conceptual query language, ConQuer (Bloesch & Halpin, 1996, 1997; Halpin & Bloesch, 1998), is both formal and readily understandable to non-technical users. Although textual languages are needed for completeness, it is much easier for a modeler to think of a rule in the first place if it is part of his/her graphical rule language. Although the UML notation can be extended to cater for the extra ORM constraints, some of these require either radical surgery or awkward changes to the UML metamodel (see later).

BINARY ASSOCIATIONS, MULTIPLICITY AND VERBALIZATION

Domain experts or subject matter experts are people who understand (at least collectively) the universe of discourse (UoD) or application domain. Hence clear communication between modelers and domain experts is critical in the conceptual analysis phase. Domain experts are often technically unskilled in modeling notations, so business rules should be verbalized in natural language for model validation. This section discusses verbalization of binary associations and their associated multiplicity constraints, and lays some groundwork for the next section's critique of UML's application of these constraints to *n*-ary associations.

Consider an application domain where each person must drive a car, and each car is driven by zero or more people. For a given state of the database, the *population* of a type is the set of instances of that type that are present in the database. For this UoD, each population of the drives association is a total function (mandatory $n:1$ relation) from the population of Person to the population of Car. A significant sample population is displayed in the instance diagram at the top of Figure 1.

Figure 1(a) depicts this binary association in UML. Classes are depicted by named rectangles, and *binary associations* by connecting lines. The association ends correspond to roles in ORM, and may be given a role name (e.g., "carDriven"). The association itself may be given a name (e.g., "Drives") as well as a direction marker to indicate the direction in which the association should be read. If an association name is supplied, the association can be verbalized as a sentence type (e.g., Person drives Car).

The association roles (ends) may be adorned with *multiplicity constraints* that specify the possible multiplicities. For example, "1..*" means one or more (at least one), "0..1" means zero or one (at most one), "1" abbreviates "1..1" (exactly one) and "*" abbreviates "0..*" (zero or more). Both UML and ORM allow multiplicities to include combinations of numbers and number ranges (e.g., "1, 2, 3, 5..100"), even if these would be rarely used.

For binary associations in UML, the number of times an object must play the role at one end of an association is marked at the *opposite end* of the association. Reading left-to-right, each person is associated with 1 (exactly one) car in this association. Hence the multiplicity constraint on the Car role may be *verbalized*: **each** Person drives **exactly one** Car. Reading right-to-left, each car is associated with * (zero or more) persons in this association. The "*" constraint on the Person role may thus be verbalized: **it is possible that more than one** Person drives **the same** Car. A role's default multiplicity is "*" (i.e., or "0..*").

The previous verbalizations were developed by us for use in ORM, and rely on singular terms being used for class names (e.g., "Person" not "Persons") for natural phrasing. Words shown in bold type have formal meaning, allow-

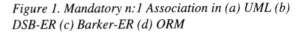

Figure 1. Mandatory n:1 Association in (a) UML (b) DSB-ER (c) Barker-ER (d) ORM

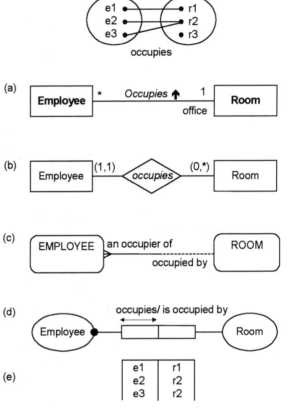

ing an ORM tool to automatically generate an ORM diagram from the textual formulation of the association and its constraints. Although UML does not have any formal verbalization, a request for proposal has been issued for a "Human Usable Textual Notation," so something like this could eventually be added to UML. ORM's verbalization patterns could provide a good basis for extending UML in this way.

Figure 1(b) depicts the same association in an ER notation proposed by Dey, Storey and Barron (1999) for work with binary and n-ary (n > 2) associations. In this notation, which we'll call "DSB-ER" after its authors, entity types are depicted as named rectangles and binary relationships are depicted as named diamonds, as in Chen's original ER (Chen, 1976). The parenthesized constraints are called *participation constraints*. The association and its constraints may be verbalized as before. As with some other versions of ER, this notation indicates the minimum and maximum number of times each instance of an object type plays a given role by marking the constraint on that role itself ("the *immediate role*"). Hence the "(1, 1)" and "(0, *)" on the left and right roles correspond to UML's "1" and "*" placed on the right and left roles respectively (the opposite).

Figure 1(c) shows the same example in the ER notation popularized by Richard Barker (1990) and Oracle Corporation. Unlike UML and DSB-ER, but like ORM, the Barker notation supports *forward and inverse readings* of binary relationships. This useful practice facilitates reading in different directions around a schema, and often leads to improved verbalization of rules. Some UML users have added their own notations in this regard, such as appending reverse readings in parentheses to the association name (Eriksson & Penker, 2000), but this is not included in the UML specification. We recommend that UML metamodel be extended to allow inverse readings for binary associations, and to provide a standard syntax for their display.

Unlike the UML and DSB-ER notations, Barker-ER uses *separate notations for minimum and maximum cardinalities*. Minimum cardinalities of 0 (optional) or above (mandatory) are specified as optional and mandatory roles. A role that is *optional* for its entity type is designated by a dashed line-half, and a role that is *mandatory* is depicted by a solid line-half: these are specified on the near role. A maximum cardinality of 1 is the default (no explicit mark), and a maximum cardinality of many is depicted as a crows-foot: these are shown on the far role as in UML.

Barker (1990) suggests the following naming scheme for relationships. Let *A R B* denote an infix relationship *R* from entity type *A* to entity type *B*. Name *R* in such a way that each of the following four patterns results in an English sentence: **each** *A* (**must** | **may**) **be** *R* (**one and only one** *B* | **one or more** *B-plural-form*). Use "must" or "may" when the first role is mandatory or optional respectively. Use "one and only one" or "one or more" when the cardinality on the second role is one or many respectively. Although awkward for verbalizing relationship types or instances, this scheme enables cardinality constraints to be verbalized in a natural way. For example, the constraints in Figure 1(c) verbalize as: **each** Person **must be** a driver of **one and only one** Car; **each** Car **may be** driven by **one or more** Persons. This verbalization convention is good for basic multiplicity constraints on infix binaries. However it is less general than ORM's approach, which applies to instances as well as types, for predicates of any variety, with no need for pluralization.

Figure 1(d) shows the same association in ORM. Entity types appear as named, solid ellipses, and relationships as named sequences of one or more roles, with each role depicted as a box connected by a line to its object type. A relationship is called a *fact type* unless it is used simply to provide a primary reference scheme. For binary associations, forward and inverse readings may be provided, separated by a slash if shown together on the same line. As in UML, each role may also be named, although ORM tools typically store role names in dialog boxes rather than display them on the diagram. If a role connector has a black dot, this means that the role is *mandatory* (i.e., it must be played by each instance in the population of the object type). By default, a role is optional (no black dot). ORM constraints were designed to facilitate validation using sample populations. An arrow-tipped bar over one or more roles is a *uniqueness constraint* declaring that each entry in the population of that role sequence is unique (occurs there exactly once). Any relationship may be populated with a table where each column corresponds to the role in that position. So the constraint over the left role of Figure 1(d) indicates that entries in the left column of Figure 1(e) must be unique, unlike the right column. If the association were instead many-to-many, the constraint would span both roles and only the ordered pairs making up the table rows must be unique.

Of the four notations, only UML depicts a mandatory role by a minimum multiplicity > 0 on the opposite role. The next section shows that this leads to problems for *n*-ary associations. Of the four approaches discussed, only the ORM notation generalizes to cater for all mandatory and frequency constraints on *n*-ary associations.

DATA USE CASES, N-ARY ASSOCIATIONS AND MULTIPLICITY PROBLEMS

In UML, use cases illustrate ways in which the required information system may be used. Although useful in requirements analysis, their focus on *process* modeling makes them less suitable for developing a *data* model. It seems obvious that a data model should be seeded by data requirements, i.e., examples of information that the system is expected to manage. In ORM these examples have traditionally been called "information samples familiar to the domain expert." By analogy with the UML term, we call them *data use cases*. They can be output reports or input screens, and since they exist at the external level, they can present information in many ways (e.g., tables, forms, graphs, diagrams).

Regardless of the external appearance of a data use case, a domain expert should be able to verbalize its information in terms of natural language sentences. The modeler should then transform that informal verbalization into a formal yet natural verbalization that is clearly understood by the domain expert. These two verbalizations, one by the domain expert transformed into one by the modeler, comprise steps 1a and 1b of ORM's conceptual analysis procedure. Here data populations are verbalized as fact instances that are then abstracted to fact types. Constraints and derivation rules are then added and themselves validated by verbalization and population. This approach has proven very effective in practice, and is an ideal precursor to the specification of a UML data model.

As an example, suppose that our system is required to output reports like those shown in Figure 2. We ask the domain expert to read off the information contained in them, and then we rephrase this in formal English. The domain expert might verbalize the facts on the top row of report (a) thus: Archery is new (it's the first year it's included in the rankings); the U.S. ranks first in archery, and scored 10 points for that. As modelers, we note that Rank functionally determines Points in the population, so ask: Does the Rank (e.g. 1) determine the Score (e.g., 10)? The domain expert replies Yes. If he/she answers incorrectly, the error can be detected later by ORM's arity-check (Halpin, 1995).

We now rephrase the information into elementary facts: the Sport named 'Archery' is new; the Country coded 'US' has the Rank numbered 1 in the Sport named 'Archery'; the Rank numbered 1 earns the Score 10 points. Similarly, the top row of the second table may be verbalized as: the Country coded 'AD' has the CountryName 'Andorra.' If reference schemes are agreed to up front (e.g., Sports are identified by name), these verbalizations can be abbreviated (e.g., the Sport 'Archery' is new). Once the domain expert agrees with the verbalization, we abstract from the fact instances to the fact types.

Figure 2. Two Sample Output Reports for a Data Use Case

(a)

Sport	Rank	Country	Points
Archery *	1	US	10
Baseball	1	US	10
	2	JP	5
Cricket	1	AU	10
	1	GB	10
...	...	...	...

* new

(b)

Country	
Code	Name
AD	Andorra
AE	United Arab Emirates
...	...
ZW	Zimbabwe

The conceptual schema may now be drawn and populated with sample facts. For discussion purposes, we consider the ORM solution (Figure 3) before the UML solution. Simple reference schemes may be abbreviated in parenthesis (e.g., "Country(code)" abbreviates the injective association Country has Countrycode). Value types need no reference scheme, and appear as named, dashed ellipses (e.g., CountryName). Here we have one unary fact type, Sport is new, two binary associations Country has CountryName, Ranks earns Score and one ternary association Country has Rank in Sport.

ORM allows mixfix predicates, which are sentences with object placeholders (denoted by "…") that may appear anywhere in the sentence. In this example, the ternary predicate is "… has … in …". Mixfix predicates allow verbalization of sentences of any arity in any natural language, along with their associated constraints and derivation rules. Other approaches use a simple name for the verb phrase or assume binary infix predicates, which support only SVO (Subject Verb Object) languages, not SOV languages (e.g., Japanese) or VSO languages (e.g., Tongan). In principle, mixfix predicates could be used in UML, by extending its metamodel with positional information to provide a role order for predicate readings.

A sample fact table has been added for each fact type in Figure 3, to help validate the constraints. ORM schemas can be represented in diagrammatic or textual form, and ORM tools can automatically transform between the two representations. Models are *validated* with domain experts in two ways: *verbalization* and *population*. For example, the constraints on the rank association in Figure 3 verbalize as: *each Rank earns **exactly one** Score; **each** Score refers to **at most one** Rank*. The 1:1 nature of this association is illustrated by the population, where each column is unique.

A sample row for rank 3 has been added to illustrate the mandatory and optional nature of the roles played by Rank (a rank's score must be recorded even if no country achieves this rank—this rule was not evident from the original sample, but is obtained when checking constraints with the domain expert). Although the sample population suggests that we are interested in only the top two countries for each sport, the domain expert indicates this is not so. With regard to ranks then, the original sample population was not fully significant. If the set of possible ranks for which scores are allocated is fixed, this list could be added as a value constraint.

The uniqueness constraint on the first and last roles of the ternary association has a *positive verbalization* of: *each Country has **at most one** Rank in each Sport*. This constraint is satisfied by the sample population, where the Country-Sport value

Figure 3. ORM Schema for Figure 2, with Sample Population

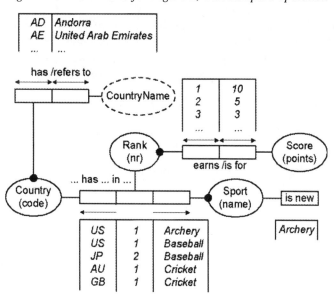

pairs are unique. To double check a constraint in ORM, a *negative verbalization* of the constraint may be given, as well as a *counter-example* to test whether the constraint may be violated. For example, the uniqueness constraint on the ternary may also be verbalized thus: ***it is impossible that the same*** *Country* ***has more than one*** *Rank* ***in the same*** *Sport*. Adding the counter-row (US, 2, Archery) to the sample population of the ternary gives the US two ranks in archery, and hence violates the uniqueness constraint. Such counter-examples make it easier for domain experts to see whether the constraint being tested really is a rule.

In ORM, all fact types are elementary, and no attributes are used, so populations never contain null values. Closed or open world semantics may be chosen, but the default semantics is closed world. For example Baseball appears in the population of Sport but does not play the role "is new," so we know it is not new. This approach is more natural to the domain expert than assigning False to a boolean attribute, as in UML (see later). For this reason, and to support natural verbalization, *we suggest that UML be extended to allow unary associations*. The UML 1.3 specification requires each association to have at least two roles (association ends), as shown in the metamodel fragment Figure 4(a). Weakening the "2..*" multiplicity constraint to "1..*" as in Figure 4(b) would permit unary associations, which could be displayed using some suitable graphical syntax (e.g., a named line). A decision regarding open or closed world semantics would also be needed.

ORM allows *n* readings for any *n*-ary predicate, one starting at each role. Apart from facilitating constraint declaration, this allows us to navigate through the information model from any starting position using natural sentences, which is especially useful for conceptual queries (Bloesch & Halpin, 1996, 1997). In principle, the UML metamodel could be extended to support this.

Figure 4. Modification to the UML Metamodel (a) to Allow Unary Associations (b)

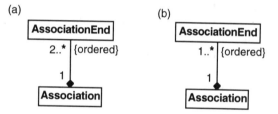

Figure 5 shows a UML schema for our sport ranks UoD. The binary fact types in the ORM schema of Figure 3 are modeled here as attributes. In the absence of any standard UML syntax for primary identification or uniqueness constraints on attributes, we use our own notations "{P}" and "{U1}" respectively. Notations for these constraints are needed if UML is to be used to completely model even simple database applications.

The Country-Sport uniqueness constraint in the ORM ternary is modeled in UML using the 0..1 multiplicity constraint on the role played by Rank. The "*" multiplicities indicate the absence of any other uniqueness constraint. If an *n*-ary fact type is elementary, any internal uniqueness constraint

Figure 5. UML Schema for Figure 2

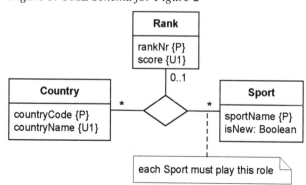

must span either *n*-1 or *n* roles. The UML notation for multiplicity constraints can express these cases, but cannot express uniqueness or frequency constraints on fewer than *n*-1 roles. Hence unlike ORM it cannot be used to specify compound fact types that may be required for derivation or denormalization. The DSB-ER notation was developed to cater for cardinalities on *n*-aries, but is even worse than UML in this regard since it cannot express composite uniqueness and frequency constraints at all. The Barker-ER notation is binary only, but would suffer the same problem if extended to *n*-aries.

Surprisingly, the *simple mandatory role constraint on Sport cannot be expressed by a multiplicity constraint* in UML. It might be thought that this constraint can be expressed by changing the multiplicity on the Country role to 1..*. But this would mean that each Sport-Rank pair formed from the populations of Sport and Rank must be associated with at least one country. But this is not true, since the role played by Rank is optional. For example, the pairs Archery-2 and Archery-3 have no associated country in the sample population. As discussed later, any attempt to redefine the semantics of multiplicity constraints in terms other than the populations of its object types leads to other problems.

This exposes a fundamental problem with the scaleability of UML's multiplicity notation, at least with regard to mandatory roles. Although it caters adequately for binaries, it cannot always express a simple mandatory constraint for a role within an *n*-ary association. In UML a multiplicity constraint on a single role indicates the number of instances playing that role that are associated in the association with each tuple from the Cartesian product of the populations of the other *n*-1 roles. Hence, UML multiplicity constraints can specify mandatory role constraints in an *n*-ary association if and only if at least *n*-1 of the roles in the association are mandatory. *If fewer than n-1 roles are mandatory, this cannot be captured by a multiplicity constraint.*

Obviously this has no impact for binaries, but for ternary and longer associations, some cases cannot be captured (the longer the association, the more cases there are). Some examples are shown in Figure 6. If we are to use an *n*-ary in UML, the only thing we can do in such cases is to add a textual description of the constraint in a note, as shown earlier in Figure 5. *This problem is a direct consequence of choosing to attach minimum multiplicity to a role other than the immediate role.* The DSB-ER and ORM notations can express mandatory constraints on roles of *n*-aries, and the Barker-ER notation could be extended to do so, since each attaches minimum multiplicity to the immediate role.

Figure 6. Some Mandatory Role Cases That UML Cannot Depict Graphically

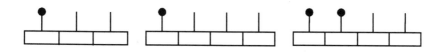

Even for *n*-ary associations where *n*-1 or *n* roles are mandatory, UML cannot express these mandatory constraints graphically without asserting a much stronger constraint (each tuple in the unrestricted Cartesian product of the other role populations must play in the association). While this strong constraint does imply the individual mandatory constraints, it is likely to be far too strong in practice except for pathological cases, or for cases where populations of the object types are tightly restricted by value constraints (the latter cases can often be handled in ORM using frequency constraints).

In some cases, we can cater for fewer than *n*-1 mandatory roles in UML by binarizing the *n*-ary. For example, Figure 7 expresses the fact type *Country is ranked in Sport* as a binary association, which is objectified as the association class Ranking. The mandatory role for Sport is now catered for by the 1..* constraint on the role for Country.

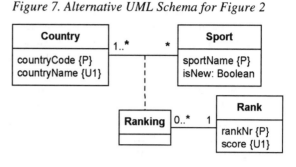

Figure 7. Alternative UML Schema for Figure 2

Unfortunately, this approach has other problems. To begin with, it is often too far removed from natural conceptualization. If the domain expert thinks in terms of a ternary, why should we force him/her to rethink the model in terms of binaries? More importantly, this solution does not always work in UML. For example, suppose we have the additional constraint that no ties are allowed when sports are ranked. There is no graphic symbol in UML to express this rule on the binarized solution (although it can be expressed on the ternary solution).

The only clean way to express the no-ties rule with the binarized model would be to extend UML with the additional notion of an external multiplicity constraint that can span model elements from different associations. ORM already includes such a constraint. For example, Figure 8 shows the binarized solution in ORM with an external uniqueness

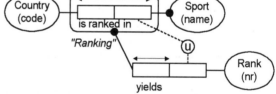

Figure 8. Nested ORM model with External Uniqueness Constraint to Forbid Ties

constraint (circled "u") to indicate that each Sport-Rank pair is associated with at most one Country in the overall association. ORM shows an objectified association by enclosing the association in an envelope. Although this works, it is more awkward to think about than the ternary solution for this case.

Now consider the report shown in Table 2. This example illustrates the no-ties rule on the ternary, as well as another defect of multiplicities in UML. In this UoD, no ties are allowed, and we are interested only in the first two ranks. Moreover, we are able to list a sport before any other details (e.g., rankings) are known for it. If a sport is ranked, we must know both its first and second place getters.

Figure 9 shows an ORM schema for this situation, as well as sample populations for the ternary association and the object type Sport. The "!" on Sport indicates it is an independent object type (instances of it can exist without playing any fact role). A meta-rule in ORM implies that any

Table 2. A Data Use Case for a Somewhat Different UoD

Sport	Rank	Country	Points
Aikido	?	?	?
Archery	1	US	10
	2	GB	5
Baseball	1	US	10
	2	JP	5
Basketball	?	?	?
Cricket	1	AU	10
	2	GB	5
...	...	...	...

Figure 9. ORM Schema for Table 2 with Some Sample Data

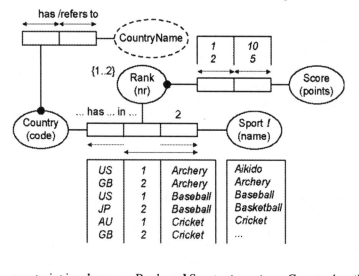

population object must play in some fact unless it is declared independent. There is no space here to extol the virtues of this rule, but its practical utility is such that we believe it should be added to UML.

In the ternary association, the uniqueness constraint over the roles played by Rank and Sport enforces the no-ties rule. In ORM the positive verbalization of this constraint is: **given any** Rank **and** Sport, **at most one** Country has **that** Rank in **that** Sport. This is satisfied by the sample population. The negative verbalization of the constraint is: **it is impossible that more than one** Country has **the same** Rank in **the same** Sport. The negative verbalization is facilitates using *counter-examples* to check the constraint. For instance, if we gave both Australia and Great Britain the rank 1 in cricket (as in Figure 3), this would violate the constraint.

Note the frequency constraint of 2 on the Sport role. This means any sport that plays that role does so exactly twice. In the context of the uniqueness constraints and the value constraint of {1..2} on Rank, this ensures that both ranks are recorded for any ranked sport. Again, the population clarifies the constraint. Some sports (e.g., Aikido) have not yet been ranked. Figure 10 shows the UML solution. The frequency constraint cannot be expressed via a multiplicity constraint, so is added informally in a note.

Multiplicity constraints of 0..1 are used to express the two uniqueness constraints. This works because uniqueness is a case of maximum multiplicity. The frequency constraint of 2 cannot be expressed on a ternary in UML because it involves, in ORM terms, a minimum occurrence frequency of 2. An occurrence frequency constraint of n means: if it plays the role, it does so n times. *Given any n-ary association ($n > 2$), UML multiplicity constraints cannot express a minimum occurrence frequency above 1 for any role* (or combination of fewer than n-1 roles). Although UML multiplicity constraints can express minimum occurrence frequencies above 1 for combinations of n-1 roles within n-ary

Figure 10. UML Schema for Table 2

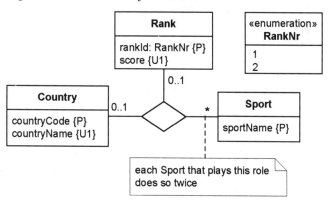

associations, they simultaneously require far stronger constraints to be asserted on the Cartesian products, and hence such usage is likely to be pathological.

ORM allows mandatory and frequency constraints over a set of roles (possibly from different associations). Uniqueness constraints are just frequency constraints of 1 with a special notation because of their importance and ubiquity. These constraints are orthogonal, and apply to associations of any arity. UML's multiplicity constraints can express simple mandatory and frequency constraints for binary associations, but cannot express mandatory role constraints or minimum frequencies above 1 for fewer than n-1 roles in n-ary associations. So UML's multiplicity notation is far weaker than ORM's mandatory and frequency constraint notation.

In summary, the whole notion of a minimum multiplicity above 0 is largely problematic for n-aries in UML. The UML 1.3 specification offers only the following description for the semantics of multiplicities in n-ary associations: *"The multiplicity of a role represents the potential number of instance tuples in the association when the other n-1 values are fixed"* (OMG, 1999, p. 3-73). *Consider a ternary association R(A, B, C). Let pop(A), pop(B) and pop(C) be the populations of A, B and C (in the database, not necessarily just in R), and pop(rA), pop(rB) and pop(rC) be the populations of the roles in R. Let R have multiplicities *, *, 2..* on the roles of A, B, C respectively. What does the 2 mean? For consistency with the meaning of multiplicities for binary associations, we should define it thus: each pair (a, b), where a is in pop(A) and b is in pop(B), is associated in R with at least 2 instances from pop(C). But as we've seen this reading fails if we replace 2 by 1. Moreover, such a constraint (for a frequency ≥ 2) is in practice virtually useless, since it far too strong to apply except in pathological cases. To base the constraint on the types rather than populations would be even worse.*

What is really needed is a way to define the constraint in terms of R's population. For example, each pair (a, b) that occurs in the projection pop(R)[a, b] is associated in R with at least 2 instances from pop(C). This corresponds to an ORM minimum frequency constraint of 2 on (rA, rB). Although useful and desirable, this definition is inconsistent with the whole approach to multiplicity constraints in UML, since it entails that minimum multiplicities of 0 could never occur.

Note that internal frequency (and uniqueness) constraints in ORM can be efficiently implemented and validated because they apply just to the local population of their predicate. Mandatory constraints refer to the population of an object type, so are ontologically distinct as well as harder to enforce. Because of their global impact, mandatory constraints should be considered more carefully. For such reasons, the separation of mandatory and frequency constraints is highly desirable.

How can we address these problems with UML multiplicities on n-ary associations? Ideally, multiplicity constraints for associations should be replaced by ORM's mandatory and frequency/uniqueness constraints, at least for n-ary associations. However such a radical change is unlikely to ever happen, and would cause backward compatibility headaches. We could try adding extra constraints for mandatory and frequency for n-ary associations. This would achieve the required expressibility but would make UML even more unnecessarily complex than it is now (e.g., the concept of mandatory role would be dealt with by a multiplicity constraint on binaries but by a mandatory constraint on n-aries). A third solution is to use ORM for the original analysis where the constraints can be easily declared and validated, then map the ORM model to UML where the constraints would appear in notes. Since the ORM notation is easily mastered, and requires no change to the UML notation, the third solution seems attractive and could be automated.

Figure 11. The Exclusion and Equality Constraints in (a) Are Lost in the UML Model (b)

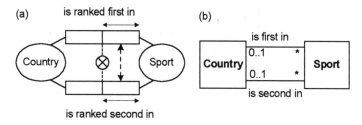

As a final comment on the no-ties example, we might try to overcome the problem of expressing the frequency constraint in UML by transforming the ternary into two binary associations: Country is first in Sport; Country is second in Sport, as shown in Figure 11.

However apart from the fact that this transformation doesn't scale (e.g., large numbers of ranks), there are now two constraints that get lost. The ORM model in * MERGEFORMAT Figure 11(a) includes the missing constraints. The pair-exclusion constraint (circled "X") enforces the no-ties rule that no country can be ranked first and second in the same sport. The equality constraint (dashed line with arrowheads) indicates that if a sport has a winner, it also has a runner-up, and vice versa. Although these constraints can be added informally in notes to the UML diagram, it would be better to extend the UML metamodel to support them. Currently UML is unorthogonal and restrictive with regard to constraints. It supports an exclusive-or constraint, but no exclusive constraint and no inclusive-or constraint. It also supports a subset constraint between full associations but not between parts of associations (e.g., single roles). The UML specification also contains inconsistencies in its handling of these constraints (e.g., Halpin, 2000, Figure 10).

Figure 12. The ORM Constraints (a) May Be Stored in an Extended UML Metamodel Fragment (b)

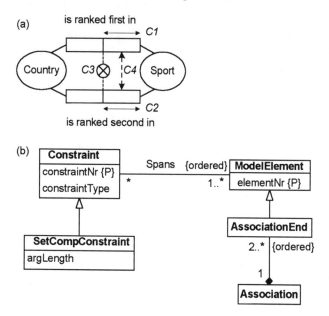

As one possible way of extending the UML metamodel to capture most of the ORM constraints, consider Figure 12. Here the ORM roles and constraints are numbered to provide efficient internal identification (e.g., for a CASE tool).

The four ORM constraints may now be stored as the object-relation shown in Table 3. The exclusion and equality constraints have their argument length recorded. The actual arguments of these two constraints may now be derived by "dividing" the role lists by this number. Thus the arguments of exclusion constraint are the role pairs (r1, r2) and (r3, r4) whereas the

Table 3. Meta-Table for Storing ORM Constraints

Constraint:

constraintNr	constraintType	roles	argLength
C1	uniqueInternal	r2	
C2	uniqueInternal	r4	
C3	exclusion	r1, r2, r3, r4	2
C4	equality	r2, r4	1

arguments of the equality constraint are the simple roles r2 and r4. The constraint type may now be used to determine the appropriate semantics.

Although this metamodel extension would allow capture of most ORM constraints in a UML-based repository, it does not in itself enable such constraints to appear on a UML class diagram. For that, several new UML notations would be required, and this task is significantly complicated by the fact that UML allows roles within ORM relationships to be expressed as attributes. Moreover, as the UML metamodel fragment indicates, UML associations must have at least two roles (association ends), so some changes are needed to deal with unaries (as discussed earlier).

CONCLUSION

We've seen that fact-orientation, as exemplified by ORM, provides several advantages for conceptual data analysis, including expressibility, validation by verbalization and population at both fact and constraint levels, and semantic stability (e.g., avoiding changes caused by evolution of attributes into associations). ORM also has a mature formal foundation that may be used to refine the semantics of UML.

Object-orientation, as exemplified by UML, also provides advantages such as compactness, and the ability to drill down to detailed implementation levels for object-oriented code. If UML is to be used for conceptual analysis of data, some ORM features can be adapted for use in UML either as heuristic procedures or as reasonably straightforward extensions to the UML metamodel and syntax. These include mixfix verbalizations of associations and constraints for associations, and exploitation of data use cases by populating associations with tables of sample data using role names for the column headers.

Nevertheless, there are some fundamental aspects that need drastic surgery to the semantics and syntax of UML if it is ever to cater adequately for non-binary associations and some commonly encountered business rules. For example, this chapter revealed some serious problems with multiplicity constraints on n-ary associations, especially concerning non-zero minimum multiplicities. For instance, UML multiplicity constraints can't express mandatory or minimum occurrence frequency constraints over fewer than n-1 roles within n-aries. Moreover, UML's treatment of set-comparison constraints is defective. Although it would be possible to fix these problems in UML by changing its metamodel to be closer to ORM's, such a drastic change to the metamodel may well be ruled out for pragmatic reasons (e.g., maintaining backward compatibility and getting the changes approved).

Unlike UML, ORM is based on a small set of orthogonal concepts that are easily mastered. UML modelers who are willing to learn ORM can get the best of both approaches by using ORM as a front-end to their information analysis and then mapping the ORM models to UML, where the additional constraints can be captured in notes or formal textual constraints. This option will become more attractive once commercial tools provide automatic transformation between ORM and UML.

ACKNOWLEDGMENT

This chapter is based in part on my shorter paper "Augmenting UML with Fact-Orientation" which appeared in the proceedings of the workshop "UML: A Critical Evaluation and Suggested Future," HICCS-34 conference (Maui, January 2001), © 2000 IEEE.

REFERENCES

Barker, R. (1990). *CASE*Method: Tasks and Deliverables*. Wokingham, England: Addison-Wesley.

Bentley, J. (1988). Little languages. In *More Programming Pearls*. Reading: Addison-Wesley.

Blaha, M. & Premerlani, W. (1998). *Object-Oriented Modeling and Design for Database Applications*. New Jersey: Prentice Hall.

Bloesch, A. & Halpin, T. (1996). ConQuer: A conceptual query language. In B. Thalheim (Ed.), *Proc. 15th International Conference on Conceptual Modeling ER'96* (pp. 121-133). Berlin: Springer.

Bloesch, A. & Halpin, T. (1997). Conceptual queries using ConQuer-II. In D. Embley & R. Goldstein (Eds.), *Proc. 16th Int. Conf. on Conceptual Modeling ER'97* (pp. 113-126). Berlin: Springer.

Booch, G., Rumbaugh, J. & Jacobson, I. (1999). *The Unified Modeling Language User Guide*. Reading: Addison-Wesley.

Campbell, L., Halpin, T. & Proper, H. (1996). Conceptual schemas with abstractions: Making flat conceptual schemas more comprehensible. *Data & Knowledge Engineering*, 20(1), 39-85.

Chen, P.P. (1976). The entity-relationship model—towards a unified view of data. *ACM Transactions on Database Systems*, 1(1), 9-36.

Dey, D., Storey, V.C. & Barron, T.M. (1999). Improving database design through the analysis of relationships. *ACM Transactions on Database Systems*, 24(4), 453-486.

Embley, D. (1998). *Object Database Management*. New Jersey: Addison-Wesley.

Eriksson, H. & Penker, M. (2000). *Business Modeling with UML – Business Patterns at Work*. John Wiley.

Falkenberg, E. (1976). Concepts for modelling information. In G. Nijssen (Ed.), *Modelling in Data Base Management Systems* (pp. 95-109). Amsterdam: North-Holland.

Fowler, M. with Scott, K. (1997). *UML Distilled*. New Jersey: Addison-Wesley.

Halpin, T. (1995). *Conceptual Schema and Relational Database Design*, 2nd edition (revised 1999). Bellevue: WytLytPub.

Halpin, T. (1998a). Object Role Modeling (ORM/NIAM). In P. Bernus, K. Mertins & G. Schmidt (Eds.), *Handbook on Architectures of Information Systems* (pp. 81-101). Berlin: Springer-Verlag.

Halpin, T. (1998b). *Object Role Modeling: An Overview*. [Online]. Available: http://www.orm.net/overview.html.

Halpin, T.A. (1998-9). UML data models from an ORM perspective: Parts 1-10. *Journal of Conceptual Modeling*. Minneapolos: InConcept. [Online]. Available: http://www.orm.net/uml_orm.html.

Halpin, T.A. (1999). Data modeling in UML and ORM revisited. In *Proc. EMMSAD'99: 4th IFIP WG8.1 Int. Workshop on Evaluation of Modeling Methods in Systems Analysis and Design.* Heidelberg, Germany.

Halpin, T.A. (2000). Integrating fact-oriented modeling with object-oriented modeling. *Information Modeling in the New Millenium*, M. Rossi & K. Siau (Eds.), Hershey, PA: Idea Group Publishing.

Halpin, T.A. & Bloesch, A.C. (1998). A comparison of UML and ORM for data modeling. In *Proc. EMMSAD'98: 3rd IFIP WG8.1 Int. Workshop on Evaluation of Modeling Methods in Systems Analysis and Design.* Pisa, Italy.

Halpin, T.A. & Bloesch, A.C. (1999). Data modeling in UML and ORM: a comparison. *Journal of Database Management*, 10(4), 4-13.

Halpin, T. & Proper, H. (1995a). Subtyping and polymorphism in object-role modeling. *Data & Knowledge Engineering* 15(3), 251-281.

Halpin, T. & Proper, H. (1995b). Database schema transformation and optimization. In *OOER'95: Object-Oriented and Entity-Relationship Modeling* (pp. 191-203). Berlin: Springer.

ter Hofstede, A. (1993). *Information Modelling in Data Intensive Domains.* Doctoral Dissertation, University of Nijmegen.

ter Hofstede, A., Proper, H. & van der Weide, T. (1993). Formal definition of a conceptual language for the description and manipulation of information models. *Information Systems,* 18(7), 489-523.

ISO (1982). *Concepts and Terminology for the Conceptual Schema and the Information Base*, (Ed. J. van Griethuysen), ISO/TC97/SC5/WG3-N695 Report. New York: ANSI.

Jacobson, I., Booch, G. & Rumbaugh, J. (1999). *The Unified Software Development Process.* Reading: Addison-Wesley.

Kobryn, C. (1999). UML 2001: A standardization odyssey. *Communications of the ACM,* 42(10), 29-37.

Levesque, H. (1984). A fundamental trade-off in knowledge representation and reasoning. In *Proc. CSCSI-84* (pp. 141-152). London, Ontario.

Muller, R.J. (1999). *Database Design for Smarties.* San Francisco: Morgan Kaufmann.

OMG. (1999). *OMG Unified Modeling Language Specification*, version 1.3. [Online]. Available: http://www.omg.org/uml.

Rumbaugh, J., Jacobson, I. & Booch, G. (1999). *The Unified Modeling Language Reference Manual.* Reading: Addison-Wesley.

Warmer, J. & Kleppe, A. (1999). *The Object Constraint Language: Precise Modeling with UML.* Reading: Addison-Wesley.

Chapter XII

The Whole-Part Relationship in the Unified Modeling Language: A New Approach

Franck Barbier
University of Pau, France

Brian Henderson-Sellers
University of Technology, Sydney, Australia

Andreas L. Opdahl
University of Bergen, Norway

Martin Gogolla
University of Bremen, Germany

*This study of the semantics of the Whole-Part relationship in OO modeling is based upon, extends and, specifically, formalizes earlier analyses of the semantics of UML's Aggregation and Composition (white and black diamonds, also called shared aggregation and composite aggregation). Although UML is nowadays regarded as a standard and is widely used as an OO modeling language, the way the Whole-Part relationship is formalized is unsatisfactory. Here, we provide a rigorous specification of various forms of the Whole-Part relationship using OCL (Object Constraint Language). The first part of the specification is based on the differentiation between **primary characteristics** (applicable to all Whole-Part relationships) assigned to a new Whole-Part metatype in the UML and **secondary features**, which are possessed by subtypes of this metatype and permit the representation of several "flavors" of the Whole-Part relationship. This UML-compliant style of specification, based on the use of OCL as well as metamodeling, allows us to directly incorporate our results into the UML metamodel, in particular revising UML's definition of Composition.*

INTRODUCTION

The Whole-Part (WP for short) relationship in OO modeling has been a subject of keen interest since, among others, its appearance in OMT (Rumbaugh, Blaha, Premerlani, Eddy & Lorensen, 1991). Named "aggregation" in OMT, this relationship is considered to be important for object modeling, although neither OMT nor its successor UML (OMG, 1997, 1999) provide well-grounded semantics. As it happens, UML supports two inconsistent kinds of WP relationship despite the fact that, both inside and outside the world of OO software engineering, numerous high-quality contributions exist on this very old research theme. This chapter is aimed at rectifying the current ambiguities and confusion in UML's white and black diamonds (shared aggregation and composite aggregation, respectively) and thus hopes to influence the next versions of the UML standard. We purposefully use a UML-compliant style of specification, i.e., the use of OCL (Warmer & Kleppe, 1998) which is part of UML, complementing the metamodel, which is the primary way in which the UML's semantics are currently described.

The second section of this chapter, named "Background," is a concise overview of the WP relationship in OO modeling. In the third section called "Foundation," we present and formalize a minimal set of characteristics for the WP relationship. In particular, we analyze this set according to three viewpoints: ontological, mathematical and software engineering-based considerations. In the fourth section named "Properties of the WP Relationship in OO Modeling," we specify in OCL the key features (e.g. separability, existence dependency) for possible subtypes of the WP relationship. We finally conclude in the fifth and last section ("Conclusion and Future Trends") by showing how this work can be used to modify the next version of the UML.

BACKGROUND

A WP relationship is a binary relationship from a set called **Whole** to a set called **Part**. A tuple is then (w, p) with w being an instance of **Whole** and p an instance of **Part**. These two sets are not necessarily disjoint. For instance, the **Programming statement** object type can be linked to itself by using a WP relationship. In OO modeling, a given object type **T** in a given object model **M** corresponds to a set of potential instances that, by definition, conform to **T**. **T** plays the role of either **Whole** or **Part** or both depending upon which **T** is involved in one or more WP relationships. Throughout this chapter, we deal with the generic terms **Whole** and **Part** in order to talk about "the" WP relationship as a metatype (called **Whole-Part** on the left side of Figure 1) from which "a" WP relationship in a specification model **M** is known to be its instance ("model level" on the right side of Figure 1). One major challenge of this chapter is then to supply robust criteria for distinguishing *without ambiguity* a WP relationship from an ordinary binary relationship (also called binary association in UML [OMG, 1999] or referential relationship in OML [Firesmith, Henderson-Sellers & Graham, 1997]) or, more accurately, to distinguish it from a *non*-WP relationship. In the UML 1.3 documents, it is written that: "An association may represent an aggregation, i.e., a whole/part relationship." and "Only binary associations may be aggregations." (OMG, 1999, pp.2-57). Therefore, in Figure 1, depicted using the UML's style of notation (white diamond or Aggregation for convenience to mean simply WP relationship), we show a WP relationship between **X** and **Y** as an instance of the **Whole-Part** metatype. As a result, a WP linkage (tuple) between **x** (an instance of **X**) and **y** (an instance of **Y**) is also an instance of the WP relationship between **X** and **Y**.

Figure 1. OO Metamodeling for the WP Relationship

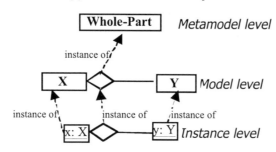

Overview of the WP Relationship in Object Modeling

Until now, the OO modeling domain has not really taken advantage of all the available knowledge related to the WP relationship. As a result, the semantics of the WP relationship remains inevitably fuzzy and convoluted in many object modeling languages, notably UML. In order to correct this, we focus our investigation on what constitutes an adequate subset of the WP characteristics for OO modeling. Such a definition has been sketched in Henderson-Sellers and Barbier (1999a) and applied to UML in Henderson-Sellers and Barbier (1999b, 1999c). In this chapter, the novelty is that we provide an OCL specification in addition to that initiated in Gogolla and Richters (1998), such that our research results become a candidate and credible proposition for the next versions of UML.

In order to formalize an appropriate subset of the WP problematics for OO modeling, concordant with the literature, we classify the properties generally assigned to the WP relationship. In Saksena, Larrondo-Petrie, France and Evett (1998) Henderson-Sellers and Barbier (1999a), it is shown that some of these are recurrent and unanimously recognized as key properties, which are vital for *any* true WP relationship. We call them "primary" properties by arguing that no well-grounded definition of the WP relationship is acceptable if it does not possess these primary characteristics (Table 1, line 1). The rest form a set of "secondary" properties (Table 1, line 2) which permit specialized types of the WP relationship to be characterized. There are also a number of consequent properties (Table 1, line 3) that are, by definition, deduced from the primary and/or secondary properties.

In metamodeling, we necessarily view primary properties as axiomatic characteristics of the WP relationship. As a result, primary properties are assigned to an abstract **Whole-**

Table 1. Primary and Secondary Characteristics (there are other secondary characteristics, not shown here, related to implementation)

Primary Characteristics	Whole-part, emergent property, resultant property, irreflexivity at instance level, antisymmetry at instance and type level; therefore asymmetry at instance level.
Secondary Characteristics	Encapsulation (visibility), overlapping lifetimes (9 cases), transitivity, shareability, configurationality, separability, mutability.
Consequent Properties	Propagation of operation(s), ownership, abstraction, existential dependency, propagation of destruction operation.

*Figure 2. Four Special Sorts of the WP Relationship: The Arrow Points to the **Part** Type, Thus Replacing the Semantically Vague UML Notation (white diamond) in Figure 1*

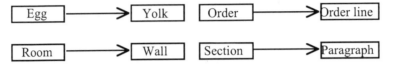

Part metatype which itself needs to be added to the current (version 1.3) UML metamodel. By use of inheritance, subtypes of the WP relationship can be derived from this metatype. Subtypes differ by the secondary properties that they possess. For example in Figure 2, one may say that the four WP relationships conform to the **Whole-Part** metatype while each is an instance of a distinct subtype determined by its secondary properties. For instance, **Room-Wall** is an instance of a subtype that possesses the secondary characteristic (Table 1) of shareability, i.e. the same wall can be a component of more than one room. This is clearly not true of the **Egg-Yolk** WP relationship. In the third example, canceling an order leads to the destruction of its order lines (coincident lifetimes) while breaking an egg does not result in destroying the yolk. So, parts sometimes outlive wholes, sometimes not. As a final example here, a given paragraph can be separated from a given section in order to dynamically become part of another section while it would be an error to do the same for a yolk, a wall or an order line because they participate in frozen structures.

Scope and Aim of the Study

The scope of our study on the WP relationship is confined to OO modeling with the underlying motivation of seeking high quality in the OO models that are thus built. In fact, OO analysts/designers use the WP relationship not only to precisely describe the requirements that their applications must meet, but they also rely on the WP relationship as a tool for arranging/organizing their models better. This especially introduces a higher level abstraction, the **Whole**, and allows the modeler to cope with various granularities. Indeed, these two facets have been noted previously: "These two goals are difficult to separate by looking at a finished model, as this not only attempts to reflect the structure of a problem domain, but is also "designed" to be understandable, manageable, reusable, resilient to change (…)" (Civello, 1993). In the same line of reasoning, Artale, Franconi, Guarino and Pazzi (1996) underline that the accepted and unified GEM (General Extensional Mereology) theory is "(…) inappropriate when considering real domains of application of the theory." They next state that any OO framework for the WP relationship will only be suitable provided that *reusability*, *understandability* and *extensibility* are direct consequences of the use of the WP relationship in the models that are built in this way.

Thus, in a model such as in Figure 2, an OO modeler expects to find recurrent forms of analysis and design or modeling patterns and idioms whose implementation is similar from one application to another. For instance, detecting that **Section-Paragraph** is an occurrence of a special WP relationship that has separability as a secondary characteristic can benefit from acquired knowledge on a previously encountered modeling pattern. The high frequency of a property like separability in real-world situations may then require a dedicated notational element in an OO modeling language, for instance as proposed by Saksena, Larrondo-Petri, France and Evett (1998). A complete and consistent subtype of the **Whole-Part** metatype can embody a modeling pattern and, provided that it is implemented, be (re)used to code the structure of this pattern. So, understandability and reusability naturally increase, subject to the constraint that only a small number of subtypes of the WP relationship are separately identified and rigorously specified. As for extensibility, any subtype may itself be extended/restricted by inheritance.

Odell (1994) and Henderson-Sellers (1997) have both echoed the reputable work of Winston, Chaffin and Herrmann (1987) and, moreover, showed the context in which the WP relationship shall be used for OO modeling. Saksena, France and Larrondo-Petrie (1998) proposed a necessary and sufficient set of properties for the WP relationship in OO modeling. This set of papers has been reviewed and even completed by Henderson-Sellers and Barbier (1999a) by using earlier discussions on conceptual/formal OO modeling (including Kilov & Ross, 1994; Dong & Duke, 1995; Lano, 1995; Firesmith & Henderson-Sellers, 1998). Concurrently, implementation of models was also discussed by Kolp and Pirotte (1997) and Barbier (1998). Regarding the continuing lack of solution in the latest UML reviews (Booch, Rumbaugh & Jacobson, 1999; Rumbaugh, Jacobson & Booch, 1999), this chapter attempts to bring to a closure the continuing debate on WP relationships and the notions of "aggregation."

Formalism

The specification of candidate properties for the **Whole-Part** metatype on the left side of Figure 1 is done in this chapter using the latest version of OCL (OMG, 1999). OCL is named by its authors a "lightweight" specification language. It can be used to write logical expressions on types in models but, as we do in this chapter, on metatypes in metamodels too. However, as observed by Henderson-Sellers and Barbier (1999b, 1999c), the current UML metamodel fragment relating to the WP relationship is defined by means of **AssociationEnd** and its metaattributes. In fact, there is currently no distinct metatype that embodies the WP relationship. Another detrimental factor here is the lack of OCL constraints on the "aggregation" and "changeability" attributes of the **AssociationEnd** metaclass. Indeed, we have demonstrated in Barbier and Henderson-Sellers (1999, 2000) that such a situation allows the creation and use of inconsistent forms of the WP relationship. Next, writing OCL is not sufficient in itself because the **Whole-Part** metatype does not exist at this time in the UML metamodel, being simulated via attributes on **AssociationEnd** (as noted earlier). Therefore, we show in this chapter all the benefits related to the possible introduction into the UML of a WP relationship metatype perhaps along the lines suggested in Figure 3. That is the reason why we need a modified version of the UML metamodel fragment relating to the WP relationship as a basis for our proposed revision. Moreover, we provide the **Whole** and **Part** types in Figure 3 with specific OCL capabilities (see the section called "Axioms") in order to underpin this proposition. Indeed, **Whole** and **Part** both inherit from **Classifier** (Figure 3). As an existing metatype in the UML metamodel, **Classifier** allows us to use **Whole** and **Part** in OCL expressions (OMG, 1999, pp.7-3).

OCL

An OCL expression (see appendix for more details) begins with the word *context* followed by the name of a type, **T** for example, as well as an invariant symbolized by *inv*. This symbol is optionally followed by an invariant name, as well as an invariant content (mandatory). The rest of the expression (invariant content) then describes an anonymous instance of **T**. Formulae are based on properties borne by **T**. Traditional logical operators (forAll which is equivalent to, exists which is equivalent to $, etc.) are used as well as other constructs like those related to object collections (iterate, select…), those based on typing (oclIsTypeOf, oclIsKindOf…) and so on. Here is a sample:

> **context** Egg **inv** *An invariant related to Figure 2*:
>   yolk→size = 1
> — "self.yolk→size = 1" is an equivalent expression
> — "yolk" is a navigation and yields a singleton set for any
> — instance of **Egg** via the "→" operator which acts on sets

Another possible expression archetype in OCL refers to pre-conditions and post-conditions for user-defined operations on types. This applies only for observer functions, i.e. those which are free from side effects. Here is an illustration:

> **context** Egg::freshness() : Boolean
>   **post:** result = yolk.freshness() **and** white.freshness()
> — We assume here the existence of another WP relationship, i.e. **Egg-White**

The great peculiarity of OCL is that it basically relies on textual material. In particular, this generates a suitable object-oriented "flavor," close to OO programming languages, in order to write more comprehensive formal specification expressions.

Starting Basis

Regarding a common WP relationship, as in the middle of Figure 1 or as may be drawn in a model (Figure 2), we introduce the following invariant:

> **context** Whole-Part **inv**:
>   WPWhole.instance→forAll(w | w.part→oclIsTypeOf(Set(Part)) = **true**)

This invariant means that for any instance of the **Whole** type in the context of a given WP relationship (i.e., a given instance of the **Whole-Part** metatype), we get the set of **Part** instances linked to this instance of **Whole** in using the part navigation.

We also make the assumption of the existence of navigation in the opposite direction in order to obtain another useful invariant:

> **context** Whole-Part **inv**:
>   WPPart.instance→forAll(p | p.whole→oclIsTypeOf(Set(Whole)) = **true**)

Figure 3. A revised Version of the UML Metamodel Fragment Related to the WP Relationship – A Possible Contribution to UML Version 2.0

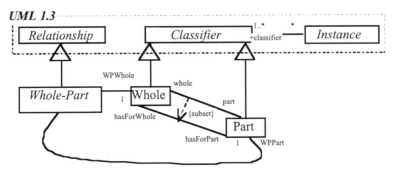

Nevertheless, **Whole** and **Part** are just roles played by types in models. So, a given type **T** in a given model **M** may act as a **Whole** in one WP relationship, a **Part** in another one, a **Part** in a third one and so on.

Axioms

We need three axioms in order to build our specification. The first one, called *Snapshot*, is the consistent relation between the part and the whole navigation directions:

>   **context** Whole-Part **inv** *Snapshot*:
>   WPWhole.instance→forAll(w | w.part→forAll(p | p.whole→includes(w)))
>   WPPart.instance→forAll(p | p.whole→forAll(w | w.part→includes(p)))

The second axiom named *History* introduces the hasForPart and hasForWhole navigation directions as well as their mutually consistent relation. As was the case for the part and whole navigation directions, we *axiomatically* view hasForPart and hasForWhole as predefined navigation directions assigned to the **Whole** and **Part** types, respectively, with the following restrictions:

>   **context** Whole-Part **inv** *History*:
>   WPWhole.instanceÆforAll(w |
>   w.hasForPart→forAll(p | p.hasForWhole→includes(w)))
>   WPPart.instance→forAll(p |
>   p.hasForWhole→forAll(w | w.hasForPart→includes(p)))

Finally, the relation between the two kinds of navigation is required:

>   **context** Whole-Part **inv** *Inclusion*:
>   — {subset} constraint in Figure 3
>   WPWhole.instance→forAll(w | w.hasForPart→includesAll(w.part))
>   WPPart.instance→forAll(p | p.hasForWhole→includesAll(p.whole))

This third and last axiom shows that, at any time, the parts of a given whole make up a set which is by definition included in the set of all the parts linked to this whole during its lifecycle. In other words, the evaluation result of the w.part expression depends upon the moment the evaluation occurs. However, computing w.hasForPart is free from temporal concerns: it yields all the part objects connected with w, even those separated from w before its death. Note that in OCL, the c.instance expression in which c is an instance of **Classifier** is based on the existing meta-relationship between **Classifier** and **Instance** in the UML metamodel (Figure 3). This yields the set of all instances of c. In contrast, the predefined allInstances operator in OCL is only directly applicable to types and not to instances such as c.

FOUNDATION

We may identify three facets of the WP relationship, as represented in the literature.

The first one is the ontological point of view. The second one comes from mathematics while the third one adds software engineering-based constraining features to the WP relationship. It seems reasonable to consider that all the listed features discussed hereafter constitute the set of primary properties for the WP relationship in OO modeling. We simply try to gather together a minimal set of characteristics which does not contradict the numerous opinions found in the literature. Moreover, we reuse some of the results coming from Henderson-Sellers and Barbier (1999a) in which the choice of a set of primary characteristics is argued. In Henderson-Sellers and Barbier (1999a), we outline the existing widespread confusion in the semantics of the WP relationship. Indeed, opinions diverge widely on the true nature of the WP relationship due to a misuse of terminology as well as the use of secondary properties (rather than primary properties), as discussed in the section called "Properties of the WP Relationship in OO Modeling."

Ontology

In his paper, Varzi (1996) states the historical foundation of what he calls the theory of Parthood or Mereology as well as the theory of Wholeness or Topology. A very wide range of disciplines has contributed to create the existing knowledge base on the WP relationship, including ontology/philosophy, linguistics, mathematics and cognitive science. Opdahl, Henderson-Sellers and Barbier (2001) re-analyze the impact of ontology and apply it to the OO framework elaborated in Henderson-Sellers and Barbier (1999a).

In ontology, the two most reputable features of the WP relationship are *emergent* and *resultant*. In the case of an egg for instance, its freshness is emergent in the sense that it depends upon the laying date, while its taste is resultant because it directly depends upon its yolk and its white.

Expressing these notions in a rigorous manner leads to the following:

Emergent: for several WP relationships owning the same **Whole** type, this type offers *at least one* emergent property. In other words, for any instance of the **Whole** type, the value of this property is not computed in any way from the properties of the **Part** types.

Resultant: for several WP relationships owning the same **Whole** type, this type offers *at least one* resultant property. In other words, for any instance of the **Whole** type, the value of this property is necessarily computed from some of the properties of the **Part** types.

It is important to note that *emergent* and *resultant* are not defined according to a single WP relationship but to a bundle of WP relationships. For example, we must consider two WP relationships (i.e., **Egg-Yolk** and **Egg-White**) in order to establish the taste of an egg. Hence, a bundle of WP relationships is such that the **Whole** type is the same for each WP relationship in the bundle. Formally, we then have:

```
context Whole-Part inv:
    let bundle = Whole-Part.allInstances→select(wp |
            self.WPWhole = wp.WPWhole) in ...
```

Next, within OCL, by definition, the attributes plus the operations plus the structural relationships possessed by a type make up its properties. We can then complete the last OCL expression as follows:

```
context Whole-Part inv Emergent:
    let bundle = Whole-Part.allInstances→select(wp |
```

```
        self.WPWhole = wp.WPWhole) in
    bundle→forAll(wp |
        (self.WPWhole.attributes→union(self.WPWhole.operations→union
        (self.WPWhole.associationEnds)))→exists(e |
        not
        (wp.WPPart.attributes→union(wp.WPPart.operations→
        (wp.WPPart.associationEnds)))→includes(e)))
```

Due to the current limitations of OCL, note that we just provide a syntactical definition of *emergent*. Indeed, we only ensure that a given property (at least one) of the **Whole** type does not match any property among the sum of properties for each **Part** type in the bundle. A semantic definition must in fact verify that the *value* of any emergent property is not computed by means of properties of parts. The reflection capabilities of OCL do not allow the expression of such a semantic constraint at this time.

Finally, we provide a similar syntactical characterization of *resultant*:

```
    context Whole-Part inv Resultant:
        let bundle = Whole-Part.allInstances→select(wp |
            self.WPWhole = wp.WPWhole) in
        bundle→forAll(wp |
            (self.WPWhole.attributes→union(self.WPWhole.operations→union
            (self.WPWhole.associationEnds)))→exists(r |
            (wp.WPPart.attributes→union(wp.WPPart.operations→
            (wp.WPPart.associationEnds)))→includes(r)))
```

Mathematics

An agreed characterization of the WP relationship is based on the binary nature of the WP relationship. In an equivalent style, one may also use predicates (as in Bourdeau & Cheng, 1995) so that the signature of the WP relationship is: WP: Whole, Part → Boolean. In fact, this mathematical foundation must remain as simple as possible, as occurs for relational theory. In this respect, we take up the pseudo-binary approach from Kent (1990). This approach may be illustrated by the fact that a synergetic relation between n sorts of thing in the real world (e.g., **Chassis**, **Engine**, **Wheel**...) can be modeled by n binary relationships from each sort to a type which acts as a controller. In the previous example, **Car** is obviously the controller type.

We may note that in Kilov and Ross (1994), although a binary approach is chosen, the flavor of the WP relationship proposed and called "composition" is formalized in quite a different way, i.e., a binary relationship from the set **Car** to the set corresponding to the Cartesian product of three types: **Chassis**, **Engine** and **Wheel**. In such an approach, a tuple is then as follows: (aCar, (aChassis, anEngine, aWheel)). In Barbier and Henderson-Sellers (2000), this approach is recognized as problematic at implementation time and, more generally, does not seem natural and direct for OO modelers.

Therefore, we choose a more comprehensive approach in first analyzing the mathematical properties of the WP relationship between instances of **Whole** and **Part**. Next, at the type level, we raise some problems related to software engineering concerns. Thus, at the instance level, we notice that the WP relationship is asymmetric (asymmetry ⇔ irreflexivity ∧ antisymmetry). We clearly reject transitivity as a primary characteristic since it has been clearly shown on many occasions that only very specific cases of the WP relationship are transitive (Markowitz, Nutter & Evens, 1992; Motschnig-Pitrik, 1996), despite that fact that transitivity has been considered as axiomatic in Mereology theory (see also discussion in Opdahl, Henderson-Sellers and Barbier, 2001). For irreflexivity, we have:

> **context** Whole-Part **inv** *Irreflexivity*:
>   WPWhole.instance→forAll(w |
>   w.oclIsKindOf(Part) **implies not** w.part→includes(w))
>   WPPart.instance→forAll(p |
>   p.oclIsKindOf(Whole) **implies not** p.whole→includes(p))

Figure 4. Part Inherits from Whole

This means that if **Part** directly (Figure 4) or indirectly derives from **Whole, Part** is associated with itself through a WP relationship, i.e., **Part** inherits this WP relationship from **Whole**. Although this case is rare, it is one of the cases in which non-irreflexivity may occur. Thus, in the OCL constraint above, if the hypothesis is true (i.e., p.oclIsKindOf(Whole)) then one ensures that p is never linked to itself. We do the same (other possible case) whenever **Whole** inherits from **Part**. An illustration for the template in Figure 4 is **Car door-Car part** whereas **Car door** inherits from **Car part**. We then simply ensure that:

Car door.instance→forAll(cd | cd.oclIsKindOf(Car part) **implies not** cd.part→includes(cd))

Another typical example is **Tree branch-Tree branch** which leads to:

Tree branch.instance→forAll(tb | **not** tb.whole→includes(tb))

From the *Snapshot* axiom, we easily deduce that:

Tree branch.instance→forAll(tb | **not** tb.part→includes(tb))

For antisymmetry, we have:

> **context** Whole-Part **inv** *Antisymmetry at the instance level*:
>   WPWhole.instance→forAll(w |
>   w.oclAsType(Part).whole→forAll(x |
>   w.part→includes(x) **implies** w = x))
>   WPPart.instance→forAll(p |
>   p.oclAsType(Whole).part→forAll(x |
>   p.whole→includes(x) **implies** p = x))

In this OCL constraint, oclAsType is a partial function that returns an object whose type is the argument, or is otherwise Undefined in the case of non-conformance. Therefore p.oclAsType(Whole) transforms p as an instance of **Whole** if and only if p.oclIsKindOf(Whole) is true. This allows us to deal with tricky situations as in Figure 5 where non-irreflexivity and/or non-antisymmetry might occur.

*Figure 5. Special Possible Case of Non-Irreflexivity and/or Non-Antisymmetry in Which **X** Inherits from **Whole** and from **Part***

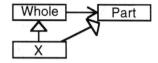

An example for the template in Figure 5 may be the **State union-State** WP relationship. Therefore **X** may be **Federal state** with USA as well as Switzerland being two instances of **X**[1]. So, as **Whole**, USA.oclAsType(State).wholeÆforAll(x | USA.partÆincludes(x) **implies** USA = x) is true because USA.oclAsType(State).wholeÆisEmpty is true. As **Part**, USA.oclAsType(State union).partÆforAll(x | USA.wholeÆincludes(x) **implies** USA = x) is true because once again USA.wholeÆisEmpty is true. A more or less utopian example is whether in the future Switzerland becomes part of the USA. The specification above precludes then that USA will not become at the same time part of Switzerland. This corresponds to asymmetry, i.e. if WP(USA, Switzerland) is true, WP(Switzerland, USA) is false.

Software Engineering

Despite some authors such as Halper, Geller and Perl (1998) who prefer to stress the part-whole relationship, most authors consider the dominant position of the **Whole** type compared to the **Part** type (see use of arrows in Figure 2). This is especially true and obvious in the OO field because one accurately wants the **Whole** type to play an extra role. Indeed, it limits or prevents any interaction between *anonymous* clients of **Part** instances. In contrast, clients of these **Part** objects request the whole(s) with which they are connected. Thus one delegates/propagates the request and acts as a proxy for its **Part** objects (Lewandowski, 1998). In OMT, this property is defined as follows: "*Propagation* (also called *triggering*) is the automatic application of an operation to a network of objects when the operation is applied to some starting object (…) The propagation behavior is bound to an association (or aggregation), direction and operation" (Rumbaugh, Blaha, Premerlani, Eddy & Lorensen, 1991, p.60). This last sentence helps us to understand that the propagation of operations is not a discriminator for the aggregation due to it also being related to an association.

In UML 1.3, this property of propagation is more strongly connected with Composition: "(…) a composite implies propagation semantics (i.e., some of the dynamic semantics of the whole is propagated to its parts). For example, if the whole is copied or destroyed, then so are the parts as well (because a part may belong to at most one composite)" (OMG, 1999, pp.2-57). More generally, in component-based client/server computing (Lewandowski, 1998), one customarily views the WP relationship as offering strict support for the delegation of operations. In other words, a **Whole** object must possess an interface so that potential requesting clients are able to call services available on its **Part** objects. All client requests are treated by the whole and forwarded (propagated) to its parts.

In addition, **Part** objects coming from different types can interact intensively (Bock & Odell, 1998a, 1998b). For instance, **Geographical Site, Business Unit, Department, Employee** and so on may be all declared as part of **Company**. While they, together, develop an intra-communication, **Company** is responsible for offering and managing a complete interface for any service demand that originates from outside.

From a design viewpoint, one intuitively seeks to use the WP relationship as a mean for isolating clear, reasonably independent and robust modules of increasing importance for the evolving component industry. This principle is also known as that of high cohesion. Furthermore, one looks for low coupling in particular and modularity in general. In fact, based on these software quality considerations, the WP relationship is not only a semantic relationship as it is sometimes treated in the ER approach or in OODBMS (Kim, Banerjee, Chou, Garza & Woelk, 1987) but it also has architectural and behavioral consequences.

This software engineering influence has led us to specific secondary properties, for example, configurationality in OML (Henderson-Sellers, 1997). Configurationality occurs when parts not only relate to the whole but also to each other either functionally or structurally. It aims to represent the synergetic relation between complementary (in terms of supplied functions) parts of the same whole and is fairly typical of the OO modeling area. More generally, we thus focus on the restricted directionality of the WP relationship, as it happens from **Whole** to **Part**, in order to use the WP relationship in a special way. In this respect, Henderson-Sellers and Barbier (1999a) promote antisymmetry at the type level as far as the WP relationship is a coupling factor. This first-class rule simply avoids the building of tortuous models, which are, first, difficult to understand and, next, not easily implementable. So, we have:

> **context** wp1,wp2 : Whole-Part **inv** *Antisymmetry at the type level*:
> wp1.WPWhole = wp2.WPPart **and** wp1.WPPart = wp2.WPWhole **implies**
> wp1= wp2

PROPERTIES OF THE WP RELATIONSHIP IN OO MODELING

We highlight in this section, properties of the WP relationship immediately useful in object modeling. The relative importance of these properties has already been discussed by Winston, Chaffin and Herrmann (1987) and re-studied and extended for operational concerns in the OO field by Barbier and Henderson-Sellers (2000). We here offer a more concise framework in OCL.

Abstraction/Encapsulation/Visibility

Tightly linked in the field of object technology, these three keywords (abstraction, encapsulation and visibility) are often recognized as important characteristics for differentiating a non-WP relationship from a WP relationship (Civello, 1993; Henderson-Sellers & Barbier, 1999a). Roughly speaking, a **Whole** object may sometimes be considered as a juxtaposition of other objects. Called its parts, these last objects are agglomerated together in order to form an object which has no strict mapping in the real world but can play the role of a proxy for its parts.

For instance, an ATM is made up of a user interface kit, a card reader, a cash dispenser, a deposit drawer and a receipt printer without being anything else (physically) than the sum of five part objects. Nevertheless, all banking transactions are checked and processed through the ATM, which corresponds to an abstraction of its five linked devices. Thus, the bank requires that the ATM accomplishes the effective delivery of money in ignoring its functional dependency with the cash dispenser. This neglect is valid in object modeling because it permits the construction of isolated and robust packages. In an object model, such an absence of visibility of the **Bank** type on the **Cash dispenser** type can possibly be depicted by means of a WP relationship from **ATM** to **Cash dispenser**.

Beyond this example, we basically want to state that the abstraction/encapsulation/ visibility trio can or cannot be used as a first-class criterion to characterize the WP relationship. Because encapsulation is a foundation of object orientation, its impact and reciprocal influence on the WP relationship is high. We may see the WP relationship as a tool for encapsulation. We may then use it on purpose to avoid any side effect resulting from the absence of protection in the models thus built. On the other hand, we may observe that the WP relationship induces some encapsulation differences in the models based on whether it is used or not. As a result, the use of the WP relationship may occur in conjunction with very specific concerns, as for example, security preoccupations in Fernandez, Gudes and Song (1994).

More generally, Cook and Daniels (1994, pp.38-39) deal with this same idea as follows: "Encapsulation. The idea here is that the aggregate encapsulates its parts in some way. (…) the abstraction provided by encapsulation is a vital part of object theory. The idea that one object is composed of others, and that the components are not known to clients of the whole, is a powerful structuring principle in object technology." Because of the wide range of interpretations and uses of encapsulation regarding the WP relationship, we consider that the abstraction/encapsulation/visibility trio must remain a secondary property. This is confirmed by other authors who also reject it as a primary characteristic or axiom. This is the case for instance for Cook and Daniels (1994) despite their observation above.

Shareability

Shareability is, in essence, distinct from sharing in the sense that it defines the notion of a potential sharing rather than mandated actual sharing (as in the current UML Aggregation or white diamond). It is always studied for a **Whole** object which may possibly share the same **Part** object with another **Whole** object. An archetype is the **Scrabble suggestion-Letter** WP relationship in which a **Letter** object may be linked to two **Scrabble suggestion** objects. On the other hand, that a **Whole** object is linked to more than one **Part** object is a very common situation and does not lead to any specific analysis.

Most of the papers in the literature discuss this property, but few take into account its true dimension and, as a result, its significant and direct impact on the WP relationship characterization. Indeed, the use of this notion in conjunction with other candidate characteristics is a source of conflict and inconsistency, as for instance for the white diamond in UML (Henderson-Sellers & Barbier, 1999b, 1999c). In this respect, we take advantage of the research results in Kolp and Pirotte (1997 and Gogolla and Richters (1998) as well as in (Halper, Geller & Perl, 1998) which carefully deal with shareability in association with exclusiveness.

Kolp and Pirotte (1997) talk about *local/global sharing* as well as *local/global exclusiveness*. Local exclusiveness is the contrary of local sharing also called "class-exclusive" by Halper, Geller and Perl (1998). Local exclusiveness means that, for a WP relationship, the maximum cardinality near the **Whole** type is less or equal to 1, in other words:

context Whole-Part **inv** *Local exclusiveness*:
WPPart.instance→forAll(p | p.whole→size <= 1)

We can then state that if this predicate holds for a WP relationship, it is said to own the local exclusiveness property much like one interpretation of the black diamond in UML (OMG, 1997). Global exclusiveness, which is the contrary of global sharing and is also called "conceptual sharing" by Saksena, France and Larrondo-Petrie (1998) or "strong form of forbidden sharing" by Gogolla and Richters (1998), is related to the fact that a **Part** type can be involved in more than one WP relationship in a model **M** (Figure 6). In OCL, this is specified by:

> **context** wp1,wp2 : Whole-Part **inv** *Global exclusiveness*:
> wp1.WPPart = wp2.WPPart **implies**
> wp1.WPPart.instance→forAll(p |
>   wp1.WPWhole.instance→exists(w | w.part→includes(p)) **implies**
>   wp2.WPWhole.instance→forAll(w | **not** w.part→includes(p)))

An archetype that illustrates global exclusiveness is the coexistence in a model **M** of the **Car-Engine** and **Truck-Engine** WP relationships. The same engine object cannot be at the same time part of a car instance and a truck instance. In contrast in Figure 6, global sharing holds since the same article (assuming articles are conceptual not physical entities) might be shared by a journal and a compilation (example appearing in Kolp & Pirotte, 1997).

Figure 6. Global Sharing

We may also note that a WP relationship can, at the same time, possess the local exclusiveness as well as the global exclusiveness properties. For instance, a chassis cannot be part of a car and a truck at the same time (global exclusiveness); neither can it be part of two distinct cars or two distinct trucks at the same time (local exclusiveness). Thus, we suppose in the rest of the chapter that unsharing is equivalent to local exclusiveness plus global exclusiveness and that shareability is the opposite of unsharing. Regarding our definition, we may nevertheless observe that some other characterizations are clearly different. Indeed, Civello (1993, p.385) writes "*Sharing*. An object is shared if two or more objects hold references to it." Unlike Civello, most authors *implicitly* analyze shareability within the scope of the WP relationship. In fact, must we extend the scope of the study for non-WP relationships? Indeed, a **Part** object can be referenced by its whole(s) as well as other objects resulting from the existence of ordinary associations involving the **Part** type in a model **M**. This problem is discussed further in the section called "Lifetime Dependency."

Separability/Mutability

Separability (similar to replaceability in Lano, 1995, or to variance in Odell, 1994) is viewed as a key notion in the classification proposed by Winston, Chaffin and Herrmann (1987). By definition, in an ordinary binary association, the instances of the two types involved in this association are dynamically linked and separated. In other words, this association is not a frozen structure in the sense that it may evolve. In this line of reasoning, some kinds of WP relationship exhibit separability while some do not. For instance, a **Sailboat-Sail** WP relationship owns separability because we obviously need to be able to replace a ripped sail of sailboat by another one. In contrast, a **Book copy-Sheet** WP relationship is such that new manufactured sheets cannot be substituted for damaged sheets.

More precisely, a copy of, say, "OPEN Modeling Language (OML) Reference Manual" by Firesmith, Henderson-Sellers and Graham is no longer scientifically *the same book* if some pages are missing. Could we nevertheless say that this book copy minus some pages has lost its identity, a topic which needs further analysis.

This raises the problem of mutability, whereby we have to pay attention to when a **Whole** object continues or not to be the same object if any change occurs regarding its linked **Part** objects. As an illustration, Smalltalk uses the becomes: method to manage the mutation of objects. Returning to modeling, a WP relationship that supports inseparability does not prevent the growth of the number of the parts of a whole (e.g. **Human egg-Cell**). We thus consider that the most interesting formal property is immutability which then permits us to characterize a very commonly occuring type of WP relationship, called **Component-Integral Object** by Winston, Chaffin and Herrmann (1987). We then specify immutability as follows:

> **context** Whole-Part **inv** *Immutability (first part)*:
>   WPPart.instance→forAll(p | p.hasForWhole = p.whole)

Starting from this OCL expression expressing immutability, we easily prove that:

> **context** Whole-Part **inv** *Immutability (second part)*:
>   WPWhole.instance→forAll(w | w.hasForPart = w.part)

Indeed, let us suppose the following assumption:

> WPWhole.instance→exists(w |
>   WPPart.instance→exists(x |
>   w.hasForPart→includes(x) **and not** w.part→includes(x)))

From the *History* axiom in the section named "Axioms," we have:

> WPWhole.instanceÆexists(w |
>   WPPart.instanceÆexists(x |
>   w.hasForPartÆincludes(x) **implies** x.hasForWhole→includes(w)))

From the *Immutability (first part)* assertion above, we have:

> WPWhole.instance→exists(w |
>   WPPart.instance→exists(x |
>   x.hasForWhole→includes(w) **implies** x.whole→includes(w)))

Finally, from the *Snapshot* axiom in the section called "Axioms," we have:

> WPWhole.instance→exists(w |
>   WPPart.instance→exists(x |
>   x.whole→includes(w) **implies** w.part→includes(x)))

The contradiction between w.part→includes(x) and our assumption above, i.e., **not** w.part→includes(x), demonstrates that this assumption is unrealistic. Thus, immutability states that the set of **Part** objects linked to any **Whole** object is the same at any time, and vice versa. Moreover, all the **Part** objects bound to a **Whole** object remain the same from its birth until its death. Referring once again to the **Book copy-Sheet** example, we can now assume it to be immutable because destroying some pages leads not to a different book but to a thing which cannot be named a book.

In order to develop our investigation further, we nevertheless note that nothing in our specification prevents the birth of all or some of the parts of a whole to precede the birth of this whole. This is the same for the wholes of a part.

Existential Dependency

The use of existential dependency may lead to confusion since there is a potential overlap between this concept and the lifetime dependency characteristic of the WP relationship (Motschnig-Pitrik & Kaasboll, 1999). While most authors deliberately blend the notion of existential dependency with that of lifetime dependency (e.g., Halper, Geller & Perl, 1998; Motschnig-Pitrik & Kaasboll, 1999), it is, in fact, possible to make a clear distinction. This is inspired by the specification proposed by Gogolla and Richters (1998) and called essentiality by Motschnig-Pitrik and Kaasboll (1999). Therefore, the existential dependency for the part is defined in a precise manner as follows:

> **context** Whole-Part **inv** *Existential dependency for the part*:
> WPPart.instance→forAll(p |
>   WPWhole.instance→exists(w | w.part→includes(p)))

A typical example is the **Order-Order line** WP relationship in which an **Order line** object is meaningless without a pre-existing link to an **Order** object. This case is even more restrictive in the sense that an order line belongs to one and only one order. In fact, it owns the local exclusiveness plus the global exclusiveness features.

A symmetrical OCL expression can be easily introduced to describe the existential dependency for the whole:

> **context** Whole-Part **inv** *Existential dependency for the whole*:
> WPWhole.instance→forAll(w |
>   WPPart.instance→exists(p | p.whole→includes(w)))

We can, however, simply note that the existential dependency for the whole is equivalent to a cardinality which is greater or equal to 1 on the part role of the WP relationship shown in Figure 7.

Furthermore, if we want to ensure that any **Part** object can only exist with at least one connection to a **Whole** object, i.e., the existential dependency for the part, we then redraw Figure 7 as shown in Figure 8.

It is essential to observe that these two characterizations are not peculiar to the WP relationship but can also be applicable to a regular association. This is confirmed by Fowler and Scott (2000) who reject this as a discriminator for the WP relationship. They indeed consider that a "1..1" cardinality is indicative

*Figure 7. A **Whole** Object Cannot Live Without at Least One **Part** Object*

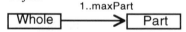

*Figure 8. A **Part** Object Cannot Live Without at Least One **Whole** Object*

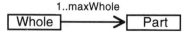

of some lifetime dependency. Moreover, Kilov & Ross (1994, pp.90-91) define "mandatory participation" as: "(…) the existence of an instance of the entity implies the existence of a corresponding instance of the association (…) The invariant for an entity with mandatory participation in an association implies that both the entity instance and the first corresponding association instance must be created in the same business process." Finally in Henderson-Sellers and Barbier (1999a), it is rigorously shown that existential dependency cannot be part of an axiomatic definition of the WP relationship due to it being inferred from other dominant primary features.

We thus propose that the existential dependency for the part according to Gogolla and Richters (1998) is equivalent to the mandatory participation for the part according to Kilov and Ross (1994). The same equivalence symmetrically applies for the existential dependency for whole. However, a deeper analysis of the idea of existence dependency is done in Snoeck and Dedene (1998). From that discussion existence dependency is seen to be strictly correlated with life span constraints, we thus now move to consideration of this important characteristic of the WP relationship.

Lifetime Dependency

Snoeck and Dedene (1998) supply a definition of existence dependency. This definition is such that some kinds of WP relationship possess this property while others do not. The generic form of this definition is: "If each object of a class A always refers to minimum one, maximum one and always the same occurrence of class B, then A is existence dependent of B" (Snoeck & Dedene, 1998, p.234). Let us consider **A** as **Part** and **B** as **Whole**. It thenbecomes clear that this definition implies what is called existential dependency for the part in the previous section. Nevertheless, it is more restrictive in the sense that the cardinality in Figure 8 should be "1..1" instead of "1..maxWhole" and immutability applies. Indeed, the definition says that we cannot substitute a distinct instance of **B** for the currently referenced instance of **B**. Furthermore, Snoeck and Dedene conclude that the life span of an existence-dependent object is contained within the life span of the object upon which it depends. That is the reason why, as for many others authors, Snoeck & Dedene provide a very constrained definition that is based on lifetime dependency.

Obviously, Snoeck and Dedene restrict the definition of existential dependency for the part from Gogolla and Richters (1998) in first assigning the local exclusiveness value ("maximum one"). They also consider the unchangeability of the whole, which, by definition, always exists and is unique. This leads to the following necessary but non-sufficient expression (see Figure 10 below for the completion of the characterization):

> **context** Whole-Part **inv** Part is existence-dependent on Whole:
> — Existential dependency for the part
> — Local exclusiveness
> — Global exclusiveness: omission in Snoeck and Dedene (1998)
> — Immutability (first part)
> — Immutability (second part): inferred from Immutability (first part)

It is important to notice that their definition does not reject the global sharing value to be set to true for a WP relationship. Indeed, they say nothing about the fact that **A** may possibly be involved (as the **Part** type) in another WP relationship. In Figure 9, this seems realistic and coherent in the sense that an ill cell can be shared both by a brain and a tumor while its life span is obviously contained within the lifecycle of its two composites.

This encourages us to scan all the possible dependency configurations between the birth and the death of a **Part** object according to those of a **Whole** object. In Figure 10, we sum up the cases

Figure 9. Global Sharing Plus Part is Existence-Dependent on Whole

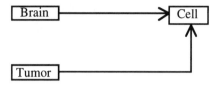

Figure 10. The Nine Cases of Lifetime Dependency

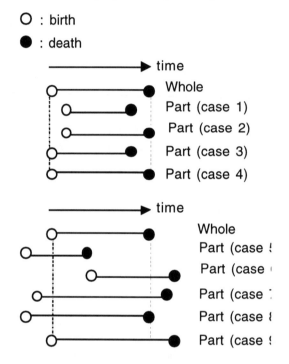

in which the life cycle of the part is included (not necessarily strictly) within the life cycle of the whole (top of figure) as well as the remaining cases (bottom of figure).

We observe that cases 1, 2 and 6 share the antecedent of the whole birth. This corresponds to the fact that any instance of **Part** is such that the commencement of its life coincides with or follows the life beginning of *any* instance of **Whole** linked to it (scenario in Figure 11). This is specified as follows:

context Whole-Part.WPWhole::creation() : Whole
   post: result.hasForPart→forAll(p | p.oclIsNew **or** p@pre.oclUndefined)
   — this means that any part of "result" is created within its own
   — creation process or does not exist at the start of the operation
   — (use of the "@pre" operator)

Compared to cases 1, 2 and 6, cases 3, 4 and 9 (Figure 10) share the coincidence of birth. This corresponds to the fact that any instance of **Part** is such that its life beginning

Figure 11. The Ellipses Mean that the Life Goes On, i.e. No Special Assumption is Made On the Object's Death

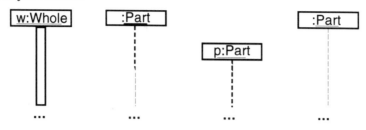

Figure 12. The Crosses Indicate the End of Life and No Assumption is Made On the Object's Birth

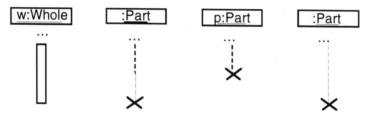

coincides with the life beginning of *any* instance of **Whole** linked to it. This is specified as follows:

> **context** Whole-Part.WPWhole::creation() : Whole
> **post**: result.hasForPart→forAll(p | p.oclIsNew)

Finally, cases 5, 7 and 8 of Figure 10 are such that they share the precedence of the part birth:

> **context** Whole-Part.WPWhole::creation() : Whole
> **post**: result.hasForPart→forAll(p |
>   p.oclIsNew **or not** p@pre.oclUndefined)

Symmetrically, we have to analyze the relation between the death of a **Part** object relative to that of a **Whole** object. In this respect, Figure 12 embodies cases 1, 3 and 5.

Thus, cases 1, 3 and 5 share the antecedent of the part death. In other words, any instance of **Part** is such that its life end coincides with or precedes the life end of *any* instance of **Whole** linked to it (scenario in Figure 12). This is specified as follows:

> **context** Whole-Part.WPWhole::deletion()
> **pre**: self.hasForPart→exists(p | p.oclUndefined)

post: self.oclUndefined **and**
               self@pre.hasForPart→forAll(p | p.oclUndefined)

Following the specification process, we have for cases 2, 4 and 8:

context Whole-Part.WPWhole::deletion()
    pre: self.hasForPart→forAll(p | **not** p.oclUndefined)
    post: self.oclUndefined **and**
               self@pre.hasForPart→forAll(p | p.oclUndefined)

For cases 6, 7 and 9, we have:

context Whole-Part.WPWhole::deletion()
    pre: self.hasForPart→forAll(p | **not** p.oclUndefined)
    post: self.oclUndefined **and**
               self@pre.hasForPart→exists(p | **not** p.oclUndefined)

Finally, there is now no difficulty in formalizing each case individually. To conclude, we merely provide an illustration, i.e., the synthesis case in which the life span of the part is contained (not strictly) within the life span of the whole (cases 1 to 4 in Figure 10):

context Whole-Part.WPWhole::creation() : Whole
    post: result.hasForPart→forAll(p | p@pre.oclUndefined)
context Whole-Part.WPWhole::deletion()
    post: self.oclUndefined **and**
               self@pre.hasForPart→forAll(p | p.oclUndefined)

Note that this specification permits us to complete what Snoeck and Dedene (1998) name "existence dependency." Moreover, it seems probable that the sum of cases 1 to 4 may be what was conceived of as Composition in UML.

CONCLUSION AND FUTURE TRENDS

This chapter provides, in a UML-compliant style, the precise specification of most of the unanimously reputable characteristics of the WP relationship in OO modeling. A set of primary properties can be assigned to an abstract **Whole-Part** metatype which is not currently included in the UML metamodel, but can easily be viewed as a subtype of the existing abstract metatype called **Relationship** (this only applies for version 1.3, not for version 1.1). Furthermore, a set of secondary features can be used to derive concrete (i.e., non-abstract) subtypes from **Whole-Part**. Since Composition in UML is very ill-defined, this allows us to fully revise this modeling construct (and propose it for inclusion in version 2.0) in order to obtain something reliable and, as a result, increase the quality of UML models which benefit from a (now accurate) use of the ideas of a WP relationship.

Concerning the perspectives of the work presented in this chapter, two ways can be explored. Further investigation relies on the mixing of several secondary properties to build direct (re)usable and implementable subtypes of the **Whole-Part** metatype. Indeed, secondary properties cannot be combined together without taking care of some possible contradictions raised by the combination. Because of lack of space, we use proofs only incidentally in this chapter (see the section named "Separability/Mutability" as an example of such a proof) but any attempt to mix properties such as shareability, separability/ mutability and so on will lead to new results and perhaps improved definitions of the kinds of WP relationship adequate for OO modeling. The other axis of exploration is the introduction of temporal logic into OCL in order to enhance the formalization of properties, especially lifetime dependency, which is recognized as a key and relevant notion for the WP relationship.

This is Contribution number 00/1 of the Centre for Object Technology Applications and Research.

ACKNOWLEDGEMENTS

We would thank Jos Warmer (father of OCL, member of the UML core team), Steve Cook (member of the UML core team) and Jean-Michel Bruel (member of the pUML group) for their advice about our use of OCL.

REFERENCES

Artale, A., Franconi, E., Guarino, N. & Pazzi, L. (1996). Part-whole relations in object-centered systems: An overview. *Data and Knowledge Engineering,* 20(3), 347-383.

Barbier, F. (1998). Systematic construction of UML associations and aggregations using cOlOr framework. *Proceedings of ECOOP'98 Workshop Reader* (pp.480-482). Heidelberg, DE: Springer.

Barbier, F. & Henderson-Sellers, B. (1999). Object metamodelling of the whole-part relationship. *Proceedings of TOOLS PACIFIC'99* (pp.127-138). Washington, DC: IEEE Computer Society Press.

Barbier, F. & Henderson-Sellers, B. (2000). The whole-part relationship in object modelling: A definition in cOlOr. *Information and Software Technology,* 43(1), 19-39.

Bock, C. & Odell, J. (1998). A more complete model of relations and their implementation: Roles. *Journal of Object-Oriented Programming,* 11(2).

Bock, C. & Odell, J. (1998). A more complete model of relations and their implementation: Aggregation. *Journal of Object-Oriented Programming,* 11(5).

Booch, G., Rumbaugh, J. & Jacobson, I. (1999). *The Unified Modeling Language User Guide.* Reading, MA: Addison-Wesley.

Bourdeau, R. & Cheng, B. (1995). A formal semantics for object model diagrams. *IEEE Transactions on Software Engineering,* 21(10), 799-821.

Cook, S. & Daniels, J. (1994). *Designing Object Systems, Object-Oriented Modeling With Syntropy.* Upper Saddle River, NJ: Prentice Hall.

Civello, F. (1993). Roles for composite objects in object-oriented analysis and design. *ACM Sigplan Notices,* 28(10), 376-393.

Dong, J., & Duke, R. (1995). The geometry of object containment. *Object Oriented Systems.* 2(1), 41-63.

Fernandez, E., Gudes, E. & Song, H. (1994). A model for evaluation and administration of security in object-oriented databases. *IEEE Transactions on Knowledge and Data Engineering,* 6(2), 275-292.

Firesmith, D., Henderson-Sellers, B. & Graham, I. (1997). *OPEN Modeling Language*

(OML) Reference Manual. Cambridge, UK: Cambridge University Press.

Firesmith, D. & Henderson-Sellers, B. (1998). Clarifying specialized forms of association in UML and OML. *Journal of Object-Oriented Programming,* 11(2), 47-50.

Fowler, M., & Scott, K. (2000).). *UML Distilled: A Brief Guide to the Standard Object Modeling Language* (2nd ed.). Reading, MA: Addison-Wesley.

Gogolla, M. & Richters, M. (1998). Transformation rules for UML class diagrams. *Proceedings of «UML»'98* (pp.92-106). Heidelberg, DE: Springer.

Halper, M., Geller, J. & Perl, Y. (1998). An OODB part-whole model: Semantics, notation, and implementation. *Data and Knowledge Engineering.* 27(1), 59-95.

Henderson-Sellers, B. (1997). OPEN relationships – compositions and containments. *Journal of Object-Oriented Programming,* 10(7), 51-55, 72.

Henderson-Sellers, B. & Barbier, F. (1999). What is this thing called aggregation. *Proceedings of TOOLS EUROPE'99* (pp.236-250). Washington, DC: IEEE Computer Society Press.

Henderson-Sellers, B. & Barbier, F. (1999). Black and white diamonds. *Proceedings of «UML»'99* (pp.550-565). Heidelberg, DE: Springer.

Henderson-Sellers, B. & Barbier, F. (1999). A survey of the UML's aggregation and composition relationships. *L'objet* 5(3-4), 339-366.

Kent, W. (1990). *Data And Reality* (5th reproduction). Amsterdam, NL: Elsevier Science.

Kilov, H. & Ross, J. (1994). *Information Modeling, An Object-Oriented Approach.* Upper Saddle River, NJ: Prentice-Hall.

Kim, W., Banerjee, J., Chou, H., Garza, J. & Woelk, D. (1987). Composite object support in an object-oriented database system. *Proceedings of OOPSLA'87* (pp.118-125). New-York, NY: ACM Press.

Kolp, M. & Pirotte, A. (1997). An aggregation model and its C++ implementation. *Proceedings of OOIS'97* (pp.211-221). Heidelberg, DE: Springer.

Lano, K. (1995). *Formal object-oriented development.* Heidelberg, DE: Springer.

Lewandowski, S. (1998). Frameworks for component-based client/server computing. *ACM Computing Surveys,* 30(1), 3-27.

Markowitz, J., Nutter, J. & Evens, M. (1992). Beyond is-a and part-whole: More semantic network links. *Computer Mathematics With Applications,* 23(6-9), 377-390.

Motschnig-Pitrik, R. (1996). Analyzing the notions of attribute, aggregate part and member in data/knowledge modeling. *Journal of Systems and Software,* 33(2), 113-122.

Motschnig-Pitrik, R. & Kaasboll, J. (1999). Part-whole relationship categories and their application in object-oriented analysis. *IEEE Transactions on Knowledge and Data Engineering,* 11(5), 779-797.

Odell, J. (1994). Six different kinds of composition. *Journal of Object-Oriented Programming,* 7(8), 10-15.

OMG. (1997). *UML Summary, Semantics and Notation Guide, version 1.1.*

OMG. (1999). *OMG Unified Modeling Language Specification, version 1.3.*

Opdahl, A. L., Henderson-Sellers, B. & Barbier, F. (2001). Ontological analysis of whole-part relationships in OO-models. *Information and Software Technology.* In press.

Rumbaugh, J., Blaha, M., Premerlani, W., Eddy, F. & Lorensen, W. (1991). *Object-Oriented Modeling and Design.* Upper Saddle River, NJ: Prentice-Hall.

Rumbaugh, J., Jacobson, I. & Booch, G. (1999). *The Unified Modeling Language Reference Manual.* Reading, MA: Addison-Wesley.

Saksena, M., France, R. & Larrondo-Petrie, M. (1998). A characterization of aggregation. *Proceedings of OOIS'98* (pp.11-19). Heidelberg, DE: Springer.

Saksena, M., Larrondo-Petrie, M., France, R. & Evett, M. (1998). Extending aggregation constructs in UML. *Proceedings of «UML» '98* (pp.435-441). Heidelberg, DE: Springer.

Snoeck, M. & Dedene, G. (1998). Existence dependency: The key to semantic integrity between structural and behavioral aspects of object types. *IEEE Transactions on Software Engineering,* 24(4), 233-251.

Varzi, A. (1996). Parts, wholes, and part-whole relations: The prospects of mereotopology. *Data and Knowledge Engineering,* 20(3), 259-286.

Warmer, J. & Kleppe, A. (1998). *The object constraint language.* Reading, MA: Addison-Wesley.

Winston, M., Chaffin, R. & Herrmann, D. (1987). A taxonomy of part-whole relations. *Cognitive Science.* 11, 417-444.

APPENDIX: A BRIEF INTRODUCTION TO OCL

Following the UML documentation, OCL was introduced in UML for a variety of reasons. First, a pure graphical model is in general not enough for a precise and unambiguous specification of a system. Often one needs to describe additional constraints about the objects, for example using a textual specification language. However, the disadvantage of traditional formal specification languages is that they are difficult to learn and to use for the average business or system modeler. OCL was developed to fill this gap with a strong emphasis on user-friendliness. OCL is a pure expression language which means that every OCL expression is free from any side effect. Therefore OCL is not a programming language. It is not possible to write program logic or flow of control in OCL. On the other hand OCL is a typed language, so that each OCL expression has a type, and types within OCL can be any kind of **Classifier** (one of the more important metaclasses in the UML metamodel).

There is a variety of places where one can use OCL in models. One may specify invariants on classes and types in class diagrams. It is also possible to formalize user-defined stereotypes by means of OCL. The description of pre-conditions and post-conditions on

Figure 13. A Simple UML Model

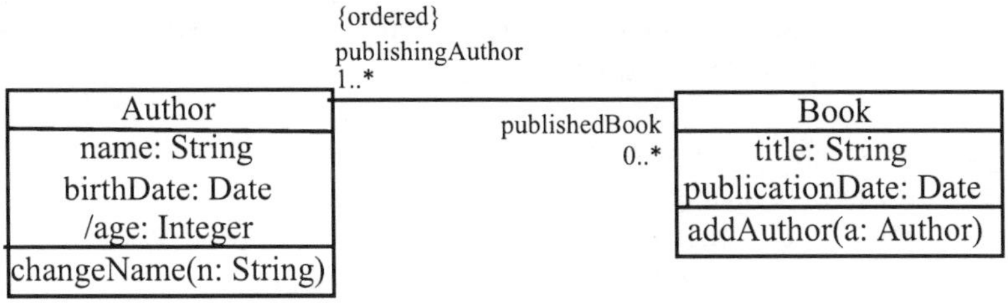

```
                          {ordered}
                          publishingAuthor
                          1..*
 ┌──────────────────┐                        ┌──────────────────────┐
 │      Author      │    publishedBook       │        Book          │
 ├──────────────────┤          0..*          ├──────────────────────┤
 │  name: String    │                        │    title: String     │
 │  birthDate: Date │                        │ publicationDate: Date│
 │  /age: Integer   │                        │  addAuthor(a: Author)│
 ├──────────────────┤                        └──────────────────────┘
 │changeName(n: String)│
 └──────────────────┘
```

operations is supported by OCL as well as the specification of guards in statechart diagrams. Furthermore the language can be used as a navigation (or query) language. Regarding the semantics of UML, OCL is used to express the well-formedness rules related to the metaclasses in the metamodel.

Let us underpin these statements by considering a class diagram (Figure 13). This class diagram introduces two classes, **Author** and **Book**, and an association between them. On the **Author** side, we find the multiplicity "1..*" indicating that a **Book** has at least one and possibly many more authors represented as an ordered list with the role name **publishingAuthor**. On the **Book** side, we see the multiplicity "0..*" allowing authors without books to exist and the role name **publishedBook**. As claimed above we can use OCL for a number of purposes.

An appropriate *invariant* in the class diagram is that an author's date of birth must precede the publication of her/his book:

> **context** Book **inv**:
> self.publishingAuthor→forAll(a | a.birthDate < self.publicationDate)

This OCL expression is formulated within the context of the class **Book**. Therefore self refers to a book. The expression self.publishingAuthor navigates through the association and yields the set of authors for the fixed book. On this set, we use the universal quantification forAll and require that each author's birthDate must be less than the publicationDate. OCL is close to first-order predicate calculus in the sense that it allows universal and existential quantification as well as the usual logical connectives **not**, **and**, **or**, **implies** to be used in an expression.

The following *derivation* rule for the age attribute of **Author** relies on the existence of a class **Date** providing an operation today() : Date that returns the current date. The **Date** class is also assumed to possess an operation yearDifference(d: Date) : Integer determining the number of years remaining between two dates.

> **context** Author **inv**:
> self.age = d.today().yearDifference(self.birthDate)
> — *this is a comment: d is an arbitrary instance of Date*

The pre-conditions and post-conditions for the operations changeName and addAuthor describe the manipulations done by these operations.

> **context** Author::changeName(n: String)
> **pre**: n <> name
> **post**: name = n

The pre-condition for changeName requires that the parameter n is different from the current name, whereas the post-condition states that after the completion of the operation, name will hold the value of the parameter n.

> **context** Book::addAuthor(a: Author)
> **pre: not** self.publishingAuthor→includes(a)
> **post:** publishingAuthor = publishingAuthor@pre→append(a)
> -- *this a comment: note that we omit "self" in the post-condition*

The pre-condition for addAuthor requires that the author to be added is not already present in the book's author list. The post-condition states that the value of publishingAuthor after the operation is equal to the value of publishingAuthor before the operation (use of the "@pre" operator) plus the parameter a appended.

To demonstrate the navigation possibility, the following expression computes for a given author the names of her/his co-authors:

> **context** Author **inv**:
> publishedBook.publishingAuthor→reject(a | a = self)→collect(a | a.name)

The term publishedBook.publishingAuthor has the type **Set(Person),** although one might expect the type **Set(Set(Person))** because publishedBook has the type **Set(Book)**. Nevertheless, nested collections are automatically flattened according to the OCL documentation. The reject expression filters the author set such that only authors different from the current author remain. The collect expression applies the attribute name to each author in the author set.

ENDNOTE

1 USA and Switzerland are officially confederations instead of federations, but in practice they both behave as federations due to the dominant position of the state union compared to each state in the union. In contrast, EU is currently a confederation and does not then conform to the "State" type.

Chapter XIII

Linking UML with Integrated Formal Techniques

Jing Liu, Jin Song Dong and Kun Shi
National University of Singapore

Brendan Mahony
Defence Science and Technology Organization, Australia

The challenge for complex systems specification is how to visually and precisely capture static, dynamic and real-time system properties in a highly structured way. In particular, requirement specifications for composite systems often involve capturing concurrent interactions between software control parts and physical system components/devices. The requirement specifications of such systems need to capture the structure and behavior of each individual physical/ software components and their communications. In this chapter, we investigate the links between the graphical notation UML and an integrated formal notation. We present an effective combination of UML and an integrated formal method for the requirement specification of a light control system.

This work is supported in part by the research grant (Integrated Formal Methods) from National University of Singapore (No. RP3991615).

INTRODUCTION

Requirements capture is a key activity in software and system engineering. The challenge for complex system requirement specification is how to precisely capture static, dynamic and real-time system properties in a highly structured way. In particular, composite systems (Feather, 1987) often involve concurrent interactions between software control parts and physical system components/devices. The requirement specifications of such systems need to capture the structure and behavior of physical/software components and their communications. Formal methods are well known for their precision and expressiveness in specifying software and system requirements (Crow & Vito, 1998, Dandenne, Lamsweerde & Fickas, 1993; Dubois, Yu & Petit, 1998; Hesketh et al., 1998; Leveson et al., 1994). However, formal specification techniques are not well integrated with existing industrial requirement analysis practices (Darimont, Heisel & Souquieres, 1999) and have a significant barrier to entry. On the other hand, though graphical notations are easy to adopt, they lack formal semantics and have scale up problems. Combinations of the two have been found successful (Grimm, 1998). To fight complexity, structured techniques (for example object-oriented methods) are also needed to properly partition the model into manageable individual components.

Following the success of conceptual modeling in databases (e.g., ER [Chen, 1976] and NIAM [Nijssen & Halpin, 1989]), many object-oriented modeling methods have been developed during the 1990s. Now those methods and notations have been merged into, the Unified Modeling Language (UML) (Rumbaugh, Jacobson & Booch, 1999). UML consists of various graphical notations which can capture the static system structure (class diagram), system component behavior (statechart diagram), system component interaction (collaboration and sequence diagram). The shortcomings of UML are:

- There is no unified formal semantics for all those diagrams. There are a few approaches to formalize a subset of UML, e.g., Evans and Clark (1998) and Kim and Carrington (1999) concentrated on class diagram semantics. Therefore, the consistency between diagrams is problematic; and
- There are limited capabilities for precisely modeling timed concurrency. For example, (in a new feature that has been added to the UML 1.3) synchronization between concurrent substates of a single statechart diagram can be captured using a synch state link. However, there is no facility to precisely model synchronous interactions between states in two different statechart diagrams.

If UML is combined with formal specification techniques, then its power can be further realized and enhanced. We believe that the best companions for UML are likely to be formal object-oriented methods. The two techniques are highly compatible and transparent to each other. One integrated formal object-oriented specification language is Timed Communicating Object Z (TCOZ) (Mahony & Dong, 1998). TCOZ combines the strengths of Object_Z (Duke, Rose & Smith, 1995) in modeling complex data and state with the strengths of Timed CSP (Schneider & Davies, 1995) in modeling real-time concurrency. In addition to CSP's channel-based communication mechanism, in which messages represent discrete synchronizations between processes, TCOZ is extended with continuous function interface mechanisms inspired by process control theory, the sensors and the actuators (Mahony & Dong, 1999). Therefore, a combination of UML and TCOZ would be a good solution to the requirement specification of timed reactive control systems.

The key technique ideas in this approach are:

- Syntactically, UML/OCL (Object Constraint Language) is extended with TCOZ communication interface types — **chan**, **sensor** and **actuator**. Upon that, TCOZ sub-expressions can be used (in the same role as OCL) in the statechart diagrams and collaboration diagrams.
- Semantically, UML class diagrams are identified with the signatures of the TCOZ classes. The states of the UML statechart are identified with the TCOZ processes (operations) and the state transition links are identified with TCOZ events/guards.
- Effectively, UML diagrams can be seen as the viewpoint visual projections from a unified formal TCOZ model.

In this chapter, we illustrate such an effective combination of UML and TCOZ through the requirement specification of a light control system (LCS). The specification/ design processes of this approach are:

1. Firstly, the UML use-case models (user-case and collaboration diagrams) are used to analyse LCS requirements so that main classes and operations will be identified (e.g., classification of the boundary and control classes). Communication links of the collaboration diagrams guide the design of communication interfaces of the TCOZ model (synchronization — channel, synchronization — sensor/actuator).
2. Then, the UML class diagrams are used to capture the static structure of the LCS systems, in which class/object relationships can be captured.
3. Based on UML class diagrams, detailed TCOZ formal models are constructed in a bottom-up style. The states, timing and concurrent interactions of the system objects are captured precisely in the TCOZ models.
4. Finally, UML state diagrams are used to visualize the behaviors (process states and events) of essential components of the LCS system, which are closely associated with the behavior parts of the TCOZ model.

The remainder of the chapter is organized as follows. Section 2 briefly introduces the TCOZ notation. A glossary is attached on page 22. Section 3 presents a brief outline of LCS and the UML use case analysis models. Section 4 presents UML class/state diagrams with TCOZ models for LCS requirements. Section 5 concludes the chapter.

TCOZ FEATURES

Timed Communicating Object Z (TCOZ) (Mahony & Dong, 1998) is essentially a blending of Object_Z (Duke et al., 1995) with Timed CSP (Scheneider & Davies, 1995), for the most part preserving them as proper sub-languages of the blended notation. The essence of this blending is the identification of Object_Z operation specification schemas with terminating CSP processes. Thus operation schemas and CSP processes occupy the same syntactic and semantic category, operation schema expressions may appear wherever processes may appear in CSP and CSP process definitions may appear wherever operation definitions may appear in Object_Z. The primary specification-structuring device in TCOZ is the Object_Z class mechanism.

In this section we briefly consider various aspects of TCOZ. A detailed introduction to TCOZ and its Timed CSP and Object_Z features may be found elsewhere. The formal semantics of TCOZ are also documented (Mahony & Dong, 1999).

A Model of Time

In TCOZ, all timing information is represented as real valued measurements in seconds, the SI standard unit of time. We believe that a mature approach to measurement and measurement standards is essential to the application of formal techniques to systems engineering problems. In order to support the use of standard units of measurement, extensions to the Z typing system suggested by Hayes and Mahony (1995) are adopted. Under this convention, time quantities are represented by the type

$$\mathbb{T} == \mathbb{R} \odot \mathsf{T},$$

where R represents the real numbers and T is the SI symbol for dimensions of time. Time literals consist of a real number literal annotated with a symbol representing a unit of time. All the arithmetic operators are extended in the obvious way to allow calculations involving units of measurement.

Interface—Channels, Sensors and Actuators

CSP channels are given an independent, first class role in TCOZ. In order to support the role of CSP channels, the state schema convention is extended to allow the declaration of communication channels. If c is to be used as a communication channel by any of the operations of a class, then it must be declared in the state schema to be of type *chan*. Channels are type heterogeneous and may carry communications of any type. Contrary to the conventions adopted for internal state attributes, channels are viewed as shared (global) rather than as encapsulated entities. This is an essential consequence of their role as communications interfaces between objects. The introduction of channels to TCOZ reduces the need to reference other classes in class definitions, thereby enhancing the modularity of system specifications. Complementary to the synchronizing CSP channel mechanism, TCOZ also adopts a non-synchronizing shared variable mechanism. A declaration of the form s : X **sensor** provides a channel-like interface for using the shared variable s as an input. A declaration of the form s : X **actuator** provides a local variable like interface for using the shared variable s as an output. Sensors and actuators may appear either at the system boundary (usually describing how global analog quantities are sampled from, or generated by the digital subsystem) or else within the system (providing a convenient mechanism for describing local communications which do not require synchronizations). The shift from closed to open systems necessitates close attention to issues of control, an area where both Z and CSP are weak (Zave & Jackson, 1997). We believe that TCOZ with the **actuator** and **sensor** can be a good candidate for specifying open control systems. Mahony and Dong (1999) recently presented detailed discussion on TCOZ sensor and actuators.

Active Objects

Active objects have their own thread of control, while passive objects are controlled by other objects in a system. In TCOZ, an identifier MAIN (non-terminating process) is used to determine the behavior of active objects of a given class (Dong & Mahony, 1998). The MAIN operation is optional in a class definition. It only appears in a class definition when the objects of that class are active objects. Classes for defining passive objects will not have the MAIN definition, but may contain CSP process constructors. If ob1 and ob2 are active objects of the class C, then the independent parallel composition behavior of the two objects can be represented as ob1 ||| ob2, which means ob1 • MAIN ||| ob2 • MAIN .

Semantics of TCOZ

A separate paper details the blended state/event process model which forms the basis for the TCOZ semantics (Mahony & Dong, 1998). In brief, the semantic approach is to identify the notions of operation and process by providing a process interpretation of the Z operation schema construct. TCOZ differs from many other approaches to blending Object_Z with a process algebra in that it does not identify operations with events. Instead an unspecified, fine-grained, collection of state update events is hypothesized. Operation schemas are modeled by the collection of those sequences of update events that achieve the state change described by the schema. This means that there is no semantic difference between a Z operation schema and a CSP process. It therefore makes sense to also identify their syntactic classes.

The process model used by TCOZ consists of sets of tuples consisting of: an initial state; a trace (a sequence of time-stamped events, including update events), a refusal (a record what and when events are refused by the process) and a divergence (a record of if and when the process diverged). The trace/refusal pair is called a failure and the overall model the state/failures/divergences model. The state of the process at any given time is the initial state updated by all of the updates that have occurred up to that time. If an event trace terminates (that is if a $\sqrt{}$ event occurs), then the state at the time of termination is called the final state.

The process model of an operation schema consists of all initial states and update traces (terminated with a $\sqrt{}$) such that the initial state and the final state satisfy the relation described by the schema. If no legal final state exists for a given initial state, the operation diverges immediately. An advantage of this semantics is that it allows CSP process refinement to agree with Z operation refinement.

Network Topologies

The syntactic structure of the CSP synchronisation operator is convenient only in the case of pipeline-like communication topologies. Expressing more complex communication topologies generally results in unacceptably complicated expressions. In TCOZ, a graph-based approach is adopted to represent the network topology (Mahony & Dong, 1998). For example, consider that processes A and B communicate privately through the interface ab, processes A and C communicate privately through the interface ac, and processes B and C communicate privately through the interface bc. This network topology of A, B and C may be described by

$$\|(A \xrightarrow{ab} B; \; B \xrightarrow{bc} C; \; C \xrightarrow{ca} A).$$

Other forms of lax usage allow network connections with multiple channels above the arrow, for example if processes D and F communicate privately through the channel/sensor_actuator df1 and df2, then

$$\|(D \xrightarrow{df_1, df_2} F).$$

LCS AND USE CASE MODEL

In most existing light control systems, all lights are controlled manually. Electrical energy is wasted by lighting rooms that are not occupied and by not adjusting light levels relative to need and daylight. LCS is an intelligent control system. It can detect the occupation of the building, then turn on or turn off the lights automatically. It is able to tune illumination in the building according to the outside light level. It gains input from sensors and actuators. The LCS presented here is a simplified version of a complex light control system presented by Feldman et al. (1999).

The Unified Modeling Language is a recent synthesis of earlier object design languages. The essential UML software process model is use-case driven. The Rational Rose2000 Enterprise case tool was used in constructing the UML models for LCS requirements.

Firstly, we identify the actor in the LCS — the occupant. The top-level use case model is depicted in Figure 1. Collaboration diagrams and sequence diagrams can be used to realize detailed use cases and they can be converted to each other. Collaboration diagrams are chosen for detailed use case analysis.

As there are many use-cases in a system, we need to prioritize them. The most essential ones are when occupants enter or exit a room. For example, when a user enters a room: a motion detector senses the presence of the person, the room controller reacts by the retrieving current daylight level and turning on the light group with appropriate illumination setting. When a user leaves a room (leaving it empty): the detector senses no movement, the room controller waits *absenT* time units and then turns off the light group. Finally, the occupant can directly turn on/off the light group by pushing the

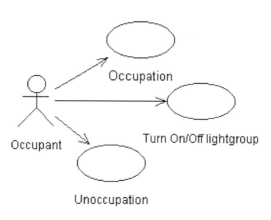

Figure 1. Top Level Usecase Diagram

button. The collaboration diagram in Figure 2 captures these use-cases. The role of message in the collaboration diagram is indicated by the associated arrow's direction (indicating the data flow direction) and the arrow's properties (synchronous/asynchronous). This provides guidelines for constructing the TCOZ communication interfaces in terms of channels and sensor/actuators.

UML AND TCOZ MODELS

In this section, UML and TCOZ are used to specify the LCS requirements. From the use case analysis activity, a few analysis classes are identified. Specifically, the boundary classes of LCS include the motion detector, the outdoor sensor and the light group. The control class is the room controller. Physical composite components, such as rooms, can be composed from the boundary objects. For example, a room can be specified as a composite object that consists of an outdoor sensor, a motion detector and a light group.

As the second step in the developing process given earlier, the UML class diagram should be used to capture all static aspects of the system, classes, relationship between classes and the overall structure of the system. This step leads to the design stage, in which

Figure 2. Concurrent Interactions

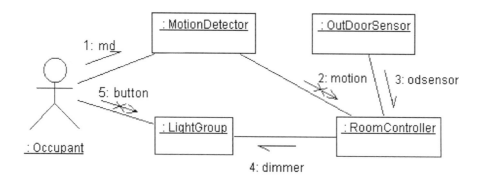

Figure 3. Light Control System Class Diagram

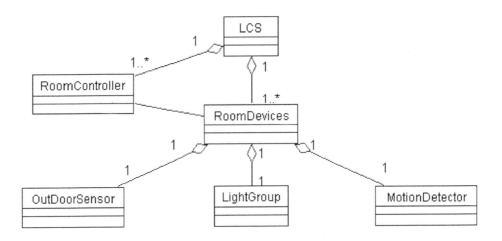

the static view of the system is presented. Based on this step, the developer can get into the system analysis and design details and build up the whole system.

Following the second step, detailed TCOZ models could be constructed in a bottom-up style. All elements in the class diagrams modeled in the previous stage, such as boundary objects in the following case study, will be specified using TCOZ. At this step, behaviors of these elements are also specified in the formal model.

The fourth step is interleaved with the third step above. Specifically, when behaviors of elements are captured in the TCOZ specifications, UML statecharts are used to visualize the dynamic view of these elements. The projection from formal model to UML statecharts should follow certain guidelines, which are interpreted later where they are applied in the case study. Frequently, these statecharts can help the developer to find obvious mistakes, such as wrong logic flows in the formal specification, then he/she can return to the third stage to modify and check again. After all elements in the system are specified, the syntactic structure of the whole system will be built up using the network topology technique in TCOZ. This specification will address the analysis (collaboration diagram) in the first step as guidelines in specifying communication interfaces.

The UML class diagram in Figure 3 depicts the structure of the LCS and provides guidelines for constructing the formal TCOZ models. The LCS system is roughly composed of RoomController and RoomDevices. RoomController serves as controlling the behaviors of the whole system. RoomDevices consists of some physical equipments, OutDoorSensor, LightGroup and MotionDetector.

Firstly, let us see how to use TCOZ to specify those boundary objects.

Boundary classes

The basic data types are defined:

$$Illumination == 1..10000 \qquad Percent == \{0\} \cup 10..100$$

The requirements of the motion detector, outdoor sensor and light group are captured by the following classes.

$\underline{\quad MotionDetector\ }\rule{0pt}{0pt}\rule{6cm}{0.5pt}$

motion : **chan**	
md : $(Mv \mid NoMv)$ **sensor**	[movement detect sensor]

$NoUser \cong md?Mv \rightarrow \text{Wait 1 s};\ motion!1 \rightarrow User \ \square\ md?NoMv \rightarrow \text{Wait 1 s};\ NoUser$

$User \cong md?NoMv \rightarrow \text{Wait 1 s};\ motion!0 \rightarrow NoUser \ \square\ md?Mv \rightarrow \text{Wait 1 s};\ User$

$\text{Main} \cong NoUser$

The purpose of the *MotionDetector* is to detect any movement and send appropriate signals to the room controllers. Timing behavior of the motion detector (when movement/ no movement is detected, system will be notified after one second) is captured in the MAIN process.

$$\mid\ convert : \mathbb{R} \rightarrow Illumination$$

The function convert is used to convert the analog signal to a digital signal.

$\underline{\quad OutDoorSensor\ }\rule{0pt}{0pt}\rule{6cm}{0.5pt}$

feel : $\mathbb{R}$ **sensor**
odsensor : *Illumination* **actuator**

$\text{Main} \cong \mu\ ODS \bullet [n? : \mathbb{R}] \bullet feel?n \rightarrow \text{Wait 10 ms};\ odsensor!convert(n) \rightarrow ODS$

The purpose of the *OutDoorSensor* class is to sense outdoor light illumination and send appropriate information to the room controller. Note that the continuous-function **sensor** interface captures exactly the analog nature of the illumination level from the outside world.

$\underline{\quad LightGroup\ }\rule{0pt}{0pt}\rule{6cm}{0.5pt}$

button, *dimmer* : **chan**	[control channels]
dim : *Percent* **actuator**	[dim value]
on : $\mathbb{B}$	

$ButtonPushing \cong button?1 \rightarrow ([dim > 0] \bullet TurningOff\ \square\ [dim = 0] \bullet TurningOn)$

$TurningOn \cong dim := 100;\ on := true$

$TurningOff \cong dim := 0;\ on := false$

$DimChange \cong [n : Percent] \bullet dimmer?n \rightarrow ([on] \bullet dim := n\ \square\ [\neg on] \bullet \text{Skip})$

$\text{Main} \cong \mu\ N \bullet (ButtonPushing\ \square\ DimChange);\ N$

The ceiling light group in the room has one related push button which is abstractly modeled as the CSP channel *button*. Another channel *dimmer* is connected to the control system component. If the occupant manually turns off the light group, there is no point in keeping the controller adjusting the dim value of the light group, so the automatic control should be correspondingly disabled. The control will be enabled when the occupant turns on the light group. The Boolean variable—*on* is specified to record the control state. The behavior of a light group can be visualized by the UML statechart diagram in Figure 4, where TCOZ processes and events are corresponding to UML state and state transitions. The overall process behavior is illustrated well by the statechart diagram. The statechart diagram indeed provides visual aid to the formal TCOZ model. Some guidelines to build the statechart are as follows: first of all, we consider each operation in TCOZ model as a

Figure 4. State Diagram for a Light Group

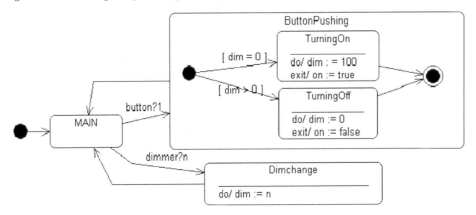

state/substate, which may have its own actions or fix some values for a span of time. MAIN is modeled as the state that the startstate leads to. Secondly, events and guards in TCOZ model are viewed as triggers which cause transition of states in the statechart (such as *button?1* and *[dim=0]* in Figure 4), which totally match the definition of trigger in UML statechart. Thirdly, sometimes, operations can call other operations (this doesn't happen in this simple case study). In this case, the called operations serve as the substates of the former ones and they compose a composite state in the statechart. If this composite state is too large, we can use the submachine to model it, and then just put the submachine state there and the diagram for the submachine elsewhere. This is useful when two or more operations call a shared complex operation (mapping to large composite state).

Physical Composite Components

Requirement specifications specify not only the software requirements but also their environment, usually physical systems/devices. Physical devices, like boundary objects, have been specified in the previous section. In this section, the room devices are specified as:

RoomDevices

$outdoorsensor : OutDoorSensor_\copyright$
$motiondetector : MotionDetector_\copyright$
$lg : LightGroup_\copyright$

$\text{MAIN} \; \widehat{=} \; outdoorsensor \; ||| \; lg \; ||| \; motiondetector$

The subscript '$\copyright$' indicates that the referenced objects (*outdoorsensor*; *motiondetector*; *lg*) are contained in their corresponding *RoomDevices* object. Object containment ensures that no object directly or indirectly contains itself; and no object is directly contained in two distinct objects. (For a detailed discussion see Dong & Duke, 1995). The behavior of a room is that all its components are concurrently and independently running which is captured by the interleave operator |||. Due to the space limitation of the chapter, we omit some minor issues of the LCS. Our main aim here is to demonstrate the approach.

Light Control System

The satisfaction relation between dim values for lights and outdoor light illumination is specified as:

$$\mid \quad satisfy : Percent \leftrightarrow Illumination$$

The room controller is used to control the room light groups. It is specified as:

```
__RoomController _____
  _____    _Adjust _____
 | dimmer, motion : chan               |  | dim! : Percent on dimmer     |
 | odsensor : Illumination sensor      |  |_____|
 | absenT : T                          |  | dim! satisfy olight           |
 | olight : Illumination               |  |_____|
 |_____|
  Ready ≙ motion?1 → On
  Regular ≙ μR • [n : Illumination] • odsensor?n → olight := n; Adjust; R
  On ≙ Regular ∇ motion?0 → OnAgain
  OnAgain ≙ (motion?1 → On) ▷{absenT} Off
  Off ≙ dimmer!0 → Ready
  MAIN ≙ Off
_____
```

The behavior of the room controller can be visualized through the UML state diagram in Figure 5. Note here MAIN is just the operation *Off*, and some operations consist of only one other operation and events/guards(such as Ready). In these cases, two more guidelines for visualization are introduced. One, in order to avoid visualizing the behavior as a single large state MAIN, MAIN is identified with the single operation that MAIN represents and then model it as the content of the single state MAIN. This is demonstrated in Figure 5. Two, in the case the specification of one operation consists of only one other operation and events/ guards leading to it, instead of using the substate technique, we model the two operations as two separate states with events/guards as the triggers between them (see *Ready* and *Off* in Figure 5) . The aim of this reduction way is also to avoid unnecessary composite states.

Now the whole light control system is defined by inclusion of the physical system part and composition of all the room controllers.

Figure 5. State Diagram for Room Controller

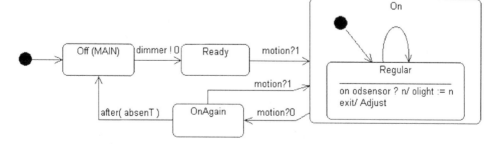

$$\boxed{\begin{array}{l} \underline{LCS} \\[4pt] \hline rd\_rc : RoomDevices \rightarrowtail RoomCtrller \\[4pt] \hline \text{MAIN} \cong \|_{(d,c):rd\_rc}(d \xrightarrow{dimmer,motion,odsensor} c) \end{array}}$$

The attribute *rd_rc* captures the one-to-one relationship between rooms and their corresponding controllers.

The behavior of the system is the multi-threaded concurrent interaction between the physical system components and their corresponding controllers, which is captured by the distributed TCOZ network topology operator. Note that although the TCOZ model is precise, the data/control flow direction and properties (sync/async) are not obvious in the network topology expression, it is implicitly captured by the input '?' and output '!' parameters and their types in lower level components. The collaboration diagrams (e.g., Figure 2) complement this.

RELATED WORKS AND FUTURE TRENDS

Linking formal and informal methods has been an active area in recent years (Araki, Galloway & Taguchi, 1999; Bryant & Semmens, 1996). From a technical point of view, our approach lies in this area. Others have studied Z and Fusion (France et al., 1997), VDM++ (Durr & Katwijk, 1992) and OMT , LOTOS (Wand, Richter, & Cheng, 1997) and OMT, and UML and Object-Z (Dupuy, Ledru & Chabre-Peccoud, 1997). The main difference is that our approach addresses not only the static aspects but also the dynamic aspects, e.g., TCOZ class behaviors are closely associated to the UML statechart and collaboration diagrams. Another difference is due to the TCOZ integration of state-based (Object Z) and event-based (Timed CSP) formalisms, whereas Z, Object-Z and VDM++ are only state-based. The process algebra aspects (processes/events) in TCOZ further link to the dynamic behavior (states/transitions) of UML statechart diagrams.

One further research topic is to develop systematic translation techniques/tools between UML and TCOZ. Since the current TCOZ specifications are constructed by using Latex (which often considered as). We are currently investigating an XML format of TCOZ specification and a translation tool from Latex to XML. Since UML 1.3 has already support for XMI (XML Metadata Interchange), then the next step is to implement the idea/ guidelines of this chapter in an semi-automatic tool to translate/project between TCOZ (XML) models and the UML (XMI) models. It is also possible to do some forms of analysis/ reasoning using the TCOZ model. For example, the model is constructed such that the question of consistency of the requirement model is equivalent to the TCOZ model being free from deadlocks. The absence of deadlocks can be checked by CSP analysis tools such as FDR (Roscoe, 1994). Projection from subset of TCOZ to FDR checkable code would also be an interesting future research area.

CONCLUSION

This chapter demonstrates an effective combination of UML and an integrated formal method (TCOZ) for the requirement specification of a light control system. Through this case study, we find that UML and TCOZ are highly complementary and compatible. The interplay between UML diagrams and TCOZ logical models make the requirement documentation easy to trace and digest. UML provides visual aid to TCOZ, while TCOZ provides a single underlying formal semantic model for all UML diagrams. From another point of view, UML diagrams can be seen as the different viewpoint projections (static, behavior, communication...etc.) of the formal unified (TCOZ) model. The formal model ensures that UML diagrams are consistent. Perhaps this work provides a complementary approach to viewpoints work (Easterbrook, 1993; Nuseibeh, Kramer & Finkelstein, 1994).

UML use-case models (user-case and collaboration diagrams) can be used to analyze system requirements so that main classes/operations can be identified/classified. For example, after the use case analysis, boundary classes (motion detector and outdoor sensor) and control classes (room controllers) are clearly identified.

UML class diagrams can also capture the static structure of the LCS systems, which is a good starting point to construct detailed class models. It provides the basis/guidelines for TCOZ formal model construction. The TCOZ process communication primitives _ channels, sensors and actuators precisely describe concurrent (synchronous and asynchronous) interactions between physical and control system components. It is appropriate to semantically identify the concept of 'state' in UML statechart diagrams with the TCOZ concept of 'process' and identify the 'state transition' of UML with the TCOZ 'event/guard.' In this way, the essential behavior of the LCS system can be visualized/highlighted according to the TCOZ formal model. The communications (concurrent interactions) between system components can also be depicted by the collaboration diagrams.

We believe that the successful combination of UML and integrated formal methods for requirement specification will provide many useful guidelines for the system design and implementation.

REFERENCES

Araki, K., Galloway, A. and Taguchi, K. Eds. (1999). *IFM'99: Integrated Formal Methods*, York, UK. Springer Verlag.

Bryant, A. and Semmens, L. (1996). *Methods Integration'96*. Springer, Leeds, UK.

Chen, P.P. (1976). The entity_relationship model: Towards a unified view of data. *ACM Trans. on Database Systems*, 1, p. 9-36.

Crow, J. and Vito, B. D. (1998). Formalizing space shuttle software requirements: four case studies. *ACM Trans. Software Engineering and Methodology*, 7(3), pp. 296-332.

Dardenne, A., van Lamsweerde, A., and Fickas, S. (1993).Goal_directed requirements acquisition. *Science of Computer Programming*, 20, pp. 3-50.

Darimont, R., Heisel, M. and J. Souquieres. (1999). Requirements and Elicitation & Specification. *FM'99 tutorial notes*.

Dong, J.S. and Duke, R. (1995). The Geometry of Object Containment. *Object_ Oriented Systems*, 2(1), pp. 41-63, Chapman & Hall.

Dong, J.S. and Mahony, B. (December 1998). Active Objects in TCOZ. In J. Staples, M. Hinchey, and S. Liu, Eds., *the 2nd IEEE International Conference on Formal Engineering Methods (ICFEM'98)*, 16-25. IEEE Computer Society Press.

Dubois, E., Yu, E. and Petit, M. (1998). From Early to Late Formal Requirements: a Process_Control Case Study. In *The 9th IEEE International Workshop on Software Specification and Design (IWSSD'98)*, pp. 34-42. IEEE Computer Society Press.

Duke, R., Rose, G. and Smith, G. (1995). Object_ Z: a Specification Language Advocated for the Description of Standards. *Computer Standards and Interfaces*, 17, pp. 511-533.

Dupuy, S., Ledru, Y. and Chabre-Peccoud, M. (1997). Integrating OMT and Object-Z. *BCSFACS/EROS ROOM Workshop*, London (UK).

221-Durr, E. and Katwijk, J. (1992). VDM++ _ - A Formal Specification Language for Object Oriented Designs. In *the International Conference on Technology of Object_Oriented Languages and Systems (TOOLS'Europe92)*, pp.63-78. Prentice_Hall.

Easterbrook, S. (1993). Domain modeling with hierarchies of alternative viewpoints. In *Frist Intl. Symposium on Requirement Engineering. IEEE*.

Evans, A. S. and Clark, A. N. (1998). Foundations of the unified modeling language. In D. J. Duke and A. S. Evans, editors, *BCS_FACS Northern Formal Methods Workshop, Electronic Workshops in Computing*. Springer Verlag.

Feather, M. (1987). Language Support for the Specification and Development of Composite Systems. *ACM Trans. Prog. Lang. and Syst.*, 9(2), pp. 198-234.

Feldmann, R. L., Munch, J. Queins, S., Vorwieger, S. and Zimmermann, G. (1999). Baselining a Doman-Specific Software Development Process. *Tech Report SFB501 TR_02/99*, University of Kaiserslautern.

France, R., Bruel, J. M., Larrondo-Petrie, M., Grant, E. and Saksena, M. (November 1997). Towards a Rigorous Object-Oriented Aalysis and Design Method. In M. Hinchey and S. Liu, editors, *the IEEE International Conference on Formal Engineering Methods (ICFEM'97)*, pp. 7-16, Hiroshima, Japan, IEEE Computer Society Press.

Grimm, K. (1998). Industrial requirements for the efficient development of reliable embedded systems. In J. P. Bowen, A. Fett, and M. G. Hinchey, editors, *ZUM'98: The Z Formal Specification Notation*, volume 1493 of Lect. Notes in Comput. Sci., pp.1-4. Springer-Verlag,. Extended abstract.

Hayes, I. J. and Mahony, B. P. (1995). Using units of measurement in formal specifications. *Formal Aspects of Computing*, 7(3).

Hesketh, J., Robertson, D., Fuchs, N. and Bundy, A. (1998). Lightweight formalisation in support of requirements engineering. *Automated Software Engineering*, 5, pp.183-210.

Kim, S. K. and Carrington, D. (1999). Formalizing UML Class Diagram Using Object Z. In R. France and B. Rumpe, Eds., *UML'99, Lect. Notes in Comput. Sci.* Springer-Verlag.

Leveson, N., Heimdahl, M., Hildreth, H. and Reese, J. (1994). Requirements specification for process control systems. IEEE Trans. Software Eng., 20(9).

Mahony, B. and Dong, J. S. (1998). Network Topology and a Case Study in TCOZ. In J. Bowen, A. Fett, and M. Hinchey, editors, *The 11th International Conference of Z Users*, volume 1493 of Lecture Notes in Computer Science, pp. 308-327, Berlin, Germany, Springer-Verlag.

Mahony, B. and Dong, J. S. (1999). Overview of the semantics of TCOZ. In Araki et al. [1], pp. 66-85.

Mahony, B. and Dong, J. S. (1999). Sensors and Actuators in TCOZ. In J. Wing, J. Woodcock, and J. Davies, editors, *FM'99: World Congress on Formal Methods*, volume 1709 of Lect. Notes in Comput. Sci., pp.1166-1185, Toulouse, France, Springer_Verlag.

Mahony, B. P. and Dong, J. S. (1998). Blending Object Z and Timed CSP: An introduction to TCOZ. In K. Futatsugi, R. Kemmerer, and K. Torii, editors, *The 20th International Conference on Software Engineering (ICSE'98)*, pp. 95-104, Kyoto, Japan, IEEE Computer Society Press.

Nijssen, G. M. and Halpin, T. A. (1989). *Conceptual Schema and Relational Database Design: a fact oriented approach*. Prentice Hall.

Nuseibeh, B., Kramer, J. and Finkelstein, A. (1994). A framework for expressing the relationships between multiple views in requirement specifications. *IEEE Trans. Software Eng.*, 20(10), pp.760-773.

Roscoe, A. W. Model checking CSP. (1994). In *A Classical Mind: Essays in Honour of C.A.R. Hoare*. Prentice Hall.

Rumbaugh, J., Jacobson, I. and Booch, G. (1999*). The Unified Modeling Languauge Reference Manua*l. Addison-Wesley.

Schneider, S. and Davies, J. (1995). A brief history of Timed CSP. *Theoretical Computer Science*, p.138.

Zave, P. and Jackson, M. (1997). Four dark corners of requirements engineering. *ACM Trans. Software Engineering and Methodology*, 6(1), pp. 1-30.

Wand, E., Richter, H. and Cheng, B. (1997). Formalizing and integrating the dynamic model within OMT. *19th International Conference on Software Engineering*, Boston(USA).

A TCOZ GLOSSORY

Notation	Explanation
c : **chan**	declare c to be a channel
a : **actuator**	declare a to be a actuator
s : **sensor**	declare s to be a sensor
SKIP	terminate immediately
WAIT t	delay termination by t
$a \rightarrow P$	communicate a then do P
$c?a$	input a on channel c
$c!a$	output a from channel c
$[b] \bullet P$	enable P only if b
$P; Q$	perform P until termination, then perform Q
$P \square Q$	perform the first enabled of P and Q
$[i : I] \bullet P$	perform P with first enabled value of i (external choice)
$(\parallel p_1, \ldots, p_n \bullet \ldots; p_i \xrightarrow{A} p_j; \ldots)$	network topology abstraction with parameters $p_1, \ldots, p_n$ and network connections including p_i communicating with p_j on private channels from A
$P \parallel\!\parallel Q$	P and Q running without sychronisations
$P \vartriangleright\{t\} Q$	if P does not begin by time t, perform Q instead
$P \triangledown e \rightarrow Q$	perform P until exception e, then transfer control to Q

Chapter XIV

Seamless Formalizing the UML Semantics Through Metamodels[1]

José Luis Fernández Alemán and Ambrosio Toval Álvarez
University of Murcia, Spain

Evolution...is – a change from an indefinite, incoherent homogeneity, to a definite coherent heterogeneity.
Herbert Spencer (1820-1903), First Principles (1862) ch.16

Despite the fact that the Unified Modeling Language (UML) has been adopted by the Object Management Group (OMG[2]) as the standard notation for use in Object-Oriented (OO) Systems Development, it still does not have a truly formal semantics. There is currently much effort directed towards formalizing particular aspects or models of UML. However, the literature gives little insight into the appropriate strategy for tackling this problem within an integrated basis including the language evolution. This chapter identifies and discusses three feasible strategies which can be applied to formalize UML. One of these strategies is selected to underpin the four-layer architecture on which UML is based. The approach is based on the soundness of algebraic specification theory, which, in addition, provides suitable theorem-proving capabilities for exploiting the UML formal model obtained. The formal models proposed are specified using an executable algebraic specification language called Maude.

INTRODUCTION

The UML (Object Management Group, 1999a; 1999b) has been adopted by the OMG as the standard OO Systems Development language. This language is experiencing a growing popularity, and it is an unavoidable reference in analysis and design of information systems, both in academia and industry. The UML stems from the merging of six earlier proposals and the invaluable contributions of about 40 authors.

In spite of that, the UML has often come under strong criticism since its appearance. The main reason for this has been the ambiguity and the lack of a formal definition of its semantics, which is still not sufficiently precise. For example, the UML static semantics is described by a semi-formal constraint language, the object constraint language (OCL), and the UML dynamic semantics is expressed in natural language. Particular problems concerning ambiguity, inconsistency and incompleteness have been identified (Reggio & Wieringa, 1999). This situation has hindered the construction of rigorous methods, precise UML artifacts and software tools to animate and formally manage UML models.

Unlike other modeling languages, UML has a distinguishing characteristic called extensibility, i.e., the ability to extend the language with new syntax and semantics features using its basic set of elements or building blocks. The UML modeling language supports extensibility by three extension mechanisms: *Stereotype*, *Constraint* and *TaggedValue*. Extensibility is sometimes considered to be a feature used mostly by academic or sophisticated users. Beware that mechanism extensions comprise less than 10% of the effort in building class diagrams (Fowler & Scott, 1997). In addition, the lack of CASE tools including this capability and the difficulty of precisely defining additional semantics to the UML result in the poor use of extensibility by most analysts.

The formalization of a modeling language can help to identify and remove these problems and also allows us to rigorously verify and manipulate the system models constructed. Thus, the goal is to combine the intuitive appeal of visual notations with the precision of formal specification languages. This chapter identifies and discusses three feasible strategies, which can be applied to formalize the UML. One of these strategies is selected and tailored to the UML four-layer metamodeling architecture. In contrast to other related approaches, we present a proposal for the integral formalization of the UML diagrams and their interrelations.

The UML syntax, static semantics and dynamic semantics are included in the same formal model in a seamless way. This means that the evolution of the UML metamodel is supported and formally described, which is a novelty from a theoretical viewpoint compared with other approaches. Therefore, the semantic framework provided faces up to the unpredictable and changeable nature of the UML, without limiting its ability to adapt the UML for needs of a particular domain.

In order to illustrate the approach, we present some examples concerning one of the UML diagrams, the Class Diagram. However, this approach is applicable to any other UML diagram or model, for example the UML Statechart Diagram (Fernández & Toval, 2000a).

The rest of the chapter is organized as follows: the second section discusses some issues that provide rationale for the framework presented, and presents a brief review of related work. We then proceed by introducing the main features of Maude through some examples that are used to present our proposal in the next section, which identifies three feasible strategies to formalize the UML. This section describes a procedure to formally support the extensibility mechanisms. The fifth section focuses on emerging trends in formalizing UML, and outlines the effort to be made in the future. The final section presents some concluding remarks. Previous background in algebraic specifications will help to understand the remaining sections, but this is not essential, provided that the reader refers to Appendix A.

SOME BACKGROUND

As said above, many problems have been identified concerning the UML semantics. A number of inconsistencies with the UML's extension mechanisms have also been identified (Alhir, 1999; Dykman, Griss & Kessler, 1999). Each extension mechanism implementation can show different semantics, leading to different or ambiguous interpretations. The formalization of these mechanisms provides a unique interpretation, thus helping to identify and remove ambiguities. Before UML appeared, we addressed this problem, putting forward a set of extension mechanisms in providing an OBJ3 formalization (Toval, Ramos & Pastor, 1994) for the object-oriented specification language OASIS (Pastor, Hayes & Bear, 1992).

Well-known formal languages, such as Z, VDM, CSP or LOTOS, have been typically used to formalize graphical notations associated with software engineering methodologies. Languages based on logic, such as Z or VDM, allow us to suitably describe the structure of a system. On the other hand, other languages based on process algebras, such as CSP or LOTOS, permit us to appropriately represent the behavior of a system. In many cases, formal languages such as CASL-LTL (Reggio, Astesiano & Choppy, 1999) and Object-Z have been defined as extensions of the original languages to cover missing aspects. However, none of these include the ability to directly handle extensibility mechanisms or specify metaprogramming applications necessary to formalize the extension of the UML metamodel.

In order to be able to cope with all the expressive richness of UML, we needed a powerful formal language, Maude[3] (Clavel et al., 1999). Maude is a mathematically well-founded language, based on equational (Goguen & Meseguer, 1988) and rewriting (Meseguer, 1992) logic. In addition, the Maude specifications can be executed using the Maude interpreter. Maude is an extension of OBJ3, with a much greater performance. Both structure and behavior of a system can be suitably defined in Maude and, unlike other formal specification languages, it offers an excellent feature, reflection, to cope with changes in the UML metamodel at modeling time. Reflection is the ability of a logic to be interpreted in itself. This is crucial to deal with metaprogramming and metamodeling issues.

Recently, the formalization of UML has increasingly been drawing considerable attention. Many contributions on this subject have been identified in a recent survey by Whittle (2000), which reflects the current state of the art in formalizing UML. In this matter, one of the most relevant research groups is the pUML[4] group (The precise Unified Modeling Language group, 2000). Research directly related to ours, but using the formal language Z, has been reported by this group (Evans, 1998; Evans & Clark, 1998; France, 1999). The primary goal of the pUML group is to define precise semantics for the UML language and develop mechanisms that allow developers to rigorously analyze the UML models.

Formalizing the UML metamodel and its evolution particularly the UML extensibility mechanisms has thus far received little attention. Although there has been some research effort directed towards formalizing particular extension mechanisms (Araújo, Moreira & Sawyer, 1999), no one has addressed the extensibility of the UML within a global framework. The formalizing process presented is holistic (the whole formal model provides support for most UML diagrams) and seamless (one can navigate from the dynamic semantic aspects at the UML object layer towards the model, metamodel and metamodel evolution ones).

MAUDE, A HIGH-PERFORMANCE LANGUAGE

In order to help us understand the next section, some basic notions regarding the formalism used are presented. Maude is a formal specification language that supports both equational and rewriting logic computation. Maude evolved from OBJ3, therefore, we will briefly describe some of the differences between the underlying formalism in OBJ3 and Maude. We will also show how reflection is exploited in Maude's design, thus extending the basic functionalities of the language Core Maude. The Maude features will be illustrated with some of the definitions and the algebraic specifications used later. A detailed description of order-sorted equational logic and rewriting logic can be found in the references quoted in Appendix A.

Maude Principles

Maude is an extension of OBJ3 (Goguen & Malcom, 1996), which is based on equational logic and provides parameterized programming, multiple inheritance and a *large-grain* programming technique, to support the scalability of the specification and appropriately manage the complexity of a system. Maude allows us to specify concurrent and distributed object-based systems. A recent study (Ölveczky & Meseguer, 1999) has also applied Maude's rewriting logic to real-time systems by simply adding syntactic sugar.

Maude's equational logic, called *membership equational logic*, extends OBJ3's equational logic by supporting *membership axioms*. The new characteristic of this logic is that a condition can be given to establish whether a term (see Appendix A) has a certain sort (see Appendix A). This kind of axiom can be applied to the verification of properties concerning the UML static semantics. As an example, checking the orthogonality property in a UML statechart diagram is shown in Figure 1. A UML statechart diagram consists of a state hierarchy, a transition list and an argument list. The constructor *statechart,* which takes three arguments (elements of sorts *State, TransitionList* and *ArgumentList*), is defined in the module *STATECHART*. The membership axiom shown in Figure 1 is introduced by the keyword *cmb* and imposes the orthogonality condition (operation *isOrthogonal(E, TL)*) to allow a statechart (*statechart (E, TL, AL)*) to have the sort *Statechart.* A more detailed description of this property can be found in a related paper (Fernández & Toval, 2000a), which chooses another alternative to explicitly show the unsatisfied constraint.

Maude Functional Modules

Maude's functional modules are theories in membership equational logic. Figure 2 shows a functional module, where the abstract syntax of a type in UML is described. A UML

Figure 1. Algebraic Specification of the UML Statechart Diagram

```
(fmod STATECHART is sort Statechart .
 protecting STATE . protecting TRANSITIONLIST .
 protecting ARGUMENTLIST .
 op statechart : State TransitionList ArgumentList -> Statechart .
 op isOrthogonal : State TransitionList -> Bool .
 var E : State . var TL : TransitionList . var AL : ArgumentList .
 cmb statechart (E, TL, AL) : Statechart if isOrthogonal(E, TL) .
 endfm)
```

Figure 2. Algebraic Specification of a UML Type.

```
(fmod TYPE is sort Type .
 including TYPENAME . *** Importing modules TYPENAME
 including ATTRIBUTELIST . ***        ATTRIBUTELIST
 protecting OPERATIONLIST . *** and OPERATIONLIST
 op type : TypeName AttributeList OperationList -> Type .
 op getTypeAttribute : Type -> AttributeList .
 op getTypeName : Type -> TypeName .
 var TN : TypeName . var AL : AttributeList .
 var OL : OperationList .
 eq getTypeAttribute (type (TN, AL, OL)) = AL .
 eq getTypeName (type (TN, AL, OL)) = TN .
 endfm)
```

type describes the common properties (attributes and operations) of a set of objects without defining their physical implementation. Therefore, a type comprises a name, a list of attributes and a list of operations. The sort *Type*, the constructor *type* and the query operations *getTypeName* and *getTypeAttribute* are declared in the functional module *TYPE*. The last operation takes one argument, an element of sort *Type*, and yields its list of attributes. The sorts *TypeName, AttributeList* and *OperationList* are declared, respectively, in the modules *TYPENAME, ATTRIBUTELIST* and *OPERATIONLIST*, which are imported by protecting and including declarations.

As an example, the term *tl* (Figure 3) of sort *TypeList* represents a list of types: *Company, Bank* and *Person. TypeList* is a sort declared by importing the parameterized

Figure 3. Term Representing a List of Types.

```
tl = type ( 'Company, attribute ('Inc, 'Bool)
                 attribute ('NumberEmployee, 'Integer), noOperation )
       type ( 'Bank, attribute ('Internet, 'Bool), noOperation )
       type ( 'Person, attribute ('Male, 'Bool) attribute ('Age, 'Integer) ,
                 operation ('Income, parameter ('date, 'Date),'Integer) )
```

Figure 4. A UML Class Diagram.

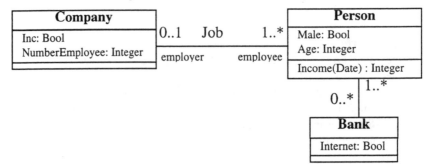

module *LIST* instantiated with the module *TYPE*. An alternative graphical representation is shown in Figure 4. For example, the type *Person* has two attributes, *male* and *age*, and one operation, *income*.

Maude System Modules

The second kind of module in Maude is the system module, which is based on rewriting logic. A rewrite theory allows us to specify states of a system, modeled by a UML diagram, as an abstract data type and its local state transitions by rewrite rules.

The basic functionality of the language, *Core Maude*, is extended by reflection to Full Maude. Full Maude, which is written in Core Maude, is a metaprogramming application that includes object-oriented modules, parameterized modules, views and module expressions in the OBJ style. Object-oriented modules are system modules with some syntactic sugar that allow us to specify in the OO style.

An extract of an object-oriented module called *COMPANY* (denoting companies) is shown in Figure 5. The declaration of a class named *Company* with two attributes called *name* of sort *Qid* (quoted identifier) and *numberEmployees* of sort *MachineInt* (machine integer) is introduced by the keyword *class*. The message declarations are introduced by the keyword *msg* (message *addEmployee*) or *msgs* if multiple messages with the same arity are defined. The labeled rewrite rules, which are introduced by the keyword *rl* (rule), specify in a declarative way the behavior associated with the messages. For instance, the rule labeled *addEmployee* specifies the behavior of objects in class *Company*, which may receive messages for changing their number of employees. The *rew* (rewrite) command is used to rewrite a term representing a configuration of a concurrent object system. For example, when a company called *Hero* with object identifier (OI) 1 receives a message *addEmployee (1, 5)*, the value 5 is added to its attribute *numberEmployees* (Figure 5).

Notice that the subsort relationship *MachineInt < Oid* is introduced, indicating that machine integers can be viewed as object identifiers. All object-oriented modules implicitly

Figure 5. Specification in Full Maude of an Object-Oriented Module Named COMPANY.

```
(omod COMPANY is
    protecting QID .
    protecting MACHINE-INT .
    subsort MachineInt < Oid .
    class Company | name : Qid, numberEmployees  : MachineInt .
    msg addEmployee : Oid MachineInt -> Msg .
    var OI : Oid .    var QI : Qid .    var MI, MI2 : MachineInt .
    rl [addEmployee] : addEmployee (OI, MI2)
    < OI : Company | name : QI, numberEmployees : MI >
 => < OI : Company | name : QI, numberEmployees : MI + MI2 > .
 endom)
(rew < 1 : Company | name : 'Hero, numberEmployees : 14 >
     < 2 : Company | name : 'Juver, numberEmployees : 24 >
                              addEmployee (1, 5) . )
Result Configuration :
 < 1 : Company | numberEmployees : 19 , name : 'Hero >
 < 2 : Company | numberEmployees : 24 , name : 'Juver >
```

include the *CONFIGURATION* predefined functional module which defines the basic concepts of concurrent object systems. Some of these definitions are left unspecified such as the sort *Oid*, which is fully defined and used in the module *Company*. Other examples can be found in Maude's documentation (Clavel et al., 1999).

Reflection, A Key Feature of Maude

Once the ability of Maude to specify both the structure and behavior of a system has been demonstrated, the outstanding and key feature of Maude, on which our proposal is based, can be introduced. Rewriting logic is reflective (Clavel & Meseguer, 1996); this means that there is a rewrite theory, called *universal theory* U, that can represent any rewrite theory R (including U itself) as a term ^R, any terms t, t_1 in R as terms ^t and $^t_1$, and any pair (R, t) as a term (^R, ^ t), in such a way that the following equivalence is satisfied:

$$R \_ t \rightarrow t_1 \iff U \_ (^R, ^t) \, \text{Æ} \, (^R, ^t_1)$$

This equivalence has a great practical interest in formalizing the UML four-layer architecture, as it provides the basis for the *navigation* through the UML metalayers. The *universal theory* U is implemented in Maude through the functional module *META-LEVEL*. Subsequently, an extract of the signature of U is presented in which terms and functional modules are reified as elements of the data types *Term* and *FModule*. Figure 6 shows the operators used to represent terms of any sort and functional modules.

The declaration of subsorting *Qid* < *Term* is used for representing variables as quoted identifiers. The first operator, *{_}_*, is used for representing constants by pairs (constant name and constant sort), both in quoted form. The next operator, *_[_]*, denotes the recursive construction of terms out of subterms. The first argument represents the top operator in quoted form, and the second argument represents the list of subterms. Finally, the term list concatenation operator, *_ _*, is declared. On the other hand, a functional module is metarepresented by eight elements: a name (sort *Qid*), a list of imported modules (sort *ImportList*), a sort declaration (sort *SortDecl*), a set of subsort declarations (sort *SubsortDeclSet*), a set of operator declarations (sort *OpDeclSet*), a set of variable declarations (sort *VarDeclSet*), a set of membership axioms (*MembAxSet*) and a set of equations (*EquationSet*). The description of these sorts is omitted here, but it can be found in Maude's documentation (Clavel et al., 1999).

Figure 6. Operators of the Universal Theory U to Represent Terms.

```
fmod META-LEVEL is
...
  sort FModule .
  subsort Qid < Term .*** variables
  subsort Term < TermList .
  op {_}_ : Qid Qid -> Term . *** constants
  op _ [ _ ] : Qid TermList -> Term . *** operators
  op _,_ : TermList TermList -> TermList [assoc] . *** list of terms
  op error* : -> Term .
  op fmod_is_ _ _ _ _ _ _endfm : Qid ImportList SortDecl
                    SubsortDeclSet OpDeclSet VarDeclSet
                    MembAxSet EquationSet -> FModule .
```

In order to illustrate the meta-representation of a term using the module *META-LEVEL* presented above, the module *TYPE* defined in Figure 2 is used. A term of sort *TypeAttribute* (Figure 7) and its meta-representation (Figure 8) are shown as an example.

In metaprogramming applications such as the one proposed in this chapter, rewrites and reductions at both high level (universal theory U) and low level (rewrite theory R) are necessary. In order to increase the efficiency of metalevel computations, descent functions are defined in the metalevel theory M, which is an extension of the universal theory U. As an example, a meta-reduction using the descent function *meta-reduce* is shown:

Maude> (down TYPE : red meta-reduce (TYPE, up(TYPE, tn)) .)

Result AttributeList: attribute ('Male , 'Bool) attribute ('Age , 'Integer)

where the function *meta-reduce* takes two arguments: the first argument is the meta-representation of module *TYPE* obtained by the constant *TYPE* declared in importing the module *META-LEVEL[TYPE]* (high level), and the second argument is the meta-representation of the term *tn* of sort *TypeAttribute* (Figure 8) included in the module *TYPE* (low level). The meta-representation of the term *tn* in the module *TYPE* is obtained by the *up* command. Finally, the *down* command is used to return the term from its meta-representation, thus obtaining the attributes of the type *Person*.

FORMALLY MODELING THE UML

When we come face to face with the problem of formally modeling the UML (or even a part of it), we must remember the existing problems, referred to in the previous section, in relation to the current version of the language. The first question that arises is whether it is actually feasible to define the semantics for all the language and its architecture. Probably, the definitive answer for this question can only be given constructively (Kent, Evans & Rumpe, 1999).

A lot of effort is required to tackle the task of obtaining a formalization of a language like UML. Moreover, the semantics provided by the formal model should be accepted by the software engineering community. The formal framework that we report in this chapter can cope with the current semantics of UML, and it also serves as a basis for its future versions. This is due to the fact that this framework includes the meta-metamodel of UML.

Figure 7. Term of Sort Type

```
tn = getTypeAttribute (
     type ( 'Person, attribute ('Male, 'Bool) attribute ('Age, 'Integer,),
           operation ('Income,  parameter ('date, 'Date), 'Integer) ) )
```

Figure 8. Metaterm of Sort Term.

```
^tn= 'getTypeAttribute [ 'type [{ ''Person } 'Qid , '__ [
'attribute [ { ''Male } 'Qid , { ''Bool } 'Qid ] ,
'attribute [ { ''Age } 'Qid , {''Integer } 'Qid] ] ,
'operation [ { ''Income } 'Qid , 'parameter [{ ''date } 'Qid ,
                  { ''Date } 'Qid ] , { ''Integer } 'Qid ] ] ]
```

Subsequently, three approaches to formalize a modeling language like UML are presented. One of these approaches is chosen and tailored to the UML four-layer metamodeling architecture. Finally, a description of the formal specification supporting our selection is accomplished.

Identifying and Selecting Feasible Formalizing Strategies

Formal techniques can be applied to a modeling language according to different purposes such as verification, prototyping, code generation and document generation. With the appearance of the UML, another relevant aspect raises: evolution. The UML models allow us to describe information from the real world, that is to say, data. The data used to describe other data are called metadata. In the same way, the concepts used to describe metadata are called meta-metadata. The extensibility mechanisms incorporated in UML offer the possibility of adding new meta-metadata in the UML metamodel, thus supporting the evolution of the language. Therefore, if formalizing a language is, intended both the meta-metadata and its evolution should be taken into consideration. Regarding the meta-metadata that can be represented, three strategies are identified:

1. *Modeling strategy.* The formalization is accomplished using a translational strategy, that is to say, by mapping each UML element to some formalism element.
2. *Metamodeling strategy.* The formalism is used to specify the modeling language metamodel.
3. *Meta-metamodeling strategy.* The formalism is used to specify the modeling language metamodel and its evolution.

The following paragraphs will explain the above three strategies.

Modeling strategy

In this approach a correspondence between each element in the modeling language and some particular expressiveness, feature or construct in the formal language is established (Bourdeau & Cheng, 1995; France, Bruel & Larrond-Petrie, 1997; Wang, Richter & Cheng, 1997). Concerning the UML four-layer architecture (see Table 1), the core UML model layer is supported by the mapping accomplished, the domain model layer is covered by a formal specification in the formalism, and the user object layer relies on the elements (for example, terms of a sort or elements of a set) belonging to the constructs of the formalism. However, the meta UML model is not formally supported in the initial specification. If a new modeling element is included in the modeling language, analysts must search for suitable formal language features that best fit to describe both its syntax and semantics, thereby modifying the initial formal specification (Araújo et al., 1999).

For example, if an algebraic language such as Larch, CafeOBJ, CASL or Maude is used, an attribute or an operation of a class can be denoted as an operation symbol in the formal language. Therefore, an algebraic specification corresponds to a domain model (Figure 5 shows an example of this approach). Otherwise, if a language based on set theory and predicate logic such as Z is used, a class in a class diagram can be represented by a state schema in Z, and an attribute of a class can be denoted as a state variable. Likewise, an operation of a class can be defined by an operation schema from the relationship between the state after and before executing the operation. Therefore, a set of schemas in Z corresponds to a domain model or diagram in UML.

Metamodeling strategy

In the metamodeling approach, the modeling language metamodel is represented by a formal specification (Evans & Clark, 1998; Fernández & Toval, 2000a; Grima & Toval, 1994). In the Maude case, the domain model layer and the user object layer are specified by terms. For instance, Figure 3 and Figure 10 show terms of the domain model layer and the user object layer, respectively. The modeling language syntax and dynamic semantics are described by what we call the *syntactic specifications*[5] and *semantic specifications,*[6] incorporating the static semantics by equations or axioms in the syntactic specifications. For example, the algebraic specification representing the UML types in Figure 2 is a syntactic specification, and the algebraic specification representing the UML objects in Figure 9 is a semantic specification.

Equations can also be used to obtain equivalent diagrams according to various purposes (Fernández & Toval, 2000d; Lano & Bicarregui, 1998) such as model enhancements, refinements, reverse engineering, reductions and, in general, any kind of transformation regarding a metric.

As an example, a pair of modules (Figure 9) is presented, namely, *OBJECT* that specifies objects of a type, and *SYSTEMOBJECTS* that specifies the whole population of objects. The constructor *object* allows us to represent objects of UML types made up of an identifier, the name of a type (to which the object belongs) and a nonempty list of values associated with the type attributes. The operation *newObject* yields a list of objects constructed by adding an object to a list of objects. Both are arguments of the operation *newObject*.

Any error condition can be specified according to the UML semantics. For example, consider that the values of the new object and the attribute types associated with the type of

Figure 9. Algebraic Specification of the UML Objects.

```
(fmod OBJECT is sorts Object .
        protecting OID .
        protecting TYPENAME .
        protecting VALUELIST .
op object : Oid TypeName NEValueList -> Object .
endfm)
(view Object from TRIV to OBJECT is sort Elt to Object .  endv)
(fmod SYSTEMOBJECTS is protecting TYPELIST .
including LIST[Object] * (sort List[Object] to ObjectList,
                    sort NonEmptyList[Object] to NEObjectList) .
op newObject : Object TypeList ObjectList -> ObjectList .
op errorAttributes : -> ObjectList .
op nonCompatibleType : ValueList AttributeList -> Bool .
var OI:Oid . var TN:TypeName . var NEVL:NEValueList .
var TL:TypeList . var OL:ObjectList .
eq newObject (object (OI, TN, NEVL), TL, OL) =
    if (length (getTypeAttrs (TN, TL)) =/= length (NEVL)) or
      (nonCompatibleType (NEVL, getTypeAttrs (TN, TL)))
      then errorAttributes
      else object (OI, TN, NEVL) OL  fi .endfm)
```

the new object (operation *nonCompatibleTypes (NEVL, getTypeAttribute (TN, TL)))* are not compatible, or the number of object values and the number of type attributes (operation *length (getTypeAttribute (TN, TL)) =/= length (NEVL))* are not equal. In both cases, the operation *newObject* yields the term *errorAttributes* of sort *ObjectList*. This element is the canonical term that represents the set of terms denoting objects with incorrect values according to the UML language. As an example of an instance of the model shown in Figure 4, and partially formalized in Figure 3, the term *ol* of sort *ObjectList* is given in Figure 10. This term represents the addition of eight objects in the modeled system. For instance, the person represented by the object with object identifier 8 is male and his age is 20.

From an evolution viewpoint, this approach suffers from the same problem as the previous one. In this case, the evolution problem is translated to the specifications representing the language metamodel. Therefore, it is necessary to modify the initial metamodel formal specification to allow new modeling elements to be included. Nevertheless, the syntactic and semantic evolution of the domain models is formally supported, in such a way that a class or an object may be included in the system. Likewise, a correct evolution of the instances of the models built under the language can be ensured, assuming that a rigorous formalization of the metamodel has been constructed. In our opinion, the second approach has several advantages over the first one:

1. The algebraic specification is fixed and independent of the size or the complexity of the system modeled.
2. Incorporating a new layer to support the modeling language metamodel evolution is plausible.
3. Considering the system evolution, the terms representing instances of the diagrams do not grow as rapidly as in the case of the first approach.
4. Possible changes in the language are focused on the metamodel formal specification. Schema evolution issues can be dealt with through constant and operation symbols in the same specification. Using the first approach, these changes should be spread out over all the algebraic specifications describing the domain models.

Meta-Metamodeling Strategy

The third strategy copes with the issue of evolution in its two dimensions (modeling and metamodeling) (Toval & Fernández, 2000) by a two-level approach. The modeling language syntax and semantics are described by the lower level in the same way as the metamodel strategy mentioned above. The higher level formally supports the evolution of the modeling language metamodel and enables us to establish rules that must be satisfied by this metamodel. The inherent duality of the modules representing the metamodel, which

Figure 10. Term Representing the Addition of a Set of Objects

```
ol = newObject (object ( 8, 'Person, (true 20)), tl,
  newObject (object ( 7, 'Person, (true 22)), tl,
  newObject (object ( 6, 'Bank, (false)), tl,
  newObject (object ( 5, 'Bank, (false)), tl,
  newObject (object ( 4, 'Company, (true 260)), tl,
  newObject (object ( 3, 'Person, (true 26)), tl,
  newObject (object ( 2, 'Company, (false 1000)), tl,
  newObject (object ( 1, 'Person, (false 25)), tl, noObject).
```

Table 1. Representing the Four-Layer Metamodeling Architecture of UML in Maude

The UML layer	Maude formal layer	Example
Meta UML model	The module META-LEVEL	MetaClass, MetaAttribute, MetaOperation
Core UML model	Syntactic and semantic specifications	Type, Attribute, Operation
Domain model	Terms (of syntactic specifications)	Person, Name, Age
User objects	Terms (of semantic specifications)	<John, 14>, <Joy, 34>

can be seen as theories or terms, is reflected in this approach. If they are considered as modules, reasoning about domain models can be performed. If they are dealt with as terms, metamodel evolution can be attained. Table 1 shows the correspondence between the UML conceptual framework and the formal framework proposed.

In order to gain some insight into the formal framework that supports the UML four-layer architecture, some examples are given as follows. A term belonging to the user object layer and representing eight specific objects of the system is shown in Figure 10. The problem domain concept *Person* represented in the UML domain model is shown in Figure 7. The construct *Type* of the core UML model is specified in the module described in Figure 2. Examples concerning the meta UML model will be addressed in the following section.

A Formal Proposal to Cope with the UML Extension Mechanisms

The meta UML model or UML meta-metamodeling layer (the UML highest abstraction level) provides the expressiveness needed to define the UML metamodel and its evolution. This allows the UML to be customized and adapted to the analyst's modeling requirements, thus providing the possibility of developing UML CASE tools that support evolution. To attain this purpose, an extension of the module *META-LEVEL* is defined. An example of extension through tagged values is provided. In order to show the feasibility of the proposal, a subset of the UML Class Diagram is also formalized and extended by the constructs defined for meta-metamodeling.

Preparing the Formal Framework for Evolution

The first step is to define a collection of basic operations in an extension of the module *META-LEVEL* to cope with the meta UML model layer (see Table 1). Some of these operations, *addSorts*, *addSubsort*, *addOperation*, *addVariable*, *addDomainSort*, *updateEquations*, *addEquation* and *addConstants*, and most of their associated equations are shown in Figure 11.

A functional module is metarepresented by terms of sort *FModule* (see Figure 6), included in the predefined *META-LEVEL* module. By the declaration *protecting META-LEVEL[TYPE]* in Figure 11, the constant *TYPE* of sort *Module* (supersort of *FModule* to metarepresent system modules) is declared. A new equation making the constant *TYPE* equal to the metalevel representation of the user-defined module with name *TYPE* (declared in Figure 2) is also implicitly included. This constant will be used to extend the meta-

Figure 11. Extension of the Module META-LEVEL.

```
(fmod META-LEVEL-EXTENSION is  protecting META-LEVEL[TYPE] .
*** Add a set of sorts
  op addSorts : FModule QidSet -> FModule .
*** Add a subsort relationship
  op addSubsort : FModule QidList QidList -> FModule .
*** Add an operation
  op addOperation : FModule Qid QidList Qid AttrSet -> FModule .
*** Add a variable declaration
  op addVariable : FModule Qid Qid -> FModule .
*** Add a sort to the domain of an operation
  op addDomainSort : FModule Qid Qid -> FModule .
  op newSortList : OpDeclSet Qid Qid -> OpDeclSet .
*** Update the equations that contain the operation represented by ModelElementName
  op updateEquations : FModule ModelElementName Qid -> FModule .
*** Add an equation.
  op addEquation : FModule Term Term -> FModule .
*** Add a constant for each quoted identifier from an identifier list
  op addConstants : FModule QidList TagName -> FModule .
  op addConstant : QidList TagName -> OpDeclSet .

  var QS : QidSet .  var QS1 : QidSet .  var QI : Qid .  var QI1 : Qid .  var QI2 : Qid .
  var QI3 : Qid .  var QI4 : Qid .    var IL : ImportList .  var SD : SortDecl .
  var TE1 : Term .  var SSDS : SubsortDeclSet .  var ODS : OpDeclSet .
  var VDS : VarDeclSet . var TE2 : Term .  var MAS : MembAxSet .
  var EqS : EquationSet .   var AS : AttrSet .  var AS1 : AttrSet .  var QL : QidList .
  var QL1 : QidList .  var MEN : ModelElementName .    var TN : TagName .

  eq addSorts (fmod QI is IL sorts (QS) . SSDS ODS VDS MAS EqS endfm, QS1)
    = fmod QI is IL sorts(QS ; QS1) . SSDS ODS VDS MAS EqS endfm .

  eq addSubsort (fmod QI is IL SD SSDS ODS VDS MAS EqS endfm, QL1, QL)
    = fmod QI is IL SD subsort QL1 < QL . SSDS ODS VDS MAS EqS endfm .

  eq addOperation (fmod QI is IL SD SSDS ODS VDS MAS EqS endfm, QI1, QL, QI2, AS)
    = fmod QI is IL SD SSDS ODS  op QI1 : QL -> QI2 [AS] .VDS MAS EqS endfm .

  eq addVariable (fmod QI is IL SD SSDS ODS VDS MAS EqS endfm, QI1, QI2)
    = fmod QI is IL SD SSDS ODS VDS var QI1 : QI2 . MAS EqS endfm .

  eq addDomainSort (fmod QI is IL SD SSDS ODS VDS MAS EqS endfm, MEN, TN)
    = fmod QI is IL SD SSDS newSortList (ODS ,MEN, TN) VDS MAS EqS endfm .
  eq newSortList (op QI3 : QL1 -> QI4 [AS1] . ODS, MEN, TN) =
      if QI3 == MEN then op QI3 : QL1 TN -> QI4 [AS1] . ODS
      else  op QI3 : QL1 -> QI4 [AS1] . newSortList (ODS, MEN, TN)        fi .

  eq addEquation (fmod QI is IL SD SSDS ODS VDS MAS EqS endfm, TE1, TE2) =
      fmod QI is IL SD SSDS ODS VDS MAS eq TE1 = TE2 . EqS endfm .

  eq addConstants (fmod QI is IL SD SSDS ODS VDS MAS EqS endfm, QL, TN) =
        fmod QI is IL SD SSDS ODS addConstant(QL, TN) VDS MAS EqS endfm .
  eq addConstant (nil, TN) = none .
  eq addConstant (QI QL, TN) =  op QI : nil -> TN [none] . addConstant (QL, TN) .
endfm)
```

representation of the module *TYPE*.

The second step is to describe the constructs for supporting the UML extension mechanisms (*Stereotype*, *Constraint* and *TaggedValue*) by using the extended module *META-LEVEL*. To illustrate our proposal, the operations (*tagging*) and equations describing the syntax and semantics of a UML tagged value are shown in Figure 12. A tagged value allows properties to be attached to a modeling element (Figure 13 shows an example). Note that, according to the formal framework proposed in this chapter, the syntax of a modeling element is represented by the signature of a Maude operation (see the operation *type* in Figure 2). In order to add a new property (sort *TagName*) to a modeling element (sort *ModelElementName*), a new sort (the tag name) must be introduced in the Maude operation domain using *addDomainSort*. If the type of the tagged value is string, integer or bool, a new sort (*TagName*) and a subsort relationship (*Qid < TagName or MachineInt < TagName or Bool< TagName*) are declared using *addSorts* and *addSubsort*. If the type of the tagged value is enumeration, a new sort is declared and a constant operation is defined for each literal using *addConstants*. Notice that the operation *tagging* is overloaded, thus making use of one of the Maude features.

To complete this specification, a variable of the new sort must be declared using *addVariable* and the equations that include the modified operation must be updated using *updateEquations*. The *built-in* operation *index*, which appends the result of an integer expression at the end of a quoted identifier, is used to obtain variable names.

Tagged Values: An Example of Extension

A virtual machine of the UML metamodel is implicit in the executable Maude specification. The constructs describing the UML extension mechanisms presented in the previous section allow us to perform modifications of the UML metamodel at the meta-metamodel layer, thus modifying the virtual machine. As an example, a new property, *author*, attached through a tagged value to a type called *Person* is displayed in Figure 13.

This extension (Figure 14) is accomplished using the operation *tagging* which takes four arguments in matching the top operation in Figure 12 due to operator overloading. The

Figure 12. Formal Specification of the Construct for Tagging UML Model Eements

```
op tagging : FModule ModelElementName
             TagName TagType -> FModule .
op tagging : FModule ModelElementName
             TagName TagType QidList-> FModule .
var MEN : ModelElementName .  var TN : TagName .
var FM : FModule .  var QL : QidList .
eq tagging (FM, MEN, TN, 'string)
   =  updateEquations( addDomainSort( addVariable( addSubsort (
      addSorts (FM, TN), 'Qid, TN),
            index (TN, 1), TN), MEN, TN), MEN, index (TN, 1)) .
eq tagging (FM, MEN, TN, 'enumeration, QL)
   =  updateEquations( addDomainSort( addVariable( addConstants (
      addSorts (FM, TN), QL, TN), index (TN, 1), TN), MEN, TN),
                                   MEN, index (TN, 1)) .
```

first argument is the functional module *TYPE* that includes the formal specification of the UML types. The second argument is the operation name *type* that formally describes the modeling element tagged. The third and the fourth argument are the name and the type, *Author* and *string*, of the tagged value. The operation *tagging* returns the meta-representation of the module that includes the formal specification of the tagged UML types. The resulting module is shown in Figure 14 for the purposes of readability, where the sort *Author* and the subsort relationship *Qid < Author* are declared. The sort *Author* is introduced in the domain of the operation *type*, and a variable, *Author1*, is declared. The subterms formed with the operation *type* and appearing in the equations are updated with the new variable *Author1*.

The formal representation of a particular tagged type, equivalent to the UML graphical representation shown in Figure 13, is given in Figure 15.

Notice that the new UML modeling element preserves all the initial properties. As an example, the query operation *getTypeName* is applied in Figure 16 to the term *t* in Figure 15. The function *meta-reduce* takes two arguments: the first argument is the meta-representation of module *TYPE* modified (*tagging(TYPE, 'type, 'Author,*

Figure 13. An Example of Tagged Value in UML.

Person { author = John }
Male : Bool Age : Integer
Income (Date) : Integer

Figure 14. Operation That Tags a Type and Resulting Algebraic Specification of the Tagged Type.

(red tagging(TYPE, 'type, 'Author, 'string) .)

(fmod TYPE is sorts Type Author .
          subsort Qid < Author .
including TYPENAME . *** Importing modules TYPENAME,
including ATTRIBUTELIST . ***   ATTRIBUTELIST
protecting OPERATIONLIST . *** and OPERATIONLIST
          op type : TypeName AttributeList OperationList Author -> Type .
op getTypeAttribute : Type -> AttributeList .
op getTypeName : Type -> TypeName .
 var TN : TypeName . var AL : AttributeList.
          var OL : OperationList . var Author1 : Author .
  eq getTypeAttribute (type (TN, AL, OL, Author1)) = AL .
  eq getTypeName (type (TN, AL, OL, Author1)) = TN .
     endfm)
Figure 15. Term of Sort Tagged Type.

     t = type ('Person, attribute ('Male, 'Bool) attribute ('Age, 'Integer,),
        operation ('Income, parameter ('date, 'Date), 'Integer) , 'John)

Figure 16. A Meta-Reduction of a Term of Sort TypeName

> (red meta-reduce (tagging(TYPE, 'type, 'Author, 'string),
> 'getTypeName ['type [{ ''Person } 'Qid , '__ [
> 'attribute [{ ''Male } 'Qid , { ''Bool } 'Qid] ,
> 'attribute [{ ''Age } 'Qid , {''Integer } 'Qid]] , 'operation [
> { ''Income } 'Qid , 'parameter [{ ''date } 'Qid , { ''Date } 'Qid] ,
> { ''Integer } 'Qid], { ''John } 'Qid]])) .)
> Result Term : { ''Person } 'Qid

'string) and the second argument is the meta-representation of a term of sort *TypeName*. As the reduction is made at the high level, the resulting term is the meta-representation of the type name *Person*.

Formally Describing Semantic Extensions

The previous example illustrates the feasibility of extending UML with new syntactic elements. In order to gain insight into the benefits from the approach, an extension that includes semantics aspects is also presented. In particular, a new attribute, named *changeability*, is defined for the Core UML model element *Attribute*. This property specifies whether the attribute value may be modified after the object is created. The values for *changeability* consist of the literal *frozen* (the attribute value cannot be altered after the object has been instantiated and its values initialized) and *changeable* (no restriction on modification is imposed). The syntax of the new property is included in the module *ATTRIBUTE* by the operation *tagging* which takes five arguments (Figure 17). The first argument is the functional module *ATTRIBUTE* that includes the formal specification of the UML attributes. The second argument is the operation name, *attribute*, that formally

Figure 17. Operation Describing the Syntax of a New Property for the Model Element Attribute *and Resulting Algebraic Specification of the New Extension*

> (red tagging(ATTRIBUTE, 'attribute, 'Changeability, 'enumeration, 'frozen
> 'changeable) .)
>
> (fmod ATTRIBUTE is sorts Attribute Changeability .
> including ATTRIBUTENAME. including TYPENAME .
> op frozen : -> Changeability .
> op changeable : -> Changeability .
> op attribute : AttributeName TypeName Changeability -> Attribute .
> op getTypeName : Attribute -> TypeName .
> op getAttributeName : Attribute -> AttributeName .
> var NA : AttributeName .   var NT : TypeName .
> var Changeability1 : Changeability .
> eq getTypeName (attribute (NA, NT, Changeability1)) = NT .
> eq getAttributeName (attribute (NA, NT, Changeability1)) = NA .
> endfm)

describes a UML attribute. The third and the fourth argument are the name and the type (*Changeability and enumeration*) of the tagged value, respectively. The fifth argument provides the literal list (*frozen* and *changeable*) of the enumeration type. The resulting module is also shown in Figure 17.

The dynamic semantics of the new property, *Changeability*, is described in the module *SYSTEMOBJECTS* (Figure 18), which belongs to the semantic specifications in Table 1. This module specifies the population of objects existing in the system, and includes operations to modify the attribute values of objects. Operations such as *changeAttributeValue* and constant operations such as *errorFrozenAttribute* are introduced in the module *SYSTEMOBJECTS*, giving rise to *extendedSystemObjects* (Figure 19). To achieve this aim, the metalevel operations defined in an extension of the module *META-LEVEL,* similar to the one described in Figure 11, are used. The constant *errorFrozenAttribute* represents all the terms denoting modifications that violate the constraint specified in the equation given for *changeAttributeValue*. The operation *changeAttributeValue* checks the value of *changeability* associated with the attribute *AN* (operation *isAttribChangeable*). If that value is *changeable*, the modification of the attribute is performed (operation *changeObjectList*). On the contrary, if that value is *frozen*, the constant *errorFrozenAttribute* is returned.

For the sake of space, the equations for the auxiliary operations *typeAttribbyName* (yielding the type attributes using a type name), and *objectTypeNamebyOid* (yielding the type name of an object using an object identifier) are not given. In a related paper (Toval & Fernández, 2000), an example about detecting the change of an attribute labeled as *frozen* is studied in more detail.

Finally, the whole meta-metamodeling strategy applied to the UML Class Diagram is shown in Figure 20. A particular domain model is initially represented by a UML class diagram using the functional requirements previously elicited. Then, this model is transformed and represented in an alternative and equivalent way by a formal term (see terms *TermMI1... TermMIm* and *TermM1... TermMn* in Figure 20) associated with the syntactic specification signatures. On the other hand, the instance of a model corresponds to the problem elements (see a desk and a strawman in Figure 20). They can also be represented

Figure 18. Definition of the Operations errorFrozenAttribute *and* changeAttributeValue

```
*** constant symbol indicating that the modification of
*** an attribute labeled as frozen is not permitted
op errorFrozenAttribute : -> ObjectList .
*** modify the value of an attribute
op changeAttributeValue : TypeList ObjectList Oid
                          AttributeName Value -> ObjectList
var OI : Oid .   var TL : TypeList .   var AN : AttributeName .
var V : Value .   var OL : ObjectList .
eq changeAttributeValue (TL, OL, OI, AN, V) =
    if         isAttribChangeable (typeAttribbyName (
          objectTypeNamebyOid (OI, OL), TL), AN)
    then    changeObjectList (typeAttribbyName (
          objectTypeNamebyOid (OI, OL), TL), OL, OI, AN, V)
    else    errorFrozenAttribute fi .
```

by formal terms (see terms *TermOI1... TermOIi* and *TermO1... TermOj* in Figure 20) associated with the semantic specification signatures.

IncorrectDiagram and *CanonicalTermM1... CanonicalTermMn* in Figure 20 are formal terms which represent the minimal formal interpretation obtained after a reduction process. *IncorrectDiagram* denotes all the different incorrect UML class diagrams (terms *TermMI1... TermMIm*) according to the UML syntax and static semantics. They are converted (or "reduced," in algebraic terminology) to a unique, minimal term with the same semantics, in this case the term *IncorrectDiagram*. However, all the correct UML class diagrams (terms *TermM1... TermMn*) are converted to the terms *CanonicalTermM1... CanonicalTermMn*. These are equivalent to the original ones regarding the syntactic specification equations that contain the UML static semantics. The relationships between the terms *TermOI1... TermOIi, TermO1... TermOj*, and the reduced terms *IncorrectObject, CanonicalTermO1... CanonicalTermOj* can be considered in the same way.

The metamodel evolution is specified by an extension of the module *META-LEVEL*. The terms and the modules from the lower level, which represent particular domain models and core UML model elements, are reified as terms at the higher level. Likewise, descent functions such as *meta-reduce* are used to efficiently compute reductions at the meta UML model layer. As a result, both extension of the core UML model layer and of the domain model layer are supported in a seamless fashion. In the same way, the lowest layer in the UML four-layer metamodeling architecture (the User Object UML layer) can also be integrated into the meta-metamodel formalization. In this case, the evolution theories are semantic specifications instead of syntactic specifications. For clarity, the relationships between the meta-metamodel and the user objects are not shown in Figure 20.

FUTURE TRENDS

Since most practitioners apply only a subset of the elements of modeling languages, the current trend in Software Engineering is to use simpler and shorter notations and methods. One solution to this problem may be found by defining a UML core (such as Core Modeling Language (Alhir, as cited in Alhir, 1999), not yet out) containing the most used constructs as well as extensibility mechanisms to tailor the UML to the needs of a specific application domain of interest. The formalization of this kernel can be undertaken by using

Figure 19. Extension of the Module SYSTEMOBJECTS

```
eq extendedSystemObjects = addEquation (addOperation(
                              addOperation (SYSTEMOBJECTS
,'errorFrozenAttribute, nil, 'ObjectList, none)
,'changeAttributeValue, 'TypeList 'ObjectList 'Oid
        'AttributeName 'Value, 'ObjectList, none)
,'changeAttributeValue [ 'TL , 'OL , 'OI , 'AN , 'V ]
  , 'if_then_else_fi [' isAttribChangeable [ ' typeAttribbyName
  [ ' objectTypeNamebyOid [ 'OI , 'OL ] , 'TL ] , 'AN ] ,
   ' changeObjectList [ ' typeAttribbyName
  [ ' objectTypeNamebyOid [ 'OI , 'OL ] , 'TL ] , 'OL , 'OI , 'AN , 'V] ,
    { ' errorFrozenAttribute } 'ObjectList ] )
```

Figure 20. UML Metamodel

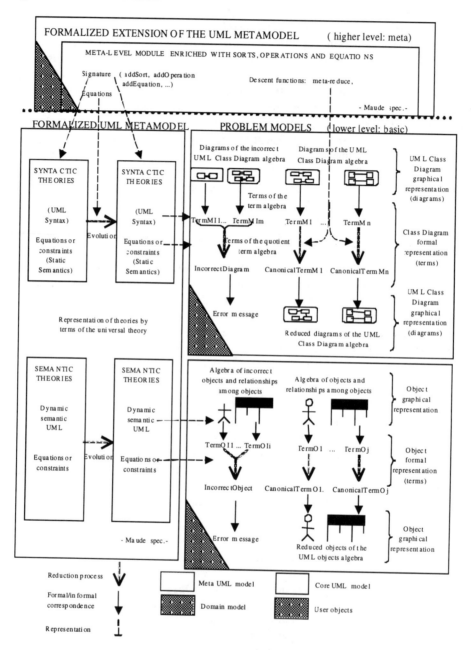

a minimum set of algebraic concepts, which may result in a standardized algebraic approach. This possibility depends on the expressiveness of the set of UML views and diagrams chosen to describe the real world. Nevertheless, the evolution issue must be dealt with by using a suitable formal language supporting reflection. It may also have practical consequences, since extensibility has been recognized as a key matter for the development of next-generation UML-based CASE tools, components, frameworks and other model-based reusable software (Dykman et al., 1999).

The evolution of the UML metamodel gives rise to several problems such as ensuring the consistency between the existing UML models (prior to evolution) and the new metamodel. Current research on schema evolution should be considered and applied to this framework. A wide range of possibilities have also opened up: exploring the proof of properties about the metamodel such as detecting deficiencies or design errors of the metamodel, and supporting rules that describe its appropriate evolution.

To our mind, the approach presented in this chapter represents a promising approach for not only formally supporting the UML evolution, but the MOF evolution as well. Since the number of MOF meta-levels is not fixed, the meta-level of the top of the MOF architecture can vary. All the MOF meta-levels can be specified using various reflection levels, by taking advantage of the fact that the universal theory U can be self-represented.

Note that this chapter deals with the technical aspects of the underlying formal models. Nevertheless, the practical use of our research assumes that a software tool is available to hide the formal concepts from modelers. A prototype of this tool is already working (Fernández & Toval, 2000b), which takes UML diagrams edited by Rational Rose" (in XMI format) and produces their equivalent formal representation.

CONCLUSIONS

A formal framework that supports the UML four-layer metamodel architecture has been presented and described in the executable formal language Maude, as a result of analyzing feasible strategies to formalize the UML language. The most innovative aspect in the approach reported involves undertaking the formalization of the UML metamodel evolution. To attain this formalization, the reflection property, which is naturally supported by the underlying logic for Maude, plays a central role.

Formal support for the syntax and semantics of the UML diagrams at different levels is thereby provided. The specification of a given system, constructed by one or more UML diagrams, can be translated into an equivalent formal representation. Thus, the UML model (through its equivalent formal representation) can be mathematically manipulated and verified. Modeling a particular criteria to transform diagrams (e.g., metrics, heuristics and so on) is made possible (Fernández & Toval, 2000d). General tests in both static and dynamic aspects according to the UML syntax and semantics, as defined in UML's documentation, are examples of verification (Fernández & Toval, 2000a; 2000c). Likewise, modeling and proving specific properties related to the domain of the particular system under development are also feasible. We consider the variety of UML diagrams within the whole UML language in a homogeneous and modular way. This makes proving UML inter-model properties possible, in addition to those properties related to just one model. Extensibility mechanisms and new elements resulting from the UML metamodel evolution can also be jointly managed because the formal model incorporates the metamodel evolution within the same framework.

In order to make this environment more usable and accessible, we are now in the process of integrating the formal specifications with Rational Rose and other commercial modeling tools via a standard XMI interface. In the same direction, we have proposed, in conjunction with other researchers, a process model based on a combination of rapid and evolutionary prototyping (Moros, Nicolás, Molina & Toval, 2000).

REFERENCES

Alhir, S. S. (1999, January 3). Extending the unified modeling language (UML). Retrieved 1999 from the World Wide Web: http://home.earthlink.net/~salhir/extendingtheuml.html.

Alhir, S. S. (in press). The Core Modeling Language. <http://home.earthlink.net/~salhir/#thecml>.

Araújo, J., Moreira, A., & Sawyer, P. (1999). Specifying persistence, class views and excluding classes for UML. In *Proceedings of the 12th International Conference on Software & Systems Applications*, December 8-11. Paris, France.

Bourdeau, R. H., & Cheng, B. H. C. (1995). A formal semantics for object model diagrams. *IEEE Transactions on Software Engineering, 21*(10), 799-821.

Clavel, M., Durán, F., Eker, S., Lincoln, P., Martí-Oliet, N., Meseguer, J., & Quesada, J. (1999, January). *Maude: Specification and Programming in Rewriting Logic.* Computer Science Laboratory SRI International. Retrieved from the World Wide Web: http://maude.csl.sri.com/manual/.

Clavel, M., & Meseguer, J. (1996). Reflection and strategies in rewriting logic. In Meseguer, J. (Ed.), *Proceedings of the 1st Intl. Workshop on Rewriting Logic and its Applications*, September 3-6. California. Vol. 4 of Electronic Notes in Theoretical Computer Science, (pp. 125-147). Elsevier.

Dykman, N., Griss, M., & Kessler, R. (1999). Nine suggestions for improving UML extensibility. In *Proceedings of the UML'99 Conference*, October 28-30. Vol. 1723. Lecture Notes in Computer Science.

Evans, A. S. (1998). Reasoning with UML class diagrams. In *2nd IEEE Workshop on Industrial-Strength Formal Specification Techniques*, October 20-30. Boca-Raton. IEEE Press.

Evans, A. S., & Clarck, A. N. (1998). Foundations of the unified modeling language. In *2nd Northern Formal Methods Workshop*, Ilkley, Electronic Workshops in Computing. Springer-Verlag.

Fernández, J. L., & Toval, A. (2000a). Can intuition become rigorous? Foundations for UML model verification tools. In *International Symposium on Software Reliability Engineering (ISSRE 2000)*, October 8-11. San Jose, California: USA. IEEE Press.

Fernández, J. L., & Toval, A. (2000b). Formally modeling and executing the UML Class Diagram. In Rodríguez, M.J., & Paderewski. P. (Eds.), *Proceedings of the V Workshop on Models Environments and Tools in Requirements Engineering (MENHIR 2000)*, March 30-31. E.T.S.I. Informática, Universidad de Granada (Spain).

Fernández, J. L., & Toval, A. (2000c). Rigorous software modeling also improves dependability: The UML CASE, (Tech. Rep. LSI 3-00). University of Murcia (Spain): Department of Computer Science.

Fernández, J. L., & Toval, A. (2000d). Rigorously transforming UML Class Diagrams. In Rodríguez, M. J., and Paderewski. P., (Eds.), *Proceedings of the V Workshop on Models Environments and Tools in Requirements Engineering (MENHIR 2000)*, March 30-31.

E.T.S.I. Informática, Universidad de Granada (Spain).

Fowler, M., & Scott, K. (1997). *UML Distilled Applying the Standard Object Modeling Language*. Addison-Wesley.

France, R. B. (1999). A problem-oriented analysis of basic UML static requirements modeling concepts. In *Proceedings of the OOPSLA'99*, November 1-5. Denver, Colorado.

France, R. B., Bruel, J. M., & Larrond-Petrie, M. M. (1997). An integrated object-oriented and formal modeling environment. *Journal of Object-Oriented Programming, 10*, (7), 25-34.

Goguen, J. A., & Malcom, G. (1996). *Algebraic Semantics of Imperative Programs*. MIT Press.

Goguen, J. A. & Meseguer, J. (1988). *Order-Sorted Algebra I*. (Tech. Rep.). Stanford University: SRI International.

Grima, A. & Toval, A. (1994). An algebraic formalization of the Objectcharts notation. In *Proceedings of the GULP-PRODE 1994*, The 1994 Joint Conference on Declarative Programming, September. Valencia (Spain): Department of Technical University of Valencia.

Kent, S., Evans, A. & Rumpe, B. (1999). UML semantics FAQ. (In conjunction with *ECOOP'99*). Retrieved 1999 from the World Wide Web: http://www.cs.ukc.ac.uk/people/staff/sjhk/detail/ecoop99/UMLsemanticsFAQ/index.html.

Lano, K.C. & Bicarregui, J.C. (1998). UML refinement and abstraction transformations. In *ROOM 2 Workshop*, May 29. Bradford University.

Martí-Oliet, N. & Meseguer, J. (1996). Rewriting logic as a logical and semantic framework. In Meseguer, J. (Ed.), *Proceedings of the 1st Intl. Workshop on Rewriting Logic and its Applications*, September 3-6. California. Vol 4. Electronic Notes in Theoretical Computer Science. Elsevier.

Meseguer, J. (1992). Conditional rewriting logic as a unified model of concurrency. *Theoretical Computer Science, 96*(1), 73-155.

Moros, B., Nicolás, J., Molina, J. G. & Toval, A. (2000). Combining formal specifications with design by contract. *Journal of Object-Oriented Programming, 12*(9), 19-21.

Object Management Group, (1999a, June). *UML Notation Guide Version 1.3*. Retrieved from the World Wide Web: http://www.rational.com/uml/index.jtmpl.

Object Management Group, (1999b, June). *UML Semantics Version 1.3*. Retrieved from the World Wide Web: http://www.rational.com/uml/index.jtmpl.

Ölveczky, P.C. & Meseguer, J. (1999, December 18). *Specification of Real-Time and Hybrid Systems in Rewriting Logic*. Preprint submitted to Elsevier Preprint. Retrieved from the World Wide Web: http://maude.csl.sri.com/papers/realtime.

Pastor, O., Hayes, F. & Bear, S. (1992). OASIS: An object-oriented specification language. In *Proccedings of the the CAISE-92 Conference*. Springer-Verlag.

Reggio, G., Astesiano, E. & Choppy, C. (1999, December 2). CASL-LTL a CASL extension for dynamic systems. Summary. Retrieved August 2000 from the World Web Site: ftp://ftp.disi.unige.it/person/ReggioG/ReggioEtAll99a.ps.

Reggio, G. & Wieringa, R. J. (1999). Thirty-one problems in the Semantics of UML 1.3 dynamics. In *Workshop "Rigorous Modeling and Analysis of the UML Challenges and Limitations," OOPSLA'99*, November 2. Denver, Colorado.

The precise Unified Modeling Language group. (2000, August 15). Homepage. <http://www.cs.york.ac.uk/puml> [2000, Aug. 17].

Toval A., Fernández J. (2000). Formally modeling UML and its evolution: A holistic approach. In *Proceedings of the Formal Methods for Open Object-Based Distributed Systems. (FMOODS 2000)*, September 6-8. Stanford, California: Kluwer Academic Publishers.

Toval, A., Ramos, I. & Pastor, O. (1994). Prototyping object-oriented specifications in an algebraic environment. In Lecture Notes in Computer Science, (LNCS), (Vol. 856, pp. 310-320). Springer-Verlag Series.

Wang, E. Y., Richter, H. A. & Cheng, B. H. C. (1997). Formalizing and integrating the dynamic model within OMT. In *Proceedings of the IEEE International Conference on Software Engineering*, May. Boston. Retrieved from the World Wide Web: http://web.cse.msu.edu/~chengb/pubs.html.

Whittle, J. (2000). Formal approaches to systems analysis using UML: A survey. *Journal of Database Management, 11*(4), 4-13.

ACKNOWLEDGEMENTS

We would especially like to thank our colleague Isidro Ramos. He has given us valuable guidance on this research. We would also like to thank José Meseguer from SRI International Computer Science Laboratory and Roel J. Wieringa from the University of Twente for their comments on various papers in connection with this chapter. The authors gratefully acknowledge the contributions made by the anonymous reviewers, whose suggestions helped us improve the presentation of this chapter. Thanks are also given to Pilar González Férez and Mike McCammon, who helped us prepare this chapter.

APPENDIX A. ORDER-SORTED ALGEBRAIC SPECIFICATION

In order to help to understand the underlying theoretical concepts in Maude, this appendix provides some basic background on order-sorted algebraic (OSA) specification theory. With this purpose we use a simple example: the stack specification. A more detailed description can be found in any book or paper related to the topic (e.g., Goguen & Meseguer, 1988; Meseguer, 1992; Goguen & Malcom, 1996). An OSA signature Σ, is a tuple (OP, S, $\leq$) where OP denotes a set of operation symbols and (S, $\leq$) is a partially ordered set of sorts, that is to say, $\leq$ in S is reflexive, transitive and antisymmetric in the sense that x$\leq$y and y$\leq$x implies x=y. Each sort denotes a collection of distinguished and homogenous data items (see sorts *Stack* and *NeStack* in Figure A1). Let s, s_1, s_2, ..., s_n be sorts, a function symbol can be a constant symbol f: $\rightarrow$ s, such as *empty* : -> *Stack* (Figure A1, *op* stands for operation), or a function symbol whose arity is n, f: s_1, s_2, ..., $s_n \rightarrow$ s, such as *top_* : *NeStack* -> *Nat*. The set of Σ-terms of sort s, denoted T_Σ, is defined by the following two conditions:

1. $\forall$s | s $\in$ S, if f $\in$ OP and f is a constant symbol f: $\rightarrow$ s, then f $\in T_\Sigma$. Given the constant symbol *empty : -> Stack*, then *empty* is a term.

2. $\forall$n | n $\in$ N, if f $\in$ OP and f is a function symbol, f: s_1, s_2, ..., $s_n \rightarrow$ s, with $t_i \in T_{OP,si}$ (terms of sort s_i), then $f(t_1, .., t_n) \in T_\Sigma$. For example, *push(5, empty)* is a term where *5* is a term of sort *Nat*, and *empty* is a term of sort *Stack*.

Given a signature Σ, a model for Σ is named a Σ-algebra (or just an algebra) and consists of:

1. For each sort s where s $\in$ S, a set I_s, termed the carrier set.

2. For each constant symbol f: $\rightarrow$ s, a constant $f_s \in I_s$ (the interpretation of f in I_s).
3. For each function symbol f: $s_1, s_2, ..., s_n \rightarrow s$, a function f_s: $Is_1, Is_2, ..., Is_n \rightarrow Is$ (the interpretation of f in I_s).

OSA is suitable to handle cases where elements of a sort also belong to another one. For example, nonempty stack elements (*NeStack*) are also considered of sort *Stack* (Figure A1, *subsort* stands for subsorting). To model UML concepts and their relationships, we can state that types and implementation classes are both classes in the UML metamodel: *Type ImpClass < Class*; another example shows more technical use of subsorting: to permit an object to be dealt as a (unitary) list of objects (implicit in Figure 9, *Object < ObjectList*). An order-sorted algebraic specification is a pair (Σ, E) where Σ is an OSA signature and E is a set of equations. For example, *top push (X, S) = X*, is an equational axiom (Figure A1, *eq* stands for equation). *X* and *S* are variables of sorts *Nat* and *Stack* (*var* stands for variable). The sort *Nat* is declared in the module *NAT*, which is imported by means of the declaration *protecting NAT*. Finally, the whole algebraic specification of a stack is shown in Figure A1, where the module *STACK-OF-NAT* is declared (*fmod* stands for functional module).

A Σ-algebra that fulfills the equations is called a SPEC-algebra or model for the algebraic specification. At the level of the corresponding algebras, this subsort ordering is interpreted as set-theoretic inclusion of the data, represented by a subsort into the data represented by its supersort (e.g., any element of the carrier set of subsort *Object* is an element of the carrier set of supersort *ObjectList*).

The algebraic specification language Maude is based upon both equational and rewriting logic. Maude's equational logic, called membership equational logic, is an extension of OBJ3's order-sorted equational logic (sorts can be ordered by a partial order relation), and its operational semantics is based on rewriting. Maude functional modules are executed by interpreting the equations of a specification as a left-to-right term rewriting system. This "reduction process" finishes when a term is reached to which no equation can be applied. The resulting term is named the "canonical term" and the term algebra modulo the congruence generated by the rules of deduction is named the "quotient term algebra" and represents the minimal formal interpretation model. Thus, Maude programs are executable order-sorted algebraic specifications, and computation becomes an efficient form of equational deduction by rewriting. Rewriting logic is also a good logical framework in which many other logics can be represented (Martí-Oliet & Meseguer, 1996), endowing Maude with high expressive power.

Figure A1. Algebraic Specification of a Stack in Maude.

```
(fmod STACK-OF-NAT is sorts Stack NeStack .
    subsort NeStack < Stack .
    protecting NAT .
    op empty : -> Stack .
    op push : Nat Stack -> NeStack .
    op top_ : NeStack -> Nat .
    op pop_ : NeStack -> Stack .
    var X : Nat .    var S : Stack .
    eq top push (X, S) = X .
    eq pop push (X, S) = S .
endfm)
```

ENDNOTES

1   Partially Granted by the CICYT (Science and Technology Joint Committee), Spanish Ministry of Education and Ministry of Industry, project MENHIR TIC97-0593-C05-02 "OM: Constructing Trusted Information Systems from OO Specifications."

2   The Object Management Group (OMG) was founded in 1989 by computer companies and was formed to create a component-based software marketplace by introducing standardized object software.

3   Maude interpreter has been available since January 1999 and is a more powerful language than OBJ3. Currently, Maude is freeware and runs under Linux.

4   The pUML group is made up of international researchers and practitioners who are interested in providing a precise and well-defined semantics for UML.

5   A syntactic theory is a module that represents the syntax and static semantics of the UML modeling elements.

6   A semantic theory is a module that represents the dynamic semantics of the UML modeling elements.

© *Rational Software Corporation.*

Chapter XV

An Interactive Viewpoint on the Role of UML

Dina Goldin and David Keil
University of Massachusetts, Boston, USA

Peter Wegner
Brown University, USA

The role of the Unified Modeling Language (UML) is to model interactive systems, whose behaviors emerge from the interaction of their components with each other and with the environment. Unlike traditional (algorithmic) computation, interactive computation involves infinite and dynamic (late binding) input/ output streams. Tools and models limited to an algorithmic paradigm do not suffice to express and manage the behavior of today's interactive systems, which are capable of self-reconfiguring and adapting to their environment.

Whereas procedural languages may express precise designs of closed processes, UML's objective is to provide support for the analysis and specification of increasingly complex and inherently open systems. Interactive systems require dynamic models where interaction has first-class status, and where the environment is modeled explicitly, as a set of actors whose roles constrain the input patterns through use cases.

UML's interaction-based approach to system modeling fits well with the encapsulation-based, object-oriented approach to implementation. By coupling these approaches, the software engineering process can promise to provide a more complete solution to system design and implementation, leading the way for widespread adoption of networked and embedded intelligent agent technology. A theoretical framework for modeling interactive computing can strengthen the foundations of UML and guide its evolution.

INTRODUCTION

The *Unified Modeling Language* (UML) emerged in response to a need for a notation (a visual language) that can express the behaviors of today's *interactive* computing systems and that can guide in constructing them. In the UML framework, software design entails building an object-oriented representation of a system, as well as of its *environment*, e.g. its users (modeled as *actors*).

Interactive systems of the kind modeled with UML represent a new paradigm in computation that inherently cannot be modeled using traditional, or *algorithmic*, tools. At the heart of the new computing paradigm is the notion that a system's job is not to *transform* a single *static* input to an output, but rather *to provide an ongoing service* (Wegner, 1997). The service-providing nature of present-day information systems was specifically noted by the Object Management Group in defining the UML standard (OMG, 2000).

When a system is viewed as a service provider, the interaction between the system and its environment becomes an integral part of the computing process. UML presents a uniform domain-independent framework for modeling the different interactions present in today's systems: those among objects or software components, those between users and applications, those over networks (including the Internet) and those among embedded devices.

Programs that work non-interactively, transforming a given input to an output by a series of steps, represent the traditional, or *algorithmim,* paradigm of computation (Figure 1). Theoretical tools for modeling algorithmic computation include *Turing Machines* (Hopcroft & Ullman, 1979), recursive function theory and the lambda calculus, which all define the same set of *computable* functions (Turing, 1936). Algorithmic computation is present throughout interactive systems modeled by UML, at the low implementation level, but the entire system is more than merely such computation. Models of interactive computation are more recent; they include the Calculus of Communicating Systems (CCS) and the *pi*-calculus (Milner, 1990, 1999), input/output automata (Lynch et al., 1994) and Interaction Machines (Wegner & Goldin, 1999b, 1999c) that maintain persistent state information between interaction steps.

Figure 1. Algorithmic Computation

A software system modeled by UML is a *computing entity*. System components and objects are also computing entities:

> **Computing entity**: a finitely specifiable software system, component or object that is being modeled by UML. Entities may contain sub-entities, or be a part of a larger entity.

Once a system is implemented, its *external behavior* emerges out of its interactions with its environment:

> **Environment of an entity**: the producer of *inputs* for the computing entity, and the consumer of its *outputs*; it is outside the entity, interacting with it via inputs and outputs.
>
> **Actor**: an active role player in a given entity's environment; for a system, actors are usually system users, but they may be other systems, software or hardware.

The desired behavior of a computing entity is determined by the service that it provides to its environment, whether it is the user or other computing entities.

A system's internal behavior, which affects the external behavior indirectly by affecting the values of outputs, emerges out of the internal interactions among its components. In this sense, systems and their components are like organizations and their subunits (departments, teams or individuals), which function through the interactions among these subunits, and between the organization and the external world.

Given the similarity between the properties of software systems and business organizations, it is not surprising that UML is also applied to model organizations in the context of business process reengineering (Jacobson et al., 1995). However, the present work's focus is on software systems. In particular, we discuss how UML reflects a paradigm shift from algorithms toward interaction:

- through use case diagrams and other interaction-based diagrams, UML models a system whose behavior is defined by its observable external interaction with its environment (actors);
- subsystems, and objects internal to a system, have their own interactions with their environments, modeled in UML with state, activity and interaction diagrams;
- UML models external occurrences with *events*, which may trigger actions;
- concurrency and parallelism can give rise to *multi-actor interaction*, which is a richer kind of behavior than *sequential interaction* and is modeled in UML in various ways;
- interaction machines provide a theoretical foundation for formalizing interactive computation.

THE BEHAVIOR OF SYSTEMS

The service-providing role of systems and subsystems modeled by UML is explicitly noted by OMG (2000). In requesting an instance of service, the actor is not concerned with the implementation details or the internal computations of the system, *within the active sub-system boundary*. Nobel prize winner Herbert Simon noted 30 years ago that computers, just like mechanical systems and social organizations, are defined by their behavior, not their internal structure:

"almost no interesting statement that one can make about an operating computer bears any particular relation to the specific nature of the hardware. A computer is an organization of elementary functional components in which, to a high approximation, only the function performed by those components is relevant to the behavior of the whole system." (Simon, 1970, p. 18)

When discussing computers, Simon mostly referred to hardware systems. Computing at that time followed a strictly algorithmic paradigm, with procedural code executed in batch mode. It was hard if not impossible to imagine today's component-based distributed software systems, which UML was created to model, ones that fit Simon's notion of a *complex system* – an interactive system whose behavior emerges out of its interactions. By shifting the focus to the relationships between actors and the computing entity (agent), UML is able to specify software systems that fit Simon's description of a complex system.

The use-case concept models a system and its behavior by specifying the *nouns*, the actors and the entities, rather than the *verbs*, or procedures. This is an *object-oriented* approach to design. A system or subsystem is specified through its external behavior rather than its internal structure; externally determined patterns of interaction are not constrained by any specific algorithm specification. The modeling is at the level of *interfaces*, which specify interactions. The behavior is not modeled explicitly, but emerges as a result of interactions between the system and its environment.

The implementation/interface distinction corresponds to the duality of *internal hidden structure* (configuration and values) versus *external observable behavior* (external interactions). This duality holds both for actors in the environment and the entities in the computing system:

> *The internal structure of an actor is not necessarily known to the entity with which the actor interacts, and vice versa.*

Two systems or interactive entities may be considered equivalent if their behavior *is observationally indistinguishable* to the actors. In CCS, this means that a relation exists between their *states* (Milner, 1990). This relative notion of equivalence, defined in terms of *observable behavior*, was first proposed by Moore (1956) in the context of *finite discrete transducers*, which can be considered the simplest interactive systems (Goldin & Keil, 2000). When two entities have the same observable behavior with respect to their environment, they are *indistinguishable*, or equivalent. By explicitly modeling the external behavior of actors vis-à-vis the computing system, UML has the capability to specify when two systems are equivalent, i.e., when their behavior is indistinguishable.

Equivalent systems can be substituted for each other while preserving behavioral equivalence of the overall system. This allows for component interchangeability. Providing a well-founded notion of equivalence for computing entities goes a long way towards the formalization of interactive computing.

By focusing on the behavior, UML abstracts away the implementation details. On the other hand, *object-oriented* (OO) programming languages specify the *implementation* of interactive systems, components and objects; their *encapsulation* mechanism is central to this implementation. However, the specification stops at the system's boundaries, without a way to model its interactions with the environment. Thus, they do not have the capability to specify equivalence of computing systems they implement.

The interaction-based UML approach to system modeling fits well with the encapsulation-based OO approach to implementation. By marrying these approaches, the software engineering process can provide a complete solution to system design and implementation.

THREE VIEWS OF SYSTEM MODELING

In object-based models, the computing entities, or components, are "small" objects with *sequential* interface and interaction protocols. That is, the input tokens (*events* and *messages*) are supplied to each entity via a single stream that serializes the tokens. The entity must act on each input before consuming the next one. On the other hand, applications like distributed airline reservation systems have "heavy" components with multiple interfaces and concurrent interaction protocols. The latter are examples of concurrency and multi-actor interaction, discussed later in this chapter.

The gap between static structure and dynamic behavior is greater for interactive computing entities than for algorithms, due to two distinct levels of execution dynamics: the external dynamics of communication are entirely separate from the internal dynamics of algorithm execution. To account for this, UML provides several views of system

Figure 2: The Three Views of System Modeling in UML

Structural modeling	**static view**: describes relations among interactive components (*nouns*); static description of objects, operations and relations among objects by *class diagrams, object diagrams* and *component diagrams*.
Behavioral modeling	**dynamic view**: describes interactions within the system (*inter-object dynamics*) with *use case, sequence, collaboration* and *state-transition diagrams*.
	functional view: describes behavior of specific functions or methods (*intra-object dynamics*); modeling algorithmic transformation behaviors with *activity diagrams* and *narratives*.

modeling: a *static view* for describing static object structure, a *dynamic view* that describes interactions and a *functional view* that describes transformation behavior of operations (Reed, 1998; Jacobson et al., 1993; Rumbaugh et al., 1990).

These three views represent projections of the system onto different conceptual dimensions, analogous to database views. Together, they provide a robust modeling framework that can be coupled with a variety of object-oriented programming environments, as pointed out by Jacobson et al. (1993). They reflect the fact that *nouns* (agents, entities) provide a more direct and more expressive model of the real world than *verbs* (procedures, methods), and the further fact that nouns are modeled computationally by the patterns of actions (verbs) that they support. UML supports modeling of nouns and their actions along all three dimensions: the static object model expresses relations among nouns, the dynamic model expresses patterns of interaction and the functional model specifies the effect of individual actions.

The three-view approach to system design clearly indicates the role of algorithms as recipes for low-level transformations of the primitive elements of interaction patterns. Interactive computation can be broken up into algorithmic steps, but viewing it as nothing more than that would "miss the forest for the trees."

Though there is a resemblance among static, dynamic and functional models (Figure 2) and corresponding levels of modeling for algorithms, it is only superficial. Consider state diagrams in UML. Like *flow diagrams* (or *flowcharts*), they have a starting state and depict flows of control. But flow diagrams have actions as nodes and control paths as edges, while state diagrams have internal object states as nodes and observable input/output actions as edges. The *state transitions* in state diagrams represent a change in internal action state in response to an external event. State diagrams also resemble deterministic finite automata (DFAs). UML state transitions may involve input or output; thus UML state machines are *transducers*, not recognizers or generators. Also, both the number of different transition labels and the number of different states in state diagrams is not finitely bounded, as it is for DFAs.

Similarly, object interaction histories are very different from algorithm execution histories. Algorithm execution histories specify internal instruction sequences, while system interaction histories specify observable events in real or digital worlds.

An interaction history, which is a trace of interactions during a single (finite) computation, can be viewed as a test case for the system, analogous to instruction execution histories of algorithm computations.

Just as no amount of testing can prove correctness of algorithms, interaction histories can only show the existence of desirable behaviors and cannot prove absolute correctness.

General patterns of interaction depend both on the system and its environment. Because the behavior of actors in the environment is not completely known, these patterns are not finitely describable. The behavior of entities that interact with open environments that change unpredictably during the process of computation cannot be described by algorithms (Wegner, 1998). This impossibility result is in spite of the finiteness of the UML model for the system whose behavior we are trying to describe.

The problem of driving home from work provides an illustration:

How can a completely automatic car get us from work to our house?

This problem is solved by combining algorithmic knowledge (a high-level mental map) with interactive visual feedback of road conditions and topography. In a toy world without traffic or bad weather, interactive feedback could be replaced by a more detailed algorithmic specification of the problem. In this case, it is possible to provide enough information up front so that the automatic car, like a blindfolded person, can "know" without any feedback when to turn the steering wheel or to slow down. However, in the real world, where every pothole and pebble affects the car's trajectory in a chaotic fashion, the complexity of such an algorithmic specification is enormous. The presence of traffic and the effect of weather conditions make the algorithmic specification impossible.

Before UML, the non-algorithmic aspect of interactive system behavior forced the literature on design patterns (Gamma et al., 1994) to resort to informal verbal descriptions of problem and solution structure, when specifying reusable patterns of object and component interaction. Design patterns are behaviorally simple interaction patterns, but interaction patterns are too low level to capture user-level regularities; they are the machine language of design patterns. UML provides a higher level notation for describing design patterns.

The fact that interactive systems cannot be described algorithmically, in a formalism that is equivalent to Turing computability, is an *incompleteness* result. The incompleteness of interactive system behaviors implies that proving correctness is not merely hard but impossible. We must be satisfied with filtering out as many errors as possible, by applying better testing strategies, or by creating better software tools for program examination and analysis, but we cannot hope to prove the nonexistence of all incorrect behaviors.

MODELING INTERACTION IN UML

Use Cases: A System and Its Environment

One of the driving notions behind UML is *use cases*. Use cases encapsulate units of service in a computing entity: a system, a subsystem, or a class. They are descriptions of a category of externally required functionality embodied in transactions or interactions, involving *actors*. A *use case* is an abstraction representing the *input sources* of the system; usually, this means the users, though other sources of input are possible. Use cases restrict or constrain the user, known as *actor*, to a particular *role*, e.g., customer, vendor, line supervisor. The actor interacts with the system by exchanging *messages* (OMG, 2000).

A use case can be clearly distinguished from a subroutine call or a step in an algorithm. The step is chosen deterministically by the system design, whereas the use case instance is initiated by the external actor. To the system, the structure or state of the actor is unknown. "Since an actor is outside the entity [in a use case], its internal structure is not defined, but only its external view as seen from the entity" (OMG, 2000, p. 2-125).

As a result, the actor's decisions driving the course of the computation are seen by the system as arbitrary. To the system, the actor acts as a non-deterministic source of inputs. *The system must be designed without having complete knowledge of its environment.*

Likewise, to the actor, the system is defined by its behavior rather than by its internal structure. The actor is not presumed to have any information about the implementation of the system. Systems that have the same behavior appear *equivalent*, or interchangeable, to users (see "The Behavior of Systems").

The actor may dynamically change during the computation. For example, it might be influenced by the system's outputs. Thus the system cannot anticipate a priori the contents of the actor's messages. In a real-world setting, the system input generated by the users in most scenarios is indeed affected by earlier system output. The semantics of the interaction sequence thus may include a bi-directional relation of causality between system input and system output. This is an interactive phenomenon, contradicting a basic premise of algorithmic computation, where input entirely precedes the computation, and output follows it.

Collaboration Diagrams: Internal vs. External Interaction

We now turn to *internal interactions* within a computing entity. Here the actors are computing entities within the modeled system, components or objects. Unlike external actors, internal actors are under the control of the system; their behavior is specified by the system. Internal interaction is *symmetric* (mutual), where the entities serve as each other's actors. From the system's point of view, there is no inherent distinction between actors and "actees" for these interactions. This symmetry is reflected in UML *collaboration and sequence diagrams* that model internal interactions.

UML's support of *collaboration* is an important feature. A collaboration defines a set of *roles* and specifies the interactions of the entities that are playing those roles (OMG, 2000). Collaboration can be viewed as a *constraint* on behavior, for computing entities as well as human beings; for example, the need for collaboration in the workplace or family constrains our behavior (Wegner, 1997). The simplest collaboration diagram may simply define a path between interacting objects to denote that instances of the classes exchange messages in the collaboration.

Sequence diagrams focus on time sequencing rather than role playing. They depict the time-ordering of the message passing between interacting entities over their lifetime, focusing on the control aspect. In either collaboration or sequence diagrams, there is no built-in duality of entity vs. environment. For each entity, the others form its environment, but the overall model takes a neutral stance. This is in contrast to the entity-centric *asymmetric* point of view taken in *use cases*, where the actors are not necessarily under the system's control (e.g., they can be human beings, or physical sensors).

Use cases can also be applied to modeling internal interactions; from a computing entity's point of view, interactions with internal agents are no different than with external ones. Use cases specify proper entity behavior in response to the actors, but they make no guarantees about the actors' behavior. Some behaviors such as collaboration cannot be modeled with use cases. It is not enough to hope that the actors will collaborate; the model must explicitly specify it. This can only be done when the model can assume that all parties to the interactions are under the system's control.

EVENT-DRIVEN COMPUTING

A notion supported by UML, inherited from the Common Object Resource Broker Architecture (CORBA), is that of an *event*. In a single-user GUI-driven system (such as one with the *model/view/controller* architecture), the system receives events from an *event stream* and handles each one in turn. In a system modeled by UML, events can also be internal to the system, triggering changes to components and objects. Events act as *input tokens* for the entities; when the same event affects multiple entities, it acts as input for each of them.

Events decouple control from statement execution to a greater extent than procedure calling; the analogy here is to *asynchronous* vs. *synchronous* computation. *Exceptions* in traditional programming languages are a restricted form of events that cause the normal flow of control to be modified when exceptional actions are required. Event models elevate the exception mechanism to be the primary control structure and generalize it so that occurrence of an event can cause multiple components to be notified of its occurrence.

Streams are distinct from strings or sequences due to their dynamic nature; each element in the stream is not available until the previous one is processed; this is known as a *lazy evaluation* mechanism. Lazy evaluation allows each input token to be produced interactively, after the previous token has been processed. As a result, an interactive input stream between an actor and the system is theoretically infinite: it can always be dynamically extended. For example, the user of a workstation may choose to work a little longer before logging off. This is analogous to interactive hardware devices (transducers), which generally do not enforce a finite restriction on the length of input: they stop only when the power is turned off. The fact that UML can model open-ended event loops means that it can model non-algorithmic behaviors. Algorithms, defined as plans for finite processes, cannot express computation over dynamically supplied infinite input streams; by definition, they have finite input and output. A *stream* of input or output tokens is circularly defined as a pair (*token, stream*). It is an element of a *non-well-founded set*, and its definition is *coinductive*, giving a consistent meaning to such circularity (Barwise & Moss, 1996; Jacobs & Rutten, 1997; Rutten, 1997; Wegner & Goldin, 1999c).

CONCURRENCY AND MULTI-ACTOR INTERACTION

Once we accept the idea that interactive behaviors are richer than algorithms, we can distinguish two levels of interactive expressiveness, *sequential* vs. *multi-actor*. In a *sequential interactive entity* such as an abstract data type, there is a single input (event) stream, representing non-concurrent interaction with a single actor. A *multi-actor interactive entity* processes multiple concurrent interaction streams, each one representing interaction with a separate autonomous actor. The actors interact with the entity simultaneously and independently (autonomously), without necessarily any awareness of the presence of other actors. Moreover, the number of actors can change dynamically: actors can start and terminate their interaction with the entity without the awareness of other actors. UML use cases allow for multiple concurrent actors.

A multi-actor interactive entity is a composite entity, with multiple sub-entities. Some of its sub-entities interact with these external actors, while others only interact internally. Just as actors can come and go, so can these sub-entities; they can be born or die. Interaction streams, too, can be created, rerouted or destroyed. As a result, the design of multi-actor interactive entities involves active management of interaction, at a level unseen in sequential interaction. The different vertical columns in UML sequence diagrams represent the multiple concurrent sub-entities of a multi-actor system.

The need for active management of interaction, and for dynamic reconfiguration of interactive entities, makes multi-actor interaction harder to formalize and to model than sequential interaction. On the other hand, it allows the set of behaviors for multi-actor systems to be strictly richer than for sequential systems. Evidence for greater expressiveness of multi-actor interaction comes from transaction theory (where the class of *non-serializable transactions* is known to be richer than the *serializable transactions*), and from concurrency theory (where *true concurrency* is not believed to be reducible to *interleaving concurrency*) (Pratt, 1995).

Multi-agent interaction precisely characterizes concurrent distributed systems: it is precisely the interactive aspect of concurrent and distributed computation that makes it more expressive, and more difficult to formalize (Wegner & Goldin, 1999c). When a modeling notation includes restrictions on concurrent behavior that force it to become serializable, its expressiveness is reduced. It is challenging to find clean notations for specifying concurrent behaviors that capture the full expressiveness of these behaviors. UML provides support for concurrency (multi-actor interaction), but it is not surprising that there are weaknesses in this support (McLaughlin & Moore, 1998), since the formalization of multi-actor interaction is still immature.

Work is under way to use wireless communication and the Internet to enable greater interaction among embedded sensors and controllers. The streams of data flowing past each device, such as those inside cars and appliances, can be harnessed for the benefit of other devices in the network. This is the theme of Estrin et al. (in CACM, May 2000). Although this phenomenon has been labeled "beyond interaction" (where interaction is presumed to be associated with human-computer communication, as in Tennenhouse, 2000), communication among embedded devices fits precisely into our notion of interaction, and can in principle be modeled by a language like UML.

Concurrency is an area where UML filled a particularly significant gap left by the notations of structured and object-oriented design. Older design notations, such as pseudocode, module hierarchy charts and class diagrams, do not support concurrent interacting processes, as UML does. Undoubtedly UML will need further development in this area, after its application to real-world concurrent design problems reveals the weak points of the original UML notation. No matter how it evolves, UML will have taken its place in computing history as pioneering notation for interactive system design.

A PARADIGM SHIFT

The need for new notations for modeling software and information systems arose from the ever-increasing level of complexity of today's systems. The recent rise of the World Wide Web further compounded our expectations of software system capabilities, by providing them with a virtual environment far more complex than heretofore. As the level of complexity increases, so does the level of abstraction. Structured programming's emphasis on the sequence-branch-loop trio of control structures gave rise to structured flow-charting. Top-down design gave rise to module-hierarchy diagramming. Object-based programming brought forth class diagrams. The entity-relationship diagram came in part out of the linking of database relations.

UML developed as these approaches showed their limits at modeling concurrent distributed systems that offer replication and load balancing while trying to ensure security and fault tolerance. What is modeled today are systems that offer tangible user services, not just transform data, and where interaction is pervasive.

The interactive, indeed multi-interactive, aspects of today's computing were highlighted by Cris Kobryn, one of those involved in UML's development. He noted that UML emerged under the impetus of the urgent need to add a superstructure for interprocess communication and distributed system services to the infrastructure supplied by the widely used Common Object Resource Broker Architecture (CORBA). CORBA's Interface Definition Language (IDL) could not specify the use cases, collaborations, state transitions and work flows that can be found in a complex system, such as an interactive software system or a business organization (Kobryn, 1999).

The paradigm shift from algorithms to interaction is intimately related to the evolution of practical computing. The technology shift from batch-oriented, procedural mainframe-based technology of the 1960s to object-oriented, GUI-driven, distributed workstation-based technology of today and to mobile, embedded, pervasive, adaptive computing agents of tomorrow is fundamentally a shift from algorithms to interaction.

yesterday: batch-oriented, procedural mainframe-based technology
today: object-oriented, GUI-driven, distributed workstation-based technology
tomorrow: mobile, embedded, pervasive, adaptive computing agents

The implicit contract between *computing entities* (such as systems or objects) and their clients (users or other entities) has changed from a sales-like contract, to transform inputs to outputs, into a marriage-like contract to provide continuing services over time (Wegner, 1997). Computing agents express persistent services over time (marriage) which cannot be modeled by time-independent input-output actions (sales). The folk wisdom that marriage contracts transcend sales contracts translates to the formal result that interactive systems cannot be modeled by algorithms.

Expressiveness, or power, of finite computing agents is defined in terms of the agent's ability to make observational distinctions about its environment. This notion of expressiveness applies equally to people and to computers. People who see are more expressive than otherwise-identical blindfolded people because they can make visual distinctions, while telescopes and microscopes increase expressiveness by allowing people to make still finer distinctions.

The ability of interactive agents to make finer distinctions than algorithmic processes is illustrated by *question answering*. Interactive questioning forces the *answerer* to commit to earlier answers before seeing later questions; it also allows the *questioner* to base later questions on the answers to earlier ones. For example, if an investigator (questioner) is interrogating a suspect (answerer), the investigator can learn more by interactive questioning with follow-up questions than by asking the suspect to fill in a questionnaire, which has the status of a multi-part single question. That is, there can be cases where suspects are able to fill out any questionnaire without implicating themselves, but where an interactive interrogation can exploit weaknesses in their story and establish their guilt.

The idea that interaction is not expressible by or reducible to algorithms was first proposed by Wegner in 1992 at the closing conference of the fifth-generation computing project in the context of logic programming (Wegner, 1996). Reactiveness of interactive computation, realized by commitment to a course of action, analogous to the suspect's commitment to earlier answers, was shown to be incompatible with logical completeness, realized by backtracking. Logic programming corresponds to closed-system computing, whereas interactive systems, modeled by UML, are inherently open.

Brooks' belief that there is no silver bullet to guarantee adherence to system specification (Brooks, 1995) can be restated in terms of the impossibility of algorithmic specification of interactive systems. In fact, a proof of irreducibility of interactive specifications to algorithms can actually be interpreted as a proof of the nonexistence of silver bullets. The irreducibility of interaction to algorithms also explains a common remark that "everyone is in favor of object-oriented programming but no one knows just what it is." If "knowing what it is" means reducing object-oriented programming to algorithms, then the reduction is bound to fail. But if we enlarge the class of things that "count" as explanations of object-oriented programming to include interactive models such as specified with UML, then we can succeed.

INTERACTION MACHINES: A MODEL OF INTERACTIVE COMPUTATION

Interactive computational models provide a formal framework for interactive computation, just as Turing Machines (TMs) model algorithmic computation. TMs have a tape which initially contains a finite input string, and a state transition mechanism that reads a character from the tape, performs a state transition, optionally writes a character on the tape, and repositions the reading head. When the machine halts (goes into a "halting" state), the contents of the tape represents its output.

Sequential interaction machines (SIMs) model objects and software components. Persistent Turing Machines (PTMs), a formalization of SIMs based on Turing Machines, treat each Turing Machine computation as a "macrostep" in an interactive computational process over a dynamically generated stream of input strings (Goldin & Smolka, 2000). An essential feature of

Figure 3. Sequential Interaction

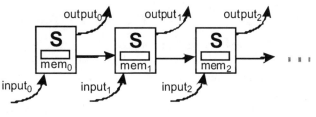

PTMs is a persistent internal worktape, so the initial TM configuration (which includes the contents of this tape, known as *memory*) changes for every macrostep.

SIMs model *sequential interactive entities* such as abstract data types, where there is a single input (event) stream, representing non-concurrent interaction with a single actor. A *multi-actor interactive entity*, whether it is a system or a component, processes multiple concurrent interaction streams, each one representing interaction with a separate autonomous actor. Multi-actor interaction machines (MIMs) are more expressive than SIMs. Multi-actor interaction is more expressive than sequential interaction, explaining why true concurrent distributed computation cannot always be simulated by interleaving computations.

A computing system is said to be *open* if the course of its computation can be affected by external events, and *closed* otherwise. The distinction between closed and open systems is precisely that between algorithmic and interactive computing. Turing machines are closed systems because their rules of engagement require all inputs to be supplied on an input tape before the beginning of the computation. Algorithms are closed because they shut out the world during computation. Interactive computing is open in allowing external agents to observe and influence computation.

Models of interaction provide a unifying conceptual framework for the description and analysis of object and component-based architectures. They are a tool for exploring software design models like UML, models of distributed objects and interoperability like CORBA, design patterns, coordination languages like Linda and Gamma, and agent-based artificial-intelligence models of planning and control.

The irreducibility of interactive systems to algorithms was noticed by Manna and Pnueli (1992) for reactive systems, by Milner (1990) in the context of process models and by Wegner (1998) in the context of interaction machines. The approach in Wegner (1998) differs from related work by focusing on models of interaction and notions of expressiveness that are language-independent as well as domain-independent. Subsequent work (Wegner & Goldin, 1999b, 1999c; Goldin, 2000) has led to the development of Persistent Turing Machines (PTMs) as a canonical model of sequential computation, of an expressiveness hierarchy for sequential computation and of the result that multi-stream interaction machines (MIMs) are more expressive than sequential interaction machines (SIMs).

Turing's proof that algorithms, Turing Machines (TMs) and the lambda calculus are equally expressive (Turing, 1936) suggested that the question of the correspondence between formal models and our intuitive notion of computing had been settled once and for all (*Church's thesis*), and channeled research to questions of design, performance and complexity for a fixed notion of computability. But the pendulum is starting to swing back; as a result of the irreducibility of interaction to algorithms, we know that software systems cannot be modeled by TMs, and their behavior cannot inherently be expressed by first-order logic. New classes of models are needed to express the technology of interaction, and UML is intended to fill that need.

CONCLUSION

UML provides a solution to the challenge posed by Milner in 1975, that functions cannot express meanings of processes (Milner, 1975; Wegner, 1998). UML models nonalgorithmic computation of interactive systems that operate in open noncomputable environments.

Interactive computational models are common nowadays in software engineering, operating systems and artificial intelligence. The evolution in AI from logic and search to agent-oriented models is not merely a tactical change but is a strategic paradigm shift from algorithms to more expressive interactive models that fundamentally increases expressive power. The reasoning/interaction dichotomy is precisely that between "good old-fashioned" AI (GOFAI) and "modern" agent-oriented AI. This paradigm shift is evident not only in research (such as the StarLogo system [Starlogo, 2000]) but also in textbooks that systematically reformulate AI in terms of intelligent agents (Russell & Norvig, 1995). UML might prove useful in the AI area, as a vocabulary for intelligent agent design.

With the systems modeled by UML, we see a re-introduction of side effects, once banished. Side effects were shunned because they can produce behavior that is not functionally formalizable, just as GOTOs can ("Goto considered harmful"). Formalizability, or the ability to formally prove various properties of the system, is an attractive feature of algorithmic computation, and it was felt that any computation with side effects could (and should) be transformed to an equivalent one without. With interactive computation, side effects are inevitable; e.g., when method invocation changes the state of the method's owner. Rather than view interactive computation as "undesirable" due to its nonformalizability, we must take it as a challenge to find new, non-algorithmic tools and methods for formalizing computation, ones where side effects have a place.

It's interesting to note that Turing's seminal paper was not intended to establish TMs as a comprehensive model for computing, but on the contrary to show the limitations of TMs and equivalent formalisms, i.e., their ability to carry out Hilbert's programme (Turing, 1936). Turing actually mentioned the irreducibility to TMs of interactive choice machines (*c-machines*), though he never proved it. This early reference to interactive computation has basically gone ignored by the community that Turing founded.

It is tempting to assume that interactive models of computation such as c-machines have not been studied due to lack of their intellectual merit. However, there is a different explanation: that the theory community has lacked the proper conceptual tools to make progress on these ideas. The claim that interactive computation is more expressive than algorithms opens up a research area that had been considered closed. Much work needs to be done on both the foundations and applications of interactive computing, to provide a systematic foundation for interactive software technology (Wegner, 1999). UML provides a large step forward in motivating and enabling this work.

REFERENCES

Barwise, J., & Moss, L. (1996). *Vicious Circles* (CSLI Lecture Notes #60). Stanford: CSLI Publications.

Brooks, F. (1995). *The Mythical Man-Month: Essays on Software Engineering*. Reading, MA: Addison-Wesley.

Davis, M. (Ed.) (1965). *The Undecidable*. New York: Raven.

Estrin, D., Govindan, R., & Heidemann, J. (Guest Eds.). (2000). Embedding the Internet (special multi-article section). *Communications of the ACM, 43*(5), pp. 39ff.

Fowler, M. (1997). *UML Distilled: Applying the Standard Object Modeling Language*. Reading, MA: Addison-Wesley.

France, R., Evans, A., Lano, L., & Rumpe, B. (1998). The UML as a formal modeling notation. *Computer Standards and Interfaces, 19*, pp. 325-334.

Gamma, E., Helm, R., Johnson, R., & Vlissides, J. (1994). *Design patterns: Elements of reusable object-oriented software*. Reading, MA: Addison Wesley.

Goldin, D. (2000). Persistent Turing Machines as a model of interactive computation. Paper presented at *Int'l Symposium on Foundations of Information Knowledge Systems*, FOIKS'00, Cottbus, Burg, Germany February.

Goldin, D., & Keil, D. (2000). *Minimal Sequential Interaction Machines*. Technical report, University of Massachusetts Boston Department of Math and Computer Science, 6/00 (*www.cs.umb.edu/~dqg/papers/minimal.ps*).

Goldin, D., & Smolka, S. (2000). Turing machines, transition systems, and interaction. Computer Science Technical Report 00-7, University of Massachusetts-Boston, October.

Hopcroft, J., & Ullman, J. (1979). *Introduction to Automata Theory, Languages and Computation*. Reading, MA: Addison-Wesley.

Jacobs, B., & Rutten, J. (1997). A tutorial on (co) algebras and (co) induction. *EATCS Bulletin, 62*.

Jacobson, I., Christerson, M., Jonsson, P., & Overgaard, G. (1993). *Object-Oriented Software Engineering: A use Case Driven Approach*, revised 4th printing. Reading, MA: Addison-Wesley.

Jacobson, I., Ericsson, M., & Jacobson, A. (1995). *The object advantage: business process reengineering with object technology*. Reading, MA: Addison-Wesley.

Kobryn, C. (1999). UML 2001: A standardization odyssey. *Communications of the ACM, 42*(10) (Oct.), pp. 29-37.

Lynch, N., Merritt, M., Weihl, W., & Fekrete, A. (1994). *Atomic transactions*. San Mateo: Morgan Kaufmann.

Manna, Z., & Pnueli, A. (1992). *The temporal logic of reactive and concurrent systems*. New York: Springer-Verlag.

McLaughlin, M., & Moore, A. (1998). Real-time extensions to UML. *Dr. Dobb's Journal*, December.

Milner, R. (1975). Processes: A mathematical model of computing agents. In *Logic Colloquium'73*. Amsterdam: North-Holland.

Milner, R. (1990). Operational and algebraic semantics of concurrent processes. *In* van Leeuwen, J., Ed., *Handbook of Theoretical Computer Science*. Cambridge: MIT Press.

Milner, R. (1999). *Communicating and Mobile systems: The pi-calculus*. Cambridge: Cambridge University Press.

Moore, E. (1956). Gedanken-experiments on sequential machines. In Shannon, C. E., & McCarthy, J., Eds., *Automata Studies*. Princeton: Princeton University Press.

Object Management Group. (2000). *Unified Modeling Language specification*. Ver. 1.3, March.

Pratt, V. (1995). Chu spaces and their interpretation as concurrent objects. *In* van Leeuwen, J., Ed., *Computer science today: Recent trends and developments* (Lecture Notes in Computer Science #1000).

Reed, P. (1998). The Unified Modeling Language takes shape. *DBMS Magazine*, 7.

Rumbaugh, J., Blaha, M., Premerlani, W., Eddy, F. & Lorensen, W. (1990). *Object-Oriented Modeling and Design*. Englewood Cliffs: Prentice Hall.

Russell, S. & Norvig, P. (1995). *Artificial intelligence: A modern approach*. Reading, MA: Addison-Wesley.

Rutten, J. (1997). A tutorial on coalgebras and coinduction. *EATCS Bulletin, 62*.

Schneider, G., & Winters, J. (1998). *Applying use cases: A practical guide*. Reading, MA: Addison-Wesley.

Selic, B. (1999). Turning clockwise: Using UML in the real-time domain. *Communications of the ACM*, 42 (10) (October 1999), pp. 46-54.

Simon, H. (1970). *The sciences of the artificial*, 2nd Edition. Cambridge: MIT Press.

Starlogo site at MIT Media Lab. (2000). Downloaded March from *http://starlogo.www.media.mit.edu/ people/starlogo*.

Tennenhouse, D. (2000). Proactive computing. *Communications of the ACM, 43*(5) (5/00), pp. 43-50.

Texel, P., & Williams, C. (1997). *Use cases combined with Booch/OMT/UML: Processes and products*. Upper Saddle River, NJ: Prentice Hall PTR.

Turing, A. (1936). On computable numbers with an application to the Entscheidungsproblem.

Proc. London Math Soc., 2(42), pp. 230-265. Reprinted in Davis, M. (1965), *The Undecidable*, New York: Raven.

Wegner, P. (1996). Interactive software technology. In Tucker, A., *Computer Science and Engineering Handbook*. Boca Raton: CRC Press LLC.

Wegner, P. (1997). Why interaction is more powerful than algorithms. *Communications of the ACM, 40*(5) (5/97), pp. 80-91.

Wegner, P. (1998). Interactive foundations of computing. *Theoretical Computer Science, 192*, pp. 315-351.

Wegner, P. (1999). Draft of ECOOP '99 banquet speech. *www.cs.brown.edu/people/pw*.

Wegner, P., & Goldin, D. (1999a). Interaction as a framework for modeling. *Lecture Notes in Computer Science* #1565. Berlin: Springer.

Wegner, P. & Goldin, D. (1999b). Interaction, computability and Church's Thesis, May, accepted for publication in *Computer Journal*.

Wegner, P., & Goldin, D. (1999c). Coinductive models of finite computing agents. *Electronic Notes in Theoretical Computer Science, 19*.

Zdonik, S., & Maier, D. (1990). *Readings in object-oriented database systems*. San Mateo: Morgan Kaufmann.

About the Authors

José Luis Fernández Alemán is an assistant lecturer at the University of Murcia in Spain. He received a BSc with honors in computer science from the University of Murcia. His research interests are in the area of analysis and design methodologies, formal methods and system prototyping. His work includes several projects involving formal methods, and the construction of trusted information systems from OO specifications. He is currently a doctoral student in the Computer Science and System Department at the University of Murcia. He can be contacted at the Faculty of Computer Science, Campus de Espinardo 30080, University of Murcia, Murcia, Spain; aleman@dif.um.es.

Ambrosio Toval Álvarez is a professor at the University of Murcia in Spain. He holds a BSc in Mathematics from the Complutense University of Madrid, and received a PhD in Computer Science (cum laude) from the Technical University of Valencia (both in Spain). He is involved in a variety of applied research and development projects with industry, and conducts research in the design and implementation of prototyping tools and software formal models. He is currently director of the Computer Science and System Department at the University of Murcia. Dr. Toval won the 1988 "NIXDORF National Award for Technological and Managerial Creativity" and the 1988 "Spanish Ministry of Education and Science National Award." His current research interests include requirements engineering, formal methods and specifications executability. He can be contacted at the Faculty of Computer Science, Campus de Espinardo 30080, University of Murcia, Murcia, Spain; atoval@dif.um.es.

Franck Barbier is professor of Computer Science at University of Pau (France). He is the scientific consultant of Reich Technologies, a French company among the 17 companies that built UML 1.1 in 1997. He has recently applied UML in three important projects related to the domains of Flight Management Systems, Submarine Telecommunications Network Management and Oil Exploration Systems. He is also a permanent member of the French OO journal, *L'objet (Hermes Science),* and edited in 2000 a special issue on Object Modeling and UML.

Silvia Clérici is an associate professor at the Department of Software of the Technical University of Catalonia (UPC). She received the degree in Computer Science from the University of Buenos Aires and the doctorate degree from the UPC. She also taught at the University of Buenos Aires and the University of Belgrano (Argentina). Her research interest is on formal methods and algebraic specification languages, being an active researcher in several European projects in this area. She is currently working on the formal basis of object-oriented methodologies.

Stefan Conrad is an associate professor for practical computer science at the Ludwig-Maximilians-University of Munich, Germany. His main working areas are database design, database integration and methods for information system development. He received the PhD degree in 1994 at the University of Technology in Braunschweig, Germany, with a thesis on verification techniques for an object-oriented specification approach to information systems. In 1997 he received the Habilitation degree at the University of Magdeburg, Germany. His Habilitation thesis dealt with problems of and concepts for building federated database systems. Before he moved to Munich, he spent a year at the University of Linz, Austria, as visiting professor and temporary chair for "Data & Knowledge Engineering."

Jin Song Dong received the BinTech degree (with first class honors) and the PhD degree from The University of Queensland in 1992 and 1995, respectively. From 1995-1998, he was a research scientist and then a senior research scientist at the CSIRO Mathematical and Information Sciences in Australia. In 1998, he joined the faculty of the Computer Science Department of the National University of Singapore. His research interests include formal methods, real-time specification, object orientation, programming language semantics, safety critical systems and open distributed systems. He is member of the IEEE. His recent papers can be found at http://www.comp.nus.edu.sg/~dongjs/.

Liliana Favre is an associate professor at UNCPBA (Universidad Nacional del Centro de la Pcia. de Buenos Aires) in Argentina. She is researcher of CIC (Comisión de Investigaciones Científicas de la Pcia. de Buenos Aires) in Argentina. Her research interests are in the area of specification and formal methods, especially algebraic methods for software specification and design.

Martin Gogolla is a full professor of Computer Science at the University of Bremen, Germany. His research interests include object-oriented design, formal methods in system design, semantics of languages and formal specification. Before joining the University of Bremen he worked for the University of Dortmund and the Technical University of Braunschweig. His professional activities include: publications in journals and conference proceedings; publication of two books; speaker to university and industrial colloquia; referee for journals and conferences; organizer of workshops and conferences; member in national and international program committees.

Dina Goldin <http://www.cs.umb.edu/~dqg> is an assistant professor of Computer Science at the University of Massachusetts Boston specializing in applied theory. She holds an NSF CAREER grant for research in Constraint Query Algebras. Recently, her interest has turned to models of interactive computation, an exciting new research area pioneered by Peter Wegner. In 1999, Dr. Goldin was an ECOOP tutorial speaker and a VLSI program committee member. Prior to working in academia, she was a software engineer at PTC, a successful start-up CAD/CAM company. Dr. Goldin is an author of numerous papers in refereed proceedings and journals. She holds a BS from Yale University, and an MS and a PhD in Computer Science from Brown University.

Pramila Gupta is a lecturer and course adviser for IT and IS courses in the Faculty of Informatics at the Melbourne International Campus of Central Queensland University, Rockhampton, Australia. She has research interests in information modelling and database management systems. Her doctoral thesis draws on theories in the areas of linguistics and psychology, with the aim of providing sounder theoretical foundations to information systems in general and to conceptual modelling techniques in particular. She has presented at NLDB '96 and ACIS '95 and published working papers at Swinburne University of Technology. Ms. Gupta received her Bachelor of Engineering in Electronics (Honours) in 1972 from Birla Institute of Technology, Pilani, India and her Graduate Diploma in Business Information Technology in 1991 from Swinburne University of Technology.

Terry Halpin, BSc, DipEd, BA, MLitStud, PhD, is Technical Lead in Database Design, Enterprise Framework and Tools Unit, Microsoft Corporation, Redmond, Washington, USA. After a lengthy career as an academic in computer science, which he combined with industrial work on database modeling, he moved to industry full time. His recent positions include head of database research at Asymetrix Corporation, research director of InfoModelers Inc. and director of Database Strategy at Visio Corporation, which was acquired by Microsoft Corporation. His research focuses on conceptual modeling and conceptual query technology for information systems, using a business rules approach. His doctoral thesis provided the first full formalization of Object-Role Modeling (ORM/NIAM), and his publications include four books and more than 90 technical papers. His latest book, *Information Modeling and Relational Databases*, will be published by Morgan Kaufmann in 2001.

Brian Henderson-Sellers is director of the Centre for Object Technology Applications and Research, and professor of Information Systems at the University of Technology, Sydney (Australia). He is author of nine books on object technology and is well known for his work in OO methodologies (MOSES, COMMA and OPEN) and in OO metrics. He has been regional editor of *Object-Oriented Systems*, a member of the editorial board of Object Magazine/Component Strategies and *Object Expert* for many years. He was the Founder of the Object-Oriented Special Interest Group of the Australian Computer Society (NSW Branch) and chairman of the Computerworld Object Developers' Awards committee for ObjectWorld '94 and '95 (Sydney). He is a frequent, invited speaker at international OT conferences.

Rolf Hennicker is assistant professor in the Department of Computer Science at the Ludwig-Maximilians-Universität München where he finished his Habilitation thesis in 1997. He has been working for more than 15 years in several areas of software development, including formal methods, object-oriented software engineering and software reusability. Mr. Hennicker has participated in many national and international projects, and has several times been a visiting professor at the University of Augsburg and at the Ecole Normale Supérieure de Cachan.

Wolfgang Hesse received a diploma degree in Mathematics in 1970 and a Dr. rer. nat. (PhD) degree in Computer Science in 1976. From 1970 to 1979, he worked as a research scientist at the University of Technology, and from 1979 to 1988 as a senior and chief consultant with a major software house in München. Since 1988 he is a professor of Computer Science at the Philipps University of Marburg. His main fields of professional interest are software engineering, information systems and social aspects of computer science. Dr. Hesse is prime author of two books on software development, co-editor of the *Informatik-Spektrum*, a member of the German Society of Informatics (GI), and the German Association of Computer Professionals for Social Responsibility (FIFF) and a member of the IFIP Working group 8.1 and its task group FRISCO (Framework of Information System Concepts).

David Keil is the acting chair in Computer Science at Framingham State College and a researcher at the University of Massachusetts Boston. He is a co-author of *Introduction to Computer Programming Using Turbo Pascal* (West, 1995), one of the first textbooks to present object-oriented concepts at the CS I level. Interactive computation has been the focus of his recent research. Mr. Keil has a master's degree in Computer Science from Boston University.

Cornel Klein received his Master in Computer Science at the Munich Institute of Technology in 1993. He then joined the group of Prof. Dr. Manfred Broy, where he has been working in distributed systems, formal specification techniques and on the formal foundation of visual modeling languages such as the UML. In 1998, he earned his PhD in the area of scenario-based specification techniques. Since 1998 he is working in the Strategic Product Development Department of Siemens Information & Communication Networks, where he is investigating new concepts and prototypes for future telecommunication systems. He has gained experience in the field of IP-based network services, intelligent networks and advanced service architectures. He is currently active in the area of mobile agents and active networks.

Nora Koch received her degree in Computer Science at the University of Buenos Aires, Argentina in 1985. She is currently a researcher at F.A.S.T. Applied Software Technology GmbH and a PhD candidate at the Institute of Computer Science, Ludwig-Maximilians-University (LMU), Munich. She has been involved in a variety of European and German research projects focusing on Web engineering and UML. Prior to working at F.A.S.T, she was an assistant professor at the University of Buenos Aires and a researcher at the LMU in Munich. Her main research interests are in the areas of software development methodologies, adaptive hypermedia and user modeling. Her recent publications on these subjects can be found at http://www.pst.informatik.uni-muenchen.de/~kochn.

John Krogstie is currently senior researcher at SINTEF Telecom and Informatics, which is part of Scandinavia's largest research institute. He had earlier worked nine years for Andersen Consulting within development and deployment of methodology, knowledge management and process improvement. He has a PhD and an MSc in information systems from NTNU, the Norwegian University of Science and Technology, where he also currently holds a position as adjunct associate professor. His main research areas are modeling of information systems, knowledge management and computer-supported cooperative work.

Patricia Lago is assistant professor in the Department of Control and Computer Engineering of Politecnico di Torino. She received the master's degree in Computer Science from the University of Pisa in 1992 and PhD from Politecnico di Torino in 1997. She has one year at the Computer Science Department at University of Dortmund, and one semester at the Norwegian University of Science and Technology, working as a guest researcher in the field of software process modeling and transactions. She worked in several European projects. Her interests focus on software engineering methodologies, software architectures and object-oriented technology.

Jing Liu received the BSc degree from Huazhong University of Science and Technology in 1999. Since then, he has been a research scholar and postgraduate student in the Computer Science Department of the National University of Singapore. His research interests include formal methods and linking formal methods with graphical notations such as UML.

Brendan Mahony received the BSc degree from The Australian National University in 1984 and the BA degree with first class honors from The University of Queensland in 1987. In 1991, he was awarded a PhD at The University of Queensland, after studying techniques for the specification and design of real-time systems. He continued these studies as a research fellow at The University of Queensland. Since 1995, he has been employed by the Defence Science and Technology Organisation, researching the application of state machine formalisms to the analysis of safety and security critical systems. In 1997-1998, he spent a year with CSIRO's Mathematical and Information Sciences in Canberra, as the CSIRO/DSTO fellow.

Andreas L. Opdahl is professor of Information Science in the Department of Information Science at the University of Bergen (Norway). He is the author, co-author or co-editor of more than 30 journal articles, book chapters, refereed archival conference papers and books within requirements engineering, enterprise modelling, ontology of information systems and other areas. Dr. Opdahl is a member of IFIP WG8.1 on Design and Evaluation of Information Systems. He is one of the organizers of the REFSQ workshop series and serves regularly on the program committees of several international conferences and workshops.

Andreas Rausch received his master's in Computer Science from the Munich Institute of Technology in 1996. He has been leading various industrial software projects, developing business-oriented information systems. He is one of the four founders of the software house 4Soft GmbH, Munich. For the past three years, he has been working on his PhD about Componentware, Evolution-Based Development of Software Architectures. This is undertaken at the chair of Prof. Dr. Manfred Broy, Munich Institute of Technology. There, he has been part of a large interdisciplinary research project FORSOFT, subproject A1, working on the Methodology of Component-Based Software Development. Currently, he is leading the subproject ZEN that is concerned with the foundations of software engineering.

Devang Shah holds a master's in Software Engineering from Carnegie Mellon University (August 2000). Prior to joining Carnegie Mellon University, he worked as a consultant with a number of companies including Oracle Corporation on the Oracle Database and Oracle Financials suites of products. He also holds a bachelor's degree in Computer Science from the University of Bombay (May 1995). His areas of interest include OOAD, UML, use of formal methods in software development, distributed databases and transaction processing systems. He is currently employed as a Consultant by C-Bridge.

Kun Shi received the BSc degree from Nankai University in 1997. From 1997-1998, she was a system engineer at Motorola, Semiconductor Product Section, China IT. Since 1999, she has been a research scholar and PhD candidate in the School of Computing, National University of Singapore. Her research interests include functional programming language, program transformation and formal methods.

Keng Siau is a JD Edwards professor and an associate professor of Management Information Systems (MIS) at the University of Nebraska, Lincoln (UNL). He is also the editor in chief of the *Journal of Database Management*. He received his PhD degree from the University of British Columbia (UBC) where he majored in Management Information Systems and minored in Cognitive Psychology. He has published more than 30 journal articles, and these articles have appeared in journals such as *MISQ, IEEE Computer, Information Systems, ACM's Data Base, Journal of Database Management, Journal of Communications of the ACM, Information Technology, International Journal of Human-Computer Studies, Transactions on Information and Systems* and others. In addition, he has published over 50 refereed conference papers in proceedings such as *ICIS, ECIS, HICSS, CAiSE, IRMA, AMCIS* and *HCI*. He has edited two books, three journal special issues and five proceedings – all of them related to systems analysis and design. Dr. Siau primary research interests are object-oriented systems development using Unified Modeling Language (UML), Web Database, Enterprise E-Business, Enterprise Resource Planning (ERP) and Web-based systems development. He has served as the organizing and program chairs for the International Workshop on Evaluation of Modeling Methods in Systems Analysis and Design (EMMSAD) (1996 – 2000). More information about him can be obtained at URL: http://www.ait.unl.edu/siau.

Marc Sihling received his master's in Computer Science at the Munich Institute of Technology in 1996 and joined the research project FORSOFT on the side of Prof. Manfred Broy. In his team the focus was set on a methodical guidance for Componentware. At this time, he held UML courses for various industrial partners and co-founded the software startup company 4Soft GmbH. At the moment, he is working on his PhD thesis in the field of component framework and architecture integration. Moreover, he is project leader of the ARTWORK project concentrating on multi-view development of turbines.

Sandra Slaughter (PhD, University of Minnesota, 1995) is an assistant professor in the Graduate School of Industrial Administration at Carnegie Mellon University. Her research focuses on productivity and quality improvement in the development and maintenance of information systems and on effective management of information technology professionals. Currently, she is conducting research on software process improvement, the evolution of information systems in organizations and the compensation, mobility and careers of IT professionals. She has published articles in leading research journals in management and software engineering, including *Information Systems Research, Management Science, Communications of the ACM*, and *IEEE Transactions on Software Engineering*. She serves as an associate editor for both *Information Systems Research* and *MIS Quarterly*.

Jim A. Sykes is a senior lecturer in the School of Information Technology at Swinburne University of Technology. He earned a BE from Melbourne University in 1969 and a PhD from the University of New South Wales in 1974, both in the field of electrical engineering. In 1978 he joined Control Data Australia and worked in a range of analyst and marketing roles. From 1981 he worked as a consultant and software developer where his experience included database design and application development for financial and stockbroking applications. He joined Swinburne University in 1989. His research interests centre on modelling for information systems, with special interests in component-based development, the Unified Modelling Language and the role of natural language.

Klaus Turowski is an assistant professor at the University of Magdeburg in the Department of Business Information Systems. Prior to assuming his current position, he worked at the University of Münster, where he received a Dr. rer. pol. (PhD in Business Information

Systems). In addition, he holds a Dipl-Wi-Ing. (diploma degree in Industrial Engineering and Management) from the University of Karlsruhe. He is speaker of working group 5.10.3 *Component-Oriented Business Application Systems* of German Informatics Society (GI). His main research interests are component-based business application systems and inter-organizational integration. Besides his theoretical background, he has been working in a variety of consulting projects concerning process management, service level management, application outsourcing and ERP-systems, especially SAP R/3.

Peter Wegner is professor emeritus of Computer Science at Brown University. He has served as the editor-in-chief of the ACM *Computing Surveys* from 1995 to 1999, and has edited numerous books related to object-oriented programming and to research directions in computing. Dr. Wegner is a leading international authority on software technology research and education. His work on interactive computation is motivated by his career-long desire to bridge the gap between "top-down" and "bottom-up" computer science. Originally referring to system specification vs. implementation, this dichotomy has crystallized for him in the '90s as "interaction" vs. "algorithms."

Zhaojun Wen graduated in 1991 from the South China University of technology and obtained a bachelor's degree in electronic engineering. In 2000 he received his master's degree in computer science at the Maximilian University of Munich. Since May 2000 he is a researcher in the group of Manfred Broy at Munich University of Technology. His research is in the field of software and systems engineering of agent-based systems and embedded systems.

Index

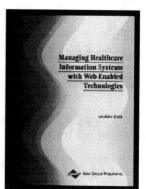